FINANCE AND CULTURE IN NINETEENTH-CENTURY BRITAIN

FINANCE AND CULTURE IN NINETEENTH-CENTURY BRITAIN

Edited by
George Robb

Volume I
Public Finance and Company Promotion

Routledge
Taylor & Francis Group
LONDON AND NEW YORK

First published 2026
by Routledge
4 Park Square, Milton Park, Abingdon, Oxon OX14 4RN

and by Routledge
605 Third Avenue, New York, NY 10158

Routledge is an imprint of the Taylor & Francis Group, an informa business

British Library Cataloguing-in-Publication Data
A catalogue record for this book is available from the British Library

ISBN: 978-1-032-44854-1 (set)
ISBN: 978-1-032-44855-8 hbk (vol I)
ISBN: 978-1-003-71389-0 ebk (vol I)

DOI: 10.4324/9781003713890

Typeset in Times New Roman
by Apex CoVantage, LLC

CONTENTS

TIMELINE: FINANCE AND CULTURE IN NINETEENTH-CENTURY BRITAIN

1801	London Stock Exchange founded as a closed market with 550 members
1802	London Stock Exchanges moves into a purpose-built building in Capel Court
1808	Henry Day's pamphlet, *A Defense of Joint-Stock Companies,* advocates for a lessening of legal restrictions on creating public companies
1811	Company shares quoted on the London Stock Exchange for the first time
1812	First set of Rules and Regulations adopted by the Stock Exchange to govern its members and their transactions
1814	De Berenger fraud perpetrated to manipulate the price of government securities
1823	London Stock Exchange opens separate trading room for foreign securities
1825	Bubble Act of 1720 repealed, greatly facilitating the creation of new joint-stock companies
	Times of London begins regular financial column
1826	First financial crisis of the nineteenth century
1837	Financial crisis
1840	Exposure of the West Middlesex Life and Fire Assurance Company as a fraud
1843	900 joint-stock companies listed on the Stock Exchange. Stock Exchange begins publication of a daily Official List of share prices
	The Economist founded by James Wilson
1844	Act for the Registration, Incorporation and Regulation of Joint Stock Companies; Creation of Registry Office
1845–46	Railway Mania; emergence of several provincial stock exchanges
1847–48	Financial Crisis
1849	Shareholders' investigations reveal widespread fraud by directors of railway companies, especially George Hudson, the "Railway King"

1850	London Stock Exchange has 800 members Walter Watts, clerk at Globe Assurance Company, convicted of embezzling £70,000; sentenced to ten years transportation, but committed suicide while in prison. Emma Robinson's novel, *The Gold Worshippers*, criticizes reckless and fraudulent activities associated with the Railway Mania; her villain Humson is a thinly disguised George Hudson
1855	Limited Liability Act
1856	New Companies Act passed, superseding 1844 Act and streamlining company formation William James Robson, clerk at Crystal Palace Company, convicted of embezzling £27,000; sentenced to twenty years transportation Leopold Redpath, registrar of Great Northern Railway, convicted of embezzling £220,000; transported for life John Sadleir, MP, director of the Tipperary Joint-Stock Bank, revealed to have embezzled £200,000; committed suicide before he could be tried
1857	Financial Crisis Charles Dickens' novel *Little Dorrit* dramatizes the frauds of John Sadleir through the character of Mr. Merdle
1859	David Morier Evans publishes *Facts, Failures, and Frauds,* detailing several notorious frauds involving British joint-stock companies
1860	George Pullinger, chief cashier of the Union Bank of London, convicted of embezzling £263,000; sentenced to twenty years imprisonment
1861	Walter Bagehot assumes editorship of the *Economist,* a position he holds until his death in 1877
1862	Companies Act, extends provisions of 1856 Companies Act to banks and life insurance companies
1863	Emma Galton publishes first guide for women investors, *A Guide to the Unprotected*
1866	Financial Crisis precipitated by the collapse of Overend, Gurney, and Company
1867	Companies Act specified contents of prospectuses Completion of transatlantic telegraph cable, allowing for greater integration of London and New York Stock Exchanges
1870	London Stock Exchange has 1,471 members London Institute of Accountants established
1872	Stock-tickers installed in the London Stock Exchange
1874	City editor of the *Times,* Marmaduke Sampson, resigned when it was revealed that he had been paid by promoters to endorse the shares of certain companies

1875	Parliamentary Committee on Loans to Foreign States criticizes the Stock Exchange's reckless flotation of loans to Latin American governments
	Anthony Trollope's *The Way We Live Now* presents an especially bleak view of company promotion; the novel's villain, Augustus Melmotte, is based on Albert Grant
1877	Twycross v. Grant: landmark legal case which establishes that company promoters are responsible for information in prospectuses; prospectuses must disclose all contracts that affect the company in a significant material way
1878	City of Glasgow Bank failure; the bank's directors are convicted for publishing false balance sheets
	The Statist is founded by Sir Robert Giffen and Thomas Lloyd
	Royal Commission on the Stock Exchange issues Report which is critical of deceptive practices involving company flotations
1879	Companies Act, requires compulsory yearly audit for banks and facilitates the conversion of unlimited companies to limited liability
	Director and Office of Public Prosecutions established; began initiating criminal proceedings against fraudulent financial undertakings
1880	Institute of Chartered Accountants in England and Wales established
1884	*Financial News* founded by Harry Marks
1885	London Stock Exchange building expanded in size
1886	Flotation of Guinness Brewery as a joint-stock company begins trend for converting private industrial firms into public companies
1888	*Financial Times* founded by Douglas MacRae
	Amy Bell establishes brokerage business in London, becoming Britain's first woman stockbroker
1890	London Stock Exchange has 3,233 members
	Barings Crisis: major London banks unite to prevent the failure of Barings Bank, averting a financial panic
	Companies Winding-Up Act facilitated company liquidation under court supervision
	Director' Liability Act made company directors criminally liable for publication of false statements
1892	Collapse of Liberator Building Society amid revelations of fraud
	Investors' Review established
1893	Gilbert and Sullivan operetta *Utopia, Limited* burlesques the craze for joint-stock company flotations
1894	Company Law Amendment Committee appointed by Commons, under the chairmanship of Lord Davey
	London Stock Exchange refuses to give outside brokers access to current share prices via the stock-ticker

1895	Trial and conviction of Jabez Spencer Balfour, director of Liberator Building Society, for falsification of accounts; he is sentenced to fourteen years' imprisonment
1896	London Stock Exchange building expanded in size. Commons passes Company Bill based on recommendations of Davey Committee, sends Bill to the Lords 1896–1900 Lords Committee debates Company Bill for four years
1897	24,000 joint-stock companies listed on the Stock Exchange
1898	Bankruptcy of company promoter Ernest Terah Hooley reveals fraudulent practices associated with the company flotations of the 1890s
1900	London Stock Exchange has 4,315 members
	Harry Marks sued for publishing fraudulent financial information in the *Financial News*
	Companies Act significantly tightens Britain's hitherto permissive company law
1902	John A. Hobson's book, *Imperialism: A Study,* argues that the expansion of the British Empire was driven by the need for new financial investments
1904	Company promoter Whitaker Wright tried and convicted for issuing false balance sheets; he was sentenced to seven years' imprisonment, whereupon he committed suicide by taking poison
1905	London Stock Exchange building expanded in size

GENERAL INTRODUCTION

FINANCE AND CULTURE IN NINETEENTH-CENTURY BRITAIN

The twenty-first-century financial world that we now inhabit had its origins in nineteenth-century Britain with industrialism, corporate expansion, and a robust securities market. New developments in limited liability and financial journalism democratized investment, rendering Victorian Britain a nation of shareholders. The City of London and the London Stock Exchange sat at the very center of international finance, much like the New York Stock Exchange does today. As historian Paul Johnson emphasizes in *Making the Market,* "most of the market institutions that we take for granted today – limited companies, shares, stock markets, accountants, financial newspapers – were Victorian creations."[1]

The history of nineteenth-century finance is also the history of culture and cultural change. Finance cut across all aspects of life. It was central to many social and political issues, including the "woman question" (should women invest their own money?) and Liberal reform (did a laissez-faire economy adequately protect ordinary investors?). The ups and downs of the stock market were also central to the plots of Victorian novels and plays, where a financial panic could imperil domestic security.

This multi-volume collection of primary source materials documents the origins, growth, and impact of Britain's financial system, focusing especially on such themes as innovations in public finance, the growth of joint stock companies and the stock market, the role of the London Stock Exchange, the rise of the popular investor and new sources of financial information, and the risks associated with finance and investment, including financial panics, crashes, and fraud. Sources will explore not only the significance of finance and investment to British society, and the role of financial agents like stockbrokers, company promoters, and investment advisors, but will also consider debates concerning the desirability of certain kinds of investments and the morality of the market. Popular attitudes and ideas about joint-stock companies, the share market, speculation, and investors will also be examined.

Historians' interest in modern British financial history has grown steadily since the 1960s, and has experienced an especially remarkable expansion during the twenty-first century. Pioneering work by economic historians such as B.C. Hunt and H.A. Shannon in the 1930s examined the development of joint-stock companies and the impact of limited liability on company formation during the nineteenth century.[2] This work, however, ran counter to the fields of political, diplomatic, and military history that still dominated the profession. The rise of social history during the 1960s and 1970s encouraged a new generation of business historians to investigate the impact of nineteenth-century financial developments on broad social and economic changes like industrialism, imperialism, and class formation. Important new work, such as Leslie Hannah's *The Rise of the Corporate Economy* and Philip Cottrell's *Industrial Finance,* demonstrated the importance of public finance and popular investment to the building of a national railway network, overseas expansion, and the rise of "big business" generally.[3]

During the 1980s and 1990s research on financial history expanded significantly both in amount and scope. A multi-volume *Dictionary of Business Biography,* edited by David Jeremy, revived interest in many important, but largely forgotten, company promoters, financiers, and stockbrokers.[4] Histories of the Stock Exchange by Ranald Michie and of the City of London by David Kynaston documented the importance of the stock market and money market in making London the center of international finance during the nineteenth century.[5] New work by Wayne Parsons on the financial press, George Robb on financial crime, and Timothy Alborn on joint-stock politics explored the complex relationship between high finance, the state, mass media, and ordinary investors.[6] Boyd Hilton and G.R. Searle scrutinized contemporary attitudes to business and finance, especially the widespread debates over the morality of the market, while Michael Edelstein, Lance Davis, and Robert Huttenback examined the role of investors in financing British imperial expansion.[7]

During the twenty-first century, scholars have revisited old themes in financial history and pioneered new fields of scholarship, complexifying our understanding of nineteenth-century finance and investment. James Taylor and Paul Johnson, for example, re-examined the messy and contentious development of joint-stock enterprise in nineteenth-century Britain. In *Creating Capitalism,* Taylor argues that historians have understated contemporary resistance to the corporate form, and in *Making the Market,* Johnson contends that the problems of modern capitalism derive from Victorian business practices and customs.[8] Taylor, along with Sarah Wilson, has also revised Robb's earlier work on white-collar crime, by de-emphasizing the influence of laissez-faire attitudes and instead stressing the state's "discovery" of financial fraud in the 1850s and its growing willingness to prosecute corporate wrongdoing.[9]

Much of the new financial history has focused on the lives and behavior of ordinary investors. Who were they? What were their sources of information? How capable were they in navigating the treacherous financial waters of the share market? A number of scholars, such as Timothy Alborn, James Freeman, and Robin Peason have studied shareholders' meetings and attempts by shareholders to influence corporate governance.[10] Much new and original work has especially highlighted women shareholders. Articles and books by Janette Rutterford, Josephine Maltby, and Nancy Henry have documented the number and significance of women investors as well as contemporary debates over the propriety of women managing money or speculating in the stock market.[11] James Taylor's recent *Sexism in the City* explores the City's longstanding prejudices against women while also recovering the forgotten histories of Britain's first women stockbrokers.[12]

Another new contribution to financial history is the work of literary scholars who have increasingly focused on representations of finance, the stock market, and speculation in nineteenth-century journalism and imaginative literature. Mary Poovey's influential *Genres of the Credit Economy* demonstrated how new types of financial writing, like the money column in daily papers and investment guide books, normalized and legitimated the workings of high finance by translating "the arcane jargon of the financial world into a language that any middle-class reader could appreciate."[13] Many other scholars, such as Paul Delany, Tamara Wagner, Nancy Henry, and Francis O'Gorman, have examined how Victorian novels engaged with financial themes.[14] Novelists often employed financial plots, especially involving the stock market, to examine issues of risk and social instability. Far from normalizing high finance, the novels of the period usually depicted corporate capitalism as dangerous and disreputable.

This four-volume collection will explore the many topics and themes identified by financial historians and literary scholars of nineteenth-century Britain by assembling a wide variety of original documents and literary sources from the period. Each volume will focus on a different aspect of British finance and culture and will include a volume introduction that places the source material in a broader historical context. Volume 1, *Public Finance and Company Promotion,* considers the debates surrounding joint-stock companies and limited liability as well as examining early financial manias and the new figure of the company promoter. At the beginning of the nineteenth century most commercial capital was raised privately and locally by individual businessmen or partnerships. Many people felt that public companies were unnecessary, that they had unfair advantages over private businesses, and that they encouraged fraud. These objections faded over time as public finance sustained a tremendous growth of joint-stock banks, insurance companies, and railways. The "Railway Mania" of the 1840s initiated corporate investment on a massive scale. For the first time the Stock Exchange dealt heavily in company shares instead of government securities, and the railway companies drew in the whole nation of investors. Company legislation at mid-century accelerated the formation of new companies by streamlining the registration process and limiting the liability of individual shareholders. From the 1860s onwards, there was a steady and tremendous growth of joint-stock companies, but attitudes about corporate finance and company promoters still included a great deal of fear and loathing.

The second volume, *The World of the Stock Exchange,* focuses on the London Stock Exchange, its brokers, and its modes of business, as well as public debates over the morality of speculation and the probity of stockbrokers. During the nineteenth century the London Stock Exchange dominated national finance. Most public companies sold their shares through the Exchange, and its members were an exclusive fraternity, governed by their own rules and resistant to outside interference. As the Railway Mania expanded stock trading, a dozen provincial stock exchanges sprang up around the country, and thousands of outside brokers, not bound by the rules of the London Stock Exchange, solicited customers. The stock market was the subject of endless fascination and commentary, with general attitudes to stock trading and stockbrokers varying considerably over time. Frequent financial crises in the early nineteenth century led many commentators to denounce the Stock Exchange as a dangerous and dishonest gambling casino. As the share market grew in size and importance, as financial panics happened less frequently, and as the London Stock Exchange came to dominate international finance, attitudes to the stock market grew more accepting, even favorable.

The third volume, *Shareholders and the Culture of Investment,* examines the impact of public investment on British men and women during the nineteenth century, as well as what it meant for Great Britain to be a nation of shareholders. The size, composition, and investment choices of British shareholders changed dramatically over the course of the century. In 1800 investors were a small body of mostly aristocratic men and wealthy Londoners whose capital was sunk in a handful of government securities. By 1900 British investors had spread across the country and the empire, and their numbers had swelled to include much of the middle class and large numbers of women. Investment choices had also multiplied exponentially and now included a vast array of domestic, foreign, and colonial banks, railways, industrial firms, utilities, mines, and government loans. As shareholders grew in numbers, wealth, and political influence, they were served by new kinds of financial advisors and guidebooks, a specialized financial press, and newfangled trust companies, which sought variously to educate novice investors, minimize shareholder risk, and promote a more positive image of the stock market and share trading. A new culture of investment developed whereby prospectuses, stock certificates, dividends, shareholder meetings, and the financial columns of newspapers became a normal part of British middle-class life.

The fourth and final volume, *Financial Crises and Financial Fraud,* investigates the widespread fear generated by the series of speculative manias and financial panics which roiled the British economy during the nineteenth century alongside the frequent occurrence of frauds and embezzlements perpetrated by company promoters and directors. The tremendous growth of big business and the novelty of the corporate form created a world of new opportunities for criminal exploitation. The exposure of financial frauds, particularly at times of speculative panics, led to serious debates in the press and parliament, as well as in imaginative literature, over standards of business morality and the role of the state in policing commercial integrity. Government reluctance to interfere in purportedly private disputes between investors and company directors eroded over the course of the nineteenth century as the amount of national wealth invested in joint-stock companies increased dramatically. Financial frauds now seemed to threaten the nation's entire system of credit and business stability, prompting the state to regulate financial transactions more carefully and to prosecute financial infractions more vigorously.

This collection includes a wide variety of primary sources covering many different aspects of the corporate economy, the stock market, and popular investment in nineteenth-century Britain. Sources are included from every decade of the century, encompassing a broad range of opinion. Among the diverse material in the collection are several government documents, including companies acts, law reports of corporate litigation, and parliamentary debates, hearings, and reports concerning different aspects of company law and public finance. There are examples of documents created by joint-stock companies and financial agents, such as prospectuses, minutes of shareholders' meetings, and the rules and regulations governing the London Stock Exchange. Examples are also included of stock portfolios from both individual and corporate investors.

The collection further contains various types of print publications such as pamphlets and magazine articles. Pamphlets (short unbound booklets) were cheap to produce and often employed for polemical purposes. Several examples are given here from contemporary "pamphlet wars" over financial controversies, such as the debate on limited liability. During the nineteenth century, the mass circulation monthly magazine emerged as an important vehicle for publishing serialized fiction and articles about contemporary issues and events. Popular periodicals like the *Edinburgh Review*, *Blackwood's Magazine*, the *Nineteenth Century*, and the *Contemporary Review* frequently covered financial issues, treating them as matters of national importance that deserved serious discussion. The collection includes several examples of journal articles on topics such as the stock market, company law reform, investment options, and financial fraud.

These volumes also contain many sources from popular literature, including poetry, plays, short stories, sketches, and novels. Nineteenth-century literature was fascinated by the workings of the stock market, which it tended to present in a rather negative light. Some of the era's most popular and celebrated novelists, Dickens, Trollope, Thackeray, and Mrs. Henry Wood, dramatized the vicissitudes of the share market and detailed the frauds of villainous financiers who epitomized a society obsessed with material success at any price. Themes of financial insecurity permeated Victorian fiction, where a financial crash or an embezzling trustee might scatter ruin in their wake.

Many of the literary and journalistic depictions of the stock market and corporate culture included in this collection express negative views about finance capitalism. The novelists and journalists who wrote these pieces, along with other like-minded clergymen, academics, and civil servants, were collectively part of a professional middle class that was frequently at odds with a commercial middle class of merchants, industrialists, and financiers. The historian Harold Perkin was among the first to elaborate how nineteenth-century bourgeois society was riven by a struggle between the ideals of business people, who favored a society based on individualism, competition, and entrepreneurship, and the ideals of professionals, who condemned such a society as selfish and soulless, and instead promoted the virtues of education, expertise, and service to the community.[15] In their debates with financiers over issues like speculation and company promotion, professionals often had the last word.

Financiers attempted to counter negative views of the stock market by penning boosterish pamphlets and defensive magazine articles, but they had less access to popular media and were less experienced in engaging in public debates than their literary opponents. Financiers had better luck neutralizing bad publicity through the promotion of new types of economic writing, like advice books for investors and a specialized financial press. Stock market guidebooks and financial newspapers, usually produced by brokers and businessmen, sought to normalize securities investment, presenting it as a socially acceptable activity. They emphasized the key role of the stock market in underwriting Britain's industrial development and imperial expansion and they depicted securities trading as a rational, safe, and patriotic practice. Several examples of this kind of pro-finance writing are included here.

In selecting specific sources for inclusion in this collection, a number of guiding principles have been followed. Chronologically, examples are given from across the century. Ideologically, examples have been chosen to illustrate both continuity of opinion and the evolution or change over time in attitudes about financial matters. Sample sources have also been selected that represent a wide variety of viewpoints and that illustrate widespread contemporary opinion (elite and popular) and well-known debates. To illustrate these selection principles, let us consider one type of financial source included in the collection: investment guidebooks. Several examples of such guides are included, ranging across time from the 1790s to the early 1900s. The examples chosen illustrate the evolution of guides from brief, bare-bones listings of financial securities available for purchase to more lengthy, elaborate, and entertaining compendiums, full of detailed advice, outspoken opinion, and City gossip. The guides included here also offer a wide range of recommendations to investors, from conservative and cautious advice in favor of low-risk government securities and corporate bonds to more risk-friendly advice on how to speculate.

All the sources in this collection are reproduced as closely to the originals as possible. Original spelling and punctuation have been retained. Writers in the nineteenth century frequently sprinkled their texts with French and Latin phrases, sometimes German and Greek. The original foreign phrases have been retained, with translations provided in footnotes. Otherwise, footnotes within the sources have been kept to a minimum, except in cases where obscure references needed to be explained for a clearer understanding of the text. Brief sources, such as magazine and newspaper articles, short stories, and business documents, have been included in their entirety. Longer sources, like novels, guidebooks, and parliamentary papers, have been excerpted, though in most cases the excerpts represent continuous blocks of text. In cases where portions of text are omitted, this is indicated by ellipses (. . .).

Each individual source in the collection begins with a short introduction that identifies when it was created and where it first appeared. Brief background information is also provided about the author or institution that generated the source. This information is intended to help readers critically assess the assumptions, biases, and subjective viewpoints of the source material. The primary goal of this collection is to provide a wide variety of historical sources and guidance in reading them. Readers will be able develop a fuller and more nuanced understanding of the financial developments that transformed nineteenth-century Britain through the study of the documents assembled in this collection.

Notes

1 Paul Johnson, *Making the Market: Victorian Origins of Corporate Capitalism* (Cambridge: Cambridge University Press, 2010), p. i.

2 B.C. Hunt, *The Development of the Business Corporation in England, 1800–67* (Cambridge: Havard University Press, 1936), and H.A. Shannon, "The Coming of General Limited Liability," *Economic History* 2 (1931), pp. 267–91. Other important pioneering work in financial history includes W.T.C. King, *History of the London Discount Market* (London: Routledge, 1936), and J.H. Clapham, *An Economic History of Modern Britain,* 3 Vols. (Cambridge: Cambridge University Press, 1926–38).

3 Leslie Hannah, *The Rise of the Corporate Economy* (London: Methuen, 1976) and Philip Cottrell, *Industrial Finance, 1830–1914* (London: Methuen, 1980). Other pathbreaking financial studies from the 1960s and 1970s include E.V. Morgan and W.A. Thomas, *The Stock Exchange: Its History and Functions* (London: Elek Books, 1962), P.G.M. Dickson, *The Financial Revolution in England: A Study of the Development of Public Credit, 1688–1756* (London: Macmillan, 1967), M.C. Reed, *Investment in Railways in Britain, 1820–1844: A Study in the Development of the Capital Market* (Oxford: Oxford University Press, 1975), and Philip Cottrell, *British Overseas Investment in the Nineteenth Century* (London: Macmillan, 1975).

4 David J. Jeremy, ed., *Dictionary of Business Biography,* 6 Vols. (London: Butterworths, 1984–86).

5 Ranald C. Michie, *The London Stock Exchange: A History* (Oxford: Oxford University Press, 1999), and David Kynaston, *The City of London,* 4 Vols. (London: Chatto and Windus, 1994–2001).

6 Wayne Parsons, *The Power of the Financial Press: Journalism and Economic Opinion in Britain and America* (New Brunswick: Rutgers University Press, 1989), George Robb, *White-Collar Crime in Modern Britain: Financial Fraud and Business Morality, 1845–1929* (Cambridge: Cambridge University Press, 1992), and Timothy Alborn, *Conceiving Companies: Joint-Stock Politics in Victorian England* (London: Routledge, 1998).

7 Boyd Hilton, *The Age of Atonement: The Influence of Evangelicalism on Social and Economic Thought* (Oxford: Clarendon Press, 1986), G.R. Searle, *Morality and the Market in Victorian Britain* (Oxford: Clarendon Press, 1998), Michael Edelstein, *Overseas Investment in the Age of High Imperialism: The United Kingdom, 1850–1914* (New York: Columbia University Press, 1982), and Lance E. Davis and Robert A. Huttenback, *Mammon and the Pursuit of Empire: The Economics of Imperialism* (Cambridge: Cambridge University Press, 1988).

8 James Taylor, *Creating Capitalism: Joint-Stock Enterprise in British Politics and Culture, 1800–1870* (London: Royal Historical Society, 2006), and Johnson, *Making the Market* (2010).

9 James Taylor, *Boardroom Scandal: The Criminalization of Company Fraud in Nineteenth-Century Britain* (Oxford: Oxford University Press, 2013), and Sarah Wilson, *The Origins of Modern Financial Crime: Historical Foundations and Current Problems in Britain* (London: Routledge, 2013).

10 Mark Freeman, Robin Pearson, and James Taylor, *Shareholder Democracies?: Corporate Governance in Britain and Ireland before 1850* (Chicago: University of Chicago Press, 2012) and Timothy Alborn, ed., *British Shareholder Meetings in the Long Nineteenth Century* (New York: Routledge, 2024). See also Janette Rutterford, "The Shareholder Voice: British and American Accents, 1890–1965," *Enterprise and Society* 13 (March 2012), pp. 120–53.

11 Janette Rutterford and Josephine Maltby, " 'The Widow, the Clergyman and the Reckless': Women Investors in England, 1830–1914," *Feminist Economics* 12 (January/April 2006), pp. 111–38, Josephine Maltby and Janette Rutterford, " 'She Possessed Her Own Fortune': Women Investors from the Late Nineteenth Century to the Early Twentieth Century," *Business History* 48 (April 2006), pp. 220–53, Nancy Henry, " 'Ladies do it?': Victorian Women Investors in Fact and Fiction," in Francis O'Gorman, ed., *Victorian Literature and Finance* (Oxford: Oxford University Press, 2007), pp. 111–31, and David R. Green, Alastair Owens, Josephine Maltby, and Janette Rutterford, eds., *Men, Women and Money: Perspectives on Gender, Wealth, and Investment* (Oxford: Oxford University Press, 2011).

12 James Taylor, *Sexism and the City: Women Stockbrokers in Modern Britain* (Oxford: Oxford University Press, 2025).

13 Mary Poovey, *Genres of the Credit Economy: Mediating Value in Eighteenth- and Nineteenth-Century Britain* (Chicago: University of Chicago Press, 2008), p. 247.

14 Paul Delaney, *Literature, Money and the Market: From Trollope to Amis* (Basingstoke: Palgrave, 2002), Tamara Wagner, *Speculation in Victorian Fiction: Plotting Money and the Novel Genre, 1815–1901* (Columbus: Ohio State University Press, 2010), Nancy Henry, *Women, Literature and Finance in Victorian Britain: Cultures of Investment* (Basingstoke: Palgrave Macmillan, 2018), and Francis O'Gorman, ed., *Victorian Literature and Finance* (Oxford: Oxford University Press, 2007). See also Silvana Colella, *Charlotte Riddell's City Novels and Victorian Business: Narrating Capitalism* (London: Routledge, 2016), and Ranald C. Michie, *Guilty Money: The City of London in Victorian and Edwardian Culture* (London: Pickering and Chatto, 2009).

15 Harold Perkin, *Origins of Modern English Society* (London: Routledge, 1969), chapter 4.

INTRODUCTION TO VOLUME I

Public Finance and Company Promotion

The Industrial Revolution called into being a complex economy increasingly dependent on finance and investment. The most significant aspect of the new financial structure was the rise and proliferation of the joint-stock company, an organization formed through the public issuance of capital shares to a number of investors. Unlike private businesses or partnerships, there was virtually no limit to the amount of wealth that joint-stock companies could draw upon.

From the 1820s to the 1840s, public finance sustained a tremendous growth of banks, insurance companies, and especially railways. Corporate investment on the scale that we know it today began with the "Railway Mania" of the nineteenth century. For the first time the Stock Exchange dealt significantly with company shares instead of government securities, and the railway companies drew in the whole nation of investors.

Company Acts in the 1840s and 1850s greatly accelerated the formation of new joint-stock companies by simplifying the registration process and limiting the liability of individual investors. Company registrations grew from a few hundred a year in the 1830s to almost 5,000 a year by the 1890s.

FINANCE, INVESTMENT, AND JOINT-STOCK COMPANIES

At the beginning of the nineteenth century, most commercial capital was raised privately and locally by individual businessmen or partnerships. The investing class was a small, elite group whose main avenues of investment were either land or government securities. Since the creation of a permanent national debt in the 1690s, government securities had emerged as an important alternative to land as a form of investment. The funded debt, or "the funds" in popular parlance, was a useful outlet for superfluous wealth from rents or commercial profits. It was more liquid and easily divisible than land and could be readily transferred from person to person. Most aristocratic landholdings were indivisible and inherited by the eldest son. Younger sons could find employment in the civil service, military, or the professions, but government securities provided income, and dowries, for daughters. Heiresses might boast of having so much money "in the funds." In

1750 the British government consolidated most of its borrowings into a single loan which paid investors a fixed rate of 3%. The consolidated debt, or "consols," remained the most important financial security until the proliferation of railway shares in the 1840s. In the mid-eighteenth century, the funded debt had reached £78 million and some 60,000 Britons owned shares of it.[1] During the Napoleonic Wars, massive government borrowing swelled the funded debt to £475 million, creating a larger and more permanent market in government securities.[2]

As the number of fundholders grew, so too did the need for information and advice on how and where to acquire government securities. The first financial guide books had emerged in the eighteenth century and the genre remained popular throughout the nineteenth century and beyond. Thomas Fortune published his *Epitome of the Stocks and Public Funds* in 1796, and it was still in print in 1817. (pp. 3–15) Fortune was a stockbroker and he sought to normalize securities' investments. His guide described the different types of government stock available for purchase as well as the brokerage fees required and the dates when dividends were paid.

While government securities were an important, and uncontroversial, type of investment in the early nineteenth century, this was far from being the case for joint-stock companies and their shares. Although we take public companies for granted today, they were viewed by most Britons, including many people in the business community, as unnecessary, dangerous, and disreputable. As historian James Taylor notes, during the first half of the nineteenth century, the ideas that

> any collection of individuals associating in the form of a company should be able to sue in the courts as an autonomous entity, that individuals should be able to transfer into and out of the company at will, that they should bear only a limited responsibility for the actions of the company, that such responsibility should cease immediately on the sale of their shares and that such companies should continue to exist after all the original members had long since died, were alarming and unfamiliar concepts.[3]

Joint-stock companies seemed to fly in the face of personal responsibility and to possess unfair advantages over private traders.

Much of the opposition to companies derived from memories of the South Sea Bubble of 1720, a financial crisis still invoked in debates a century later. The South Sea Company had been chartered by the government in 1711 to carry on trade with South America. It did lackluster business until the directors of the Company devised an ingenious scheme for converting part of the government's funded debt into South Sea stock. This procedure would allow the government to reduce its debt while increasing the Company's capital and prestige. To facilitate their plan, directors bribed Members of Parliament and Court officials and also bought up blocks of South Sea shares to boost the price. At the time of the conversion, in 1720, South Sea stock rose precipitously, inspiring a mania for new companies.[4]

A multitude of joint-stock promotions mushroomed around the South Sea Company, hoping to emulate its success. Most of these companies were hopelessly ill-conceived and many outright swindles. This onrush of dubious promotions alarmed prudent businessmen and politicians. The South Sea Company, however, was more worried about competition from this new issue market, and it lobbied its allies in the government to pass the so-called Bubble Act of 1720, forbidding further company formation without Royal Charter or Parliamentary sanction. Yet by this time the damage had already been done.

Shares in the South Sea Company and its host of imitators were desperately oversubscribed with little chance of repaying the initial investment. Many speculators had purchased shares on borrowed money, paying small deposits in hope of reselling before the next payment was due. As demands for payment mounted, people had to sell shares in order to meet obligations or repay loans. Prices fell and in turn more shares were thrown upon the market. Thus the bubble burst in the autumn of 1720.

The inevitable crash brought ruin to thousands of humble investors as well as a number of prominent merchants and tradesmen. Criminal allegations were leveled against the South Sea Company, and many of its directors fled abroad. Sir Robert Walpole became a power in the state by his deft screening of the Crown and other members of the Court involved in the Company. The South Sea catastrophe exercised a psychological restraint on joint-stock organization for over a century, associating it in the public mind with fraud and duplicity. The Bubble Act rendered incorporation impossible without the trouble and expense of a private bill in Parliament. Fortunately the requirements of eighteenth-century commerce were not so complicated as to demand incorporation. Most businesses could be accommodated by private firms or partnerships.

The Industrial Revolution quickened the pace of earlier financial developments. Industry required new refinements in banking and credit, and enterprises such as canals, docks, gas-works, and railways could only be financed through the flotation of public companies. The steady proliferation of joint-stock companies during the nineteenth century constitutes a second financial revolution which in size, numbers of people involved, and real operation was more profound than eighteenth-century financial developments. Company shares came to compete with government securities, and, in 1811, industrial shares were quoted on the Stock Exchange for the first time, making them as accessible as Treasury stock. A growing middle class desired more lucrative avenues of investment beyond the 3% interest paid by government securities.[5]

By the early nineteenth century, some business people began railing against the strictures of the Bubble Act. One such complaint was Henry Day's pamphlet, *A Defense of Joint-Stock Companies* (1808). (pp. 17–21) Day, a solicitor for a brewery, situated his advocacy for companies within larger arguments in favor of free trade and against undue government interference in private enterprise. As he argued:

> It would be ridiculous to talk of the freedom of trade in a country, which owes its present aggrandizement to trade, if we were to be told that any

> sums, however large, might not be raised for legal speculations, by any number of subscribers, and that the whole might not divide the profits in proportion to their respective contributions!
>
> (p. 17)

As *laissez-faire* principles gained ground over the course of the nineteenth century, restrictions on incorporation became harder to maintain.

The debate over joint-stock companies reached a crescendo in 1825, during a period of intense commercial and financial speculation. Between 1824 and 1825, 624 new companies were promoted with a nominal capital of £370 million.[6] Parliament became so swamped with applications for incorporation that it repealed the Bubble Act as a hindrance to economic development. Parliamentary sanction was no longer necessary for company formation, but limited liability for shareholders, traditionally inseparable from the joint-stock company form, was henceforth a privilege only doled out by private Act or Royal Charter to a small number of companies.[7]

The stimulus for the 1825 boom, like that of the South Sea Bubble a century earlier, was the fabled wealth of Latin America. In 1824 and 1825 the British public raised £17.5 million in loans for the newly independent South American republics, and this was soon followed by a tremendous investment in South American mining companies. In turn, large numbers of British railway, insurance, and gas company schemes jumped on the bandwagon. The 1825 mania spawned an intense newspaper and pamphlet debate over the propriety of company formation in general and the legitimacy of the current promotions in particular.[8]

Among the most scathing condemnations of the new company mania was the anonymously published work, *The South Sea Bubble and the Numerous Fraudulent Projects to Which it Gave Rise in 1720* (1825). (pp. 23–30) The author, like many commentators at the time, invoked the South Sea catastrophe "as a beacon to the unwary against modern schemes equally visionary and nefarious." The London merchant William Clay also denounced the current spate of company promotions in *Remarks on Joint-Stock Companies by an Old Merchant* (1825). (pp. 31–80) Clay believed that these promotions encouraged a reckless spirit of gambling and a feckless desire to get rich quick without the necessary hard work.

The advocates for joint-stock formation countered that companies were an economic innovation that would unleash stagnant capital and enrich all classes of society. In *The Influence of Interest and Prejudice Upon Proceedings in Parliament* (1825), the solicitor Alexander Mundell argued that most politicians were ignorant of the principles of political economy and were therefore incapable of framing effective commercial laws. (pp. 39–42) Although he saw reckless stock market speculation as a social ill, he did not think parliament could, or should, do much about it. In a true system of free trade, investors must exercise more caution as to where they place their capital and not rely on the faulty enactments of legislators for protection.

Unsurprisingly, most participants in the debate over joint-stock companies came from elite backgrounds, but there was also a working-class argument in favor of incorporation. The socialist Abram Combe, for example, believed that joint-stock companies had great potential for social improvements by enabling large numbers of working people to pool their modest resources for cooperative endeavors. In *The Sphere of Joint-Stock Companies* (1825), Combe explains how he helped to organize a socialist commune in Scotland, financed by the creation of a joint-stock company. (pp. 43–7)

As it transpired, comparisons between the 1720 South Sea Bubble and the 1825 company boom proved accurate. In both cases, shares were outrageously overvalued and often purchased on borrowed money. In 1825 the drain on bullion for foreign loans and overseas mining companies led the Bank of England to restrict credit and, with this restriction, the whole speculative structure collapsed. Of the 624 companies floated in two years, only 127 still existed in 1827. The surviving companies had a nominal value of £103 million though only £15 million had been paid up. Another 118 companies had issued shares and taken in some £2 million, but were abandoned within a few months of formation – a category which smacked strongly of fraud.[9]

The 1825 crash was one of the worst financial crises of the nineteenth century. Dozens of banks across the nation failed, and the companies which managed to survive the crisis, saw their share prices plumet. The writer Thomas Love Peacock, who at the time worked for the East India Company in London, witnessed the financial wreckage firsthand. He reflected on the crisis in his poem "Chorus of Bubble Buyers," told from the point of view of the ruined investors:

> Now curst be the projects, and curst the projectors,
> And curst be the bubbles before us that rolled,
> Which, bursting, have left us like desolate spectres.
> Bewailing our bodies of paper and gold.

The ghost-like speculators now plan to haunt the stock exchange as a warning against similar delusive schemes. (pp. 49–51)

Ironically, some of the failures of 1825 paved the way for further joint-stock promotions. Widespread bank failures underscored the weaknesses of the English banking system, where all banks were privately owned, since the Bank of England had secured a national monopoly on joint-stock banking in 1708. With trade expanding, the burdens placed on the private banks became too great for their limited resources. Critics contrasted the English banks with their Scottish counterparts, which had long been organized along the joint-stock principle, and which weathered the 1825 crisis without a hitch. Therefore, in 1826 Parliament passed an Act permitting joint-stock banks to be formed in England, outside a sixty-five-mile radius of London. The restriction was in deference to the Bank of England's monopoly, but even this last bit of favoritism was eliminated in 1833 with the renewal of the Bank's Charter.[10]

Joint-stock banks experience a boom in the 1830s, increasing from 32 in 1833 to 79 in 1836 to 115 in 1841. Between 1825 and 1843, ninety-three private banks reorganized themselves along joint-stock lines.[11] This explosion of joint-stock banks, along with a concurrent rise in insurance companies and railways, created tremendous new investment opportunities for the propertied classes. New investment guides sprang up, offering up-to-date information on the latest securities, such as Charles Fenn's *A Compendium of the English and Foreign Funds, and the Principal Joint Stock Companies* (1838) (pp. 53–8). Fenn, a stockbroker, supplied investors with a detailed list of all the new joint-stock banks, the price of their shares, and the amount of their most recent dividends.

As joint-stock companies increased in number, their proponents sought a more rational and systematic means of company formation. Forming joint-stock companies under the registration process laid down by the Companies Acts only became the norm after the middle of the nineteenth century. The two decades from 1825 to 1844 were a nebulous period for public companies. Even with the repeal of the Bubble Act in 1825, the legal position of joint-stock companies remained unclear. There were no special laws regulating company formation, which was left to the inadequate provisions of the common law. Anyone could promote a company for any purpose. Directors were under no obligation to report to shareholders, to publish accounts, or even to audit the company's books. In this atmosphere of confusion fraud flourished. As economist J.R. McCulloch complained in the *Edinburgh Review* in 1836:

> If [companies'] power of doing good, when rightly applied and conducted, be great, their power of doing mischief, when in the hands of craft and perverted to improper purposes, is ten times greater. They then become the most prolific sources of bankruptcy and ruin; enriching a select coterie of knaves and jobbers, while they involve thousands, who were led to believe that they would add prodigiously to their wealth, in irremediable poverty and beggary.[12]

This complaint was far from academic, for the 1830s witnessed a growing number of frauds, especially among life insurance companies.

These frauds alerted Parliament to the need for company regulation, and in 1841 a Select Committee was appointed "to inquire into the state of the law respecting joint-stock companies with a view to the prevention of fraud." The first sittings dealt primarily with life insurance frauds, but in 1843 the Committee was reconstituted under the chairmanship of Gladstone, then President of the Board of Trade, and the focus was broadened to include the possible regulation of all joint-stock enterprise. The Committee solicited testimony from businessmen and lawyers with expertise in company matters, and the picture which emerged was from far from reassuring.[13]

In its Report of 1844, the Committee listed a number of unsavory practices whereby dishonest promoters deceived the public. Companies, for example, would often use, without permission, the names of famous people in their advertisements. Promoters would further "puff" their concerns by falsely advertising the amount of capital subscribed or else getting reports of pretended meetings inserted into papers. Companies might try to project a façade of respectability by opening accounts at the Bank of England or selecting "offices in respectable situations, and fitted out in a respectable manner." To bring in more money directors sometimes published false accounts or else paid unearned dividends out of capital. Directors could ward off inquiries by creating fictitious votes or proxies to outvote actual shareholders, and if directors conducted their business at a distance, through agents, or under assumed names, inquiries would be doubly difficult.[14]

The Committee was optimistic about its ability to combat fraud, arguing in its Report that "publication of the Directors, of the Shareholders, of the amount of capital, and whether subscribed or not subscribed, nominal or real, would baffle every case of fraud which has come under the notice of your Committee." Publicity was to be the antidote to fraud, and in June of 1844 the Committee's recommendations were embodied in "An Act for the Registration, Incorporation, and Regulation of Joint Stock Companies." (pp. 59–91) The Act provided a Registry Office to coordinate company matters. Henceforth, before any new company could advertise to the public, it had to inform the Registrar of its name and purpose, and the names and addresses of its promoters. At this point the company was *provisionally* registered. It had thereafter to inform the Registrar of its place of business, the names of its directors, and the names of all shareholders. Provisionally registered companies could only require a 5% deposit on shares. Furthermore, new companies were required to file with the Registry Office copies of every prospectus or advertisement issued.[15]

To achieve complete registration, a new company had within a year to present the Registrar with its Deed of Settlement, specifying the amount of nominal capital, the total number of shares, the names and addresses of shareholders, the number of shares held by each member, and the deposits paid on those shares. The Deed had to be signed by at least one-fourth of the shareholders holding at least one-fourth of the total shares. Once a company was fully incorporated, it still had to meet certain requirements of the Act. Half-yearly returns of members had to be sent to the Company Registry Office. All companies had to draw up a yearly balance sheet of assets and liabilities which was to be signed by the company auditor and at least three directors, presented at a yearly meeting of shareholders, and then filed with the Registrar. To insure full publicity, the documents of any company were open to inspection at the Registry Office for the fee of one shilling.[16]

The Company Act of 1844 revolutionized business organization. At the time of the Act there were some 900 English joint-stock companies in existence. In the next ten years, another 900 were registered. This figure does not include railway companies, which were outside the jurisdiction of the Company Act and which also experienced a phenomenal boom in 1845. The mid-forties marked a "take-off" period for joint-stock promotions, as clearly discernible today as it was to contemporaries.[17]

THE RAILWAY MANIA

As financial journalist David Morier Evans wrote in 1859,

> it is with the railway mania of 1845 that the modern form of speculation may be said to begin, and the world has not yet recovered from the excitement caused by the spectacle of sudden fortunes made without trouble and obscure individuals converted, as if by magic, into *millionaires*.[18]

Railways transformed English finance as surely as they transformed the English landscape. In 1845 Parliament sanctioned 2,816 miles of new railway lines, an amount equal to all the miles sanctioned between 1821 and 1843. An additional 4,540 miles were sanctioned in 1846. At its peak in 1846–47, railway expenditure absorbed almost 7% of national income.[19]

Railways broadened the base of investment. For the first time, the Stock Exchange dealt significantly with company shares instead of government bonds. The Mania of the mid-forties drew in the whole nation of investors. The aristocracy and gentry became heavily involved in railway shareholding since they were often given large blocks of shares to secure their goodwill for lines crossing their estates. At mid-century the economist Thomas Tooke observed:

> In every street of every town persons were to be found who were holders of Railway shares. Elderly men and women of small fortunes, tradesmen of every order, pensioners, public functionaries, professional men, merchants, country gentlemen – the mania had affected all.

All propertied people, that is. Or in the words of business historian J.H. Clapham, railway shares had become "a universal family investment for all families which had anything to invest."[20]

As demand for shares grew, the Railway Mania gave birth to a network of provincial stock exchanges and a new financial press. In 1844-45, existing stock exchanges in Manchester and Liverpool shot up in size and level of business and new exchanges were formed in Glasgow, Birmingham, Leeds, Edinburgh, Bristol, and Newcastle. With these provincial stock exchanges linked to London by telegraph, Britain now had a national capital market. With new companies being created daily, the first financial periodicals sprang up to offer up-to-date information about railway investments. Among the various railway papers were the *Railway Magazine,* the *Railway Times, The Railway Monitor,* a special section of the *Economist,* and *Railway Intelligence,* published by the London Stock Exchange.[21]

As the financial data on railway companies grew increasingly complex, enterprising publishers began summarizing basic information in guide books for investors. Henry Tuck, the publisher of the *Railway Times* created one of the first and most popular guides, *The Railway Shareholder's Manual* (1845). (pp. 95–100)

Tuck provided basic information about individual railway companies, including the extent of their lines, share prices, amount of paid-up capital, and dividends paid.

Investors dreamed of riches and contemporaries were fascinated by stories about railway millionaires. Fortunes were made by enterprising new men such as the engineer George Stephenson or the contractor Samuel Morton Peto. The parvenu *par excellence*, however, was George Hudson, the "Railway King." A Yorkshire draper turned banker and railway promoter, Hudson parlayed his shrewd business sense into a railway fortune, a country estate, and a seat in parliament. Hudson was chairman of several important lines, including the York and North Midland and the Eastern Counties. For a time, he seemed to have the Midas touch. The mere mention of Hudson's name in connection with a proposed railway would guarantee full subscription of its shares. Hudson was courted by some of the highest in the land, eager for his financial advice, though others mocked his Yorkshire brogue and lack of gentlemanly polish.[22]

The idea of an obscure person elevated to sudden wealth through railway investments was certainly ripe with comic possibilities. W.M. Thackeray's "Diary and Letters of C. Jeames de la Pluche" appeared in *Punch* during 1845–46, the height of the mania, satirizing the misadventures of a London footman, whose £20 speculation in railway shares escalates to half a million. (pp. 101–8) Jeames Plush becomes director of numerous railway companies and sets himself up as a gentleman – newly styled James de la Pluche. Soon Jeames is pompously boasting (in Cockney dialect) of his financial eminence:

> Railway Spec is going on phamously. You should see how polite they har at my bankers now! Sir Paul Pump Aldgate & Company. They bow me out of the back parlor as if I was a Nybobb. Everybody says I'm worth half a million. The number of lines they're putting me upon is inkumseavable.

Thackeray's burlesque, like many other literary accounts of railway tycoons, depicts railway promoters as vulgar upstarts, blissfully unaware of their own shortcomings.

If the idea, however improbable, of working-class speculators disturbed Victorian sensibilities, the spectacle of female financiers was even more unsettling. There is no question that many women eagerly participated in the Railway Mania. The press frequently commented on the phenomenon, and railway share registers contain the names of numerous women. Even the Bronte sisters in remote Haworth bought shares in Hudson's York and North Midland Railway.[23] John Sheehan's comic fable, "The Railway Queen" (1845), includes unflattering portraits of women speculators, who are vain, frivolous, and ignorant. (pp. 109–15) Sheehan's unease at women avidly pursuing gain on the stock market was consistent with Victorian stereotypes that idealized women as modest, self-effacing, and spiritual. Advice books cautioned women from investing their own money, recommending instead that they put their financial affairs in the hands of a male relation or family friend.

The very immensity of railway promotions was in itself overwhelming. The *Times* saw the nation "stifled in the froth of a thousand schemes."[24] Among the hundreds of proposed railway lines dangled before the British public were some that were outright frauds. Investors, however, were ill-equipped to separate the wheat from the chaff. Parliament could barely cope with the hundreds of railway bills before it in 1845 and 1846. The public had little access to good financial advice or even to accurate financial data.

The ease with which railways could be promoted ensured an abundance of new companies. In 1846 the M.P. Thomas Duncombe complained to the Commons:

> Any man might go and get any scheme, how absurd soever, provisionally registered on paying £5. In November and September last, every man who dreamed almost of a railway got it registered. It would generally be found that most of the parties who registered were only solicitors or surveyors.[25]

Railway companies were a source of limitless fees for lawyers, engineers, and surveyors. It was of little regard to some of these men whether or not the proposed lines were feasible or the resulting companies successful. Money was to be made simply in drawing up maps, prospectuses, and articles of association. An abortive company was almost as profitable to lawyers as a successful one. In the general rush to make money discrimination was thrown to the winds.

Railway promotion took on a life of its own. People stopped asking whether a given line was viable or whether it met any real need. If money could be made, practical questions were ignored. In 1846, John Hawkshaw, Engineer of the Manchester and Leeds Railway, estimated that half of the lines projected that year were launched by mere speculators who had no intention of actually constructing railways. These railways were proposed for the sole purpose of securing deposits from prospective shareholders. Provisional Committees would squander deposit money in fees to themselves and their cronies, leaving deceived subscribers in the lurch.[26]

Railway promoters were not the only persons attempting to manipulate the share market to their advantage. Many legitimate promoters were themselves victimized by unprincipled speculators who specialized in applying for shares which they never intended to keep, but only to sell for a quick profit. Speculative abuses in railway shares were facilitated by the practice of only requiring a small deposit on each share (usually 5%) and leaving the remainder to be "called-up" as needed. Anyone with a few pounds could thus become a gambler in shares. The term "stag" was coined in the 1840s to describe those people who applied for railway shares only to resell them. Stags dealt not only in shares but also in letters of allotment – letters which informed prospective shareholders how many shares had been assigned them as well as the deposit required to receive those shares. Letters of allotment were not valid securities, and their sale was illegal, though stags traded in them extensively during the Mania.[27]

This share-dealing spirit possessed all classes and changed the nature of railway enterprise. Speculation became the driving force behind railway promotion. In the words of Samuel Smiles,

> many people, utterly ignorant of railways, knowing and caring nothing about their general national uses, but hungering and thirsting after premiums, rushed eagerly into the vortex of speculation. They applied for allotments, and subscribed for shares in lines, of the engineering character or probable traffic of which they knew nothing. 'Shares! shares!' became the general cry.[28]

Interestingly, Smiles characterized the Mania as a "vortex," as if it were a force of nature over which people could exercise little control.

Promotion followed promotion in a veritable Niagara of new companies. Above all else, the ball had to be kept rolling by launching fresh projects for expansion. Yet, as a few killjoys began pointing out in the autumn of 1845, the Mania could not be kept up indefinitely. In October 1845, the *Economist* argued that the nation did not possess sufficient capital to pay for all proposed railway construction. In November, the *Times* estimated that the cost of an additional 620 new railway schemes was £563 million, or more than two-thirds of the total National Debt. This money could not be raised, the *Times* insisted, without "the most ruinous, universal, and desperate confusion."[29] Henry Wilson, a surveyor, published his own lengthy warning to investors: *The Railway Panic: Hints to Railroad Speculators* (1845). (pp. 117–23) Wilson was a strong believer in railways as engineering marvels and commercial improvements, but he believed that reckless share speculations endangered the solvency of the entire railway network.

The construction of railway lines proceeded faster than new traffic, while over-speculation guaranteed a steady stream of bubble promotions. Many proposed lines were redundant. According to the *Economist,* "we see nine or ten proposals for nearly the same line, all at a premium, when it is well known that only one can succeed, and the rest must, in all probability, be minus their expenses." Such reckless speculation led the *Times* to characterize the Railway Mania as "a tale of national delusion."[30]

In 1846 the Mania fizzled out. Over-subscription had taken its toll, and investors now sold shares to meet calls on other shares. Hundreds of proposed lines collapsed as their scrip became unsaleable. In his *History of the English Railway,* published in the aftermath of the Mania, John Francis argued that "no other panic was ever so fatal to the middle class. It reached every hearth, it saddened every heart in the metropolis. Entire families were ruined."[31]

The English public now regarded the Railway Mania as a monstrous plot for the extortion of money. After the crash, a number of newspapers and journals printed cartoons which showed savage, anthropomorphic trains devouring shareholders.[32] Several books and pamphlets were now published, detailing the disreputable methods employed by railway promoters. Among the most influential and widely read of these exposés was Arthur Smith's *The Bubble of the Age* (1848). (pp. 125–30) Smith contended that many railway companies inflated the value of their shares by paying unearned dividends out of capital rather than from genuine profits. The firms then concealed their financial jugglery by publishing false accounts.

The surviving railway companies struggled to adjust investors' expectations as it became clear that the nation's traffic would not sustain the high dividends which shareholders had become accustomed to during the Mania. By the late 1840s railway share values had dropped precipitously. The twelve principal railway companies had paid an average dividend of 7.6% in 1846. By 1848 the average dividend had fallen to 5.3% and by 1849 to 3.2%. Irate shareholders began to scrutinize accounts more closely, and in the late 1840s Committees of Investigation were set up at a number of railways. These committees uncovered an alarming amount of fraud and mismanagement, especially at the firms managed by George Hudson, the "Railway King."[33]

In 1849 the York and North Midland Railway's Committee of Investigation released its report detailing Hudson's misdeeds. Under his chairmanship, no proper books or accounts had been kept, and records of much company business reposed in Hudson's mind alone. Without company sanction, Hudson and other directors had appropriated thousands of shares for themselves. Hudson also overstated traffic receipts and understated working charges so as to pay unearned dividends. Similar revelations at other lines led to Hudson's financial downfall, social disgrace, and eventual exile from England.[34]

The nation's wrath now fell upon its former hero, as Hudson was made the scapegoat for all the excesses of the Railway Mania. The historian and social critic Thomas Carlyle denounced Hudson as a false messiah in his withering essay "Hudson's Statue." (pp. 131–6) Hudson represented the crass materialism and relentless pursuit of wealth that Carlyle saw as the new spirit of the age. Hudson, however, could not have succeeded in his villainy had so many people not been willing to worship at his shrine. Greedy speculators were as much at fault as Hudson, and they should examine their own motives before singling out their former idol for blame: "One sordid, hungry *canaille* are they all. Why should this, the chief terrier among them, be set upon by all the dog fraternity?"

Literary depictions of the Railway Mania were equally harsh. Emma Robinson dissected railway promotion in her allegorical novel, *The Gold Worshippers* (1851). Her story follows the rise of the railway magnate Humson and his accomplice Lawless as they lead the Gullible family to ruin. In Robert Bell's novel, *The Ladder of Gold* (1850), the Hudson-like protagonist, Richard Rawlings, rises from provincial clerk to railway millionaire. (pp. 137–43) Rawlings' success owes no small part to ruthless business practices. He rides roughshod over company meetings, going so far as to hire Irish thugs to silence dissident shareholders.

In a lengthy article in the *Edinburgh Review,* "Railway Morals and Railway Policy" (1854), philosopher Herbert Spencer evaluated recent railway investigations by shareholders and Parliament. (p?) He detailed many of the sharp business practices and frauds that had been exposed, and, like Carlyle, saw the problem as systemic. He attributed corruption in railway management to a "corporate conscience" which allowed company directors to distance themselves from wrongful acts by spreading the responsibility widely among numerous actors.

Was the corporate economy inherently amoral and unmanageable? The Railway Mania in all its excesses seemed to suggest that this might be the case. In the following decades, the business community, the government, the press, and the investing public struggled to understand a new and increasingly complex financial system. They debated whether more financial regulation was desirable, and if so, the forms it should take. A desire for economic stability and an eagerness to inhibit financial fraud led to a further revamping of company law.

THE COMING OF LIMITED LIABILITY

By the late 1850s, limited liability was the one prize still sought by the advocates of joint-stock organization. Since 1825 most public companies had unlimited liability, meaning that directors and shareholders were liable for their companies' debts to the entire extent of their fortunes – "to the last acre and last shilling," as the popular expression went. Classic historic accounts, such as H.A. Shannon's influential 1930s article, "The Coming of General Limited Liability," have depicted limited liability as a necessary ingredient in British economic expansion that was aggressively lobbied for by business people.[35] As more recent work by James Taylor and Rob McQueen has demonstrated, many Victorian merchants and industrialists preferred private partnerships over limited liability companies, which they feared would lower barriers to competition and undermine privacy in commercial matters.[36] During the 1850s, deep divisions over limited liability played out in parliamentary investigations, in newspapers and journals, and in a vigorous pamphlet war.

The meteoric rise of railways, which all had limited liability, was accustoming Britons to the idea that a company's financial responsibility should be limited to the total amount of its capital and individual shareholder responsibility to the nominal value of their shareholding. Limited liability could be secured by any company by a private parliamentary act or a royal charter granted by the Board of Trade, but these were complicated and expensive procedures. A wealthy and influential rentier class wanted more avenues of investment offering higher rates of return than railways and government securities. They pressed for less restrictive access to limited liability.

The growing influence of free trade principles favored limited liability and pushed against excessive government regulation. At the same time that a *laissez-faire* mentality was influencing foreign trade, as in the much-celebrated repeal of the protective Corn Laws in 1846, it was also busily at work in the realm of domestic commerce. The cautionary regulations of the 1844 Company Act were unpopular with free traders, who whittled away at their provisions. In 1847 promoters were relieved of the "burdensome" task of registering prospectuses and advertisements. Although a Select Committee found in 1853 that most companies never filed annual balance sheets, Parliament refused to give the Registrar of Joint Stock Companies powers of enforcement. Indeed, the government had no duty to prosecute violators of the 1844 Act, who could only be brought to justice by aggrieved shareholders or creditors. The tradition of *caveat emptor* was well established in the common law and underscored the case for governmental non-interference in business matters.[37]

On the other hand, many Britons still saw joint-stock companies as anomalous and unnecessary entities in an economy best organized by family firms and partnerships. The incorporation of limited liability companies might be necessary in certain instances, as in the case of railways, but this privilege should not be made available to all comers and was best controlled by the state. As the historian Timothy Alborn argues, this was still "a time when it was difficult, if not impossible, for people to imagine large-scale commercial operations as belonging wholly to the social construct known as 'the market.'"[38]

Opponents of limited liability feared that it would undermine the work ethic and habits of thrift by encouraging speculative investment and a desire to get rich quick. Christian Evangelicalism, well embedded in Victorian culture, emphasized personal responsibility.[39] Like many of those hostile to limited liability, the economist J.R. McCulloch invoked religious sentiments, opposing limited companies for enabling individuals to escape their moral obligation to their debtors and to hide behind a collective corporate identity. In his anti-limited liability tract, *Considerations on Partnerships with Limited Liability* (1856), McCulloch insisted that "in the scheme laid down by Providence for the government of the world, there is no shifting or narrowing of responsibilities, every man being personally answerable to the utmost extent for all his actions."[40] Yet with the divorce of ownership and control in large companies, McCulloch's argument seemed increasingly irrelevant. The nominal owners of the company, the shareholders, were in practice a large body of passive investors who had ceased to be entrepreneurs in the usual sense of the word. They had little ability to oversee the company's affairs which were in the hands of a small body of directors. Why then should shareholders be made liable for the actions of the directors, beyond their specific capital investments?

Some advocates of limited liability characterized the current state of legislation as a "law for the rich," arguing that wealthy men could better secure the privileges of limited liability by parliamentary act or royal charter than could ordinary, working-class Britons. Christian Socialists like F.D. Maurice and John Ludlow believed that easier access to limited liability would create new business opportunities for working people.[41] A similar argument was made by the writer Henry Morley in an article, "The Penny Saved," published in Charles Dickens's journal *Household Words* in 1850. (pp. 165–70) Morley argued that an extension of limited liability would enable laborers to pool their more limited financial resources, establishing all kinds of cooperative enterprises.

In 1850, expert witnesses before the Parliamentary Committee on the Savings of the Middle and Working Classes debated whether unlimited liability deterred modest investors from buying company shares. Some witnesses believed that the current system inhibited investment and that too much of the nation's capital was lying idle. They noted that limited liability prevailed in the United States, France, the Netherlands, and Belgium, where it was of great utility in stimulating investment.[42] Lord Hobart drew upon these arguments in his 1853 tract, *Remarks on the Law of Partnership Liability.* (pp. 171–4) Hobart, who had worked at the Board of Trade, estimated that some £40 million was added to the national wealth annually. Too much of this money, he believed, was being hoarded by people wary of placing it in unlimited companies, or it was subject to capital flight, being invested in limited liability companies abroad.

Opponents of limited liability countered that Britain had a prosperous and expanding economy and that there was no evidence that business enterprises were unable to find sufficient capital. They conceded that limited liability might be appropriate for underdeveloped and newly industrializing nations, but that it was unnecessary in a mature economic powerhouse like Great Britain.

Conservative voices from the business community feared that limited liability would encourage speculation and financial fraud. In *Observations on Unlimited and Limited Liability* (1854), industrialist William Hawes argued that unlimited liability was a safer system as it made investors more prudent in the employment of their capital and less likely to do business with unknown and unproven entities. (pp. 175–85) Limited liability, by contrast, would promote reckless speculation and relieve investors of their obligation to exercise "prudence, foresight, and care" in the employment of their capital.

Advocates of limited liability admitted that the principle was likely to be abused, but as they pointed out under the current system of unlimited liability, "many reckless schemes ruinous to shareholders and injurious to the public, have been carried on."[43] The 1844 Company Act had sought to inhibit fraud, but some critics argued that it actually facilitated it. For example, the provisional registration mandated by the Act may have given an aura of authenticity to embryo companies, allowing dishonest promoters to collect share deposits only to decamp with the proceeds.

Given the deep divisions over limited liability, in 1854 the government established a Royal Commission on the Law of Partnership to consider the matter. The Commissioners examined sixty-nine legal and commercial experts, but their testimony remained divided and there was no strong consensus over whether to retain the current system or scrap it.[44] However, in the ensuing parliamentary debate over the Royal Commission's Report, most Members spoke strongly in favor of limited liability. (pp. 187–222) They argued that it would unleash even more capital for British economic expansion and innovation.

In 1855 Parliament passed a Limited Liability Act with strong support from both Liberals and Conservatives. (pp. 223–8) The Act allowed most joint-stock companies to limit their members' liability, so long as the Deed of Settlement stated clearly that the company was limited and the word "limited" always appeared at the end of the company's name. This state sanction of limited liability probably reflected the growing influence of free trade principles as well as a desire by the government to divest itself of the onerous responsibility of granting or denying limited liability to joint-stock companies on a case-by-case basis.

In 1856, Parliament repealed the 1844 Company Act, replacing it with more permissive legislation.[45] Under the 1856 Companies Act, to achieve incorporation a company need only submit a Memorandum of Association to the Registrar containing the name and object of the company, the type of liability – whether limited or unlimited, the amount of nominal capital, and the total number of shares. It was only necessary for seven people holding one share each to sign this document. Provisional registration was dropped as was the requirement for a minimum paid-up capital. Companies were still required to hold annual shareholders' meetings and to send the Registrar a yearly list of members and their holdings, but there was no longer a mandatory audit.

The liberal provisions of the 1856 Act were defended in the Commons by Robert Lowe. The science of political economy, Lowe argued, taught that

> to interfere with and abridge men's liberty, and to undertake to do for them what they can do for themselves, is really lulling their vigilance to sleep, and depriving them of that safeguard which Providence intended for them, and helping fraudulent men to mislead and delude them.[46]

The new legislation protected investors by limiting their liability, but in return, it demanded that they be more careful about deciding where and with whom to invest their money. In 1862 a consolidating Companies Act was passed which essentially recapitulated the provisions of the 1856 Act and extended its privileges to banks and insurance companies.[47]

The passage of the new Companies Acts brought a big increase in the number of joint-stock promotions. Between 1844 and 1856, 966 companies had been registered. Thereafter the numbers increased at a remarkable rate. In the six years from 1856 to 1862, nearly 2,500 companies were registered. In another six years 4,000 more companies were incorporated.[48] In an 1864 essay, "Whither is Limited Liability Leading Us?", financial journalist David Morier Evans concludes that what was until recently "considered an experiment, and an experiment of a very dangerous character," was now universally accepted. (pp. 229–34) The British were not merely establishing limited liability companies throughout the kingdom, but were investing in such concerns in the "more distant quarters of the globe."

COMPANY PROMOTION AND COMPANY PROMOTERS

New Companies Acts in 1855, 1856, and 1862 made limited liability available to all joint-stock companies and greatly simplified the process of company registration. This led to a new boom in joint-stock promotions during the 1860s and the rise of a new character – "the company promoter." Although systematic company promotion began with the Railway Mania, the professional company promoter really came into his own during the 1860s. With the upsurge in joint-stock flotations following the new company legislation, there was a greater need for financial intermediaries between the merchants, industrialists, and inventors who wanted to incorporate their businesses and the British public who wanted investment outlets for their capital. The promotion of a company required advertising skills and share-dealing expertise which many businesspeople did not possess. In France, Germany, and other continental states, investment banks supervised the majority of joint-stock flotations. In Britain, however, investment banking remained underdeveloped, so that most joint-stock companies went public through the agency of an individual promoter who would purchase the business, assemble a board of directors, draw up a prospectus and advertisements, and resell the company to the public through the issuance of shares.[49]

Almost from their first appearance, company promoters had a bad reputation. At mid-century, Evans wrote:

> The man who assumes as a calling the constitution of joint-stock associations, is most frequently looked upon as a doubtful character, who, if even to be trusted, requires looking after. He is not like an individual who, bringing a great system to bear, and having carried it out, obtains a leading appointment, and continues in the service of the company; but, in the character of "company-monger," he is merely the person who, having the idea entrusted to him, endeavors to get together a body of men who are willing, by their names and influence, to set the scheme in motion.[50]

In other words, the promoter was a salesman, and given to the flash and exaggeration of modern commercialism. It was believed by many that promoters would sell any company, however defective, so long as they could turn a personal profit.

The most important document promoters drew-up was the prospectus, a brief printed broadside or leaflet inviting subscriptions to the new company. The prospectus set forth the company's purpose, the names of its directors, and the amount of its capital. Ideally prospectuses should provide detailed financial information on the nature and value of companies' assets, though this was not required by law and in practice was rarely done. Many prospectuses contained lurid promises of success rather than substantial financial data. Worthless or failing businesses concealed their insolvency by dwelling on past performance or future hopes, assets were shamelessly overvalued, and liabilities concealed. The Overend and Gurney crash in 1866 revealed the full possibilities of such deception. (For more information about the 1866 financial crisis, see Vol. 4 of this collection, *Financial Crises and Financial Fraud*.) The prospectus for the 1865 flotation of the celebrated private discount bank Overend and Gurney had failed to list several million pounds of bad debts which were transferred to the new public company by means of a secret contract with the old firm. Parliament responded with a hastily drafted amendment to the 1867 Companies Act requiring prospectuses to list all contracts. There was considerable confusion, however, as to what constituted a contract, and some promoters avoided the new requirement by means of a waiver clause.[51]

The 1886 prospectus for the flotation of the Guinness Brewery provides a good example of the form and content of a Victorian prospectus. (pp. 237–43) Prospectuses such as this were widely disseminated by being printed in newspapers, distributed by brokers and bankers, and mailed to likely investors. As Guinness was a successful business with a long track record of profitability, the prospectus did not tamper with the financial data provided. Although the Guinness prospectus was above board, the actual flotation of the company by the promoters, in this case Baring's Bank, was far from straightforward. Baring's held back huge blocks of shares for itself and allied City firms, only releasing around 25% of the shares to the public. This artificial scarcity caused share prices to skyrocket, allowing the promoters to sell their own shares later at the inflated price.[52]

In a cautionary 1897 article, "How to Scan a Prospectus," financial journalist Hartley Withers warned investors that many prospectuses

> are interesting only as examples of audacious impudence, and as giving lamentably emphatic evidence of public gullibility: they seldom give one half the information which anyone in his senses would require before investing in a new company, and yet it must be inferred that they do not display, or conceal, their charms in vain.
>
> (p. 246)

Withers advised investors to avoid promotions where the prospectus gave gross profits rather than net profits or that lumped past profits together for several years, possibly concealing downward trends. Financial information should never be taken on faith, but should be accompanied by a signed statement from an independent accountant.

Promoters suspected that the public only read the front sheet of a prospectus to see the names of the company's directors and that to catch investors' attention, a prospectus should advertise well-known or titled directors, dubbed "front sheeters." Also known as "guinea-pig directors" since they lent their names for money (guineas), these men were the most celebrated aspect of promoters' window dressing. Their names were used to guarantee the respectability of a new company, although they usually held no financial interest in the company and were often completely ignorant of business matters. "A judicious promoter of companies," joked *All the Year Round* in 1865, "is obliged, if he wishes to bring out a really good thing, to arrange his board as a bouquet-maker does his flowers." Ideally, a directorial bouquet would have contained peers of the realm, bankers, and Members of Parliament. Celebrity directors were invaluable publicity tools, ensuring that a company was mentioned in the society columns of the papers in addition to the money article.[53]

If extravagant publicity failed to excite interest in a new company, promoters might organize "share rigs" to artificially inflate the value of company stock. Promoters would buy up their own shares using either the company's capital or borrowed money, thus creating the illusion that their shares were in demand. In 1878 the Royal Commission on the Stock Exchange condemned the practice, citing a number of disturbing examples. For instance, in 1864 promoters of the Australian and Eastern Steam Navigation Company drove up the price of their stock by having brokers purchase in the open market 19,000 of the company's 27,000 shares.[54]

A large number of corporate failures and frauds during the 1860s and 1870s led many writers and social critics to denounce company promoters and their methods as symptomatic of British moral decline. A typically cynical assessment can be found in the story "John Skeeme, the Promoter," published in Dickens's journal *All the Year Round* in 1867, in the aftermath of the 1866 financial crisis. (pp. 253–68) In this fantastic tale, John Skeeme is a domestic servant who re-invents himself as a company promoter. Skeeme makes and loses a fortune during the Railway Mania of the 1840s before recouping his millions in the limited liability boom of the 1860s. The story illustrates a whole series of dubious financial operations. In 1876, *Blackwood's Magazine* published a lengthier and even bleaker account of company promotion: Laurence Oliphant's "The Autobiography of a Joint-Stock Company (Limited)." (pp. 269–97) Imaginatively told from the company's point of view, the story detailed many of the abuses of company promoters, including fraudulent prospectuses, dummy directors, share rigs, and false accounts.

Of course, not all promoters were bent on illicit profits. The best practice was represented by men such as David Chadwick. Chadwick promoted at least forty-seven limited companies between 1862 and 1874, most of them flotations of private industrial firms. Before agreeing to float a business, Chadwick, who was also an accountant, would thoroughly examine the firm's books to assure himself of the venture's credibility. As a result of his scrutiny, Chadwick's flotations were unusually long-lived by the standards of the day. His business methods were also above reproach. He charged a commission of only 1% for converting businesses into public companies, shares were offered through private circulars and prospectuses sent to known investors, directors held large numbers of shares, and share rigs were not allowed. Honest promoters like Chadwick, however, created no problems and, therefore, left few records in the form of lawsuits or literary exposés.[55]

Among the most notorious and thus remarked upon early company promoters was Albert Grant. Born Abraham Gottheimer in Dublin, the son of a Jewish trader from central Europe, Grant would promote anything if he thought it would bring him a profit. Grant did not wait to be approached by industrialists or traders, but rather sought out businesses to be converted or invented wild schemes of his own to promote. Once a company was floated, Grant washed his hands of it. Grant's methods were characterized by fraud and deceit, yet so lax were the requirements of commercial law that during his active career from 1863 to 1877 he avoided criminal prosecution altogether.[56]

Grant specialized in forming foreign railways, mines, and public utilities. Many of his flotations led to legal disputes and allegations of wrongdoing. In 1866, for example, Grant purchased the Marseilles Land Company for some £400,000 but resold it to the public for more than £1 million. The difference of over £600,000 went largely in promotional fees to Grant and his cronies. Grant concealed his exorbitant profits by loading the purchase price of his promotions with overvalued assets.[57]

By the early 1870s, Grant's promotional techniques were subject to growing public scrutiny. In 1872 Grant was exposed for bribing the financial editor of the *Times* to puff one of his companies. In 1875 a parliamentary investigation revealed that Grant had inflated the value of a loan to Paraguay by buying back £300,000, or nearly one-third, of the loan. By 1877 Grant was bankrupt and his companies in disarray. Thirty-seven of his promotions, which had a total value of £25 million in 1872, were now worth only £5 million. Grant retired from the City in disgrace, hounded by his creditors.[58]

Scores of civil actions for fraud were pending against Grant in 1877. One of them, Twycross vs. Grant, concerning Grant's 1871 promotion of the Lisbon Tramway's Company, became a landmark case in company law. (pp. 299–306) The plaintiff, James Twycross, alleged that Grant had violated the 1867 Companies Act by failing to disclose in the prospectus a contract between Grant and the builders of the tramway to pay Grant £45,000. Hidden fees of this sort, in effect "kickbacks," were a common feature of company promotions, so that much of the money which investors believed went for the purchase of land, machinery, patents, or labor, went in fact into the pocket of the promoter. The courts found for Twycross, and in so doing established the principle that promoters were fully responsible for information in the prospectus and that they must disclose all contracts materially affecting the new company.

Promoters, whether they were crooked or honest, were almost all men. Perhaps the only woman promoter during the nineteenth century was Alice Cornwell. Born in England, she emigrated with her family to Australia, where her father made a fortune sinking gold mines. Alice managed her father's business interests, in 1886 returning to England, where she floated the Midas Mine on the London Stock Exchange.[59] The mystery writer Fergus Hume based his 1888 novel, *Madame Midas,* on Alice Cornwell's dramatic rise to wealth. (pp. 307–12) Embodying many of the sexist assumptions of its day, the novel portrays a woman's financial achievements as fraught with danger. In particular, a woman's romantic impulses were seen as incompatible with practical business sense.

Given the vicissitudes, real and imagined, surrounding company promotion, many sober businessmen remained suspicious of joint-stock incorporation until very late in the nineteenth century. The bulk of British promotions from the 1840s through the 1870s involved railways, banks, government loans, and utilities. Industrial firms did not enter the share market in a significant way until the 1880s and 1890s, at which time there was a new boom in home industrials. Domestic manufacturing firms quoted on the Stock Exchange increased tenfold between 1885 and 1907. This was a period of industrial amalgamation and numerous private businesses saw incorporation as a means of raising capital for expansion and acquisitions. In other businesses, founders retired and a new generation less interested in entrepreneurship, and less distrustful of the City, transferred their firms to public ownership. New technical advances in electricity and the internal combustion engine, the so-called Second Industrial Revolution, also sought financing in the share market.[60]

By late century company promotion had become so pervasive that a whole network of subsidiary services had developed to assist promoters. Advertising firms acted as intermediaries between promoters and the press, inserting prospectuses and planting positive stories in newspapers and magazines. Promoting syndicates undertook the entire costs of flotation from the printing of the prospectus and articles of association to stamp duties on contracts to lawyers' fees and accountants' charges connected with registration. By the early twentieth century, promoters were also assisted by postal publicity firms which sold lists of thousands of known shareholders.[61]

A new breed of company promoter emerged during the late Victorian period. These men, as exemplified by Harry Lawson, Ernest Hooley, and Whitaker Wright, were flamboyant figures who lived in ostentatious style, made and lost fortunes, and through it all traded on public ignorance and gullibility. (For more about Lawson, Hooley, and Wright, see Vol. 4 in this series: *Financial Crises and Financial Fraud.*) In his 1892 collection of stories depicting urban types, *Round London,* Montagu Williams includes "The Promoter" (pp. 313–19) as a well-known figure in the business world. The eponymous promoter in the story, Leopold Stiff, is a con man on a gigantic scale. His outrageous schemes eventually land him in court and prison.

Late Victorian literary depictions of the financial world frequently depict a nation intoxicated with limited liability promotions. Bracebridge Hemyng's melodramatic tale, "Promoting a Company, or, Shrimps for the Million" (1885), mocks the craze for joint-stock schemes via the preposterous "London and Provincial Shrimp Breeding, Catching, and Canning Company, Limited" which promised "the social elevation of the masses" through the provision of cheap shrimp. (pp. 321–32) The story begins as a broad burlesque of company promotion but quickly descends into tragedy with the financial ruin of a widow and orphans and the suicide of the promoter. In a somewhat lighter vein, Gilbert and Sullivan's operetta, *Utopia Limited* (1893), depicts an English company promoter transforming a remote island nation, Utopia, into a limited liability company. (pp. 333–36) Apparently nothing and nowhere was safe from "companification."

Over the course of the nineteenth century, Great Britain experienced a dramatic transformation of public finance and investment. In the early 1800s, the creation of joint-stock companies was nearly impossible, and companies themselves were looked upon with great suspicion. Government securities were the main investment opportunity apart from land. By the 1890s, hundreds of different corporate securities were now quoted on the Stock Exchange. Investing in company shares had become an ordinary part of British life. The creation of joint-stock companies had been greatly facilitated by the liberalization of company law, but attitudes about corporate finance and financiers still included much skepticism, distrust, and outright hostility. These negative attitudes were a response to a somewhat chaotic, and at times corrupt system of company promotion.

Notes

1 Mary Poovey, *The Financial System in Nineteenth-Century Britain* (Oxford: Oxford University Press, 2003), p. 13.
2 David Kynaston, *The City of London, Volume 1: A World of Its Own, 1815–1890* (London: Chatto and Windus, 1994), p. 24.
3 James Taylor, *Creating Capitalism: Joint-Stock Enterprise in British Politics and Culture, 1800–1870* (London: Royal Historical Society, 2006), p. 12.
4 This account of the South Sea Bubble is derived from P.G.M. Dickson, *The Financial Revolution in England: A Study of the Development of Public Credit, 1688–1756* (London: Macmillan, 1967), pp. 90–157, and John Carswell, *The South Sea Bubble* (London: Cresset Press, 1961), 89–156.
5 B.C. Hunt, *The Development of the Business Corporation in England, 1800–67* (Cambridge: Harvard University Press, 1936), pp. 1–30.
6 James Taylor, *Creating Capitalism: Joint-Stock Enterprise in British Politics and Culture, 1800–1870* (London: Royal Historical Society, 2006), pp. 107–9.
7 James Taylor, *Creating Capitalism: Joint-Stock Enterprise in British Politics and Culture, 1800–1870* (London: Royal Historical Society, 2006), pp. 117–21.
8 Frank Griffith Dawson, *The First Latin American Debt Crisis: The City of London and the 1822–25 Loan Bubble* (New Haven: Yale University Press, 1990).
9 B.C. Hunt, *The Development of the Business Corporation in England, 1800–67* (Cambridge: Harvard University Press, 1936), pp. 50–55.
10 Charles W. Munn, "The Emergence of Joint-Stock Banking in the British Isles: A Comparative Approach," *Business History* 30 (January 1988), pp. 69–83, and Joint-Stock Banking Act, 1826, 7 Geo. IV c. 46.
11 J.H. Clapham, *An Economic History of Modern Britain,* 3 Vols. (Cambridge: Cambridge University Press, 1926–38), Vol. 1, pp. 511–12, and P.L. Cottrell and B.L. Anderson, *Money and Banking in England: The Development of the Banking System, 1694–1914* (Newton Abbot: David and Charles, 1974), p. 249.
12 J.R. McCulloch, "Joint-Stock Banks and Companies," *Edinburgh Review* 63 (July 1836), p. 423.
13 Select Committee to Inquire into the State of the Laws Respecting Joint Stock Companies, *Parliamentary Papers*, 1844, VII, Minutes and Report.
14 Select Committee on Joint Stock Companies, *PP*, 1844, VII, Report, pp. 361–62.
15 Act for the Registration, Incorporation and Regulation of Joint Stock Companies, 1844, 7/8 Vict. c. 110, Sections IV, XIX, XXIII.
16 Joint Stock Companies Act, 1844, Sections VII, XI, XVIII, XXV, XXXVI, XLIII.
17 H.A. Shannon, "The Coming of General Limited Liability," *Economic History* 2 (1931), p. 290.
18 David Morier Evans, *Facts, Failures and Frauds* (London: Groombridge and Sons, 1859), p. 2.
19 B.R. Mitchell, "The Coming of the Railways and United Kingdom Economic Growth," *Journal of Economic History* 24 (September 1964), p. 321.

20 Thomas Tooke, *A History of Prices*, 6 Vols. (London: Longman, Orme, Brown, Green and Longmans, 1838–57), Vol. 5, p. 234, and Clapham, *Economic History*, Vol. 2, p. 357.
21 J.R. Killick and W.A. Thomas, "The Provincial Stock Exchanges, 1830–1870," *Economic History Review* 23 (April 1970), pp. 96–111, and Paul Crosthwaite, Peter Knight, Nicky Marsh, Helen Paul, James Taylor, *Invested: How Three Centuries of Stock Market Advice Reshaped Our Money, Markets, and Minds* (Chicago: University of Chicago Press, 2022), pp. 53–7.
22 A.J. Arnold and S. McCartney, *George Hudson: The Rise and Fall of the Railway King* (London: Hambledon and London, 2004).
23 Nancy Henry, "'Ladies do it?': Victorian Women Investors in Fact and Fiction," in Francis O'Gorman, ed., *Victorian Literature and Finance* (Oxford: Oxford University Press, 2007), pp. 121–22.
24 *The Times*, 31 October 1845.
25 *Hansard*, LXXXV, 1846, p. 946.
26 Select Committee on Railway Acts, *Parliamentary Papers*, 1846, XIV, Minutes, p. 103.
27 David Morier Evans, *The Commercial Crisis of 1847–48* (London: Letts, Son and Steer, 1849), Introduction.
28 Samuel Smiles, *The Life of George Stephenson* (Boston: Ticknor and Fields, 1858), p. 384.
29 *The Economist*, 11 October 1845, and *The Times*, 17 November 1845.
30 *The Economist*, 25 October 1845, and *The Times*, 17 November 1845.
31 H.G. Lewin, *The Railway Mania and Its Aftermath, 1845–52* (London: The Railway Gazette, 1939), Chapter 12, and John Francis, *A History of the English Railway: Its Social Relations and Revelations, 1820–1845*, 2 Vols. (London: Longman, Brown, Green and Longmans, 1851), Vol. 2, p. 195.
32 For examples, see James Taylor, *Creating Capitalism: Joint-Stock Enterprise in British Politics and Culture, 1800–1870* (London: Royal Historical Society, 2006), pp. 70, 88.
33 H.G. Lewin, *The Railway Mania and Its Aftermath, 1845–52* (London: The Railway Gazette, 1939), Table IX, p. 365.
34 York and North Midland Railway, Shareholders' Committee of Investigation, 1849, National Archives, Rail 770/13.
35 H.A. Shannon, "The Coming of General Limited Liability," *Economic History* 2 (1931), 267–91.
36 James Taylor, *Creating Capitalism: Joint-Stock Enterprise in British Politics and Culture, 1800–1870* (London: Royal Historical Society, 2006), pp. 8–13, and Rob McQueen, *A Social History of Company Law: Great Britain and the Australian Colonies* (Ashgate Publishing, 2009), pp. 1–15.
37 Company Law Amendment Act, 1847, 10/11 Vict. c. 78, Section IV, and Select Committee on Assurance Associations, *Parliamentary Papers*, 1853, XXI, Report, pp. 4–5.
38 Timothy Alborn, *Conceiving Companies: Joint-Stock Politics in Victorian England* (London: Routledge, 1998), p. 257.
39 Boyd Hilton, *The Age of Atonement: The Influence of Evangelicalism on Social and Economic Thought, 1785–1865* (Oxford: Clarendon Press, 1986), pp. 255–67.
40 J.R. McCulloch, *Considerations on Partnerships with Limited Liability* (London: Longman, Brown, Green and Longmans, 1856), p. 10.
41 Rob McQueen, *A Social History of Company Law: Great Britain and the Australian Colonies* (Ashgate Publishing, 2009), Chapter 3: "Christian Socialism and the Debate on Limited Liability."

42 Select Committee on the Savings of the Middle and Working Classes, *Parliamentary Papers*, 1850, XIX, Minutes, pp. 174–81.
43 Select Committee on the Savings of the Middle and Working Classes, *Parliamentary Papers*, 1850, XIX, Minutes, p. 174.
44 Royal Commission on the Law of Partnership, *Parliamentary Papers*, 1854, XXVII, Minutes and Report.
45 Joint Stock Companies Act, 1856, 19/20 Vict. c. 47.
46 *Hansard*, CXL, 1856, p. 138.
47 Companies Act, 1862, 25/26 Vict. c. 86.
48 H.A. Shannon, "The Coming of General Limited Liability," *Economic History* 2 (1931), p. 290.
49 P.L. Cottrell, *Industrial Finance, 1830–1914* (London: Methuen, 1980), Chapter 7.
50 David Morier Evans, *The City, or the Physiology of London Business* (London: Baily Brothers, 1845), p. 76.
51 David Kynaston, *The City of London, Volume 1: A World of Its Own, 1815–1890* (London: Chatto and Windus, 1994), pp. 236–43, and Companies Act, 1867, 30/31 Vict. c. 131, Section XXXVIII. See also, Janette Rutterford, " 'Propositions Put Forward by Quite Reasonable Men': Company Prospectuses and Their Contents, 1856 to 1940," *Business History* 53 (October 2011), 866–99.
52 David Kynaston, *The City of London, Volume 1: A World of Its Own, 1815–1890* (London: Chatto and Windus, 1994), pp. 405–7.
53 "Starting the Rio Grande Railway," *All the Year Round* 14 (November 1865), p. 369, and A. Still, "Front Sheet Reflections," *Journal of Finance* (November 1898), 988–92.
54 Royal Commission on the Stock Exchange, *Parliamentary Papers*, 1878, XIX, Minutes, pp. 229–34.
55 P.L. Cottrell, "David Chadwick," *Dictionary of Business Biography*, ed. David J. Jeremy (London: Butterworths, 1984), Vol. 1, pp. 625–32.
56 P.L. Cottrell, "Albert Grant," *Dictionary of Business Biography*, ed. David J. Jeremy (London: Butterworths, 1984), Vol. 2, pp. 623–9.
57 Royal Commission on the Stock Exchange, *Parliamentary Papers*, 1878, XIX, Report, p. 11.
58 P.L. Cottrell, "Albert Grant," *Dictionary of Business Biography*, ed. David J. Jeremy (London: Butterworths, 1984), pp. 626–7, and Select Committee on Loans to Foreign States, *Parliamentary Papers*, 1875, XI, Report.
59 D.M. Griffiths, "Cornwell, Alice Ann," *Oxford Dictionary of National Biography*, Vol. 13, pp. 492–93.
60 P.L. Cottrell, *Industrial Finance, 1830–1914* (London: Methuen, 1980), pp. 162–93.
61 Sir Mark Webster Jenkinson, *The Promotion and Accounts of a Public Limited Company* (London: Gee and Company, 1912), 94–5.

BIBLIOGRAPHY

Alborn, Timothy. *Conceiving Companies: Joint-Stock Politics in Victorian England.* London: Routledge, 1998.

Armstrong, John. "The Rise and Fall of the Company Promoter and the Financing of British Industry." In J.J. Van Helten and Y. Cassis, eds. *Capitalism in a Mature Economy: Financial Institutions, Capital Exports and British Industry, 1870–1939.* Cheltenham: Edward Elgar, 1990.

Arnold, A.J. and S. McCartney. *George Hudson: The Rise and Fall of the Railway King.* London: Hambledon and London, 2004.

Baskin, J.B. and P.J. Miranti, *A History of Corporate Finance.* Cambridge: Cambridge University Press, 1997.

Carswell, John. *The South Sea Bubble.* London: Cresset Press, 1961.

Cottrell, P.L. *Industrial Finance, 1830–1914.* London: Methuen, 1980.

Dawson, Frank Griffith. *The First Latin American Debt Crisis: The City of London and the 1822–25 Loan Bubble.* New Haven: Yale University Press, 1990.

Dickson, P.G.M. *The Financial Revolution in England: A Study of the Development of Public Credit, 1688–1756.* London: Macmillan, 1967.

French, E.A. "The Origin of General Limited Liability in the United Kingdon." *Accounting and Business Research* 21 (1990), 15–34.

Hannah, Leslie. *The Rise of the Corporate Economy.* London: Methuen, 1976.

Harris, Ron. "The Bubble Act: Its Passage and Effects on Business Organization." *Journal of Economic History* 54 (1994), 610–27.

Hilton, Boyd. *The Age of Atonement: The Influence of Evangelicalism on Social and Economic Thought.* Oxford: Clarendon Press, 1986.

Hoppit, J. "The Myths of the South Sea Bubble." *Transactions of the Royal Historical Society* 12 (2002), 141–65.

Hunt, B.C. *The Development of the Business Corporation in England, 1800–67.* Cambridge: Harvard University Press, 1936.

Ireland, P.W. "The Rise of the Limited Liability Company." *International Journal of the Sociology of Law* 12 (1984), 239–60.

Johnson, Paul. *Making the Market: The Victorian Origins of Corporate Capitalism.* Cambridge: Cambridge University Press, 2010.

Loftus, D. "Capital and Community: Limited Liability and Attempts to Democratize the Market in Mid Nineteenth-Century England." *Victorian Studies* 45 (2002), 93–120.

McQueen, Rob. *A Social History of Company Law: Great Britain and the Australian Colonies.* Ashgate Publishing, 2009.

Mitchell, B.R. "The Coming of Railways and United Kingdom Economic Growth." *Journal of Economic History* 24 (September 1964), 315–36.

Murphy, Anne L. *The Origins of English Financial Markets.* Cambridge: Cambridge University Press, 2009.

Poovey, Mary. *The Financial System in Nineteenth-Century Britain.* Oxford: Oxford University Press, 2003.

Reed, M.C. *Investment in Railways in Britain, 1820–1844: A Study in the Development of the Capital Market.* Oxford: Oxford University Press, 1975.

Rutterford, Janette. " 'Propositions Put Forward by Quite Reasonable Men': Company Prospectuses and Their Contents, 1856–1940." *Business History* 53 (October 2011), 866–99.

Shannon, H.A. "The Coming of General Limited Liability." *Economic History* 2 (1931), 267–91.

Taylor, James. *Creating Capitalism: Joint-Stock Enterprise in British Politics and Culture, 1800–1870.* London: Royal Historical Society, 2006.

Part 1

FINANCE, INVESTMENT, AND JOINT-STOCK COMPANIES

1

EPITOME OF THE STOCKS AND PUBLIC FUNDS

Thomas Fortune

Source: Thomas Fortune, *Epitome of the Stocks and Public Funds,* 9th edition (London: T. Boosey, 1817), pp. 9–51.

EDITORIAL HEADNOTE

First published in 1796, Thomas Fortune's popular guide went through seventeen editions into the 1850s, even after Fortune's death. Regularly updated, the later editions were compiled by the financial journalist David Morier Evans. Thomas Fortune was himself a broker, and he sought to normalize and rationalize the stock market for inexperienced investors, rather than demonize it as did other early commentators like Thomas Mortimer.[1]

In providing a detailed survey of investment opportunities, Fortune promised to furnish readers with "every necessary information for perfectly understanding the nature of those securities and the mode of doing business therein." Here, he describes all the different government securities available for investors as well as the brokerage fees required at purchase, and the dates when dividends were paid.

Note

1 Paul Crosthwaite, et al., *Invested* (Chicago: University of Chicago Press, 2022), pp. 43–47.

The Funds, of which the following sheets will give as short though as exact an account as possible, owe their foundation to the various Loans borrowed by the Government of this country from the public, through the medium of incorporated companies, or private bodies of individuals, between the close of the seventeenth century and the present time. They are commonly, although improperly, called

DOI: 10.4324/9781003713890-2

Stocks; as that term cannot be applied with any degree of propriety, except to those sums which form the capitals of the different incorporated societies, – such as the Bank, India, and South Sea Companies; together with those of the different Insurance Offices, whose Stocks or Capitals are transferable from one person to another. The remainder are public debts due from this country, borrowed at different periods, by the sanction and authority of Parliament, and funded under the various names, as may be seen in the following Table.

CAPITAL STOCKS AND PUBLIC FUNDS

Transferable at the different Offices, classed according to the Time of the Dividend or Interest becoming due upon each; together with their several Days of Transfer.

At the Bank of England	*Trans. Days*	*Divid. Due*
5 per Cent. Navy Annuities	Tu.W.Th.F.	January 5 and July 5
3 per Cent. Consols	Tu.W.Th.F.	January 5 and July 5
3 per Cent. 1726	Tu. and Th.	January 5 and July 5
Bank Stock	Tu.Th.F.	April 5 and Octo. 10
5 per Cent. 1797	Tu.Th.F.	April 5 and Octo. 10
4 per Cent. Consols	Tu.W.Th.F.	April 5 and Octo. 10
3 per Cent. Reduced	Tu.W.Th.F.	April 5 and Octo. 10
Long Annuities	Mon.Wed.S.	April 5 and Octo. 10
3 per Ct. Imp. Annuities	Mo.Wed.Fr.	May 1 and Novem. 1
Imp. Anns. For 25 Years	Tu.Th.S.	May 1 and Novem. 1
5 per Cent. Irish Anns.	Tu.Th.S.	March 25 and Sept. 29
South Sea House		
South Sea Stock	Mo.Wed.Fr.	January 5 and July 5
3 per Cent. New S.S. Anns.	Tu.Th.S.	January 5 and July 5
3 per Cent. 1751	Tu.Th.	January 5 and July 5
3 per Cent. Old S.S. Anns.	Mo.Wed.Fr.	April 5 and Octo. 10
At India House		
India Stock	Tu.Th.S.	January 5 and July 5

There are other public securities, transferable from one person to another, which do not come under any of the before mentioned heads; – such as *Exchequer Bills*, and *India Bonds*. These are very proper investments for cash that is liable to be suddenly called for, being always marketable; which, with the interest due upon them up to the very day on which they are sold, are transferable to the purchaser simply by a note or bill from the broker or holder who sells them.

GENERAL INFORMATION AND DIRECTIONS

Which, if punctually attended to, will save much Time, prevent Mistakes, and expedite all Business relative to the Public Funds, Stocks, &c.

BANK OF ENGLAND

Public or common transfers are made of all the funds transferable here between the hours of eleven and one, on the respective days annexed to them in the foregoing Table; and all dividends on the same are payable, when due, from nine in the morning to eleven, and from one to three in the afternoon, everyday in the year, Sundays and holidays excepted. – Holders of stock should particularly remember, that when the books of any stock or fund are shut, the interest or dividend up to that day on which the books were so shut, is *due*, and can be paid *only* to that stockholder in whose name the stock stands *at that time*, or his or her attorney duly authorised, and is not transferable to any other person whatever. Had this been duly attended to formerly, there would not have been occasion for so voluminous an account of unclaimed dividends which has since claimed the attention of the public.

THE SOUTH SEA HOUSE

Common transfers are made of all the funds transferable here, on their respective transfer days, between the hours of twelve and one only; and no business of any kind can be transacted after one o'clock on Saturdays. The dividends here are payable from nine to twelve o'clock, and from one till three, except on Saturdays; then only from nine till twelve.

THE INDIA HOUSE

As the joint or capital stock of this Company is the only one which is transferable here at present, the said transfers are made between the hours of eleven and one, and the dividends are paid from nine till two, except on Saturdays, when no business is done after twelve at noon; and here it will be necessary to observe, that the common or public transfers of this *Stock,* as well as those of the *Bank* and *South Sea Stock,* although made on the regular days in the Table, and within the appointed hours, yet are always attended with the following expenses:

	£	*s*	*d*
A transfer of Bank Stock, if under £25	0	9	0
If above that sum	0	12	0
A ditto of India Stock, for any sum	1	4	0
A transfer of South Sea Stock, if under £100	0	9	6
If above that sum	0	12	0

As it may be necessary, upon many occasions, to either make or obtain a transfer of some stock or fund on days or hours contrary to those mentioned in the preceding Table, persons wanting them can always be accommodated at any time during the office hours where such stock or fund is transferable; except during the first three or four weeks of the books of that stock being shut: if at the Bank, or India House, upon payment of two shillings and sixpence to the witnessing clerk; and if at the South Sea House, three shillings and sixpence for any such transfer, be the sum so transferred little or much.

The same stock cannot be *twice* transferred on the same day, either by public or private transfer; – and I would advise the purchaser, if present at the transfer, to accept the stock then transferred directly; as it saves time, and in some measure prevents mistakes thereafter; and also to sign, either as transferer or accepter, always in the same manner; and to retain the *first* description of his or her place of abode, &c., even if one or more removals has taken place: this measure will expedite business, prevent mistakes (always to be avoided, if possible) and also much trouble to the stockholder:

A lady resident in the country had requested a friend to purchase 3 per Cent. Consols for her at different times; during which period, she had changed her residence more than once; which the aforesaid friend knowing, he imagined that he was acting properly in changing the description of her abode every time that he thought it necessary. The consequence was, that, when she came to town to receive her dividends, they would only pay her according to *one* of her descriptions, she having *three different ones* in the books of that fund, answering to the different places of her abode at the time the purchases were made. As neither herself nor her friend knew in what manner to proceed (the clerks in the office being restricted from giving any information relative to the business), after much trouble, and some expense, an affidavit was obliged to be made before the Lord Mayor, by a gentleman who knew her, that she was one and the same person, although described in the books as resident at three separate and distinct places; all which trouble and anxiety might have been avoided, had the above advice been followed, of retaining the first description of a person's place of abode throughout.

It may be requisite, at this place, to take some notice of a book which has run through many editions, entitled *Every Man his Own Broker*[1]*:* the reason why I do so is, that I mean to recommend a measure exactly opposite to that author's; and, instead of advising Every Man to be his Own Broker, endeavor to persuade every man *from* being so, who does not intend to become a regular jobber in the funds, and attend constantly for that purpose, so as to be *personally known* to the clerks at the transfer books.

I will readily admit that the book in question gives ample directions how to make purchases, or to *buy,* into respective funds; but, unfortunately, it is not quite so explicit as it ought to be with respect to *selling,* a matter sometimes of more moment than the former; when the loss of an hour, or probably some minutes, may be of great consequence in obtaining a sum of money.

In the directions for selling, he (the author) not only passes over the most essential matter unnoticed, viz., the *identity of the transferer or seller being made out,* but even insinuates that government intended that every individual should transact his own business. If ever Government did intend so, it is extremely fortunate for the Bank, and the other public company concerned in the management of their funds, that such intentions never took place. What a fine field for forgery would such an indiscriminate mode of doing business have opened to the adventurous felon! Even all the restrictions now so wisely laid on cannot absolutely deter them, as the annals of Newgate can bear testimony; few years passing without one or more executions for the offence.

By the present rules, every one, male or female, making a transfer, should be known to be the person whom he or she represents by the witnessing clerk; and as this must be, in nine out of ten instances, impossible, from the multitude of people who come before him, how is this required identity to be made out? If the person who makes the transfer is not known to the clerk, it may be said, he must bring somebody to prove his identity; but if that person so brought in is also a stranger to the witnessing clerk, the transfer cannot (or at least ought not to) be made; yet all this trouble is incurred by the advice of the aforesaid author, to save a trifling brokerage.

Now my advice, in opposition to his, is, never to do any business in the funds without a Broker; who (if you always employ one and the same person) can vouch for your identity upon all occasions, and procure your business to be done without any more loss of time than what is absolutely necessary: he will also take care that you have the fair price for your stock, if a seller, and procure it for you at the same, if a buyer; neither of which, I am certain, could be done by yourself, without incurring a greater loss either way than what his commission or brokerage amounts to.

I shall now take leave of this author, and proceed to state, that the commission or brokerage, which gave him such offence, is, upon all the Government funds not terminable at any stated time, one eighth, or two shillings and sixpence, per cent. On the terminable annuities, or those which have only a specific time to run, two shillings and sixpence per cent. *on the sum laid out.* And upon India Bonds, and some Exchequer Bills, one shilling each.

I have said thus much in favour of stockbrokers from a thorough conviction of their utility in all business relative to the funds; and shall now proceed to give the remaining directions to be observed, without farther digression.

Letters of Attorney, either to sell stock or receive dividends, must be taken out at the office appointed for issuing them; and such letters (the expense of which is £1. 1*s.* 6*d.*), when executed, must be deposited in the office of that fund, or stock, to which the said letter of attorney has a reference, one day before any sale, or other business for which they were granted, can take place.

Probates of Wills must also be deposited until registered, which formerly used to cost two shillings and sixpence, but is now done gratuitously, in one general office set apart for that purpose; and not at the different offices, as heretofore was the case. If, after granting a letter of attorney for any purpose, the *granter acts personally,* such action revokes the power of the said letter, and it cannot be acted upon by the person appointed therein. A provision may be made in the funds for the benefit of any person, or persons, whether relations or others, independent of any deed or will, provided the person's name or names so to be benefited are joined with the stockholders' in a *particular* or *separate account of stock*; which, upon proof being given of death of either of the parties, becomes the property of the remaining survivor or survivors.

In trust accounts, after the acceptance of all the trustees named therein is obtained, any one of them may receive the dividends. But as the laws with respect to trust accounts were still defective, an act passed in 1796, by which it is declared, that when stock stands in the name of trustees who have become bankrupts, or lunatics; or are absent, or out of the jurisdiction of the courts of equity; or who may refuse to transfer the stock so vested in them; in any, or all of these cases, the court can order the said stock to be transferred either into the name of the Accomptant-general of the Court of Chancery, or into that of the Deputy-remembrancer of the Court of Exchequer, *in trust;* or to the parties who are entitled to the same. Or if one trustee is a bankrupt, or lunatic, or it is uncertain if he be living, and the remainder are willing to act, an order may be obtained, empowering them either to transfer the stock in question, or to receive and pay over the dividends. And in case a bankrupt refuses to transfer stock which belongs to him, the Chancellor may (upon a petition from his assignees) order the stock to be transferred into their names. And he may likewise, in certain cases, order stock standing in the names of lunatics, or their committees, to be transferred.

As the Bank is a chartered body, no property vested in the funds there can be attached, except in some particular cases; when, upon application to the Court of Chancery, it will issue a Distringas for that purpose.

It will be necessary for every person, when purchasing stock, to keep the seller's receipt for such stock, until one dividend is received upon it at least, and after that period it is the advice of many to destroy it, for fear of its creating *trouble* to the heirs, &c., of such persons, in searching the books of the different funds for the sum described in such receipt: but as I have known more than one mistake of long standing cleared up by the production of old receipts, I therefore advise their being kept; and, in order to prevent any disappointment or *trouble* to the heirs, &c. of such persons who may follow this advice, I would farther counsel them to keep a regular ledger account of all the stock bought and sold, opening a separate one for every stock, or fund, in which they may have property: this, if regularly posted up, the stock bought on one side, with its value, and that sold on the other, in like manner, will not only afford amusement for a leisure hour, but present at one view the state and amount of all property so vested, together with any loss or gain that may have accrued in those transactions.

Since the publication of the seventh Edition of this Tract, the following alterations and regulations have been made in the conducting of the public business at the Bank: – The days of transfer of some of the funds have been altered; the registering of wills, and issuing letters of attorney, instead of being done at the different offices which were relative to either. Are now collected in one point, and transacted at two new offices, appointed solely for those purposes; the receipts also which pass from the seller to the purchaser of stock have now printed on their margins the several days of transferring that particular fund to which the said receipt appertains, together with the times of the dividends becoming due thereon, and also a request that the proprietor (or buyer) of stock would accept the same in the transfer books.

I shall now proceed to give as concise an account as possible of the different Stocks and Funds separately.

FIVE PER CENTS., OR NAVY ANNUITIES

This fund was established in the year 1784; its capital on August 1st, 1817, was £134,882,348 18s. It is transferable at the Bank of England every Tuesday, Wednesday, Thursday, and Friday, between the hours of eleven and one, except when the books are shut for the dividends or interest, which becomes due January 5th and July 5th.

Letters of Attorney for transacting business in this fund, cost £1 1*s.* 6*d.*

Brokerage, 2*s.* 6*d.* per cent. on the sum bought or sold.

THREE PER CENT. CONSOLIDATED ANNUITIES[2]

In the former editions of this work I asserted that this fund began in 1727; but, upon better information since obtained, I now say that it originated in 1731, although the balance of the annuities granted by the 8th of George the First, instead of St. Chistopher's and Nevis Debentures, on which it was partly founded, and which was the last article carried to this account, were not subscribed into it until the year 1751; and it owes its name to the Consolidating Act, passed in that year. Its capital on August 1st, 1817, was £377,415, 537. 17*s.* 5 ¼ *d.* This fund is transferable at the Bank of England every Tuesday, Wednesday, Thursday, and Friday, between eleven and one, except when the books are shut. The dividends or interest is due January 5th, and July 5th.

On account of the large amount of the capital of this fund, and the great number of stockholders in consequence, an office is established for the express purpose of paying the dividends upon it: therefore they may be received every day in the week, from the hour of nine till three, contrary to all the other funds, the dividends upon which are only payable at those times when transfers are not made.

THREE PER CENT. 1726

The date shews the year of its origin. Its capital is £999,538. 9*s.* It is transferable at the Bank of England on Tuesdays and Thursdays only between eleven and one, except when the books are shut for the dividends or interest, which becomes due January 5th, and July 5th.

BANK STOCK

This Stock originated in 1694. The Charter of Incorporation bears date July 27th in that year. Its capital on August 1st, 1817, was £14,686,800. Is transferable at the Bank (being the Capital Stock of that Company) every Tuesday, Thursday, and Friday, except, as before, when the books are shut. The dividends or interest, which at present is 10 percent., becomes due April 5th, and October 10th.

Letters of Attorney cost £1. 1*s.* 6*d.*

Brokerage, 2*s.* 6*d.* per cent. on all sums bought or sold.

A transfer of this stock at all times, if under £25, costs 9*s.*; if above that sum, 12*s.*; and if private, 2*s.* 6*d.* extra.

By an act passed in the seventh year of the reign of his present Majesty, it was enacted that every person possessed of £500 of this stock is entitled thereby to vote in all elections for Governor, Deputy Governor, or Directors, provided they have been in possession of such stock, in their own right, six calendar months; "unless the said stock shall have been acquired, or shall have come by bequest, or by marriage; or by custom of the city of London; or by any deed of settlement after the death of any person who shall have been entitled for life to dividends of such stock." Two thousand pounds stock is the qualification for becoming Director, three thousand pounds for Deputy Governor; and four thousand for Governor.

FIVE PER CENT. 1797 AND 1802

This fund originated in 1796, by a voluntary subscription; but was raised for the service of the year 1797, and is since distinguished by the name of Loyalty: its capital on August 1st, 1817 was £1,058,503. 5*s.* 6*d.* It is transferable at the Bank of England every Tuesday, Thursday, and Friday, between the hours of eleven and one, except on holidays, or when the books are shut for the dividends, which become due April 5th, and October 10th.

The time having arrived for the paying off this fund at par, the holders of it were called upon by advertisement to make their election on or before Oct. 5th, 1804; either to receive £100 five per Cents. Valued at £88. 10*s.* 6*d.*, or to wait till April 1805, then to be paid off at par. But that this arrangement did not take place, the above capital of this fund remaining unpaid is a satisfactory proof.

Letters of Attorney for transacting business in this fund cost £1. 1*s.* 6*d.*

Brokerage, 2*s.* 6*d.* per cent. on the sum bought or sold.

FOUR PER CENT. CONSOLIDATED ANNUITIES

Although this fund really originated in 1760, yet being granted only for twenty-one years, and a subsequent loan of twelve millions, in 1762, for nineteen years, both were terminable, and did terminate, in 1781. We must therefore say that the present capital of the Four per cents. originated in 1777, by a loan of £5,000,000; which capital, by sundry augmentations, amounted on August 1st, 1817, to

£74,919,405. 5*s.* 1*d.* It is transferable at the Bank of England every Tuesday, Wednesday, Thursday, and Friday, except when the books are shut. The dividend or interest is due April 5th, and October 10th.

Letters of Attorney cost £1. 1*s.* 6*d.*

Brokerage, 2*s.* 6*d.* per cent. on all sums bought or sold.

THREE PER CENT. REDUCED ANNUITIES

If we date the origin of this fund from the time at which the sums forming the first part of the capital were reduced (as the name implies) to three per cent., it will be found to commence in the year 1757, having before that period borne interest at 4 per cent.; viz. from 1746 to 1750, and 3 ½ per cent. from that time until 1757, when it was reduced to 3 per cent. Its capital on August 1st, 1817, amounted to £143,306,206. 16*s.* 5*d.* It is transferable at the Bank of England every Tuesday, Wednesday, Thursday, and Friday, except when the books are shut for the dividends or interest, which is due April 5, and October 10th.

Letters of Attorney cost £1. 1*s.* 6*d.*

Brokerage, 2*s.* 6*d.* per cent. on all sums bought or sold.

LONG ANNUITIES

These annuities have been granted as douceurs at different times, and for various terms, but all terminating at one period, viz. January 1860, when they will all expire together. They amounted on August 1st, 1817, to £1,354,544. 12*s.* ½*d.* per annum.: are transferable at the Bank of England every Monday, Wednesday, and Saturday, except when the books are shut for the dividends or interest, which becomes due April 5th, and October 10th.

Letters of Attorney cost £1. 1*s.* 6*d.*

Brokerage, 2*s.* 6*d.* per cent. upon the *sum laid out*; these Annuities not being bought or sold at so much per cent., but in the same manner as land, at so many years purchase.

THREE PER CENT. IMPERIAL ANNUITIES[3]

This fund originates in a convention between his Imperial Majesty and the Government of this country, signed in May 1795. Its capital on August 1st, 1817, was £5,514,232. 3*s.* 8*d.* It is transferable at the Bank of England every Monday, Wednesday, and Friday, except when the books are shut for the dividends or interest, which becomes due May 1st, and November 1st.

By the Act of Parliament which established this and the next following fund, and which guaranteed the payment of the interest upon both to the respective holders, it was enacted, that, provided the Emperor should fail in making the necessary remittances to this country for the payment of the interest, or dividends, upon both these funds; then, and in that case, our government was authorized by the said Act to defer the payment of the said dividends until the time of paying the interest or dividends upon the 3 per Cent. Consolidated Annuities, viz. January and July. And the Emperor having so failed in making the remittances in due time for payment of the half year's interest which became due in November 1797, it was accordingly deferred until January 1798: the succeeding one, which became due in May 1798, was not paid till July; or that due in November 1798, until January 1799, and has continued so ever since.

Letters of Attorney cost £1. 1*s.* 6*d.*

Brokerage, 2*s.* 6*d.* per cent. upon all sums bought or sold.

IMPERIAL ANNUITIES FOR TWENTY-FIVE YEARS

These annuities commenced the 1st of May, 1794. They amounted on August 1st, 1817, to £229,961. 12*s.* 4*d.* per annum, and will expire April 30th, 1819. They are transferable at the Bank of England every Tuesday, Thursday, and Saturday, between the hours of eleven and one, except when the books are shut for the dividends or interest, which is due May 1st, and November 1st.*

Letters of Attorney cost £1. 1*s.* 6*d.*

Brokerage, 2*s.* 6*d.* per cent. upon the sum laid out.

*See the note to the preceding article.

FIVE PER CENT. IRISH ANNUITIES

These originate in part of two loans, borrowed for the use of the Irish Government in the years 1794 and 1795. Such of the subscribers to these loans, who, at the time the payments were made, declared their intention of receiving the dividends arising therefrom in London, were permitted to do so; and for their accommodation, under the sanction of an Act of Parliament, passed in the thirty-fifth year of his present Majesty's reign, the Bank of England undertook the management of such part, both in transferring, and in paying the dividends thereupon: to enable them so to do, they are empowered by the aforementioned Act to receive the money from the Irish Exchequer.

The dividends upon this fund are nevertheless not guaranteed by our Government, but rest solely upon the revenues of the Sister Kingdom. Its capital, if I may be allowed so to express myself, or at least that part of it transferable here, amounted, on August 1st, 1817, to £1,900,000.* It is transferable at the Bank of England every Tuesday, Thursday, and Saturday, except when the books are shut for the dividends or interest, which becomes due March 25th, and September 29th.

Letters of Attorney cost £1. 1*s.* 6*d.*

Brokerage, 2*s.* 6*d.* per cent., upon all sums bought or sold.

*Now Consolidated with the Debt of Great Britain.

LIFE ANNUITIES

In order to accelerate the liquidation of the national debt, and in aid of the funds set apart for that purpose, the legislature passed an act in 1808, being the 48th of his present Majesty, entitled an act "For enabling the Commissioners for the Reduction of the National Debt, to grant Life Annuities;" by which it was enacted, that from and after the first day of August 1808, the holders of stock in the 3 per Cent. Consolidated and the 3 per Cent. Reduced Annuities might exchange the same for Life Annuities, on one or more lives, according to the age of the respective parties, at the rates set forth in the Tables annexed to the said act; one of the clauses in which enacts, that all annuities ceasing by the death of the nominees do revert to the sinking fund. It also allows transfers to be made of the said Annuities under certain restrictions set forth therein; which transfers, when required, are made at the Bank of England.

The amount of these Annuities, August 1st, 1817, was £225,254. 13*s.* They are payable in January and July, and April and October, according to the description of Stock which the purchasers may transfer to the Commissioners, who are now authorised to grant Annuities in exchange for the following Stocks:

3 per Cent. Consols	3 per Cent. Reduced
Navy 5 per Cents	4 per Cents
Long Annuities	

SOUTH SEA STOCK

The South Sea Stock is the capital of the South Sea Company, which was established in the year 1711. The capital stock, after many reductions before 1733, was then settled, and has continued without variation up to August 1st, 1817, £3,662,784. 8*s.* 6*d.* It is transferable at the South Sea House every Monday, Wednesday, and Friday, between the hours of twelve and one, except on holidays, or when the books are shut for the dividends or interest, which is 3 ½ per cent. and is due January 5th, and July 5th.

Letters of Attorney cost £1. 1*s.* 6*d.*

Brokerage, 2*s.* 6*d.* per cent. upon the sum bought or sold.

Every transfer of this stock, if under £100, costs 9*s.* 6*d.;* if above, 12*s.;* and if a private transfer, 3*s.* 6*d.* over and above the foregoing sums.

Every person possessed of five hundred pounds of this stock, and which has been in his actual possession six months, is entitled thereby to give one vote at all elections for Governors and Directors of this Company; two thousand pounds stock entitles them to two votes; three thousand to three votes; and five thousand pounds to four votes.

Two thousand pounds stock is also a qualification for becoming Director; four thousand for Deputy Governor; and five thousand for Sub Governor.

THREE PER CENT. NEW SOUTH SEA ANNUITIES

This fund was part of the capital stock of the South Sea Company, and may be said to have its origin in the year 1757, at which time it became a 3 per cent. fund, having, previously to that period, borne interest at 4 and 3 ½ per cent. Its capital was on August 1st, 1817, £3,895,330. 2*s.* 10*d.* It is transferable at the South Sea House every Tuesday, Thursday, and Saturday, between the hours of twelve and one, except on holidays, or when the books are shut for the dividends or interest, which becomes due the 5th of January, and 5th of July.

Letters of Attorney cost £1. 1*s.* 6*d.*

Brokerage, 2*s.* 6*d.* per cent. on the sum bought or sold.

THREE PER CENT. 1751

The date shews the time when this fund commenced. Its capital on August 1st, 1817, was £857,600. It is transferable at the South Sea House every Tuesday and Thursday, from twelve till one, except on holidays, or when the books are shut for the dividends or interest, which is due the 5th of January, and 5th of July.

Letters of Attorney cost £1. 1*s.* 6*d.*

Brokerage, 2*s.* 6*d.* per cent. on the sum bought or sold.

THREE PER CENT. OLD SOUTH SEA ANNUITIES

This fund, as well as that of the New South Sea Annuities, formed part of the capital stock of the South Sea Company: its origin as a 3 per cent. fund was in 1757, having previously borne interest at 5, 4, and 3 ½ per cent. Its capital was on August 1st, 1817, £5,604,470. 2*s.* 7*d.* It is transferable at the South Sea House every Monday, Wednesday, and Friday, between twelve and one, except on holidays, or when the books are shut for the dividends or interest, which is due the 5th of April, and the 10th of October.

Letters of Attorney cost £1. 1*s.* 6*d.*

Brokerage, 2*s.* 6*d.* per cent. on the sums bought and sold.

INDIA STOCK

This Stock is the capital or trading stock of the India Company, and, with those of the Bank and South Sea Stocks, are the only three that can with propriety be called Stocks, all the rest in the Table being Funds. Without entering into a long detail of the Old and New Companies, with their junction, &c. &c. I shall only state, that its capital on August 1st, 1817 was £6,000,000.* It is transferable at the India House every Tuesday, Thursday, and Saturday, between the hours of eleven and one on the first two of those days, and from eleven till twelve only on Saturday (after which hour no business of any kind is transacted at this House), except on holidays, or when the books are shut for the dividends or interest, which becomes due January 5th, and July 5th, and are paid every day, from nine till two, except on Saturdays, as before noticed, when all business here finishes at twelve. The interest on this stock is at present 10 ½ per cent., and every transfer, be the sum more or less, costs £1. 4*s.* Private transfers, when wanted, are 2*s.* 6*d.* additional.

*By an Act of Parliament which received the Royal Assent on the 7th day of March, 1797, the Company are enabled to increase their capital to £8,000,000, but have not yet availed themselves of it.

Letters of Attorney cost £1. 1*s.* 6*d.*

Brokerage, 2*s.* 6*d.* per cent. on all sums bought or sold.

Every person possessed of one thousand pounds of this stock, in their own right, is entitled to give one vote at all elections, and upon all questions decided by the proprietary at large; three thousand entitles them to two votes; six thousand to three votes, and ten thousand to four votes, provided they have been in actual possession of the said stock twelve calendar months, with the exceptions as heretofore stated in Bank Stock; two thousand pounds stock is the qualification for the Chairman, Deputy Chairman, or Directors; and the possessor of that stock is eligible as a candidate, and may be elected to either of the preceding offices, although he has not been in possession of the said stock twelve months; but he cannot *vote* at elections until the time is expired.

Editorial Endnotes

1 By Thomas Mortimer, first published in 1761.

2 Popularly known as Consols, these were the most commonly held government securities well into the nineteenth century.

3 This fund and the following were raised to assist the Austrian Empire in the war against France. The emperor being referred to was Francis II.

2

A DEFENSE OF JOINT-STOCK COMPANIES

Henry Day

Source: Henry Day, *A Defense of Joint Stock Companies; Being an Attempt to Shew Their Legality, Expediency, and Public Benefit* (London: Longman, Hurst, Rees, and Orme, 1808), pp. 31–42.

EDITORIAL HEADNOTE

Henry Day was a solicitor for the British Ale Brewery.[1] His book is part of a larger argument in favor of free trade and against undue government interference in private enterprise. Although Day believed that irresponsible speculation was a real danger, he argued that the Bubble Act of 1720 went too far in inhibiting the formation of useful companies. Far from injuring the public, Day argued that the expansion of legitimate business corporations (like the brewery he represented) would enhance competition and undermine monopoly.[2]

Notes

1 Ron Harris, *Industrializing English Law: Entrepreneurship and Business Organization, 1720–1844* (Cambridge: Cambridge University Press, 2000), p. 238.
2 Alan Pryor, "The Industrialization of the London Brewing Trade: Part 3," *Brewery History* (2016), pp. 51–80.

It would be ridiculous to talk of the freedom of trade in a country, which owes its present aggrandizement to trade, if we were to be told that any sums, however large, might not be raised for legal speculations, by any number of subscribers, and that the whole might not divide the profits in proportion to their respective contributions!

It is indeed true, that in large pecuniary speculations, it is frequently deemed expedient to apply for acts of incorporation; but it is conceived that the advantages to be derived, may be obtained as well without such acts of incorporation as with them.

DOI: 10.4324/9781003713890-3

For if, as in the present Joint Stock Companies, the subscribers at large authorize and appoint a certain number of their own members, nominally, ostensibly, and responsibly, for the joint benefit of all, to conduct the whole concern, such individuals so nominated, would it is conceived, possess as much legal and necessary power, to act for the benefit of such concern, as they could possibly derive even from the exclusive sanction of an act of parliament.

Thus any Joint Stock Company would derive as much benefit from their agents, so chosen, under whatever denomination they may be appointed to act, whether as governors, directors, trustees, &c.; as if such persons were vested with their functions under the sanction of the legislature.

In the Golden Lane Brewery, for instance, the subscribers amount to several hundreds; but relying on the competency of Messrs. Brown and Parry, they have assigned the whole powers of management to these gentlemen; and as a proof of the judgment of the electors, and the competent eligibility of the persons so nominated, the subscription shares, which were originally only 50*l.* have within the space of two years, risen nearly to 100*l.* – the Market price within one year and half being 94*l.*

Other institutions proceed upon similar principles, with little other difference than perhaps that of their objects – how these can be deemed mischievous attempts or projects, it is difficult to determine.

If the names of the Brewers be admitted, and regularly entered at the Excise, his Majesty has sufficient security for the duties; and the Brewers may be prosecuted for any violations of the Revenue Laws. At the same time it is essential to observe, that from the large and respectable guarantee which they are required to give, there seems little danger to be apprehended on that account.

There is no necessity that the names of all the Proprietors should be known to support any action; consequently individuals have no more difficulty in obtaining redress for any civil injury from the ostensible persons acting as agents for any of the Joint Stock Companies, than they would have in proceeding against any chartered company whatever.

Another attempt has been made to intimidate the individuals embarked, or intending to embark in Joint Stock Companies, by asserting, that they could in no instance whatever exonerate themselves, or their property, from the responsibility of a partnership, after they had once signed the deed, although they had regularly assigned their shares, and had no longer any connection with the concern – such an assertion is too ridiculous to impose even upon the most implicit credulity.

As, however, such an opinion has gone abroad, and has been said even to have been sanctioned by counsel; – let us examine a little into the doctrine of the law of partnership, and see how it applies to the point in question.

In every partnership, it is well known that the property of every individual, in case of the deficiency of any of the rest of the partners, stands responsible for the debts of the firm; nor can the partners by any engagement amongst themselves, whether by deed or otherwise, exonerate themselves from such responsibility.

Any contract therefore which provides that no partner shall be responsible beyond the extent of his property in the firm, however binding upon the contracting parties composing that firm, would nevertheless be void with respect to the public.

It is certainly true, that until due notice of an alteration in the firm, or a dissolution, to all the former creditors and correspondents of the house, that not only the joint and several shares in the capital employed, but the joint and several property of all the partners not employed in trade, would be made responsible.

Hence it becomes necessary in case of dissolution, to give notice in the Gazette; but probably even this notice would not be sufficient, if the party subsequently giving such credit had never had such notice – but if, on the contrary, notice were so publicly given, and understood, of one partner disposing of his share of interest in the concern to another, it would surely be too preposterous to assert, that such partner, so transferring his share, should be responsible for debts contacted subsequently to his having formally relinquished, and completely abandoned every connection with the concern. – Such a proposition would carry the doctrine of partnership responsibility to a most monstrous and dangerous extent.

But it may perhaps be objected, that there is no parity of reasoning whatever between partnerships, consisting of a few individuals, as customarily carried on, and Joint Stock Companies, which are *sui generis*, and in their nature anomalous.

It has been elsewhere observed, that the objects the legislature had in view, were to guard the public from impositions, and at the same time to protect the rights of individuals.

Let us examine whether these points are sufficiently attended to, at least in two or three of the Institutions, the articles of which have come more particularly within my own knowledge. In those it is stipulated that the beverage brewed, shall be from Malt and Hops only, and that the brewers, if required, shall once every month take an oath before some magistrate, to verify that fact.

This regulation, it is presumed, will not be considered as "a mischievous project, injurious to his Majesty's subjects," although the present ale brewers, or perhaps the druggists, may have some cause to complain of it – these gentlemen however are probably better advised than to pray in aid of the attorney-general, armed with the two-edged sword of the 18th Geo. I.

Let us examine how far the subscribers can be injured, or to speak in the language of the enemies of these institutions, how far they can possibly become the dupes of interested projectors.

In the first place, the object of the institution is known – the regulations by which it is organized, have been assented to and approved – the shares have been limited to a reasonable number – the sums paid upon subscription, and the instalments, are easy – the subscribers have all the power of transferring their shares, under, nevertheless, some few necessary qualifications, whenever they think proper, and which they will probably do at a premium – the sums subscribed are all paid into the hands of a respectable banker – the accounts of the concern are audited every quarter, by a distinct body of gentlemen of the highest respectability, and a committee meets every week for the purpose of providing for the incidental expenses of the preceding week, and settling the accounts of the concern; and such committee has the power of ordering drafts for monies in the hands of the bankers, either for making the necessary advances, on account of the concern, or drawing to make dividends to the proprietors; and the trustees issue drafts accordingly to the persons who are to receive the money – such drafts to be made in committees assembled, and attested to the secretary.

The acting committee have also power to dismiss the brewers – to require from them any reasonable security for the integrity of their conduct – to quit the concern without interruption when discharged from office, and to pay over and transfer any balance of money, books, and vouchers in their hands.

There are some other very important regulations, which have a double tendency to guard the public, and to guarantee the subscribers against any ruinous responsibility; viz. as that no debts, except for wages of servants hired for certain periods, shall be contracted by the concern; but all Malt, Hops, &c. are to be paid for on delivery. Thus by a fundamental article in this institution, no debts can be contracted, and consequently no hazard can accrue to the public in their dealings with a company of this description.

Neither can any of the subscribers be injured – all the shares are either paid up, or in course of payment; the money is vested in the hands of respectable bankers; and such judicious checks are established with respect to drawing it out, as to render fraud next to impossible.

So little enveloped in mystery are the transactions of the directors, that every individual member may have access to their proceedings: in a word, the proceedings of the whole concern, either are, or may be known, to every individual composing it.

Surely a society so organized, cannot be deemed a nuisance, like the *sixpenny subscriptions*, before cited by Macpherson – where the projectors hired a room for a few hours, opened their books, and absconded with the money; nor is it an "extravagant or unwarrantable undertaking," to restore to the people of England their wholesome beverage, composed of genuine malt and hops, notwithstanding any clamour of the brewers, or the druggists; whose profits may be thereby in no small degree injured.

With respect to the distilleries also, it would not be deemed, it is presumed, an extravagant or unwarrantable undertaking, to substitute juniper for turpentine, and produce a more excellent spirit by that measure which can alone effect so desirable an object, viz. by establishing that competition which will inevitably produce so advantageous a change.

Any prosecution therefore against these companies, must come with a very bad grace from those overgrown capitalists who have so long assumed an exclusive right to monopolize an article of general consumption, and deal it out to the public, at any price, and of any quality they may fix amongst themselves.

Little cause indeed have the brewers or distillers, to originate a prosecution, which by sanctioning competition must destroy monopoly – little cause have the gentlemen to talk as injured individuals, on account of the aggregate capital of a company, whose capital for the benefit of the public does not amount to one fourth part of those capitals, which have enabled them to raise the price and regulate the quality, without hitherto having found any power to control their dictates: whose avaricious gains are much more their object than any advantage to the Public. Their price of gin has several times been raised, whilst malt has rather decreased than otherwise.

The immense capitals of the distillers individually, is upon an average considerably more than some of the Joint Stock Companies; and by establishing the price and quality of the article, the whole aggregate of their immense capital, is not only to the disadvantage of the public, but to the revenue; and evil that could only be counteracted by that of competition, which would result from the establishment of other distilleries.

With respect to one part of the act, which perhaps is to be perverted from its sound construction, and which will be treated upon hereafter, viz. – "unwarrantable and extravagant projects, injurious to great numbers of his Majesty's subjects, in their trade and other affairs" – in the first place, as it will be more minutely shewn, this act has no reference to any particular trade, except in the clause which gives an action with treble costs, &c.

But it is not true, that these associations can do any serious mischief to individuals in the vast state of population of this metropolis; estimating in comparative proportion the small number of Joint Stock Companies, the interest of the individual fair trader can never be injured; some overgrown capitalists, perhaps, may indeed divide less profits than they have heretofore accumulated, but of this they have no reason to complain. Instead of imitating the conduct of the foolish countryman, who prayed to Hercules to assist him, let them diminish or annihilate competition by producing a better article.

No doubt can be entertained, that Joint Stock Companies, or associated companies of any description, can only exist whilst they adhere to their original principles; the moment they deviate from these, they will read their fault in their punishment, and must either return to their original principles, or they will dwindle into oblivion.

There is then no danger either to the public or to individuals to be apprehended from these Joint Stock Companies: absurd it is therefore to call in the aid of the legislature to abolish them.

For however extensive the power, however large their avowed capital, and capable of concealed increase, yet is there little apprehension of injury to individual fair traders, from such a company, even if they were to attempt it.

3

THE SOUTH SEA BUBBLE AND THE NUMEROUS FRAUDULENT PROJECTS TO WHICH IT GAVE RISE

[Anon.]

Source: [Anon.], *The South Sea Bubble, and the Numerous Fraudulent Projects to Which It Gave Rise in 1720, Historically Detailed as a Beacon to the Unwary Against Modern Schemes, Equally Visionary and Nefarious* (London: Thomas Boys, 1825), pp. 3–7, 133–42.

EDITORIAL HEADNOTE

The collapse of the South Sea Bubble in 1720 came to symbolize the dangers of reckless speculation embodied by joint-stock companies. For the remainder of the eighteenth century and well into the nineteenth, whenever an upsurge of company formations seemed likely, commentators inevitably invoked the specter of the South Sea Bubble as a dire warning.[1]

The anonymous author of this pamphlet equates the numerous joint-stock company promotions of 1825 (mines, foreign loans, banks, etc.) with the "nefarious" speculative mania of 1720.

Note

1 Julian Hoppit, "The Myths of the South Sea Bubble," *Transactions of the Royal Historical Society* 12 (2002), pp. 141–65.

In seeking to arrest public attention, and *at this moment* to direct it to events which have occurred more than a century ago, we are influenced by one motive, and by one motive alone – the most anxious desire to avert the recurrence of such disasters, as, at that period, shook the kingdom to its centre, and spread misery and wretchedness from one quarter to the other. The same destroying spirit is again unfortunately abroad, and the same melancholy consequences will as inevitably ensue, if the nation, which it is to be hoped only slumbers, be not aroused to an immediate sense of the perils that surround it. The first acts of the fearful drama,

DOI: 10.4324/9781003713890-4

which we are about recording, passed off with as much eclat, as the performances now getting up for similar representation; the wand of the enchanter seemed but to touch any substance, and it was instantly converted into gold; and the South Sea project continued to be applauded to the very skies, by the unprincipled and the unthinking, until its fatal catastrophe plunged thousands of both into one common abyss of ruin. It was patronized by the first characters of the kingdom, by persons of both sexes, in the highest walks of society, nay by royalty itself, if the following extract from a letter of the Duchess of Ormond to Swift,[1] dated April 18, 1720, be deemed sufficient authority for such an assertion: "I want much to hear what you think of Great Britain; for all your relations here want to see you, where are strange changes every day. You remember, and so do I, when the *South Sea* was said to be my Lord Oxford's brat, and must be starved at nurse. Now the King has adopted it, and calls it his beloved child; though perhaps, you may say, if he loves it no better than his son, it may not be saying much: but he loves it as well as he does the Duchess of K-,[2] and that is saying a good deal. I wish it may thrive, for many of my friends are deep in it: I wish you were so too."

Prior, in a letter to the same distinguished person, in the May following, says, "The South Sea Company have raised their stock to three hundred and fifty;" and again, upon the 28th of February, 1720–21, speaks thus: "I am tired of politics, and lost in the South Sea. The roaring of the waves, and the madness of the people, were justly put together. I can send you no sort of news, that holds either connexion or sense. It is all wilder than St. Anthony's dream; and the *bagatelle* is more solid than any thing that has been endeavoured here this year."

A pretty convincing proof that even the retiring habits, and, generally speaking, contempt of base lucre, which characterize men of letters, were no safe-guard against the raging infection; but the following anecdotes of Gay[3] the poet, and of Chandler,[4] the celebrated non-conformist divine, place the fact in a stronger point of view.

Gay has a present of some South Sea stock from young Craggs, and once supposed himself to be worth twenty thousand pounds. His friends advised him to dispose of his share; but he dreamed of dignity and splendour, and could not bear to obstruct his own fortune. He was then importuned to sell as much as would purchase him a hundred a year for life, "which," says Fenton, "will make you sure of a clean shirt, and a shoulder of mutton every day." This counsel was rejected. The profit and principal were lost; and Gay sunk under the calamity so low, that his life became in danger. Samuel Chandler, the learned nonconformist divine, lost his whole fortune by the bubble, so that he was under the necessity of opening a bookseller's shop in the Poultry, which he kept for two or three years, whilst he continued to discharge his duty as a minister.

The designing knave of the present day is not more scrupulous, nor the visionary fool less sanguine, than the knave and the fool of the last century; whether the materials of gullibility be so easily moulded – be so tempered to the hands of the workmen, time, the great unraveller of all mysteries, is alone competent to determine. It is the duty, however, in the interim, of every man who values the prosperity, the happiness, nay, the very tranquility of his country, to exert every nerve in allaying the ferment, ere it reach the climax of delirium. In the name of common sense then, we conjure persons of all descriptions, whom our little book may attract, to ponder well upon what they shall read – to reflect that it is no idle tale, but a narration of circumstances, parallel to those now in agitation; let them not be deceived by high sounding titles – the South Sea scheme, we have shewn, was patronized by the King himself: let every man, to use a familiar expression, "look ere he leap;" and before he risk solid, substantial property upon phantoms and moonshine, bring all his faculties to the investigation; let him bear in mind, that though chance may sometimes favour the gamester, in nine hundred and ninety-nine cases out of a thousand the professed gambler dies a beggar; and, in fine, let him not forget, that the only sure road to independence is by frugal and persevering industry . . .

BUBBLES OF 1825

The following is the most extensive list of the *bubbles* now blowing, as yet published; it appeared in the *Examiner* newspaper of Sunday, Jan. 30, 1825, with the very judicious observations that accompany it. If this numerous progeny be compared with the litter of the last century, the features of resemblance will be found so strong, as to leave no doubt whatever of their common origin; and the bantlings of 1825, already exhibit the very same symptoms of premature decay, which consigned their predecessors, of 1720, to sudden dissolution and everlasting disgrace.

"We are decidedly of opinion, that on particular occasions a mere statement of matter of fact, unaided by much of other reasoning or illustration, forms a stronger appeal to common sense than the most elaborate disquisition. In the spirit of this conviction, we shall present our readers with a list of the various new schemes at present before the public for the employment of British capital, without the delivery of any opinions of our own on the comparative merit of their pretensions, beyond a remark or two on the distinctive features of the various lines of adventure. Our purpose, indeed, is rather to form a great general inference, than a series of particular conclusions – to shew by the very nature of the circumstances how necessarily the major part of this speculation must end delusively. When it is rendered unequivocally apparent, that a certain number of things cannot possibly exist together, it is trite to observe, that a portion of that number must fail in some stage or other; and that they should fail as soon as possible, is doubtless the most desirable consummation. The following is a list, and if not inclusive of *all* these projects, it is quite sufficiently so for the purpose to which we have alluded:

Railroads:	Capitals
Bath and Bristol	112,000
Birmingham and Liverpool	1,000,000
Bristol and Birmingham	800,000

Bristol Northern and Western	800,000
East London and United Dock	100,000
Grand Western	3,000,000
Grand Junction	2,000,000
Hibernian General	1,000,000
Kentish	1,000,000
Limerick and Waterford	300,000
London and Birmingham	1,500,000
London and Bristol	1,500,000
London Northern	2,500,000
London, Portsmouth, and Southampton	1,000,000
Manchester and Leeds	500,000
Manchester and Liverpool	7,000,000
Norfolk, Suffolk, and Essex	1,000,000
Royal Hibernian General	1,000,000
Surrey, Sussex, and Hants	1,500,000
Taunton	200,000
Banking, Loan, Investment, and Insurance Companies:	Capitals
Alliance Fire and Life Insurance	5,000,000
Alliance Marine	5,000,000
British Annuity	3,000,000
British Paving, Building, and Investment	2,000,000
British Shipping Loan Company	1,000,000
Crown Life Assurance	1,000,000
Equitable Investment Society	5,000,000
Equitable Loan Bank	2,000,000
Hibernian Joint Stock Company	1,000,000
Irish Investment Bank	500,000
Investment Bank	200,000
Irish Investment and Equitable Loan Bank	1,000,000
London and Manchester Equitable Loan Bank	500,000
Metropolitan Banking Company	500,000
Metropolitan Investment Society	2,000,000
Medical, Clerical, and General Life Insurance	1,000,000
Metropolitan Loan and Investment Company	1,000,000
Palladium Fire and Life Assurance	2,000,000
Protector Fire Assurance	3,000,000
Promoter Benefit Company	60,000
Provincial Bank of Ireland	2,000,000

United British and Foreign Loan Company	2,500,000
Gas Companies:	Capitals
British	400,000
Birmingham and Staffordshire	120,000
Continental	2,000,000
Gas Engine Carriage Company	200,000
Hibernian	1,000,000
London Portable Gas Company	250,000
New Imperial	250,000
Provincial	1,000,000
Phoenix	450,000
South American and Colonial	1,000,000
United General Gas	1,000,000
British and Irish Mines:	Capitals
British Mining Association	400,000
Equitable Mining	200,000
English Mining	250,000
Hibernian Mining Company	500,000
Irish Mining	
Mr. Rothschild's Welsh Mining Company	
South Wales	2,000,000
Welsh Iron and Coal	250,000
Foreign Mines, &c.:	Capitals
Anglo-Mexican	1,000,000
Anglo-Chilian	1,500,000
Arigna Iron and Coal	300,000
Bolanos	200,000
Brazilian	3,000,000
Chilian	1,000,000
Colombian	1,000,000
General Mining Association	
Gold Coast Mining	750,000
General South American	2,000,000
New Brazilian	1,000,000
Pasco Peruvian Mines	1,000,000
Pearl Fishery	725,000
Real del Monte	200,000
Rio de la Plata	1,000,000
Tlalpaxahua	200,000

United Mexican Mining Company	1,000,000
Shipping and Dock Companies:	Capitals
Bristol and English Channel Ship Company	1,750,000
Bermondsey Dock	800,000
Faversham Navigation	33,000
General Steam Navigation	2,000,000
London and Portsmouth Ship Canal	5,000,000
London, Brighton, and Devonshire Fishing Company	500,000
St. Ives New Pier	30,000
South London Dock	750,000
Miscellaneous Companies:	Capitals
Australian Agricultural Company	1,000,000
Alderney Dairy	150,000
Bognor New Town	300,000
Bread Company	200,000
British Distillery	200,000
British Iron	2,000,000
British Fishing Company	1,000,000
British Patent Brick	300,000
Canada Company	
East London Dairy	125,000
General Coal Company	500,000
General Journal Company	100,000
Great Westminster Dairy	200,000
General United Coal	1,000,000
Kent and Essex Flour Company	210,000
London Brick Company	500,000
Metropolitan Marine Bath	500,000
Metropolitan Milk	
Metropolitan Fish Company	300,000
Metropolitan Water-works Company	500,000
Metropolitan Alderney Dairy	150,000
New Corn Exchange	200,000
Royal National Bath	250,000
Sea and Inland Coal	500,000
South London Milk	100,000
Steam Washing Company	40,000
Thames Quay Company	611,000
Thames Tunnel	200,000
Westminster Fish	100,000

In addition to the foregoing projects, we acquire from the Scottish, Irish, and provincial newspapers, accounts of new kindred local speculations every day. We copy the following list, for instance, from the *Edinburgh Times*, a spirited journal of liberal principles, the first number of which was published the 22d instant:

List of the principal Joint Stock Companies, which have been publicly proposed, and, separately, or by union, established in Edinburgh, within the last two months: Edinburgh and Leith Dock Company; Edinburgh and Dalkeith Rail-road Company; Edinburgh and Glasgow Rail-road Company; Berwick and Kelso Rail-road Company; East Lothian Rail-road Company; Scottish Union Insurance Company; Commercial Marine Insurance Company; Scottish Union Banking Company; National Bank of Scotland; Scottish Union Commercial Banking Company; Scottish Wool Stapling Company; Shotts Iron Joint Stock Company; Caledonian Iron and Foundry Company; Edinburgh and Leith Glass Company; Albion Glass Company; Scottish Porter Brewing Company; Caledonian Porter Brewing Company; British Distillery Company; Joint Stock Whale Fishing Company; Edinburgh Cotton and Flax Spinning Company; Edinburgh Dairy Company, for the supply of Milk, the feeding of Veal, the making of Cheese, &c. &c.; Equitable Loan, or Pawnbroker Company; Albyn Company, for the purpose of investing money on Heritable Properties in Edinburgh, &c. &c.; Equitable Building Company, for the purpose of building Houses in the vicinity of Edinburgh for Workmen, &c. &c.; Joint Stock Company for the Manufacturing of Paper; Joint Stock Company for the Printing of Law-papers.

In short, setting aside the extreme ignorance of political economy and trading principles betrayed in much of the foregoing scheming, the amount of capital required, avowedly upwards of one hundred millions, implies a sudden transfer of property upon merely speculative views that would scarcely be warranted upon the clearest demonstration. Much of it is also for cultivation of objects which will produce little advantage to the country, even when fortunate to individuals, – such as the foreign mining adventure. The bustle of fictitiously-created property, or surplus capital, under the operation of a gradual reduction to its real value by the force of circumstance, is a curious subject for contemplation; and the proposed creation of employment for it, without demand, will not render it less so.

It is no doubt obvious, that the features of these various appeals to unemployed capital are very materially distinguished from one another. For instance, the application of scientific discoveries to the promotion of commercial facilities and local improvement, like Rail-roads and Steam Navigation, are not to be classed with schemes founded on a mere spirit of trading adventure or speculative scheming of individuals. The same observation may also be made in regard to such as rest on the presumed advantage of great works, as Docks, Ship Canals, Piers, &c. as well possibly as upon certain Banking and Assurance Schemes. In one point of view, however, they must all be regarded alike, we mean in reference to the vast transfer of capital required to carry them into simultaneous effect, and consequently, independent of legislative backwardness, the utter absurdity of a great number of them, with a view to the benefit of anybody or anything, except the projectors.

For the sake of argument, we will admit that all are feasible; what would be the consequence? At best, the most momentous transfer of property and employment in the twinkling of an eye, that was ever known in any age or nation. Strong-minded politicians might get over the fact; but how are the opposing interests to be paralysed? They cannot be made weak or inoperative; hence, even in the most favourable point of view, the delusion of so much of this giddy speculation, and its inutility to all but the adventurers and jobbers who originate it. Some of these plans are formed so entirely in a spirit of gaming adventure, as for instance the Foreign Mining adventures, that it would be as useless to offer a formal argument against the game of Blind Hazard, as against the spirit which leads people to deal with them either with a view to an immediate jobbing gain, or to the ultimate result. Persons of this description require no statements from us: but satisfied as we are that the pernicious example of much temporary gain in the buying and selling way, is tempting people both in country and town to venture their little hoards, to whom ultimate loss would be very ruinous, and to whom such loss is far more probable than to others, – we have drawn up the foregoing rapid statement, to show the utter absurdity of the prosperity of such a variety of fresh applications of capital at one time. We might venture to assert, that even some of the undertakings that will be ultimately useful, will benefit the speculators very little in a pecuniary point of view, while many of them are evident absurdities. Every body may recollect the rage for Joint Stock Companies a few years ago, which vanished away in smoke; and a contemplation of the preceding list, and of the nature of much of the specified speculation, must satisfy every reflective person that it will be so again. Of the number of projects, it would be unjust to deny that several will be useful to the country, whatever they may prove to the final shareholders; but even good effected this way often produces a very pernicious species of temporary suffering. At all events, a sober consideration of the above list will be of service to minor speculators, if we have such among our readers; and to such consideration we look for the due impression, much more than to these very cursory observations.

Editorial Endnotes

1 Jonathan Swift (1667–1745) Irish satirist and Anglican cleric.
2 Melusine von der Schulenburg, Duchess of Kendal (1667–1743) German-born mistress of George I.
3 John Gay (1685–1732) poet and dramatist, author of *The Beggar's Opera.*
4 Samuel Chandler (1693–1766) Nonconformist minister and pamphleteer.

4

REMARKS ON JOINT-STOCK COMPANIES BY AN OLD MERCHANT

[Sir William Clay]

Source: [Sir William Clay], *Remarks on Joint Stock Companies by an Old Merchant* (London: John Murray, 1825), pp. 43–60.

EDITORIAL HEADNOTE

William Clay (1791–1869) was a merchant and politician. He was the son of George Clay, a wealthy London merchant and shipowner. In 1832 Clay entered Parliament as a Whig, representing Tower Hamlets, a seat he was to hold for twenty-five years. He served on the Board of Control and was made a baronet for his service to the state in 1841. Clay published several pamphlets related to economic matters, and he was a member of the 1843 Select Committee on Joint-Stock Companies that recommended an easier and more streamlined process for incorporating joint-stock companies.[1]

In this work, published anonymously, Clay saw the profusion of joint-stock proposals as encouraging a dangerous spirit of gambling which was the antithesis of "those habits of patient and well-directed industry which can alone really advance individual or national prosperity." Far from benefitting the nation as a whole, Clay believed that the vast majority of joint-stock companies primarily enriched the promoters, lawyers, bankers, and contractors who received large salaries and commissions whether or not the companies actually succeeded.

Note

1 Francis Watt, "Clay, Sir William," *Oxford Dictionary of National Biography*, eds. H.C.G. Matthew and Brian Harrison (Oxford: Oxford University Press, 2004), Vol. 11, p. 971.

DOI: 10.4324/9781003713890-5

The discussion of the question, of how far the present abundance of schemes for Joint Stock Companies may be attributed to an unexampled redundancy of national wealth, has extended to a greater length than I had anticipated, – but it may not be perhaps without its value.

The cause, however, to which I am disposed to attribute this abundant and mushroom growth of Joint Stock Companies, is, in my opinion, so perfectly adequate to the effects we are witnessing, that it was, perhaps, superfluous to discuss the claims of any other; for whatever may be the real amount at which it could be rationally fixed, would have had any material influence upon the operation of this active and influential principle.

This cause, in my apprehension, is neither recondite or remote; it is to be found in the *enormous gains which these schemes afford the means of amassing to their projectors and promoters*. An increasing disposition amongst men of business, to participate in the operations of the Stock-Exchange, has been evident for some time past; for the last two or three years, this love of stock-jobbing has begun to pervade classes of society hitherto exempt from its influence; within these few months it seems to have gained its acme. Several reasons may be assigned for the growth of this prevailing inclination: the operations of the traffickers in the funds have, in the main, been successful ever since the peace; indeed, they are perhaps the only men of business in London of whom this can truly be said. The funds, both of this and of other countries, have greatly risen; it has been flowing water, and some individuals amongst them have realized colossal fortunes; and whilst the absence of those topics of spirit-stirring interest which public events formerly afforded, having left the daily press more at leisure to direct its attention to such subjects, has tended to foster this inclination in the public at large, the diminished profits of trade have yet more forcibly turned to such pursuits the attention of mercantile men. Foreign loans were the first objects of this spirit of speculation; its direction towards the enterprises which are the objects of our present inquiry is comparatively recent, but it seems, in pursuit of them, to have acquired tenfold animation.

The rapidity of this increase affords the clearest indication of the source from which it proceeds: it has all the characteristics of being the effect of an unusual excitation of the public mind; there exists in fact, very generally, a vague, indefinite, and feverish expectation of magnificent results to be produced by the advance of science, and the acuteness of modern research; we are thought to be on the eve of an era of such unexampled improvement in trade, science, and finance, that all the conveniences we at present possess seem stale, flat, and unprofitable in comparison; we gaze at the bright vista, which we fondly believe is opening before our eyes, of interminable prosperity and unimagined greatness, until we grow giddy with its brilliance; and even the highest and wisest amongst us seem not wholly exempt from intoxication, in contemplating its visionary glories. Certain it is, that the eagerness which is manifested by the public, to embark in whatever enterprise the ingenuity of projectors may propose, amounts at this moment to absolute infatuation; to infatuation, at least, in that larger portion of the public, who can only become subscribers to these schemes, when they bear a premium, – that smaller portion, which has an earlier acquaintance with them, may be considered, I think, as perfectly free from the imputation of simplicity.

The origin of these schemes is commonly somewhat after this fashion: – the projector or projectors, having either possessed themselves of some privilege, obtained from a foreign government to mine the soil, fish the seas, or light the towns with gas, &c., &c., or having *only surmised that they might*, could, would, or should obtain such privilege, or having devised some plausible project of public works to be executed in our own, forthwith associate to themselves twelve or twenty-four directors, of course selecting the most respectable or best known individuals whom they can persuade to undertake the office, and they are not without the power of offering inducements the most persuasive. To each of these directors a certain number of shares in the new enterprise is allotted, (I believe two hundred are considered liberal and business-like,) *at prime cost, at nothing, that is, at par*; the remainder is offered to the discerning public, at a premium varying as the degree of heat at which the thermometer of public excitation may stand at the moment, or as the moderation of the authors themselves of the lists may dictate.

Some have been disposed of at a premium of five, some of ten per cent., which last price may, perhaps, afford to the projectors something like a remuneration for their expense of thought, and their zeal and anxiety for the public good; others again have been thrown away at the paltry price of three per cent.; but all, I believe, or with very few exceptions, have been sold at a premium. I do not mean to assert, that in all the schemes it may have been part of the original plan to admit the public at a premium, upon the very opening of the lists of subscription; in some, it undoubtedly has been, as the very circular to the subscribers, that required payment of the first instalment, also demanded the premium; but it is clear that it is perfectly immaterial, whether the premium to the projectors be made a stipulation with the subscribers, and the lists be then thrown open, or whether the market be gradually supplied with as many shares as can be advantageously disposed of; this latter mode is, perhaps, the more profitable.

In one or other of these modes, either the originators of the undertaking requiring a fixed premium from those whom they admitted as subscribers, or reserving themselves the bulk of the shares to be gradually disposed of as the market might encourage the sale, has by far the larger part of these associations been formed. It was not to be expected, indeed, that when, from the state of the public mind, it was almost certain that the shares of any undertaking, at all plausible in its nature, would bear a high premium immediately upon their coming out, that persons having the means or opportunity from any pecuniary circumstances of setting such projects on foot, should give away to others enormous profits, which they had completely the power to retain themselves. It was only accordingly amongst the earliest schemes, that subscribers were admitted freely and gratuitously; latterly, I believe, that the shares of any undertaking likely to bear a premium have been sparingly bestowed, except on such persons as the interests of the undertaking rendered it necessary to conciliate.

The probability of salary, the certainty of patronage, as inducements to accept the office of director, are perhaps hardly worth alluding to, as they must have been almost wholly overlooked in the contemplation of the more immediate and substantial advantage to be derived from the sale of their shares.

The various officers and functionaries of the new company, the bankers who are to receive the deposits, the solicitors who are to manage the law proceedings, the engineers who are to direct the formation of the works, the managing director and secretary who are to receive large salaries, the contractors who are to supply the iron and other materials – these, and more than I can afford space to enumerate, have evidently sufficient inducement, in the peculiar expectation of profits which the prosecution of the undertaking may afford them in their several offices and vocations, to wish well to the enterprise, and affix their names to the prospectus; it is, however, I believe, considered the handsome mode of proceeding to allot each of these gentlemen a certain number of shares, in the proportion of their respective dignity and importance.

Thus engendered, thus patronised, thus recommended, the project is introduced to the public in a prospectus, where its advantages are described, the opposition it is likely to meet with treated lightly, and its profits calculated. These commonly are on the most magnificent scale; but then, in a spirit of moderation never sufficiently to be praised, some twenty or thirty per cent. are thrown off for contingencies, and ten or fifteen per cent. (as the case may be) left for the steady and permanent remuneration of the subscribers. These prospectuses are conceived so nearly in the same spirit, and have so strong a family likeness, that any one might serve as a specimen of the whole, the only difference being, I think, that those which relate to pursuits to be undertaken in foreign parts, treat principally of the advantages to be derived by the adventurers, whilst those which are intended for home consumption, and relate to domestic objects, have a large infusion of public spirit and regard for the public good.

I have felt a strong temptation to select some one or two of these prospectuses and reprint them, with all their array of presidents, directors, functionaries, &c. &c., as the best illustration of this short account of their common origin; but I forbear to do so for several reasons. Writing anonymously myself, I do not feel that I have a right to bring before the public the names of others. When I accuse, I trust I shall have manliness enough to affix my name to the accusation: the system is monstrous, and calls aloud, in my opinion, for legislative interference; but it is to the system I am hostile, not to the individuals. It would not be difficult to select individuals whom I might elevate, for general edification, upon no very enviable pedestal, and who, by their frequent appearance before the public, have perhaps rendered their names fairly public property; but I should feel the task to be invidious, and I think the attack would be unfair. They are justified in usage in what they have done, and there are few men who would decline profit, patronage, notoriety, and consequence, under similar temptation to accept them. Of some of the individuals concerned in these undertakings, I know enough personally to believe them incapable of doing, under any temptation, what they believe to be wrong; of others, (of all, for aught I know to the contrary,) the general voice speaks unequivocally as of men of unsullied reputation; but to such men, I should say, that they are acting most inadvertently. – Can they be ignorant that their recommendation is an inducement to the public to subscribe? – That their names give a sanction to any project to which they are affixed; and that they are looked upon, to a certain degree, as guarantees of its success? – Can they, after dwelling upon this reflection for a moment, be satisfied that the proposed undertaking is of such brilliant promise as to justify its profits being sold by anticipation (before a spade is put into the ground, or one step is taken towards its completion) for fifty or an hundred thousand pounds? For to the extent of such an assertion must they, by implication at least, fairly, I think, be considered to go, in affixing their names to the prospectus of any scheme, of which the projectors themselves sell the shares at a premium to the public.

With regard to many of these gentlemen, however, it is impossible, that with only the usual allotment of human faculties, they should have been able to afford any very attentive investigation of all the projects whereof they are directors. No one can have cast even a cursory glance over the advertisements of this nature with which the papers have for some months abounded, and not have observed how frequently the names of the same persons occur.

Now many of these individuals have public duties to perform, and others are engaged in very extensive mercantile concerns, and can hardly, therefore, be supposed to have leisure minutely to examine so many schemes, whereof each, probably, would require no little patient attention of a clear head to understand all its details, and scrutinize well the various allegations upon which must rest the probability of its success. Yet, upon such a guarantee as names thus lightly given can afford, it is expected that the public will adventure millions, and strange to say, the expectation is justified by the result; list after list is filled and overflowing, and fresh subscribers are ready, ere the ingenuity of projectors can provide food for their insatiable avidity.

Assuredly, of all the processes that have ever been devised for filling the pockets of the wise, this getting up of joint-stock companies is the most to be admired; it requires no capital, and but a moderate share of ingenuity; it incurs no risk, and looks not to distant or problematical returns. Gentlemen who have sold some thousand shares at a premium of five or ten per cent., may retain their fifty or one hundred each for decency's sake, and contemplate with a truly calm and philosophic indifference the fate of the wildest enterprise.

I have said above, that in all the prospectuses of home enterprises, credit is largely taken for the public spirit of the projectors; their concern for the public good recurs in many a well-turned paragraph.

If a rail-road is to be undertaken, they are moved thereto mainly by the "facilities which the cheap and rapid transmission of goods will afford to the internal commerce of the country." If a dock is to be excavated, the adventurers have it in view "to carry into full effect the enlightened policy of the legislature;" whilst their opponents are described as covetous persons, caring more for their own profit than the public good; and they complain that the execution of their great intentions is enviously retarded by the opposition of "private interests." – Private interests, indeed, and from what else do they expect opposition? – From what else do their own enterprises spring? – Have they really persuaded themselves that it is the pure love of their country that prompts their industry; or, having so persuaded themselves, do they expect the world will be of the same opinion? – The world will pronounce, and pronounce rightly, that it is from some view of profit or power, immediate or remote, that their zeal arises. – Do I blame their motives? On the contrary (inasmuch as an expectation of profit from the enterprise itself may form part of those motives), they are praiseworthy, and precisely what ought to actuate the promoters of such undertakings. I would only wish to banish from all discussions, – as to whether the legislature can permit an association of individuals to undertake such and such a public work for their own emolument, with advantage to the public (for that is the real question) any thing like cant.

A dock or rail-road undertaken upon motives of public spirit would be the silliest of all imaginable projects; no axiom can be less doubtful, than that such works can only be undertaken with advantage to the public, when they promise to yield a profit to the individual adventurers; and then alone can a man be sure that he is adding aught of stability to the sublime fabric of national greatness, when by honest arts he is rearing the edifice of his private fortunes.

To a consideration of the causes which have generated these innumerable projects, reflections upon what may be their consequences naturally succeed; and first, amidst the obvious results of the formation of so many joint-stock companies, may be noticed the spirit of gambling and speculation to which the jobbing incessantly going on in the shares gives rise in all classes of society – a spirit altogether foreign to those habits of patient and well-directed industry which can alone really advance individual or national prosperity. The merchant and manufacturer add to the general stock of the community every pound their operations gain; the speculator in shares can only gain by another's loss.

It may seem, perhaps, that this evil is of too subtle and evanescent a nature to be successfully grappled with by the strong arm of the law; prudence and industry cannot be inculcated by statute, nor can men be compelled by act of parliament to follow their lawful avocations; and yet, in a country which has abolished (to our honour be it spoken) lotteries, and pretends, at least, to put down gambling-houses, it might be no unworthy object of legislative interference, to check this infinitely more extensive and more pernicious gambling.

Leaving apart, however, for the present, the considerations of these obvious results from the inordinate increase of Joint Stock Companies, it may be well to advert to some other consequences of no mean importance, that we shall find to proceed inevitably from the present mode of constituting these associations. First, amongst such consequences, may be noticed, the inordinate power that it throws into the hands of a few individuals. Recent events have proved, beyond the possibility of doubt, that it is the power of two or three of these "eminent capitalists," by encouraging an undertaking which trenches upon the pursuits of some joint-stock company already in existence, to depress the stock of that company to an indefinite and great extent. New docks are proposed, rail-roads are to be undertaken, or new water-works are announced, and the stock of the docks, canals, and water-works already in existence falls twenty or thirty per cent.; and when it is considered that in such undertakings above thirty millions are invested, this fluctuation alone must be considered as no very trifling evil. It is clear that no limits can be assigned to the profits which might thus be made, at the expense of the frightened holders of these funds, if we can suppose schemes to be got up with a view to a speculation in the stock of existing companies – and whether they be got up merely with such a view or not, is much the same in the end to those who suffer by them.

Great fluctuations in the value of property are at all times to be deprecated, for the inconveniences they occasion and the sufferings they inflict; nor can any object be named more worthy the attention of a wise and paternal government than, inasmuch as can be accomplished by legislative regulations, to mitigate the effects of those fluctuations in value with which the inevitable changes of events affect more or less every species of property. In this case, the evil is not remediless, as it does not arise from uncontrollable causes: it is entirely in the power of the legislature to protect those who would suffer without its protection, a power which I apprehend it will not be the less disposed to exercise in this instance: that it will limit the influence of the great stock-jobbers, for whom, as a class of the community perfectly competent to protect themselves, there is perhaps no necessity that government should feel particularly sensitive. I cannot indeed conceive a more offensive and injurious exercise of the vast powers of capital, than would arise from its being permitted to war indiscriminately against capital already vested, and thus spread anxiety and alarm through thousands and hundreds of thousands of persons, who, far aloof from the turmoil of the Stock Exchange, and ignorant of its secrets, would yet feel that they were the sport of its operations, and could only hold their property securely, by participating in its mysteries. A large proportion, too, of the persons whose vital interests are thus made the sport of speculation, belongs to a class which may fairly be considered as entitled to somewhat more than the general protection afforded to all classes by government. The stock of these companies has become the property of persons retired from active life, of individuals of moderate fortune, of annuitants, of widows, or has been invested in the names of trustees for the benefit of minors. Such proprietors are grievously overmatched by the opponents with whom, in any struggle for their rights, they will probably have to contend. Dispersed over the kingdom, unknown to each other, without the facilities of uniting for a common object, or the habits of energy and consequent influence that attend active life, they are opposed to wealthy merchants, bankers, and members of parliament, who, assembled at boards, or divided into committees, arrange their evidence, canvass their friends, and marshal all their forces for a parliamentary conflict, secure of profit and patronage if their scheme do but proceed, and careless of its ultimate success, as they will incur no loss by its failure. It may be stated, as a general proposition, that government should in all cases, where the two classes of society above alluded to (and which might shortly be distinguished as the active and *passive* classes, passive in more senses than one) come into collision, entertain a disposition *prima facie* to shew favour to the passive class, in the certainty that the interests of their opponents will be more vigilantly protected.

It is also, perhaps, matter for consideration, whether it be wise, by taking away from all property the character of stability (the certain effect of the legislature lightly and frequently interfering with vested capital) to take away from the industrious classes of society one of the greatest incentives to exertion; and by depriving the artist, the merchant, or the professional man, in any degree of the certainty of being able to leave to his family a secure provision, to weaken insomuch a hope of all others the most potent, at once to incite and solace his labours.

It is at least matter for consideration, whether such a combination of circumstances or situation of the laws, as leaves in the hands of any dozen or score of individuals (however wealthy or important they may be upon Change) the power to injure the property and disturb the repose of thousands, without incurring themselves the slightest risk or responsibility, be a beneficial or an unavoidable state of society.

5

THE INFLUENCE OF INTEREST AND PREJUDICE UPON PROCEEDINGS IN PARLIAMENT

[Alexander Mundell]

Source: [Alexander Mundell], *The Influence of Interest and Prejudice Upon Proceedings in Parliament* (London: John Murray, 1825), pp. 11–12, 145–46, 148–55.

EDITORIAL HEADNOTE

Alexander Mundell (1768–1837) was a solicitor based in London. He was born in Edinburgh, and his father, Robert, had founded a successful publishing house, Mundell and Company. Alexander published several books related to economic questions, including *Bullion Finance* (1828) and *A Comparative View of the Industrial Situation of Great Britain* (1832). He also served as a legal advisor to the House of Lords.

In this work, published anonymously, Mundell argued that most politicians were ignorant of the basic principles of political economy and were therefore unsuited to regulate the nation's financial system. Great facility should be afforded for company formation, which in turn would enhance competition and commercial health.[1]

Note

1 James Taylor, *Creating Capitalism: Joint-Stock Enterprise in British Politics and Culture* (London: Royal Historical Society, 2006), pp. 110–11.

He who takes it upon him to frame, or to bring forward any legislative measure, ought to know the whole facts and bearings of the case, as it exists at common law, in equity, and in Acts of Parliament. If any art, or science, or trade, or manufacture is concerned, he ought to be conversant with that art, that science, that trade, or that manufacture, with reference to which this rule ought to be invariably observed, namely, that no art, or science, or trade, or manufacture should be

DOI: 10.4324/9781003713890-6

interfered with, but each should be left to the course which it would take, if there were no municipal law upon the subject. The order of nature is paramount to the order of man, and Nature never suffers any of her laws to be thwarted with impunity. A knowledge of political economy to which the attention of this country was first directed by Adam Smith, is thus necessary to the composition of many Acts of Parliament. But many of those who presume to frame, and of those who venture to legislate upon Bills in Parliament, know nothing of that science which they view with prejudice, and reject with scorn, merely because they are ignorant of it. Prejudice thus combines with interest to operate mischievously in legislation, as will be shewn in some striking instances; but it is necessary first to consider some modes of proceeding in Parliament which require alteration. . . .

To common apprehension it seems difficult to conceive why fifty persons may not associate for any commercial or other purpose as well as five, or five hundred as well as fifty, or five thousand as well as five hundred; or how the interests, separate as well as joint, of a large number of persons, may not be settled by the partnership deed equally well as the interests of a small number of persons, or how, at common law, there can be anything to prevent persons from associating in large or small numbers as they may find it convenient. In truth it is only by means of large numbers that such a capital can be raised as is required for some undertakings, and one should think it may be safely left to individuals to associate together in large or small companies as best suits the object of their association. Indeed it is difficult to see why a commercial country like this should not have the benefit of competition by large as well as small companies equally as by individuals. The division of profit will always prevent more persons from associating together than will be necessary to raise the capital required, and the capital that may be required must be various as the nature of the trade or business in which the capital is to be employed. . . .

In all commercial dealings it is part of the common law of the land that every company without regard to the number of its partners, binds all of them by the signature or use of the firm in all ordinary transactions, and, if at common law the company binds all its members by the name of the firm in all ordinary transactions, why should it not be allowed to sue and be sued in the name of the firm in the case of such transactions also?. . . .

To common apprehension, to which I again desire to appeal, it seems desirable that the public should know who are the partners of every trading or manufacturing company whatever, whether large or small. For this purpose, adopting the course taken in the case of banking companies, I should say that every company, the names of all the partners of which do not appear in the firm, should every year produce and leave with the proper officer at the Stamp Office a paper containing the signature of the firm by each partner entitled to sign it, and a list of all partners of the firm, and that a license should be taken out every year containing such firm and a list of such partners, and that the partners named therein should be deemed to be the partners of the firm for the year in which such license was issued, notwithstanding any change in the partnership; and that the company being allowed to sue and be sued in the name of the firm, mentioned in the license, the party or parties suing the company under such firm, should, by the judgement or decree pronounced, be entitled to recover not only against all the persons appearing by the license to have been the partners of the firm at the time the contract sued upon was entered into, but against all the persons appearing to have subsequently become partners by the license issued for the year in which judgement or decree was pronounced, or the intermediate licenses.

Though I do not think that the gambling speculations in joint stock companies or otherwise, which disgrace the Stock Exchange, are to be put down by parliamentary interference, yet I do not know that any harm will result, and perhaps it may tend to distinguish the good from the bad of such speculations, if it be provided that no such license shall be granted to any joint stock company where any share shall have been sold previous to the issuing of such license, and that if any such license shall have been issued where any such share shall have been previously sold, such license shall be void and null, and the person or persons applying for it, moreover, may be subjected to a penalty.

It is impossible that the question as to the legality of joint stock companies can be suffered to remain in the situation in which it now is. From a clause added to the Bubble Act Repeal Act it seems to be contemplated that they are to be legalized by charters from the crown, preserving the responsibility of the shareholders. . . .

Independently of other objections, the clause in the Bubble Act Repeal Act does not enable the king to grant the power of suing and being sued in the name of the firm, or of directors or managers, and it being necessary that the king should be enabled by Act of Parliament to grant charters preserving the responsibility of the partners, can his Majesty, by virtue of a power so limited, enable joint stock companies so incorporated to sue and be sued in the name of the firm, or of directors, or of managers? And if the transference of shares be illegal, or an abatement may be pleaded upon every change in the partnership, is this illegality or this legal consequence removed by the King's Charter? And how are the public to know who are the shareholders for the time being?

But in behalf of the whole public of the United Kingdom, I entreat that this course may be reconsidered, because it will unavoidably produce monopoly, and enable persons to obtain charters who do not deserve them, while worthy persons may be excluded. The cunning and the designing will succeed by arts to which men of open and erect fronts cannot stoop. We see how influence is exerted to obtain or to prevent the passing of Private Bills in Parliament; and can it be believed that it will not be exerted in the case of charters from the crown, to the obtaining or preventing them as may suit the interest of particular persons, and where a charter shall have been obtained for any purpose whatever will not those who shall have obtained it exert themselves to prevent all others from obtaining another for the same purpose? Men in authority and of influence are not aware how they are sometimes made the instruments of the most selfish, aye, and sometimes of the most vile and wicked purposes. . . .

In the infancy of society, it was right and proper for the Crown to grant charters, because otherwise persons and means might not have been found to institute the business intended to be conducted. But now there is no want either of persons or means to institute or conduct any business whatsoever, and if one great leviathan of a joint stock company shall arise, another as great will spring up, or the great leviathan will be beaten by a number of smaller leviathans, and perhaps all the leviathans by individuals. In these days no company should be incorporated unless by Act of Parliament, and then only where powers are required which can be granted by Parliament alone, such as companies for making canals, railways, &c.; and none of these companies should ever be suffered to prevent or oppose the establishment of any other company. Once established, their cry is "we embarked our property upon the faith of an Act of Parliament, and we are entitled to protection against the ruin that will be brought upon us by another company or other companies." Protection against what? Competition? And from ruin? How ruin? Ruin is not an object pursued by any persons whatever, though it may be occasioned by the follies of some. Incorporated companies should be placed in no other situation than that in which individuals are placed. In embarking in any trade whatever, every one knows that if it be a good trade he will be followed by others, and, if any one shall conduct it better, or shall find out a better way of conducting it, the latter will have more of the trade than the former. And is not the public thereby benefited in the competition, though it may happen that some of the competitors may fail? But it may also happen that they all prosper. The same causes which produce good management and good results in the case of individuals, cannot fail to produce the same effects in the case of companies. If every company shall engage in any undertaking, as every individual does, with the certainty that they will meet with the competition of other companies, as individuals meet with the competition of other individuals, they will be more cautious than they now are, how they embark in any undertaking at first, and more careful how they conduct it afterwards; and, being kept, as they ought to be, in a situation where they can hope to prosper only by being what they ought to be, then the probability is that they will be what they ought to be, and, if they are not, the sooner they ruin themselves or are ruined by others, the better.

6

THE SPHERE OF JOINT-STOCK COMPANIES

Abram Combe

Source: Abram Combe, *The Sphere for Joint-Stock Companies; or, The Way to Increase the Value of Land, Capital, and Labour* (Edinburgh: Bell and Bradfute, 1825), pp. iii-iv, 3–8.

EDITORIAL HEADNOTE

Abram Combe (1785–1827) was a Utopian socialist and writer. He was born in Edinburgh, the son of a brewer. He apprenticed as a tanner and in 1807 established a successful tannery business. In 1820 Combe became a disciple of Robert Owen and a strong advocate of the cooperative movement among working people. In 1825 Combe established an Owenite cooperative community at Orbiston, Scotland, financed by the creation of a joint-stock company. The community supported itself with an iron foundry, grain mill, and printing press.[1]

Combe published several pamphlets advocating socialist beliefs. He saw the joint-stock principle as an efficient method of raising capital for a cooperative purpose, rather than a means of enhancing economic competition.

Note

1 R.G. Garnett, *Cooperation and the Owenite Communities in Britain, 1825–1845* (Manchester University Press, 1972), pp. 68–93

The mode recommended in the following pages, to augment the Value of Land, Capital, and Labour, is, by a Union of Interest, to such an extent as Experience shall prove to be practical and beneficial. It is proposed that Capitalists, by a Joint Stock, shall purchase as much Land as will raise food for 1,000 or 1,500 individuals. That they shall build Dwelling-Houses, Manufactories and Workshops, and furnish these with Machinery, and all requisite utensils, &c. and then give them in lease, for a term of years, at a fixed per centage on the Cost, to a Company of

DOI: 10.4324/9781003713890-7

Tenants. My object, in what follows, is to prove that this will be exceedingly profitable to all parties, and that it can be easily accomplished. . . .

In referring to the Labour and Capital of the Employers, and Distributors or retailers, under the present system, I have endeavored to show that the other parties pay more than is necessary for this Labour and Capital. But I wish the Reader to bear in mind, that, in saying this, I do not mean that the Retailers do now receive too much for their labour; for the reverse of this is really the case. When we take into account the acuteness and unremitting attention which their occupation requires, there is perhaps no other class of community so ill requited for the labour bestowed. What is proposed under the New System will diminish the labour and anxiety of the retailers, without at all diminishing their means of obtaining comfort. Whatever diminishes labour does not necessarily diminish the comfort of any individual; on the contrary, it may be made a real blessing to Society. Experience will soon demonstrate, that the labour of the distributors may be shortened at least nine parts out of ten; and when this is done all classes will reap the benefit of it.

I have added a short account of the Establishment at Orbiston; which was founded on 18th March last, and is to be conducted on the principle here recommended. There are sixty or seventy people now employed in the erection of this building and it is expected that the Dwelling-Houses will be completed by the early part of the ensuing Spring.

Though this Establishment is conducted on an economical principle, yet no expense is spared that will add to the strength and durability of the Premises, or to the real comfort of the inhabitants.

As it is probable that what remains of the Stock of this Company will be soon taken up; and as it is also probable that other Capitalists will feel a desire to invest funds in a similar way, I am willing to receive Communications from those who are desirous of doing so, and to do anything in my power to enable them to execute their wishes.

As no individual can enjoy the happiness of which his nature is susceptible while he remains in a state of poverty, it follows that the desire of riches is both natural and beneficial. The *easiest* way of making money is by making good bargains; and the *surest* way of keeping it is by avoiding as much as possible all risk of loss. Before we can continue to make good bargains without risk of loss, it will be necessary to secure a connection with good customers. This can only be done by studying the *interest* of such customers; and we cannot injure ourselves more effectually than by attempting to over-reach them. We may fancy that we have "made" something by our success in palming a bad bargain upon such individuals, but the truth is, that, as a matter of necessity, by doing so, we must, in no slight degree, diminish their desire to deal with us. If they continue to do business with us, it must be only because they can find no other good merchant, who is more honest. We may rest assured that such customers, who are so treated, will leave us the first opportunity. We may, indeed, make good bargains with customers of another description; but those who have had most experience in this way, are well aware that little profit is made in the end by such customers. In these cases, the old proverb is almost invariably verified; for those who go, in this way, to seek wool, generally come home shorn. In fact, the whole history of business demonstrates that it is impossible to continue to make good bargains, without risk of loss, by any other way than that which leads us to study the interests of our customers.

As the proper business of Joint Stock Companies is to accomplish beneficial purposes, which are beyond the power of individuals, the first consideration ought to be – whether the object proposed can be accomplished *at all* by individual means. If this can be done *easily,* the probability is – that no Joint Stock Company will thrive; for it is indeed *not* in its proper sphere. If such a concern is liable to be injured by competition, this circumstance will greatly diminish its chance of success.

In making proposals for erecting Villages of Union and Mutual Co-operation by Joint Stock Companies, I shall consider:

1st. Whether such Company is in its proper sphere.
2d. The security it holds out for capital invested.
3d. The return it is likely to yield; and,
4th. The way by which, if found beneficial, its affairs may be most successfully conducted.

Regarding the first of these questions, it appears that no single individual could engage in such an undertaking with the same chance of success as a Company can do, let the capital of the individual be what it may, – because, from the united skill of individuals, who have experience in various departments, a concern under the direction of a Company will have advantages which no single individual could bestow; and, at the same time, the amount of capital required, is what *very few* individuals can command: while those who can do so, *fewer still* have the inclination to bestow the attention that is requisite for its success. A little serious reflection on this subject will lead us to perceive, that, of all objects, this is the most worthy the attention of a Joint Stock Company; and the discussion of the two other points will enable me to state my reason for thinking so.

The next subject for our consideration then, is, the SECURITY which the proposal holds out.

Loss in business arises to individuals from two sources. The first is from the difficulty of finding customers willing to deal with us at a profitable rate; and the other is from our customers *not fulfilling* what they engage to fulfil.

Our difficulty in finding customers arises also from two sources: – from the competition of others making the supply exceed the demand, or from our articles having gone out of use.

Regarding the effects of competition, we are, by the adoption of the proposed measures, completely secure from all injury. On the contrary, a similar establishment erected in our immediate neighborhood will increase comfort of the inhabitants, and the value of both properties, at the same time. A third and a fourth will still add to those advantages; and the value of the whole will continue to increase with their number, till the world shall be saturated with wealth. If similar exertions on the part of others tend only to increase the advantages of the inhabitants of these villages, then, as a matter of necessity, the real value of the property must increase with these advantages. This will, at any rate, secure the Capital so expended from all injury from competition.

The chances of losing customers from our article going out of use, is our next consideration. The articles upon which the Capital is expended, are, arable Land, Dwelling-houses, (constructed in the way by which the greatest amount of comfort can be obtained at the cheapest rate,) Manufactories for producing the necessaries and comforts of life, Machinery, Utensils, Furniture, &c., all situated in the most healthy, the most convenient, and the most agreeable situation which can be procured. No person who is capable of reflecting, will fail to discover that such property is almost the only species to which the objection is not applicable; for all property which is *not of this description* is truly liable to sink in value for this very reason.

We now come to our second consideration, "The chance of loss from our customers not fulfilling their engagements;" and this also arises from two sources – from inability, and unwillingness.

Regarding the first of these, we find that those who made good bargains are always most able to fulfill them. When we ascertain the rate which is demanded for the rest of land in the immediate neighborhood of towns, we find it run from ten to fourteen pounds per acre. The ground upon which dwelling-houses stand, usually exceeds one hundred pounds per acre of yearly rent. The rent charged for dwelling-houses and shops will exceed twenty per cent upon the capital expended in their erection; and the sole reason of these heavy demands being made and paid, is merely the circumstance of their being near each other. Now in the New Establishments, from the judicious arrangements that are there introduced, the property let to the tenants at the yearly rent of five per cent. on the Capital expended, would be to them a signal advantage. Even this rent, well paid, would double the transferable value of the property to an absolute certainty; while instead of this property being deteriorated by competition, the greater the influx of Capital to the same channel, the more would the value of that which was first expended be enhanced. To let such property to industrious tenants at the yearly rent of ten per cent. on the Capital expended, would be to them superior to any thing which the present system offers; in which event the original price of shares would be augmented at least three-fold. This, I think, ought to satisfy us that we should run no hazard of a fair return for our Capital, on the score of *ability* on the part of tenants; and on the score of *unwillingness*, we find that this feeling is often produced by deception on the part of the seller; or by his palming on the purchaser something of inferior value; for the individual who makes a good purchase always pays willingly.

As it appears from these considerations, that there will not, probably, be much difficulty in getting the annual payment for the use of the Stock laid out, we have only to consider the risk of losing the property altogether. This also, like everything which stands upon sound principles, will bear minute investigation. This Stock consists of Land, Buildings, fixed Machinery, Utensils, and Furniture. The land will remain secure, as nothing can injure it. It will yearly increase in value, from the superior system of cultivation which the neighborhood of two or three hundred families will necessarily introduce. The Buildings may also be considered "safe property," because they may be insured from fire, and the tenants will have no difficulty in keeping them in the best state of repair. The same may be said of the Machinery, and Utensils, and Furniture. None of this property will be liable for the debts of the tenants. However ill they may conduct their affairs, no third party can have any title to touch any of these articles, so that the Stock of the Company will be as secure as property can be *under any circumstances*. The reflection on all these statements will, I hope, lead us all to perceive that Joint Stock Companies of this description afford the best SECURITY for Capital.

As an explanation of the way by which these Companies may be carried into practice, will also shew the magnificent return which the capital so expended is likely to yield, I shall now proceed to state the mode which at present appears to me the best for that purpose. – Though this subject has occupied much of my attention, yet all I consider certain is, "that the System of Mutual Co-operation is better for *every* individual, than the System of Mutual Opposition is for *any* single individual." My opinion is, that this mode of introducing this system is the best which has yet been devised; but I am equally convinced, that, as we proceed, Experience will point out many improvements. One cheering prospect lies before us, and that is, that, in our Experiment, we shall have no enemies. We shall have the powerful Aid of the Government, as soon as our exertions exhibit their natural tendency to increase the peace and prosperity of the country; and we shall have the friendly aid of the Church as soon as we exhibit the absence of vice and immorality, and the presence of the Spirit of True Religion. If Experience should prove that efforts to introduce justice and persuasion in place of deception and force, should have an opposite tendency, we shall only have to change their direction, and to follow the present system. But even under such a result, we are cheered by the assurance that the real value of the property will be, in no shape, deteriorated.

7

CHORUS OF BUBBLE BUYERS

Thomas Love Peacock

Source: Thomas Love Peacock, 'Chorus of Bubble Buyers,' *Paper Money Lyrics,* Brimley Johnson, ed., *The Poems of Thomas Love Peacock* (London: George Routledge and Sons, 1906), pp. 308–9.

EDITORIAL HEADNOTE

The novelist and poet Thomas Love Peacock (1785–1866) was born in Weymouth into a family of wealthy glass merchants. He was privately educated, and a modest inheritance allowed him to pursue a career as a writer. His close friendship with the poet Percy Shelley introduced him to a wider and more radical literary circle. Peacock is best known for a series of satirical novels such as *Nightmare Abbey* (1818) and *Crotchet Castle* (1831), which mocked the social and political mores of the day. From the 1820s until 1856, Peacock worked as a civil servant for the East India Company in London. He drew upon his experience of the City in composing *Paper Money Lyrics*, a book of poems parodying political economy and high finance. Written in the aftermath of the 1826 financial crisis, Peacock did not publish the book until the 1837 death of James Mill, his superior at India House and a leading advocate of economic Liberalism.[1] Ironically, the book's release coincided with the financial crisis of 1837.

The "Chorus of Bubble Buyers" is written from the point of view of the deluded English investors who lost fortunes in the overhyped Latin American mining schemes of 1825, "in places we neither could utter nor spell." Grown wise too late, the bubble buyers now curse the Stock Exchange, threatening to haunt Capel Court for eternity.

Note

1 "Peacock, Thomas Love," in Ian Ousby, ed., *The Cambridge Guide to Literature in English* (Cambridge: Cambridge University Press, 1993), pp. 726–27.

DOI: 10.4324/9781003713890-8

When these practisers come to the last decoction, blow, blow, puff, puff, and all flies *in fumo*. Poor wretches! I rather pity their folly and indiscretion, than their loss of time and money: for these may be restored by industry: but to be a fool born is a disease incurable. – Ben Jonson, *Volpone.*

Oh! where are the hopes we have met in the morning,
    As we hustled and bustled around Capel Court?
When we laughed at the croakers that bade us take warning,
    Who once were our scorn, and now make us their sport.

Oh! where are the regions where well-paid inspectors
    Found metals omnigenous streaked and embossed?
So kindly bought for us by honest directors,
    Who charged us but three times as much as they cost.

Oh! where are the riches that bubbled like fountains,
    In places we neither could utter nor spell,
A thousand miles inland, 'mid untrodden mountains,
    Where silver and gold grew like heath and blue-bell?

Oh! where are the lakes overflowing with treasure?
    The gold-dust that rolled in each torrent and stream?
The mines that held water by cubic-mile measure,
    So easily pumped up by portable steam?

That water our prospects a damp could not throw on;
    We had only a million-horse power to prepare,
Make a thousand-mile road for the engine to go on,
    And send coals from Newcastle to boil it when there.

Oh! where are the bridges to span the Atlantic?
    Oh! where is the gas to illumine the poles?
They came to our visions; that makes us half-frantic:
    They came to our pockets; that touches our souls.

Oh! there is the seat of most exquisite feeling:
    The first pair of nerves to the pocket doth dive:
A wound in our hearts would be no time in healing,
    But a wound in our pockets how can we survive?

Now curst be the projects, and curst the projectors,
    And curst be the bubbles before us that rolled,
While, bursting, have left us like desolate spectres,
    Bewailing our bodies of paper and gold.

For what is a man but his coat and his breeches,
    His plate and his linen, his land and his house?
Oh! we had been men had we won our mock riches,
    But now we are ghosts, each as poor as a mouse.

But shades as we are, we, with shadowy bubbles,
    When the midnight bell tolls, will through Capel Court glide,
And the dream of the Jew[1] shall be turmoils and troubles,
    When he sees each pale ghost on its bubble astride.

And the lecturing Scots[2] that upheld the delusion,
    By prating of paper, and wealth, and free trade,
Shall see us by night, to their awe and confusion,
    Grim phantoms of wrath that shall never be laid.

Editorial Endnotes

1 Here Peacock is reflecting the popular prejudice that Jewish brokers dominated the Stock Exchange.
2 Many of the founders of Liberal political economy were Scottish: Adam Smith, John Law, Dugald Stewart.

8

A COMPENDIUM OF THE ENGLISH AND FOREIGN FUNDS, AND THE PRINCIPLE JOINT-STOCK COMPANIES

Charles Fenn

Source: Charles Fenn, *A Compendium of the English and Foreign Funds, and the Principal Joint Stock Companies,* 2nd edition (London: Effingham Wilson, 1838), pp. 98–99, 106–116.

EDITORIAL HEADNOTE

Charles Fenn was a stockbroker, whose investment guide went through seventeen editions from 1837 to 1898. Unlike similar guides from earlier in the century, which focused almost entirely on government securities, Fenn's book included considerable information about the investment opportunities of joint-stock companies, especially canals, railways, docks, insurance companies, and banks. The *Compendium* dramatized the wider investment field brought about by industrialization as well as the need for up-to-date financial information by the propertied classes.[1]

Here Fenn lists the principle English Joint-Stock Banks, the price of their shares, and the amount of their most recent dividend.

Notc

1 Paul Crosthwaite, et al., *Invested* (Chicago: University of Chicago Press, 2022), pp. 43–46.

BANKS

England and Wales

Until the year 1826, the exclusive privileges possessed by the Bank of England prevented the establishment of joint stock banks of issue in any part of England

DOI: 10.4324/9781003713890-9

or Wales. In that year an act was passed (7 Geo. IV., cap. 46), permitting the formation of these associations at the distance of 65 miles and upwards from the metropolis. By virtue of this act, joint stock banks of issue have been established in various parts of the country, none of which have received any special charter of incorporation; and, consequently, the proprietors are individually responsible for the full extent of their property, for all the liabilities of the company with which they are connected. . . .

The following particulars relating to the joint stock banks, established under the act of 1826, are chiefly taken from the returns made to the committee of the House of Commons in 1836.

Bank of Stockport – Established in 1836: 12,740 shares. £5 paid. No branches.

Bank of Birmingham – Established in 1832: capital £500,000, in £50 shares; £10 per share paid. Dividend 10 per cent. per annum on the paid-up capital. No branches.

Bank of Liverpool – Established in 1831: capital £3,000,000, in £100 shares; £10 paid. Dividend 8 per cent. per annum on the paid-up capital. No branches.

Bank of Manchester – Established in 1829: capital £2,000,000, in £100 shares; £25 paid. Dividend 7 per cent. per annum on the paid-up capital. Three branches, Stockport, Bolton, and Newtown.

Bank of Westmoreland – Established in 1833 at Kendal: capital £250,000, in £100 shares; £10 paid. Last dividend 12*s*. per share, being the profits of one year. One branch at Ulverston, Lancashire.

Barnsley Banking Company – Established in 1832: capital £300,000, in £100 shares; £10 paid. Dividend 6 ½ per cent. per annum. No branches.

Bradford Banking Company – Established in 1827: capital £500,000, in £100 shares; £20 paid. Dividend 10 per cent. per annum upon the amount paid up. No branches.

Bradford Commercial Joint Stock Bank – Established in 1833: capital £500,000, in £100 shares; £15 paid. Dividend 7 per cent. on the amount paid up. No branches.

Birmingham Banking Company – Established in 1829: capital £500,000, in £50 shares; £10 paid. Dividend 10 per cent. on the paid-up capital. No branches.

Cheltenham and Gloucestershire Bank – Established in 1836: £500,000 capital, in shares of £50; £5 paid. Dividend 5 per cent. on the paid-up capital. No branches.

Chesterfield and North Derbyshire Banking Company – Established in 1834: capital £250,000, in £100 shares; £10 paid. Dividend 6 per cent. on the paid-up capital. No branches.

Commercial Bank of England – Established in 1834: capital £500,000, in £5 shares; 52,000 of which have been issued and paid up. Dividend 6 per cent. per annum. Eighteen branches.

Coventry and Warwickshire Banking Company – Established in 1836: capital £400,000 in £50 shares; £5 paid. Dividend 8 per cent. upon the paid-up capital. One branch.

Coventry Union Bank – Established in 1836: capital £200,000, in £20 shares; £5 paid. Dividend 5 per cent. upon the paid-up capital. No branches.

Darlington District Joint Stock Banking Company – Established in 1832: capital £400,000, in £100 shares; £15 paid. Dividend 10 per cent. per annum on the paid-up capital. Four branches.

Derby and Derbyshire Banking Company – Established in 1834: capital £250,000, in shares of £50 each; £10 paid. Dividend 6 per cent. upon the amount paid up. Two branches.

Devon and Cornwall Banking Company – Established in 1832: capital £300,000, in £100 shares; £20 paid. Dividend 7 ½ per cent. on the paid-up capital. Nine branches.

Dudley and West Bromwich Bank – Established in 1834: capital £400,000, in £50 shares; £5 paid. Dividend 6 per cent. per annum on the paid-up capital. Two establishments, one at Dudley, and one at West Bromwich.

East of England Bank – Established in 1836: capital of £1,000,000, in £20 shares; £10 paid. Four branches. Dividend 5 per cent.

Gloucester County and City Bank – Established in 1835: capital £100,000, in shares of £500 each; £200 paid. Dividend £3 per share. No branches.

Gloucestershire Banking Company – Established in 1831: capital £500,000, in £50 shares; £10 paid. Dividend 10 per cent. per annum on the paid-up capital. Four branches.

Halifax Joint Stock Banking Company – Established in 1829: capital £500,000, in £100 shares; £10 paid. Dividend 12 ½ per cent. upon the amount paid up. No branches.

Hampshire Banking Company – Established in 1834: capital £300,000, in £50 shares; £5 paid. Dividend 6 per cent. upon the amount paid up. Three branches.

Huddersfield Banking Company – Established in 1827; capital £700,000, in £100 shares; £10 paid. Dividend 10 per cent. upon the paid-up capital. No branches.

Hull Banking Company – Established in 1833: capital £800,000, in £100 shares; £10 paid. Dividend 6 per cent. upon the amount paid up. Fifteen branches.

Lancaster Banking Company – Established in 1826: capital £300,000, in £100 shares; £20 paid. Dividend 10 per cent. upon the paid-up capital. Two branches.

Leamington Bank – Established in 1835: capital £200,000, in shares of £20 each; £5 paid. No branches.

Leamington Priors and Warwickshire Banking Company – Established in 1835: capital £200,000, in £20 shares; £6 paid. Four branches.

Leeds Banking Company – Established in 1832: capital £1,000,000, in £100 shares; £15 paid. Dividend 8 per cent. upon the paid-up capital. No branches.

Leeds and West Riding Banking Company – Established in 1835: capital £400,000, in £20 shares; £5 paid. Three branches.

Leicestershire Banking Company – Established in 1829: capital £500,000, in £100 shares; £15 paid. Dividend 7 ½ per cent. upon the paid-up capital. Four branches.

Lichfield, Rugeley, and Tamworth Bank – Established in 1835: capital £100,000, in £10 shares; £5 paid. Two branches.

Lincoln and Lindsey Banking Company – Established in 1833: capital £250,000, in £200 shares; £20 paid. Two branches. Dividend 10 per cent.

Liverpool Albion Bank – Established in 1836: capital £250,000, in £10 shares; £5 paid. No branches.

Liverpool United Trades' Bank – Established in 1836: capital £400,000, in £20 shares; £10 paid. No branches.

Liverpool Commercial Bank – Established in 1833: capital £500,000, in £10 shares; £10 paid. Dividend 6 ½ per cent. No branches.

Liverpool Union Bank – Established in 1835: capital £600,000, in £20 shares; £10 paid. No branches.

Manchester and Liverpool District Banking Company – Established in 1829: capital £5,000,000, in £100 shares; £15 paid. Dividend 7 ½ per cent. Fourteen branches.

Monmouthshire and Glamorganshire Banking Company – Capital £500,000, in shares of £20 each; £10 paid. Dividend 5 per cent. for the half-year ending 30th June.

National Provincial Bank of England – Established in 1834: capital £1,200,000, in 10,000 shares of £100 each, and 10,000 of £20 each; £35 paid upon the £100 shares, and £10 upon the £20 shares. Dividend 5 per cent. upon the paid-up capital. Thirty branches.

Newcastle Commercial Banking Company – Established in 1836: capital £100,000, in £10 shares; £7 10*s*. paid. Dividend 4 per cent. upon the paid-up capital.

Newcastle, Shields, and Sunderland Union Bank – Established in 1836: capital £300,000, in £10 shares; £5 paid. Dividend 10 per cent. upon the paid-up capital.

Newcastle-upon-Tyne Joint Stock Banking Company – Established in 1836: capital £500,000, in £25 shares; £5 paid. Dividend 6 percent. Upon the paid-up capital.

Northumberland and Durham District Banking Company – Established in 1836: capital £500,000, in £10 shares; £5 paid. Dividend 8 per cent. upon the paid-up capital.

North Wilts Banking Company – Established in 1835: capital £250,000, in £25 shares; £5 paid. Dividend 7 per cent. upon the paid-up capital. Eleven branches.

North and South Wales Bank – Established in 1836, at Liverpool: capital £600,000, in £10 shares; £7 10*s*. paid. Two branches.

Northern and Central Bank of England – Established in 1834, at Manchester: capital £711,860, in £10 shares; all paid. Twenty-five branches.

North of England Joint Stock Banking Company – Established in 1832, at Newcastle: capital £500,000, in £25 shares; £20 paid. Dividend £3 6*s*. per cent. upon the paid-up capital. Four branches.

Nottingham and Nottinghamshire Banking Company – Established in 1834: capital £500,000, in £50 shares; £10 paid. Dividend 5 per cent. Five branches.

Pare's Leicestershire Banking Company – Established in 1800, as a private bank, and converted into a joint stock bank in 1836. Capital £100,000, in shares of £12 10*s*. each; £2 10*s*. paid. No permanent branches.

Royal Bank of Liverpool – Established in 1836: capital £2,000,000, in shares of £1,000 each; £400 paid. No branches.

Saddleworth Banking Company – Established in 1806, as a private bank, and converted into a joint stock bank in 1833: capital £300,000, in shares of £50 each; £5 per share paid. Dividend 7 ½ per cent. upon the paid-up capital. Two branches.

Sheffield Banking Company – Established in 1831: capital £300,000, in shares of £200 each; £55 paid. Dividend 8 per cent. upon the paid-up capital. One branch.

Stamford, Spalding, and Boston Banking Company – Established in 1832: capital £150,000, in shares of £100 each; £40 paid. Dividend 7 ½ per cent. upon the amount paid up. Stations at the places mentioned in the title of the company, and three branches in addition.

Stourbridge and Kidderminster Bank – Established in 1834: capital £250,000, in £25 shares; £7 10*s*. paid. Dividend 8 per cent. upon the paid-up capital. Establishments at Stourbridge, Kidderminster, and Stratford-on-Avon: £2 10*s*. was added to the capital from the surplus profits on 28th August, 1837, making the amount paid up £7 10*s*.

Stuckey's Banking Company – Established in 1826: capital £300,000, in £100 shares; £20 paid. Dividend £2 per share. Sixteen branches, all in Somersetshire.

Sunderland Joint Stock Banking Company – Established in 1836: capital £100,000, in £10 shares; £5 paid. Dividend 5 per cent. upon the paid-up capital.

Union Bank of Manchester – Established in 1826: capital £600,000, in £25 shares; £2 10*s*. paid. No branches.

Wakefield Banking Company – Established in 1832: capital £300,000, in shares of £50 each; £8 paid. Dividend 8 per cent. upon the paid-up capital. No branches.

Walsall and South Staffordshire Bank – Established in 1835: capital £200,000, in shares of £25 each; £5 paid. One branch.

Warwick and Leamington Banking Company – Established in 1834: capital £250,000, in shares of £25 each; £5 paid. Dividend 6 per cent. upon the paid-up capital. Five establishments.

West of England and South Wales District Bank – Established in 1834: capital £1,000,000, in shares of £20 each; £10 paid. Dividend 5 per cent. upon the paid-up capital. Chief office in Bristol. Nine branches.

Whitehaven Joint Stock Bank – Established in 1829: capital £300,000, in shares of £100 each; £10 paid. Dividend 10 per cent. upon the amount paid up. One branch.

Wolverhampton and Staffordshire Joint Stock Banking Company – Established in 1832: capital £500,000, in shares of £50 each; £5 paid. Dividend 6 per cent. upon the paid-up capital. No branches.

Wilts and Dorset Banking Company – Established in 1835: capital £300,000, in shares of £15 each; £10 paid. Dividend 5 per cent. Twenty-one branches.

York Union Banking Company – Established in 1833: capital £700,000, in shares of £100 each; £10 paid. Dividend 9 per cent. upon the paid-up capital. Four branches.

York City and County Banking Company – Established in 1830: capital £500,000, in shares of £100 each; £15 paid. Dividend 12 per cent. upon the amount paid up. Five branches.

Yorkshire District Bank – Established in 1834: capital £1,000,000, in shares of £20 each; £15 paid. Dividend 8 per cent. upon the capital paid up. Head office at Leeds, eighteen branches.

The joint stock banks referred to in the preceding statement, being established at a greater distance from the metropolis than sixty-five miles, have the privilege of issuing promissory notes. The following banks, established in London and its vicinity, are not allowed this privilege.

London and Westminster Bank – Established in 1834: capital £3,000,000, in shares of £100 each; £20 paid. Dividend 5 per cent. upon the paid-up capital. Branches at No. 9, Waterloo-place; 213, High Holborn; 12, Wellington-street, Borough; 87, High-street, Whitechapel; and 155, Oxford-street.

London Joint Stock Bank – Established in 1836: capital £3,000,000, in shares of £50 each; £7 paid. Office, Princes-street, Bank.

Middlesex County Bank – Established in 1836: capital of £1,000,000, in shares of £20 each, with power to increase the capital, by additional shares, to £3,000,000.

Borough of St. Marylebone Bank – Established in 1836: capital £1,000,000, in shares of £25 each; £5 paid. Chief-office, No. 9, Cavendish-square.

9

1844 ACT FOR THE REGISTRATION, INCORPORATION AND REGULATION OF JOINT-STOCK COMPANIES

Source: Act for the Registration, Incorporation, and Regulation of Joint Stock Companies, 1844, 7/8 Vict., Cap. CX.

EDITORIAL HEADNOTE

A series of frauds involving insurance companies led Parliament to launch an investigation of joint-stock companies in 1841. In 1843 this Select Committee on Joint Stock Companies was reconstituted under the chairmanship of W.E. Gladstone, then President of the Board of Trade. The Gladstone Committee interviewed twenty-one lawyers and business people, and its recommendations were embodied in the 1844 Company Act. This Act created for the first time a systematic legal framework for incorporation under a newly created Joint-Stock Companies Registrar. Henceforth, incorporation was freely available to all, but with government oversight and publicity requirements designed to prevent fraud.[1]

Note

1 James Taylor, *Creating Capitalism: Joint-Stock Enterprise in British Politics and Culture, 1800–1870* (London: Royal Historical Society, 2006), pp. 135–43, and George Robb, *White-Collar Crime in Modern England: Financial Fraud and Business Morality, 1845–1929* (Cambridge: Cambridge University Press, 1992), pp. 16–18.

I. Whereas it is expedient to make Provisions for the due Registration of Joint Stock Companies during the Formation and Subsistence thereof; and also, after such complete Registration as is herein-after mentioned, to invest such Companies with the Qualities and Incidents of Corporations, with some Modifications, and subject to certain Conditions and Regulations; and also to

DOI: 10.4324/9781003713890-10

prevent the Establishment of any Companies which shall not be duly constituted and regulated according to the Provisions of this Act: Now be it enacted by the Queen's most Excellent Majesty, by and with the Advice and Consent of the Lords Spiritual and Temporal, and Commons, in this present Parliament assembled, and by the Authority of the same, That this Act shall come into operation at the following Times; that is to say, as to the Officers to be appointed in pursuance hereof for the Registration of Companies, and the Regulation of the Office hereby provided for that Purpose, immediately on the passing hereof; and as to all Companies to which this Act is to apply, and all other the Provisions herein-after contained, except such as relate to such Officers and Office as aforesaid, on the First Day of *November* in the Year One thousand eight hundred and forty-four.

II. And be it enacted, That this Act shall apply to every Joint Stock Company, as herein-after defined, established in any Part of the United Kingdom of *Great Britain and Ireland* except *Scotland,* or established in *Scotland* and having an Office or Place of Business in any other Part of the United Kingdom, for any commercial Purpose, or for any Purpose of Profit, or for the Purpose of Assurance or Insurance (except Banking Companies, Schools, and Scientific and Literary Institutions, and also Friendly Societies, Loan Societies, and Benefit Building Societies, respectively duly certified and enrolled under the Statutes in force respecting such Societies, other than such Friendly Societies as grant Assurances on Lives to the Extent herein-after specified;) and that the Term "Joint Stock Company" shall comprehend:

Every Partnership whereof the Capital is divided or agreed to be divided into Shares, and so as to be transferable without the express Consent of all the Copartners; and also,

Every Assurance Company or Association for the Purpose of Assurance or Insurance on Lives, or against any Contingency involving the Duration of Human Life, or against the Risk of Loss or Damage by Fire, or Storm or other Casualty, or against the Risk of Loss or Damage to Ships at Sea or on Voyage, or to their Cargoes, or for granting or purchasing Annuities on Lives; and also every Institution enrolled under any of the Acts of Parliament relating to Friendly Societies, which Institutions shall make Assurances on Lives, or against any Contingency involving the Duration of Human Life to an Extent upon One Life or for any One Person to an Amount exceeding Two hundred Pounds, whether such Companies, Societies, or Institutions shall be Joint Stock Companies or Mutual Assurance Societies, or both; and also,

Every Partnership which at its Formation, or by subsequent Admission (except any Admission subsequent on Devolution or other Act in Law), shall consist of more than Twenty-five Members:

And that, except where the Provisions of this Act are expressly applied to Partnerships existing before the said First Day of *November,* it shall be held to apply only to Partnerships the Formation of which shall be commenced after that Date: Provided nevertheless, that, except as herein-after specially provided, this Act shall not extend to any Company for executing any Bridge, Road, Cut, Canal, Reservoir, Aqueduct, Waterwork, Navigation, Tunnel, Archway, Railway, Pier, Port, Harbour, Ferry, or Dock which cannot be carried into execution without obtaining the Authority of Parliament: Provided also, that, except as herein-after is specially provided, this Act shall not extend to any Company incorporated or which may be hereafter incorporated by Statute or Charter, nor to any Company authorized or which may be hereafter authorized by Statute or Letters Patent to sue and be sued in the Name of some Officer or Person.

III. And be it declared, That the following Words and Expressions are intended to have the Meanings hereby assigned to them respectively, so far as such Meanings are not excluded by the Context or by the Nature of the Subject Matter; that is to say,

The word "Company," to mean any Joint Stock Company or other Institution, as before defined:

The Expression "Assurance Company," to mean any Assurance Company, Association, or Institution, as before defined:

The word "Directors" to mean the Persons having Direction, Conduct, Management, or Superintendence of the Affairs of a Company:

The Expression "Promoter," or "Promoter of a Company," to apply to every Person acting by whatever Name in the forming and establishing of a Company at any Period prior to the Company obtaining a Certificate of complete Registration as herein-after mentioned:

The Word "Subscriber" to mean any Person who shall have agreed in Writing to take or have taken any Shares in a proposed Company or in a Company formed, and who shall not have executed the Deed of Settlement, or a Deed referring thereto:

The Word "Shareholder" to mean any Person entitled to a Share in a Company, and who has executed the Deed of Settlement, or a Deed referring to it, or, in the Case of Mutual Assurance Societies, any Person who shall be an assured Member thereof:

The Word "Person" to apply to Bodies Politic or Corporate, whether sole or aggregate:

The Expression "Commissioners of the Treasury" to apply to the Lord High Treasurer for the Time being, or the Commissioners of Her Majesty's Treasury for the Time being, or any Three or more of them:

The Expression "Committee of the Privy Council for Trade" to mean the Lords of the Committee of Her Majesty's Privy Council for the Consideration of all Matters of Trade and Plantations:

The Expression "Secretary of the Committee" to mean One of the Joint Assistant Secretaries of said Committee of Privy Council for Trade:

The Word "Justice" to mean a Justice of the Peace for the County, City, Borough, Liberty, or Place where the Matter requiring the Cognizance of any Justice shall arise, and who shall not be interested in the Matter:

The Expression "special Authority" to mean any Deed of Settlement, Bye Laws, Letters Patent, Charter, or Local and Personal Act of Parliament by which Powers are conferred or Regulations prescribed with reference to any individual Company:

The Word "prescribed" to mean provided for by special Authority:

The Word "Month" to mean Calendar Month:

The Expression "Superior Courts" to mean Her Majesty's Superior Court of Law or Equity in *England* or *Ireland*:

The Word "Occupation," when applied to any Person, to mean his Trade or Following, and, if none, then the Rank or usual Title, as Esquire, Gentleman:

The Expression "Place of Residence" to include the Street, Square, or Place where the Party shall reside, and the Number (if any) or other Designation of the House in which he shall so reside:

The Word "Oath" to include Affirmation or other Declaration lawfully substituted for an Oath:

And generally, whensoever, with regard to any Matter, or to any Function in respect thereof, the Name of an Officer (whether a public Officer or an Officer of a Company) ordinarily having Cognizance of such Matter, or ordinarily exercising such Function, is mentioned, such Reference is to be understood to apply as well to any other Person or Officer who may have Cognizance of such Matter, or exercise such Function in respect of such Matter:

And, subject to the Context and to the Nature of the Subject Matter, Words denoting the Singular Number are to be understood to apply also to a Plurality of Persons or Things, and Words denoting Masculine Gender are to be understood to apply also to Persons of the Feminine Gender.

IV. And be it enacted, That before proceeding to make public, whether by way of Prospectus, Handbill, or Advertisement, any Intention or Proposal to form any Company for any Purpose within the Meaning of this Act, whether for executing any such Work as aforesaid under the Authority of Parliament, or for any other Purpose, it shall be the Duty of the Promoters of such Company and they or some of them are hereby required to make to the Office hereby provided for the Registration of Joint Stock Companies (and herein-after called the Registry Office) Returns of the following Particulars according to the Schedule (C.) hereunto annexed; that is to say:

1. The proposed Name of the intended Company; and also,
2. The Business or Purpose of the Company; and also,
3. The Names of its Promoters, together with their respective Occupations, Places of Business (if any), and Places of Residence;

   And also the following Particulars, either before or after such Publication as aforesaid, when and as from Time to Time they shall be decided on; viz.,

4. The Name of the Street, Square, or other Place in which the provisional Place of Business or Place of Meeting shall be situate, and the Number (if any) or other Designation of the House or Office; and also,

5. The Names of the Members of the Committee or other Body acting in the Formation of the Company, their respective Occupations, Places of Business (if any), and Places of Residence, together with a written Consent on the Part of every such Member or Promoter to become such, and also a written Agreement on the Part of such Member or Promoter, entered into with some One or more Persons as Trustees for the said Company, to take One or more Shares in the proposed Undertaking, which must be signed by the Member or Promoter whose Agreement it purports to be (but such Agreements need not be on a Stamp); and also,
6. The Names and Officers of the Company and their respective Occupations, Places of Business (if any), and Places of Residence; and also,
7. The Names of the Subscribers to the Company, their respective Occupations, Places of Business (if any), and Places of Residence; and also, before it shall be circulated or issued to the Public,
8. A Copy of every Prospectus or Circular, Handbill or Advertisement, or other such Document at any Time addressed to the Public, or to the Subscribers or others, relative to the Formation or Modification of such Company:
9. And afterwards, from Time to Time, until the complete Registration of such Company, a Return of a Copy of every Addition to or Change made in any of the above Particulars:

   And that upon such Registration of at least the Three Particulars first before mentioned the Promoters of such Company shall be entitled to a Certificate of provisional Registration.

V. And be it enacted, That if for a Period of One Month after the Particulars hereby required to be registered, or any of them, shall have been ascertained or determined, the Promoters of any Company fail to register such Particulars, then, on Conviction thereof, any Promoter as aforesaid shall be liable to forfeit for every such Offence a Sum not exceeding Twenty Pounds.

VI. Provided always, and be it enacted, That if the Promoters of a proposed Company appoint a Person, being an Attorney or Solicitor of One of Her Majesty's Superior Courts of Law or Equity, to be Solicitor for the Promoters of such Company, and return to the said Registry Office a Duplicate of such Appointment in Writing, signed by some One or more of such Promoters, together with a Duplicate of the Acceptance of such Appointment, signed by the Person so appointed, then, until a Duplicate of the Revocation or of the Resignation of such Appointment be returned in like Manner, so signed as aforesaid, or until the Decease of such Solicitor, all Returns by this Act required to be made by such Promoters shall be made by such Solicitor in their Behalf, and the Penalty herein-before imposed in respect of any Failure to make such Returns shall not be incurred by them; and that if within the Period of One Month after the Particulars hereby required to be registered, or any of them, shall have been ascertained or determined, such Solicitor fail to make such Returns, then he shall be liable to forfeit for every such Offense a Sum not exceeding Twenty Pounds; and that if it be made to appear to the Court to which he shall belong that he fraudulently omitted to make a Return of any such Particulars, then he shall be liable to be suspended from Practice for any Time to be appointed by the said Court, or to be struck off the Rolls of the said Court.

VII. And be it enacted, That it shall not be lawful for any Joint Stock Company hereafter to be formed for any Purpose within the meaning of this Act, whether for executing any such Work as aforesaid under the Authority of Parliament, or for any other Purpose, to act otherwise than provisionally in accordance with the Act until such Company shall have obtained a Certificate of complete Registration as herein-after provided; and no Joint Stock Company shall be entitled to receive a Certificate of complete Registration unless it be formed by some Deed or Writing under the Hands and Seals of the Shareholders therein; and in or by such Deed there must be appointed not less than Three Directors, and also One or more Auditors; and such Deed must set forth in a Schedule thereto, in a tabular Manner, according to the Order herein-after mentioned, the following Particulars, that is to say:

1. The Name of the Company; and also,
2. The Business or Purpose of the Company; and also,
3. The principal or only Place for carrying on such Business, and every Branch Office (if any); and also,
4. The Amount of the proposed Capital, and of any proposed additional Capital, and the Means by which it is to be raised; and where the Capital shall not be Money, or shall not consist entirely of Money, then the Nature of such Capital and the Value thereof shall be stated; and also,
5. The amount of Money (if any) to be raised or authorized to be raised by Loan; and also,
6. The total amount of the Capital subscribed or proposed to be subscribed at the Date of such Deed; and also,
7. The Division of Capital (if any) into equal Shares, and the total Number of such Shares, each of which is to be distinguished by a separate Number in a regular Series; and also,
8. The Names and Occupations and (except Bodies Politic) the Places of Residence of all the then Subscribers, according to the Information possessed by the Officers of the Company in respect of such Names and Occupations and Places of Residence; and also,
9. The Number of the Shares which each Subscriber holds, and the distinctive Numbers thereof, distinguishing the Numbers of the Shares on which the Deposit has been paid from those on which it has not been paid; and also,
10. The Names of the then Directors of the Company, and of the then Trustees of the Company (if any), and of the then Auditors of the Company,

together with their respective Places of Business (if any), Occupation, and Places of Residence; and also,

11. The Duration of the Company, and the Mode or Condition of its Dissolution:

And that such Deed must contain a Covenant on the Part of every Shareholder, with a Trustee on the Part of the Company, to pay up the Amount of the Instalments on the Shares taken by such Shareholder, and to perform the several Engagements in the Deed contained on the Part of the Shareholders; and that such Deed must also make Provision for such of the Purposes set forth in Schedule (A.) to this Act annexed as the Nature and Business of the Company may require, and either with or without Provision for such other Purposes (not inconsistent with Law) as the Parties to such Deed shall think proper; and that every Deed of Settlement must be signed by at least One Fourth in Number of the Persons who at the Date of the Deed have become Subscribers, and who shall hold at least One Fourth of the maximum Number of Shares in the Capital of the Company; and that every such Deed must be certified by Two Directors of the Company, by Writing endorsed thereon in the Form contained in Schedule (B.) to this Act annexed; and that on the Production of such Deed, setting forth such Matters and making such Provisions as are hereby required to be provided for, and being so signed and certified, together with a complete Abstract or Index thereof, to be previously approved by the Registrar of Joint Stock Companies, and also a Copy of such Deed, for the Purpose of registering the same, or as soon after such Production as conveniently may be, the Registrar of Joint Stock Companies shall grant a Certificate of complete Registration, according to the Provisions of this Act in that Behalf; and unless such Deed and other Matters be so produced, and such Conditions be so performed, it shall not be lawful for him to grant such Certificate; and that after such Certificate shall be granted it shall be taken as Evidence of the proper Provisions being inserted in such Deed, and of the Performance of the Conditions hereby required previously to the granting such Certificate of complete Registration; and that any Defect or Omission as regards the Matters hereby required in any Deed of Settlement may from Time to Time be supplied by a supplementary Deed or Deeds; and if any such supplementary Deed be not inconsistent with or repugnant to this Act, or any Act respecting Joint Stock Companies, and if it be duly registered, then it shall have the same Effect as if there were only One Deed for the Purposes of this Act; and that unless the same shall be registered it shall be of no Force or Effect.

VIII. And be it enacted, That if any Deed of Settlement or supplementary Deed of Settlement, whether made before or after the granting of the Certificate of complete Registration, appear to such Registrar of Joint Stock Companies to be insufficient by reason of the Omission or Incompleteness of any of the Provisions therein Contained for the Purposes set forth in the said Schedule

(A.), or if the Deed contain Provisions which appear to such Registrar to be inconsistent with or repugnant to this Act, or any Act for the Time being in force respecting Joint Stock Companies, then as soon thereafter as conveniently may be such Registrar shall notify the same in Writing to the Persons or to the Company by whom the Deed shall have been presented for Registration, specifying in such Notification the Particulars wherein such Deed of Settlement or supplementary Deed of Settlement is incomplete, or inconsistent with or repugnant to any such Act aforesaid.

IX. Provided always, and be it enacted, That if any Company for executing any Bridge, Road, Cut, Reservoir, Aqueduct, Waterwork, Navigation, Tunnel, Archway, Railway, Pier, Port, Harbour, Ferry, or Dock, which cannot be carried into execution without the Authority of Parliament, deposit at the proper Offices of the Two Houses of Parliament, in compliance with the Standing Orders of such Houses respectively, and at or within the Time required by such Standing Orders, such Deeds of Partnership or Subscription Contracts as shall be required to be deposited by such Standing Orders, and also return to the said Registry Office a Copy of such Deeds of Partnership or Subscription Contracts, together with such Certificate of the Receipt of such Plans, Sections, and Books of Reference as shall be appointed by the said Committee of Privy Council for Trade, then it shall be lawful for the Registrar of Joint Stock Companies and he is hereby required to accept the same instead of the Deed of Settlement by this Act required to be returned for the Purpose of obtaining a Certificate of complete Registration; and thereupon such Company shall be entitled to a Certificate of complete Registration accordingly.

X. And be it enacted, That throughout the Continuance of any Joint Stock Company completely registered under this Act, except such Companies as shall have been incorporated by Act of Parliament after complete Registration and within One Month after the Date of any new or supplementary Deed of Settlement, there shall be transmitted by the Directors of every such Company to the Registrar of Joint Stock Companies a Copy of such new or supplementary Deed of Settlement, together with a complete Abstract thereof so approved of as aforesaid; and within Six Months after any Change shall have taken place in any of the Particulars herein-before required to be set forth in the Schedule to the Deed of Settlement, except so far as respects the Shareholders thereof and their respective Shares, there shall be transmitted Returns of such Particulars, so far as the same shall have been changed; and if within such Period any such Return be not made, then, on Conviction thereof, every Director of such Company shall be liable to pay a Sum not exceeding Twenty Pounds.

XI. And be it enacted, That in the Months of *January* and *July* in every Year the Directors of every Joint Stock Company completely registered under this Act, except Companies which shall have been incorporated by Act of Parliament after complete Registration, shall make or cause to be made the following Returns to the Registrar of Joint Stock Companies; namely:

A Return according to the Schedule (E.) hereunto annexed, and containing the Particulars therein set forth, of every Transfer of any Share in such Company which shall have been made since the preceding half-yearly Return (or, in the Case of the first of such Returns made by such Company since the complete Registration thereof), and which shall have come to the Knowledge of the Directors:

And also a Return according to the Schedule (F.) hereunto annexed, and containing the Particulars therein set forth, of the Names and Places of Abode of all Persons who shall either have ceased to be Shareholders of such Company, or have become Shareholders of such Company otherwise than by a Transfer as aforesaid, since the preceding half-yearly Return, or since the complete Registration of the Company, as the Case may require, and also of the Changes in the Names of all Shareholders of such Company whose names shall have been changed by Marriage or otherwise since the last preceding half-yearly Return, or since the complete Registration of the Company, as the Case may require:

And if within any such Period any such Return be not made, then, on Conviction thereof, every Director of such Company shall be liable to pay a Sum not exceeding Twenty Pounds.

XII. And be it enacted, That if at any Time any Party to a Transfer of a Share request in Writing the Directors of any such Company to make a Return thereof, then forthwith on such Request the Directors shall make the same accordingly; and that Proof of such Transfer and such Request to the Satisfaction of the Registrar of Joint Stock Companies it shall be lawful for any such Party to make a Return of such Transfer, which shall be received, marked, and registered, and with the same Effect, as hereby provided in the Case of Returns made by such Companies.

XIII. And be it enacted, That until the Return of the Transfer or other Fact or Event whereby a Person becomes the Holder of any Shares be made, pursuant to the Provisions herein-before contained, it shall not be lawful for such Company, its Directors or Officers, if such Fact or Event be known to them respectively, to pay to any such Person any Part of the Profits of the Concern, nor for any such Person to sue for or recover any Part of the Profits arising in respect of such Shares, or in anywise to act as a Shareholder; and that until the Return of the Transfer of any Share shall have been made pursuant to the Provisions herein-before contained the Person whose Share shall have been thereby transferred shall, so far as respects his Liability to the Debts and Engagements of the Company, and also as respects the Reimbursement of any Loss, Damages, Costs, and Charges he may incur thereby, be deemed to continue a Shareholder of such Company.

XIV. And be it enacted, That annually in the Month of *January* in every Year every Company completely registered under this Act, except Companies which shall have been incorporated by Act of Parliament after complete Registration, shall make to the said Registry Office a Return of the Name and Business of the Company; and that of the Receipt of such Return the Register of Joint Stock Companies shall give a Certificate thereof; and that if within the further Period of One Month such Return be not made, then, on Conviction thereof, such Company shall be liable to pay a Sum not exceeding Twenty Pounds: Provided always, that it shall be lawful for the Lords of the said Committee, on the Application of any Company, to appoint any other Period of the Year for the making of such annual Return as aforesaid.

XV. And be it enacted, That when the Particulars and Documents severally by this Act required to be returned to the said Registry Office shall have been so returned, it shall be the Duty of the said Registrar of Joint Stock Companies and he is hereby required to cause to be written on every such Document and Return of Particulars brought to him for Registration the day of the Receipt thereof, and to cause to be marked on every such Return or Document, in Writing or otherwise, a Number denoting the Order in which the same was received, and also, upon Demand, to cause an Acknowledgement of the Receipt of such Return or Document to be given to the Person by whom the same shall be so brought; and that if such Returns or Documents be conformable to the Provisions of this Act, or of any Regulations in that Behalf, then it shall be the Duty of the Registrar and he is hereby required forthwith to register the same, and, on Demand, to grant to such Company a Certificate of provisional or complete Registration, as the Case may require, signed by him, and sealed with the Seal of his Office; which Certificate must set forth whether the Company has been constituted provisionally or completely; and that, in the Absence of Evidence to the contrary, any such Certificate, or a copy of any such Return as aforesaid, shall be received in Evidence, without Proof of the Signature thereto, or of the Seal of Office affixed thereto.

XVI. And be it enacted, That until the Company shall have obtained its Certificate of complete Registration the Promoters of the Company, or their Solicitor as aforesaid, shall make or cause to be made every Return by this Act required to be made; and after such Company shall have obtained a Certificate of complete Registration the Directors of the Company shall make or cause to be made every such Return; and One or more of such Promoters, or their Solicitor, or such Directors, as the case may be, shall sign such Return; and every such Return which shall be made after complete Registration of the Company shall be sealed with the Seal of the Company.

XVII. And be it enacted, That if the Committee of the Privy Council for Trade shall deem it expedient, then it shall be lawful for the said Committee and they are hereby authorized from Time to Time to make Regulations respecting the Form of any such Returns as are hereby directed to be made, and the Manner and Time of making them, and for those Purposes to alter and vary the Schedules annexed to this Act, and to dispense with any of the Returns hereby made necessary, or any of the Forms of Returns prescribed by this Act; and that every such Regulation shall be published in the *London Gazette*, and thereupon shall be of the like Force as if the same were contained in this Act: Provided always that nothing herein contained shall be construed to permit the said Committee to make any such Regulations which shall not apply alike to all such Companies as may be registered under the Authority of this Act, so far as may be applicable to them.

XVIII. And be it enacted, That every Person shall be at liberty to inspect the Returns, Deeds, Registers, and Indexes which shall be made to or kept by the said Register of Joint Stock Companies; and that there shall be paid for such Inspection such Fees as may be appointed by the Commissioners of Her Majesty's Treasury in that Behalf, not exceeding One Shilling for each such Inspection; and that any Person shall be at liberty to require a Copy or Extract of any such Return or Deed, to be certified by the said Registrar; and there shall be paid for such certified Copy or Extract such Fee as the Commissioners of Her Majesty's Treasury may appoint in that Behalf, not exceeding Sixpence for each Folio of such Copy or Extract; and that in all Courts of Law and Equity and elsewhere every such Copy or Extract so certified shall be received in Evidence, without Proof of the Signature thereto, or of the Seal of Office affixed thereto.

XIX. And be it enacted, That it shall be lawful for the Committee of Privy Council for Trade and they are hereby empowered to appoint a Person to be and to be called the Registrar of Joint Stock Companies, and, if the said Committee see fit, an Assistant Registrar, Clerks, and other necessary Officers and Servants; and that every such Registrar and Assistant Registrar, Clerks, and Officers shall be entitled to hold their Offices during the Pleasure only of the said Committee; and that from Time to Time it shall be lawful for the Commissioners of Her Majesty's Treasury and they are hereby authorized to fix the Salary or Remuneration of such Registrar, Assistant Registrar, Clerks, Officers, and Servants; and that, subject to the Provisions of this Act, it shall be lawful for the said Committee of Privy Council for Trade and they are hereby authorized to make Rules for regulating the Execution of the Office of the said Registrar; and that said Registrar shall have a Seal of Office to be by him used in the Authentication of all Matters relating to his said Office in respect of which such Authentication is by this Act required; and that such Assistant Registrar shall in the Absence of the Registrar be competent to do all Things which the Registrar is authorized or empowered, directed, or required to do, as fully and effectually to all Intents and Purposes, as the Registrar himself may do; and all Provisions in this Act relating to the Signature and Seal of Office of the said Registrar shall apply to the said Assistant Registrar: Provided always, that the Registrar shall not be absent from the Duties of his Office, except on account of ill Health or other urgent Cause, without express Leave in Writing of the said Committee of Privy Council for Trade for that Purpose previously obtained.

XX. And be it enacted, That from the Hour of Ten of the Clock in the Morning until Five of the Clock in the Afternoon, and at such other Times as the said Committee of Privy Council for Trade shall appoint, such Registrar, or in the unavoidable, or, as aforesaid, permitted Absence of the Registrar, then such Assistant Registrar, shall give his Attendance at the said Office every Day throughout the Year, except *Sundays, Good Friday, Christmas Day* and any other general Holiday or Fast Day appointed by Her Majesty in Council.

XXI. And be it enacted, That every Company shall pay the following Fees; (that is to say,)

For a Certificate of provisional Registration the Sum of Five Pounds:

For a Certificate of complete Registration the Sum of Five Pounds; and One Shilling additional in respect of every Thousand Pounds Value of Capital, as declared on the Formation of the Company in the Deed of Settlement, or by any other special Authority:

For an annual Certificate the Sum of One Pound:

And also such other Fees as shall be appointed to be paid in respect of any other Services to be performed by the said Registrar; and that from Time to Time it shall be lawful for the Commissioners of Her Majesty's Treasury and they are hereby authorized, in addition to the Fees hereinbefore required to be paid in respect of such Certificates, to fix such other Fees to be paid for the Services to be performed by the Registrar of Joint Stock Companies as they shall deem requisite to defray both the Expenses of the said Office and the Salaries or other Remuneration of the said Registrar and any other Persons employed under him, with the sanction of the said Commissioners of Her Majesty's Treasury, in the Execution of this Act; and that the Balance, if any, shall be carried to the Consolidated Fund of the United Kingdom of *Great Britain* and *Ireland*, and shall be paid accordingly into the Receipt of Her Majesty's Exchequer at *Westminster*; and that it shall be lawful for the said Commissioners of Her Majesty's Treasury to regulate the Manner in which such Fees are to be received, and in which they are to be kept, and in which they are to be accounted for: Provided always, that if within Two Years after a Company shall have obtained a Certificate of complete Registration such Company shall obtain an Act for the Incorporation thereof, then Three Fourths of the Fee paid by or on behalf of such Company on such complete Registration in respect of the Capital of the Company shall be reimbursed and repaid to the said Company, and that it shall be lawful for the said Commissioners of Her Majesty's Treasury and they are hereby authorized and empowered to repay the same accordingly.

XXII. And be it enacted, That if either the said Registrar of Joint Stock Companies, or any Person employed under him, either demand or receive any Gratuity or Reward in respect of any Service performed by him other than the Fees aforesaid, then for every such Offence every such Registrar or Person shall be guilty of a Misdemeanor.

XXIII. And be it enacted, That on the provisional Registration of any Company being certified by the Registrar of Joint Stock Companies it shall be lawful for the Promoters of any Company so registered to act provisionally, but not for any longer Period than Twelve Months from the date of the Certificate, unless such Certificate shall be renewed, which may be done on Application for that Purpose; and no such renewed Certificate shall be in force for a longer Period than Twelve Months from the Date thereof; and it shall be lawful for the Promoters of such Company:

To assume the Name of the intended Company, but coupled with the Words "Registered provisionally;" and also,

To open Subscription Lists; and also,

To allot Shares, and receive Deposits by way of Earnest thereon, at a Rate not exceeding Ten Shillings for Every One hundred Pounds on the amount of every Share in the Capital of the intended Company; and also, in the Case of Companies for executing any Bridge, Road, Cut, Canal, Reservoir, Aqueduct, Waterwork, Navigation, Tunnel, Archway, Railway, Pier, Port, Harbour, Ferry, or Dock, which cannot be carried into execution without the Authority of Parliament, in addition to and exclusive of such Sum of Ten Shillings *per* Hundred Pounds, such further Sum *per* Hundred Pounds on the Amount of every such Share as may be required by the Standing Orders of either House of Parliament to be deposited before the obtaining of an Act of Parliament for enabling the Company to execute such Work; and also,

To perform such other Acts only as are necessary for constituting the Company, or for obtaining Letters Patent, or a Charter, or an Act of Parliament;

But not to make Calls, nor to purchase, contract for, or hold Lands, nor to enter into Contracts for any Services, or for the Execution of any Works, or for the Supply of any Stores, except such Services and Stores or other Things as are necessarily required for the establishing of the Company, and except any Purchase or other Contract to be made conditional on the Completion of the Company, and to take effect after the Certificate of complete Registration, Act of Parliament, or Charter or Letters Patent, shall have been obtained, and, except in the Case of Companies for executing such Works as aforesaid, Contracts for Services in making Surveys and performing all other Acts necessary for obtaining an Act of Incorporation or other Act for enabling the Company to execute such Works.

XXIV. And be it enacted, That if before a Certificate of provisional Registration shall be obtained the Promoters or any of them, or any Person employed by or under them, take any Monies in consideration of the Allotment either of Shares or of any Interest in the Concern, or by way of Deposit for Shares to be granted or allotted; or issue, in the Name or on behalf of the Company, any Note or Scrip, or Letter of Allotment, or other Instrument or Writing to denote a Right or Claim, or Preference or Promise, absolute or conditional, to any Shares; or advertise the Existence or proposed Formation of the Company; or make any Contract whatsoever for or in the Name or on behalf of such intended Company; then every such Person shall be liable to forfeit for every such Offence a Sum not exceeding Twenty-five Pounds; and that it shall be lawful for any Person to sue for and recover the same by Action of Debt.

XXV. And be it enacted, That on the complete Registration of any Company being certified by the Registrar of Joint Stock Companies such Company and the then Shareholders therein, and all the succeeding Shareholders, whilst Shareholders, shall be and are hereby incorporated as from the Date of such Certificate by the Name of the Company as set forth in the Deed of Settlement, and for the Purpose of carrying on the Trade or Business for which the Company was formed, but only according to the Provisions of this Act, and of such Deed as aforesaid, and for the Purpose of suing and being sued, and of taking and enjoying the Property and Effects of the said Company; and thereupon any Covenants or Engagements entered into by any of the Shareholders or other Persons with any Trustee on the Behalf of the Company, at any Time before the complete Registration thereof, may be proceeded on by the said Company and enforced in all respects as if they had been made or entered into with the said Company after the Incorporation thereof; and such Company shall continue so incorporated until it shall be dissolved, and all its Affairs wound up; but so as not in anywise to restrict the Liability of any of the Shareholders of the Company, under any Judgment, Decree, or Order for the Payment of Money which shall be obtained against such Company, or any of the Members thereof, in any Action or Suit to be prosecuted against such Company in any Court of Law or Equity; but every such Shareholder shall, in respect of such Monies, subject as after mentioned, be and continue liable as he would have been if the said Company had not been incorporated; and thereupon it shall be lawful for the said Company, and they are hereby empowered, as follows; that is to say:

1. To use the registered Name of the Company, adding thereto "Registered;" and also,
2. To have a Common Seal (with Power to break, alter, and change the same from Time to Time), but on which must be inscribed the Name of the Company; and also,
3. To sue and be sued by their registered Name in respect of any Claim by or upon the Company upon or by any Person, whether a Member of the Company or not, so long as any such Claim may remain unsatisfied; and also,
4. To enter into Contracts for the Execution of the Works, and for the Supply of the Stores, or for any other necessary Purpose of the Company; and also,
5. To purchase and hold Lands, Tenements, and Hereditaments in the Name of the said Company, or of the Trustees or Trustee thereof, for the Purpose of occupying the same as a Place or Places of Business of

the said Company, and also (but nevertheless with a License, general or special, for that Purpose, to be granted by the Committee of the Privy Council for Trade, first had and obtained,) such other Lands, Tenements, and Hereditaments as the Nature of the Business of the Company may require; and also,

6. To issue Certificates of Shares; and also,
7. To receive Instalments from Subscribers in respect of the Amount of any Shares not paid up; and also,
8. To borrow and raise money within the Limitations prescribed by any special Authority; and also,
9. To declare dividends out of the Profits of the Concern; and also,
10. To hold General Meetings periodically, and extraordinary Meetings upon being duly summoned for that Purpose; and also,
11. To make from Time to Time, at some General Meeting of Shareholders specially summoned for the Purpose, Bye Laws for the Regulation of the Shareholders, Members, Directors, and Officers of the Company, such Bye Laws not being repugnant to or inconsistent with the Provisions of this Act or of the Deed of Settlement of the Company; and also,
12. To perform all other Acts necessary for the carrying into effect the Purposes of such Company, and in all respects as other Partnerships are entitled to do:

And the said Company are hereby empowered and required:

13. To appoint from Time to Time, for the Conduct and Superintendence of the Execution of the Affairs of the Company, a Number of Directors, not less than Three, for a Period not greater than Five Years, with or without Eligibility to be re-elected at the Expiration of the Term, as may be prescribed by any Deed of Settlement or Bye Law; and also,
14. To appoint and remove One or more Auditors, and such other Officers as the Deed of Settlement under which the Company shall be constituted may authorize:

Subject nevertheless, with respect to all such Powers and Privileges, to the Provisions of this Act, and subject also to the Provisions of the Deed of Settlement of the Company or any other special Authority: Provided always, with regard to any Company for executing any Bridge, Road, Cut, Canal, Reservoir, Aqueduct, Waterwork, Navigation, Tunnel, Archway, Railway, Pier, Port, Harbour, Ferry, or Dock, which cannot be carried into execution without obtaining the Authority of Parliament, that on the complete Registration of any such Company, and before such Company shall have obtained its Act of Incorporation or other Act whereby the Authority of Parliament shall be granted for executing such Work, it shall not be lawful for any such Company or the Directors or Officers thereof to exercise the herein-before mentioned Power to enter into Contracts, otherwise than conditionally upon obtaining such Act, or to exercise the Power to purchase and hold Lands as aforesaid, or to exercise the Power to receive Instalments from

Shareholders beyond the Sum or Per-centage necessary to be deposited in compliance with the Standing Orders of either House of Parliament, or such other Sum as may be requisite for obtaining the Act of Incorporation or other Act for granting the Authority of Parliament to execute such Work, or to exercise the Power to borrow Money, as aforesaid, or to exercise the Power to declare Dividends, as aforesaid; and subject to these last-mentioned Exceptions, all the Powers by this Enactment herein-before given to any Company completely registered, except the general Power to perform all Acts necessary for carrying on the Business of the Company, may be exercised as fully by any such Company so completely registered as by any other Company so completely registered: Provided always, that it shall be lawful for any such Company to perform all Acts which may be necessary for obtaining an Act of Incorporation or other Act for obtaining the Authority of Parliament to execute its Works as aforesaid, any thing herein contained to the contrary notwithstanding; and that upon obtaining such Act of Incorporation or other such Act as aforesaid, or at the Time of the coming into operation of such Act, as shall be thereby appointed, all the Powers which any such Company shall obtain by virtue of this Act, and all the Provisions and Regulations of this Act which shall apply to such Company, shall cease and determine, except so far as shall be otherwise provided by such Act of Incorporation or other such Act as aforesaid.

XXVI. And be it enacted, That no Shareholder of any Joint Stock Company completely registered under this Act shall be entitled to receive any Dividends or Profits, or be entitled to the Remedies or Powers hereby given to Shareholders, until he shall have executed the Deed of Settlement of the said Company, or some Deed referring thereto, and also have paid up all Instalments or Calls due from him, and shall have been registered in the Registry Office aforesaid; and further, that it shall be lawful for every Shareholder who shall have signed such Deed, and paid up such Instalments or Calls, and shall have been registered, and he is hereby entitled:

To be present at all General Meetings of the Company; and also,

To take part in the Discussions thereat; and also,

To vote in the Determination of any Question thereat, and that either in Person or by Proxy, unless the Deed of Settlement shall preclude Shareholders from voting by Proxy; and also,

To vote in the Choice of Directors, and of every Auditor to be elected by the Shareholders; Subject nevertheless to the Provisions of this Act, and of the Deed of Settlement of the Company or other special Authority, so far as such Provisions shall either regulate or restrict the Exercise of such Powers but not so as to deprive such Shareholders thereof; and further, with regard to Subscribers and every Person entitled or claiming to be entitled to any Share in any Joint Stock Company the Formation of which shall be commenced after the First Day of *November* One thousand eight hundred and forty-four, that until such Joint Stock Company shall have obtained a Certificate of complete Registration, and until any such Subscriber or Person shall have been duly registered as a Shareholder in the said Registry Office, it shall not be lawful for such Person to dispose, by Sale or Mortgage, of such Share, or of any Interest therein, and that every Contract for or Sale or Disposal of such Share or Interest shall be void, and that every Person entering into such Contract shall forfeit a Sum not exceeding Ten Pounds; and that for better protecting Purchasers it shall be the Duty of the Directors of the Company by whom Certificates of Shares are issued to state on every such Certificate the Date of the first complete Registration of the Company, as before provided; and that if any such Director or Officer knowingly make a false Statement in that respect then he shall be liable to the Pains and Penalties of a Misdemeanor.

XXVII. And be it enacted, That with regard to the Powers and Duties of Directors it shall be lawful for the Directors of any Joint Stock Company registered under the Act:

1. To conduct and manage the Affairs of the Company according to the Provisions and subject to the Restrictions of this Act, and of the Deed of Settlement, and of any Bye Law, and for that Purpose to enter into all such Contracts and do and execute all such Acts and Deeds as the Circumstances may require; and also,
2. To appoint the Secretary, if any; and also,
3. To appoint the Clerks and Servants; and also from Time to Time as they see fit,
4. To remove such Secretary, Clerks, and Servants, and to appoint others, as Occasion shall require; and also,
5. To appoint other Persons for special Services as the Concerns of the Company may from Time to Time require; and also,
6. To hold Meetings periodically and from Time to Time as the Concerns of the Company shall require; and also,
7. To appoint a Chairman to preside at all such Meetings, and in his Absence to appoint a Chairman at each such Meeting;

Subject nevertheless to the Provisions and Restrictions of this Act, and to the Provisions of the Deed of Settlement of the Company or other special Authority, but not so as to enable the Shareholders to act in their own Behalf in the ordinary Management of the Concerns of the Company otherwise than by means of Directors: Provided always, that it shall not be lawful for the Directors to purchase any Shares of the Company, nor to sell any such Shares, except Shares forfeited on the Nonpayment of Calls or Instalments, nor to lend to any of their Number, or to any Officer of the Company, any Money belonging to the Company without the Authority and Sanction of a General Meeting of Shareholders duly convened.

XXVIII. And be it enacted, That henceforth, notwithstanding any thing to the contrary in any Deed of Settlement or other Instrument by which a Joint Stock Company shall be constituted or regulated, it shall not be lawful to appoint any Person to be or to act as a Director, whether honorary or otherwise, or to hold the Office of Patron or President, or any other Office of the like Description; nor shall it be lawful for any Person to act in any such Capacity unless at the Time of such his Appointment or of such his acting he hold in his own Right at least One Share in the Capital of such Company; and that if, without having such Share, any Person be or become or act as Director, Patron, or President of such Company, or in any Office of such or the like Nature, then he shall forfeit for every such Offence a Sum not exceeding Twenty Pounds; and if any Person be announced or held out by or on behalf of the Company as a Director, Patron, or President, or as holding any Office of such or the like Description, without having so consented or acted, then each Director of such Company knowingly concurring in such Representation shall forfeit a Sum not exceeding Twenty Pounds.

XXIX. And be it enacted, That if any Director of a Joint Stock Company registered under this Act be either directly or indirectly concerned or interested in any Contract proposed to be made by or on behalf of the Company, whether for Land, Materials, Work to be done, or for any Purpose whatsoever, during the Time he shall be a Director, he shall, on the Subject of any such Contract in which he may be so concerned or interested, be precluded from voting or otherwise acting as a Director; and that if any Contract or Dealing (except a Policy of Assurance, Grant of Annuity, or Contract for the Purchase of an Article or of Service, which is respectively the Subject of the proper Business of the Company, such Contract being made upon the same or the like Terms as any like Contract with other Customers or Purchasers), shall be entered into, in which any Director shall be interested, then the Terms of such Contract or Dealing shall be submitted to the next General or Special Meeting of the Shareholders to be summoned for that Purpose; and that no such Contract shall have Force until approved and confirmed by the Majority of Votes of the Shareholders present at such Meeting; and that if at any Time any Director cease to be a Holder of the prescribed Number of Shares in the Company, or shall become a Bankrupt or Insolvent, or shall have suspended Payment, or compromised with his Creditors, or be declared a Lunatic, then it shall be unlawful for any such Director to continue as a Director, or to act as such, and the Office of such Director shall be and is hereby declared to be vacant.

XXX. And be it enacted, That notwithstanding it may be afterwards discovered that there was some Defect or Error in the Appointment of any Person acting or who may have acted as a Director of a Joint Stock Company registered under this Act, or that such Person was disqualified, yet all Acts done by him as such Director before the Discovery of such Defect or Error, either solely or with other Directors, shall be as binding on him, and on the Company, and the Directors and Officers thereof, as if such Person had been duly appointed or qualified, and, if such Acts were done *bona fide*, shall be as binding on all Persons whomsoever as if such Person had been duly appointed or qualified.

XXXI. And be it enacted, That if any such Director or other Officer or any Joint Stock Company registered under this Act wrongfully do or omit any Act, with intent to defraud the Company or any Shareholder therein, or falsify or fraudulently mutilate or fraudulently make any Erasure in the Books of Account or Books of Register, or any Document belonging to the Company, then such Director or Officer shall be deemed to be guilty of a Misdemeanor.

XXXII. And be it enacted, That if the Entry of the Proceedings of any Meeting of the Shareholders or of the Directors of any Joint Stock Company registered under this Act purport to be signed by the Chairman duly presiding at such Meeting, and sealed with the Seal of the Company, then it shall be the Duty of all Courts of Justice, Justices, and others, and they are hereby required, to receive the Book in which such entry shall be made as *prima facie* Evidence, not only of the Proceedings of the Meeting of which Entry shall be so made, but of such Meetings having been duly convened, and of the Persons making or entering such Orders or Proceedings being Shareholders or Directors, and of the Signature of the Chairman.

XXXIII. And be it enacted, That the Books of any such Company wherein the Proceedings of the Company are recorded shall be kept at the principal or only Place of Business of the Company, and at all reasonable Times such books shall be open to the Inspection of any Shareholder of the Company; subject nevertheless to the Provisions of the Deed of Settlement or of any Bye Law.

XXXIV. And be it enacted, That the Directors shall cause the Accounts of such Company to be duly entered in Books to be provided for the Purpose.

XXXV. And be it enacted, That Fourteen Days at the least before the Period at which the Accounts are required to be delivered to the Auditors as herein-after provided the Directors of such Company shall cause the Books of the Company to be balanced, and a full and fair Balance Sheet to be made up; and that previously to such Balance Sheet being delivered to the Auditors as herein-after provided the Directors, or any Three of their Number, shall examine such Balance Sheet, and sign it as so examined; and that when the Balance Sheet shall have been so examined the Chairman of the Directors shall sign such Balance Sheet, and that thereupon the Directors shall cause the same to be recorded in the Books of the Company.

XXXVI. And be it enacted, That at each ordinary Meeting of the Shareholders the Directors shall produce such Balance Sheet to the Shareholders assembled thereat.

XXXVII. And be it enacted, That during the Space of Fourteen Days previously to such ordinary Meeting, and also during One Month thereafter, every Shareholder of the Company may, subject to the Provisions of the Deed of Settlement, or of any Bye Law, inspect the Books of Account and the Balance Sheet of the Company, and take Copies thereof and Extracts therefrom; and if at any other Time Three Directors authorize in Writing any Shareholder to make such Inspection, then at such other Time the Shareholder so authorized may make such Inspection.

XXXVIII. And be it enacted, That every Joint Stock Company completely registered under this Act shall annually at a General Meeting appoint One or more Auditors of the Accounts of the Company (One of whom at least shall be appointed by the Shareholders present at the Meeting in Person or by Proxy), and shall return the Names of such Auditors to the Registrar of Joint Stock Companies; and that if an Auditor be not appointed on behalf of the Shareholders, or if he shall die, or become incapable of acting, or shall decline to act at the prescribed Period, or if such Return be not made, then on the Application of any Shareholder of the Company it shall be the Duty of the Committee of Privy Council for Trade and they are hereby authorized to appoint an Auditor on behalf of the Shareholders; and that such Auditor shall continue to act till the next General Meeting; and the due Appointment of such Auditor shall be returned to the Register of Joint Stock Companies, and that thereupon it shall be his Duty to register the same; and that it shall be lawful for the Commissioners of the Treasury and they are hereby empowered to appoint that the Company shall pay to such Auditor such Salary or Remuneration as to the said Commissioners shall appear suitable, having regard to the Duties of his Office, and that thereupon such Auditor shall be entitled to recover such Salary from the Company as to when it shall become due, according to the Terms of the Appointment thereof.

XXXIX. And be it enacted, That Twenty-eight Days at least before the ensuing ordinary Meeting at which such Balance Sheet is required to be produced to the Shareholders the Directors shall deliver to the Auditors the half-yearly or other periodical Accounts and the Balance Sheet required to be presented to the Shareholders; and that the Auditors shall receive from the Directors such Accounts and Balance Sheet, and examine the same.

XL. And be it enacted, That throughout the Year and at all reasonable Times of the Day it shall be lawful for the Auditors and they are authorized to inspect the Books of Account and Books of Registry of such Company; and that the Auditors may demand and have the Assistance of such Officers and Servants of the Company and such Documents as they shall require for the full Performance of their Duty in auditing the Accounts.

XLI. And be it enacted, That within Fourteen Days after the Receipt of such Balance Sheet and Accounts the Auditors shall either confirm such Accounts, and report generally thereon, or shall, if they do not see proper to confirm such Accounts, report specially thereon, and deliver such Accounts and Balance Sheet to the Directors of the Company.

XLII. And be it enacted, That Ten Days before the ordinary Meeting of such Company the Directors shall subject to the Provisions of any Deed of Settlement or Bye Law in that Behalf, send or cause to be sent a printed Copy of the Balance Sheet and Auditors Report to every Shareholder, according to his registered Address, and shall, at such Meeting of the Company, cause such Report to be read, together with the Report of the Directors.

XLIII. And be it enacted, That within Fourteen Days after such Meeting it shall be the Duty of such Directors and they are hereby required to return to the said Registry Office a Copy of the Balance Sheet, and of the Report of the Auditors thereon; and that thereupon it shall be the Duty of the Registrar of Joint Stock Companies and he is hereby required to register or file the same with the other Documents relating to such Company.

XLIV. And for the Purpose of regulating Contracts entered into on behalf of any Joint Stock Company completely registered under the Act (except Contracts for the Purchase of any Article the Payment or Consideration for which doth not exceed the Sum of Fifty Pounds, or for any Service the Period of which doth not exceed Six Months, and the Consideration for which doth not exceed Fifty Pounds, and except Bills of Exchange and Promissory Notes), be it enacted, That every such Contract shall be in Writing, and signed by Two at least of the Directors of the Company on whose Behalf the same shall be entered into, and shall be sealed with the Common Seal thereof, or signed by some Officer of the Company on its Behalf, be thereunto expressly authorized by some Minute or Resolution of the Board of Directors applying to the particular Case; and that in the Absence of such Requisites, or of any of them, any such Contract shall be void and ineffectual (except as against the Company on whose Behalf the same shall have been made); and that every such Contract for the Purchase of any Article the Consideration of which doth not exceed the Sum of Fifty Pounds, or for any Services the Period of which doth not exceed Six Months, and the Consideration for which doth not exceed Fifty Pounds, entered into on behalf of any Joint Stock Company completely registered under this Act, may be entered into by any Officer authorized by a general Bye Law in that Behalf; and that every such Contract, whether under the Seal or not, shall immediately after the same shall have been entered into be reported to the Secretary or other appointed Officer of the Company on whose Behalf the same shall have been entered into, who shall enter the same in proper Books to be kept for that Purpose; and that if any such Contract be not reported and entered, then the Officer by whose Default such Contract shall not be so reported or entered shall be liable to repay the Company on whose Behalf such Contract may be made the Amount of the Consideration agreed to be paid by or on behalf of such Company in respect of such Contract.

XLV. And be it enacted, with regard to Bills of Exchange and Promissory Notes made, accepted, or endorsed on the Behalf or Account of any such Company, so far as relates to the Mode of making, accepting, or endorsing the same, and to the Liability of any such Company thereon, That if the Directors of the Company be authorized by Deed of Settlement or Bye Laws to issue or accept Bills of Exchange or Promissory Notes, then every such Bill of Exchange or Promissory Note shall be accepted (as the Case may be) by and in the Names of Two of the Directors of the Company on whose Behalf or Account the same may be so made or accepted, and shall be by such Directors expressed to be made or accepted by them on behalf of the Company; and that every such Bill of Exchange and Promissory Note so made or accepted as aforesaid shall be countersigned by the Secretary or other Officer of the Company in whose Behalf the same is expressed to be made or accepted; and that every Bill of Exchange so made as aforesaid, or received by or on behalf of the Company, may be endorsed in the Name of the Company by any Officer authorized by Deed of Settlement or Bye Laws in that Behalf; and that every such Bill of Exchange or Promissory Note so made, accepted, or endorsed as aforesaid shall, immediately after the making, accepting, or endorsing of the same, be reported to the proper Officer of the Company on whose Behalf the same shall have been made, accepted, or endorsed, and such last-mentioned Officer shall enter the same in proper Books to be kept for that Purpose; and that if any such Bill of Exchange or Promissory Note be not so reported and entered, then the Officer by whose Default such Bill or Note shall not be so reported or entered shall be liable to repay to the Company the Amount which the Company shall pay or be liable to pay in respect of such Bill or Note: Provided always, that nothing herein contained shall be deemed to make any such Secretary or Officer personally liable upon any such Bill of Exchange or Promissory Note, nor be deemed to make any such Directors personally liable thereon, except as Shareholders of the Company; and that every such Company on whose Behalf or Account any Bill of Exchange or Promissory Note shall be made, accepted, or endorsed, in manner and form aforesaid, shall and may sue and be sued thereon, as fully and effectually, and in the same Manner, as in the Case of any Contract made and entered into under their Common Seal.

XLVI. And be it enacted, That all Deeds and Instruments bearing the Seal of the Company shall be signed by Two at the least of the Directors of the Company.

XLVII. And be it enacted, That all Bye Laws made by any Joint Stock Company completely registered under this Act, in pursuance of the Power hereinbefore given, must be reduced into Writing, and must be affixed thereto the Common Seal of the Company; and that such Bye Laws must be registered at the Office for Registering Joint Stock Companies, and until they be so registered they shall not be of any Force; and that such Bye Laws must be printed and circulated for the Use of the Shareholders, and a Copy thereof must be given to every Officer of the Company, and to every Shareholder who shall require the same.

XLVIII. And be it enacted, That in all Actions, Suits, and other legal Proceedings for the Enforcement of such Bye Laws, or other Penalties for the Breach thereof, the Production of a written or printed Copy of the Bye Laws of the Company, having the Seal of Office of the Registrar of Joint Stock Companies affixed thereto, shall be sufficient Evidence of such Bye Laws.

XLIX. And be it enacted, That it shall be the Duty of the Directors of every Joint Stock Company registered under this Act to keep or cause to be kept a Book, to be called the "Register of Shareholders," and from Time to Time in such Book to enter the following Particulars; that is to say:

The Names and Addresses of All Persons or Corporations being Shareholders of the Company; and also,

The Number of Shares to which such Shareholders shall be respectively entitled, distinguishing each Share by its Number; and also,

The Amount of the Instalments paid on such Shares.

L. And be it enacted, That it shall be Lawful for every Shareholder, or if such Shareholder be a Corporation then the Clerk or principal Officer of such Corporation, at all convenient Times to search the Registrar of Shareholders gratis, and to require a Copy thereof or of any Part thereof; and that the Company may demand a Sum not exceeding Sixpence for every One hundred Words so required to be copied.

LI. And be it enacted, That, on Demand of the Holder of any Share in any Joint Stock Company completely registered under this Act, the Company shall cause a Certificate of the Proprietorship of such Share to be delivered to such Shareholder, specifying the Share in the Undertaking to which such Shareholder is entitled, and the Amount paid up in respect of such Share at the Date of such Certificate, and shall have the Common Seal of the Company affixed thereto; and for such Certificate the Company may demand any Sum not exceeding One Shilling; and that such Certificate must be according to the Form in the Schedule (I.) to this Act annexed, or to the like Effect.

LII. And be it enacted, That it shall be the Duty of all Courts of Justice, Judges, Justices, and others to admit such Certificate as *prima facie* Evidence of the Title of the Shareholder to the Share therein specified; nevertheless the Want of such Certificate shall not prevent the Holder of any Share from disposing thereof.

LIII. And be it enacted, That if any such Certificate be worn out or damaged, then, upon such Certificate being produced at some Meeting of the Directors, it shall be lawful for them to order such Certificate to be cancelled; and that thereupon another similar Certificate shall, if he require the same, be given to the Party in whom the Property of such Certificate and of the Share therein mentioned shall at the Time be vested; or if such Certificate be lost or destroyed, then, upon Proof thereof, a similar Certificate shall, if he require the same, be given to the Party entitled to the Certificate so lost or destroyed; and that in either Case it shall be the Duty of the Secretary and he is hereby required to make a due Entry of the substitute Certificate in the Register of Shareholders; and for every such Certificate so given or exchanged the Company may demand any Sum not exceeding the Sum of One Shilling.

LIV. And be it enacted, That, subject to the Regulations herein contained, and to be contained in any Deed of Settlement of any Joint Stock Company completely registered under this Act, it shall be lawful for every Shareholder of such Company and he is hereby entitled to sell and transfer his Shares therein by Deed duly stamped, in which the full Amount of the pecuniary Consideration for such Sale shall be truly expressed, and which Instrument of Transfer must be according to the Form in the Schedule (K.) to this Act annexed, or to the like Effect; and that the Directors of the Company shall cause a Memorial of such Instrument of Transfer, when produced at the Office of the Company, to be entered in a Book to be called "The Register of Transfers," and the Entry thereof to be endorsed on the Instrument of Transfer; and for every such Entry and Endorsement the Company may demand any Sum not exceeding One Shilling; and that until such Instrument of Transfer shall have been produced at the Office of the Company the Purchaser of the Share shall not be entitled to receive any of the Profits of the Company, or to vote in respect of such Share; Provided always, that if at the Time of such Transfer the Shareholder shall not have paid the full Amount due and payable to the Company on every Share held by him, then he shall not be entitled to transfer any Share, unless there be a Provision to the contrary in the Deed of Settlement.

LV. And be it enacted, That if any Shareholder fail to pay any Instalment of Capital due upon or in respect of any Share held by him, when the same shall become due, it shall be lawful for any such Company and they are hereby authorized to sue such Shareholder for the Amount in an Action of Debt in any Court having competent Jurisdiction in respect of the same; and that in the Declaration in any such Action it shall be sufficient to state only that at the Time of the Commencement of the Suit the Defendant, as the Holder of certain Shares (stating how many) in a certain Company or Undertaking, as the Case may be, (naming it,) was indebted to the Company in a certain Sum (stating the Amount of the Instalments, or so much thereof as is sought to be recovered,) for certain Instruments of Capital then due and payable in respect of the said Shares, and that the Defendant hath not paid the same; and that if upon the Trial of any such Action it shall be proved that the Defendant was the Holder of any Share when such Instalments, or any of them, in respect of the same, and for which the Action is brought, became due, then such Company shall recover such Instalments, or so much thereof as is due, together with Interest for the same at the Rate of Five Pounds *per Centum per Annum*, to be computed from the Day on which such Instalment shall have become due.

LVI. And be it enacted, That if any Share be held jointly by several Persons, then any Notice required to be given shall be given to such of the said Persons whose Name shall stand first on the Register of Shareholders, and Notice so given shall be sufficient Notice to all the Proprietors of such Share, and the Person so standing first shall be entitled to vote, and to have all the Privileges hereby conferred on Shareholders.

LVII. And be it enacted, That at every principal Place of Business of any Joint Stock Company completely registered under this Act it shall be the Duty of the Directors and Officers of the Company and they are hereby respectively required to have written or printed Copies of an Index or Abstract of the Deed of Settlement, approved by the Registrar of Joint Stock Companies, and a List of the Shareholders of the Company, and the Number of Shares held by each, and also a List of the Directors and Officers thereof, and a Copy of the Bye Laws sealed with the Seal of the Company, as returned to the said Registry Office; and that if at any reasonable Time any Shareholder, or any Person authorized in Writing by him, apply at any such Place of Business of the Company to inspect the same, then on Demand thereof made during the usual Hours of Business, it shall be the Duty of the Directors or Officers and they respectively are hereby required to permit such Inspection; and that if on such Demand any such Director or Officer to whom such Demand is made do not thereupon permit such Inspection, then, on Conviction thereof, he shall be liable to pay for every such Offence a Sum not exceeding Forty Shillings.

LVIII. And be it enacted, with regard to all Joint Stock Companies to which this Act is herein-before made to apply, and which shall exist on the First Day of *November* One thousand eight hundred and forty-four, whether incorporated by Act of Parliament or by Charter, or privileged by Letters Patent, or established by virtue of a Deed of Settlement, or of any other Instrument, or by virtue of any Authority whatever, or in any other Way whatever, That within Three Months from the said First Day of *November*, the Directors, Managers, Officers, or others having the Direction, Management, Conduct, Superintendence, or Execution of the Affairs of any such Company, shall register such Company at the Office for the

Registration of Joint Stock Companies, and for that Purpose shall make or cause to be made a Return of the following Particulars, according to the Schedule (I.) hereunto annexed that is to say:

1. The Name or Style of the Company; and also,
2. The Purpose of the Company; and also,
3. The principal or only Place for carrying on its Business:

And that on such Registration every such Company shall be entitled to have a Certificate of Registration, without paying any Fee either for such Registration or for such Certificate, but such Certificate shall be for the Purpose of showing that such Company had registered, and shall not be considered as a Certificate of complete Registration, so as to confer on any such Company the Powers and Privileges of this Act; and that if within the said Period the Persons hereby required to register any such Company fail so to do, then, on Conviction thereof, every such Company so failing shall forfeit for every such Offence a Sum not exceeding Fifty Pounds.

LIX. And be it enacted, with regard to such existing Companies as aforesaid (except Assurance Companies), That if any such existing Company be so constituted as is by this Act required with regard to any future Company, or if the Deed or Deeds of Settlement of such existing Company contain the Particulars by this Act required to be contained in some one or other Deed of Settlement of such future Company, and if any other Conditions required to be fulfilled by or in respect of any such future Company, in order to obtain a Certificate of complete Registration, be fulfilled in respect of any such existing Company, then such existing Company shall be entitled to obtain a Certificate of complete Registration; but if such existing Company be not so constituted, or if such Deed of Settlement do not contain such Particulars, or if such other Conditions be not fulfilled, then, on such existing Company returning a Deed or Deeds according to the Provisions of this Act, and also, in addition to any other Matters by this Enactment required to be returned by such existing Company, such other Matters as are by this Act required to be returned by any future Company in order to obtain or before obtaining a Certificate of complete Registration as aforesaid, or such Modification of the said Deeds or Returns, or of any of them, as the Committee of Privy Council for Trade shall direct by any Regulation to be made in that Behalf, either on the Part or in respect of any One Company or of any Class of Companies, and signed by One of the Secretaries of the said Committee, such existing Company shall be entitled to a Certificate of complete Registration; and on such Certificate of complete Registration being granted by the Registrar of Joint Stock Companies it shall be lawful for such existing Company, its Shareholders, its Directors, and its Officers, and they are respectively hereby empowered, to have and exercise all such Powers and Privileges as are by this Act conferred upon Joint Stock Companies to be hereafter formed, subject nevertheless with respect to all such Powers and Privileges to the Provisions of this Act, or of any other Act to be hereafter passed for regulating the same; and that every such Company not incorporated shall be incorporated for the Purposes of this Act, as from the Date of the Certificate of complete Registration, in such Manner as herein-before provided with regard to the Companies to be formed after the First Day of *November* next; and that any Directors or other Managers of any such Company as last aforesaid, with the Consent of at least Three Fourths in Number and Value of the Shareholders of such Company present at a General Meeting summoned for that Purpose, may at any Time or Times hereafter make any Alterations in the Constitution of the said Company or otherwise as shall be necessary for enabling such Company to come within the Provisions of this Act, so as the same shall be approved of by the said Committee of Privy Council for Trade; and the Order of such Committee, signed as aforesaid, shall be sufficient Evidence of such Provisions having been complied with, and that any such Company has come within the Provisions of this Act: Provided always, with regard to existing Companies, that in the event of any such Company becoming entitled to a Certificate of complete Registration as aforesaid it shall not be necessary to pay in respect of such Certificate any higher Fee than the Sum of Five Pounds, and also the Sum of Sixpence additional in respect of every Thousand Pounds Value of Capital, as declared on the Formation of the Company in the Deed of Settlement, or by any other special Authority.

LX. And be it enacted, That so much of the Provisions of this Act as are applicable to Companies formed after the First Day of *November* next shall apply to Companies begun or formed since the passing of this Act, so far as such Provisions shall on or after the said First Day of *November* be applicable to such last-mentioned Companies.

LXI. Provided always, and be it enacted, That, notwithstanding the Incorporation of any existing Company in pursuance of this Act, every such Company, and the Members and Officers of every such Company, shall be liable to be sued in respect of any valid Obligation incurred before such Incorporation, in the same manner with the same legal Consequences as if such Company had not been incorporated.

LXII. And be it enacted, That if at any Time during the Period of Five Years from the said First Day of *November* a Memorial be presented to the Committee of Privy Council for Trade, by or on the Part of any Company, whether now existing or hereafter formed, except Assurance Companies, making Application that any of the Conditions and Regulations prescribed by this Act be dispensed with or modified, and setting forth the special Grounds of such Application, and if such Application be registered at the Office of the Registrar of Joint Stock Companies, and if, before such Application be granted, the same be Three Times advertised, at Intervals not less than One Week, in the *London Gazette*, then from Time to Time during the said Period of Five Years, and Six Months after the Expiration thereof, it shall be lawful for the said Committee and they are hereby empowered, both as regards Companies formed before this Act shall come into operation and afterwards, either to dispense with or modify such of the Conditions of this Act required to be fulfilled by any future Company for the Purpose of obtaining a Certificate of complete Registration, and such of the Regulations by this Act made for the Government or Management of such Companies, as to the said Committee shall seem fit for facilitating the Application of this Act to the Constitution and Arrangements of any such Company, but so that nevertheless the Order or Instrument by which such Dispensations or such Modification shall be made in Writing, and be registered at the Office for registering Joint Stock Companies; and this Act shall be construed as if such Modifications or Alterations were herein contained; and further, that annually it shall be the Duty of the said Committee to cause to be laid before both Houses of Parliament a Return of all such Applications for such Dispensation or Modification, and of the Orders made on such Applications.

LXIII. Provided always, and be it enacted, That nothing in this said Act contained shall extend or be construed to extend to any Partnership formed for the working of Mines, Minerals, and Quarries of what Nature soever, on the Principle commonly called the Cost Book Principle.

LXIV. Provided always, and be it enacted, That nothing in this Act contained shall extend or be construed to extend to Partnerships in *Ireland* commonly called "Anonymous Partnerships," formed under and by virtue of an Act passed in the Parliament of *Ireland* in the Twenty-first and Twenty-second Years of the Reign of His late Majesty King *George* the Third, intituled *An Act to promote Trade and Manufactures by regulating and encouraging Partnerships.*

LXV. And forasmuch as great Injury has been inflicted upon the Public by Companies falsely pretending to be patronized or directed or managed by eminent and opulent Persons, now for the Purpose of preventing such false Pretences, be it enacted, with regard to every Company or pretended Company whatsoever, whether registered or not, and whether now existing or not, That if any Person shall make any such false Pretences, knowing the same to be false in any Advertisement or other Paper, whether printed or written, and whether published in any Newspaper, or Handbill, or Placard, or Circular, then every such Person shall forfeit for every such Offence a Sum not exceeding Ten Pounds.

LXVI. Provided always, and be it enacted, That every Judgment and every Decree or Order which shall be at any Time after the passing of this Act obtained against any Company completely registered under this

Act, except Companies incorporated by Act of Parliament or Charter, or Companies the Liability of the Members of which is restricted by virtue of any Letters Patent, in any Action, Suit, or other Proceeding prosecuted by or against such Company in any Court of Law or Equity, shall and may take effect and be enforced, and Execution thereon be issued, not only against the Property and Effects of such Company, but also, if due Diligence shall have been used to obtain Satisfaction of such Judgment, Decree, or Order, by Execution against the Property and Effects of such Company, then against the Person, Property and Effects of any Shareholder for the Time being, or any former Shareholder of such Company, in his natural or individual Capacity, until such Judgment, Decree, or Order shall be fully satisfied; provided, in the Case of Execution against any former Shareholder, that such former Shareholder was a Shareholder of such Company at the Time when the Contract or Engagement for which such Judgment, Decree, or Order may have been obtained was entered into, or became a Shareholder during the Time such Contract or Engagement was unexecuted or unsatisfied, or was a Shareholder at the Time of the Judgment, Decree, or Order being obtained; provided also, that in no Case shall Execution be issued on such Judgment, Decree, or Order against the Person, Property, or Effects, of any such former Shareholder of such Company after the Expiration of Three Years next after the Person sought to be charged shall have ceased to be a Shareholder of such Company.

LXVII. Provided always, and be it enacted, That every Person against whom, or against whose Property or Effects, Execution upon any Judgment, Decree, or Order obtained as aforesaid shall have been issued as aforesaid shall be entitled to recover against such Company all Loss, Damages, Costs, and Charges which such Person may have incurred by reason of such Execution; and that after due Diligence used to obtain Satisfaction thereof against the Property and Effects of such Company, such Person shall be entitled to Contribution for so much of such Loss, Damages, Costs, and Charges as shall remain unsatisfied, from the several other Persons against whom Execution upon such Judgment, Decree, or Order obtained against such Company, might also have been issued under the Provision in that Behalf aforesaid; and that such Contribution may be recovered from such Persons as aforesaid in like Manner as Contribution in ordinary Cases of Copartnership.

LXVIII. And be it enacted, That in the Cases provided by this Act for Execution on any Judgment, Decree, or Order, in any Action or Suit against the Company to be issued against the Person or against the Property and Effects of any Shareholder or former Shareholder of such Company, or against the Property and Effects of the Company, at the Suit of any Shareholder or former Shareholder, in satisfaction of any Monies, Damages, Costs, and Expenses paid or incurred by him as aforesaid in any Action or Suit against the Company, such Execution may be issued by Leave of the Court or of a Judge of the Court, in which such Judgment, Decree, or Order shall have been obtained, upon Motion or Summons for a Rule to show Cause, or other Motion or Summons consistent with the Practice of the Court, without any Suggestion of Scire facias in that Behalf; and that it shall be lawful for such Court or Judge to make absolute or discharge such Rule, or allow or dismiss such Motion, (as the Case may be,) and to direct the Costs of the Application to be paid by either Party or to make such other Order therein as to such Court or Judge shall seem fit; and in such Cases such Form of Writs of Execution shall be sued out of the Courts of Law and Equity respectively for giving effect to the Provision in that Behalf aforesaid as the Judges of such Courts respectively shall from Time to Time think fit to order; and the Execution of such Writs shall be enforced in like Manner as Writs of Execution are now enforced: Provided that any Order made by a Judge as aforesaid may be discharged or varied by the Court, on Application made thereto by either Party dissatisfied with such Order: Provided also, that no such Motion shall be made, nor Summons granted, for the Purpose of charging any Shareholder or former Shareholder, until Ten Days Notice thereof shall have been given to the Person sought to be charged thereby.

LXIX. And be it enacted, That all Penalties and Forfeitures inflicted or authorized to be imposed by this Act, and all Costs and Expenses for which any Person may be liable under this Act or by virtue of any Bye Law, and the Recovery of which has not been otherwise specially hereinbefore provided, shall and may be recovered, by any Person who shall proceed for the same, before any Two of Her Majesty's Justices of the Peace of the County, City, or Place where the Offender or Person liable to pay such Costs or Expenses shall reside, or where the Offence shall be committed.

LXX. Provided always, and be it enacted, That all Penalties and Forfeitures recovered under this Act, and not otherwise specially appropriated, shall be applied as follows; one Half thereof shall be paid to the Person who shall sue or proceed for the same, and the other Half to Her Majesty's Use, and shall be paid to the Sheriff of the County, City, or Town where the same shall have been imposed; and that all Convictions before Justices shall be returned to the Court of Quarter Sessions under the Provisions of an Act passed in the Third Year of the Reign of His late Majesty King *George* the Fourth, intituled *An Act for the more speedy Return and levying of Fines, Penalties, and Forfeitures, and Recognizances estreated,* and shall be paid to the Sheriff of the County, City, or Town, and shall be duly accounted for by him.

LXXI. And be it enacted, That in all Cases in which any Penalty or Forfeiture or any Costs or Expences are recoverable before Two Justices of the Peace under this Act, it shall and may be lawful for any One Justice of the Peace to whom Complaint shall be made of any such Offence to summon the Party complained of, and the Witnesses on each Side, before any Two such Justices; and at the Time and Place mentioned in such Summons, or at any Adjournment of such Summons, the said Two Justices may hear and determine the Matter of such Complaint, and upon due Proof thereof, either by Confession of the Party or by the Oath of One or more credible Witness or Witnesses, give Judgment or Sentence on such Complaint, with Costs, to be allowed by such Justices, although no Information in Writing shall have been exhibited or taken; and all such Proceedings by Summons without Information shall be as good, valid, and effectual to all Intents and Purposes as if an Information in Writing had been exhibited; and all Penalties, Forfeitures, and Costs so adjudged may be levied by Distress and Sale of the Goods and Chattels of the Party offending, by Warrant under the Hand and Seal of any One Justice; and in default of such Distress the Offender may be committed to Prison by any One Justice, by Warrant under his Hand and Seal, there to remain for any Time not exceeding Three Months, unless such Penalties, Forfeitures, and Costs shall be sooner paid.

LXXII. And be it enacted, That if any Person shall be summoned as a Witness to give Evidence before such Justices of the Peace touching any Matter which such Justices are hereby authorized to inquire into, and shall neglect or refuse to appear at the Time and Place to be for that Purpose appointed, without a reasonable Excuse for such Neglect or Refusal, to be allowed by such Justices, or appearing shall refuse to be examined on Oath and give Evidence before such Justices, then every such Person shall forfeit for every such Offence a Sum not Exceeding Five Pounds, to be levied and paid in such Manner and by such Means as are herein-before directed as to other Penalties recoverable before Justices under this Act.

LXXIII. And be it enacted, That every Proceeding for any Offence punishable on summary Conviction by virtue of this Act shall be commenced within Six Months after the Commission of the Offence, and not after.

LXXIV. And be it enacted, That if any Person shall think himself aggrieved by the Judgment of such Justices, he may, within One Month next after such Conviction, and upon giving Ten Days Notice of Appeal in Writing to the Party in whose Favour such Judgment shall have been given, stating the Nature and Grounds of Appeal, and upon entering into Recognizances with Two sufficient Sureties to the Amount and Value of such Penalty and Costs, together with such further Costs as shall be awarded in case such Judgment shall be affirmed, appeal to the next General Quarter Sessions of the Peace for the County, City, or Place where such Conviction shall have been made; and the Justices at such Sessions are hereby empowered to summon and examine Witnesses on Oath, and to hear and finally determine the Matter of such Appeal, and to award such Costs as the Court shall think reasonable to the Party in whose Favour such Appeal shall be determined.

LXXV. And be it enacted, That no Conviction or other Proceeding before Justices under this Act shall be set aside for Want of Form, nor be removed by Certiorari or otherwise into any of Her Majesty's Superior Courts of Record.

LXXVI. And be it enacted, That in any Case to which a Penalty is annexed by this Act the Whole or any Part of such Penalty may be recovered by Action of Debt in any Court now or hereafter having competent Jurisdiction, by any Person who shall sue for the same; and that in every such Action for the Recovery of such Penalty, so much of such Penalty as is sought to be recovered shall be endorsed on the Writ of Summons, and the Plaintiff shall not be entitled to recover a greater Sum than the Sum so endorsed; and if the Party suing for any such Penalty recover the same, or any Part as aforesaid, he shall be entitled to full Costs of Suit.

LXXVII. And be it enacted, That it shall not be lawful for any Person to commence or prosecute any Action, Bill, Plaint, Information, or Prosecution in any of Her Majesty's Superior Courts for the Recovery of any Penalty or Forfeiture incurred by reason of any Offence committed against this Act, unless the same be commenced or prosecuted in the Name and with the Consent of Her Majesty's Attorney General; and that if any Action, Bill, Plaint, Information, or Prosecution, or any Proceeding before any Justices as aforesaid, shall be commenced or prosecuted in the Name of any other Person than is in that Behalf before mentioned, the same shall be and are hereby declared to be null and void.

LXXVIII. And be it enacted, That with regard to every Act, Instrument, or Writing by this Act required or authorized to be done or to be made or executed by the Committee of Privy Council for Trade, that if the same purport to be so done, made, or executed by or on behalf of the said Committee, and be signed by One of the Secretaries of the said Committee, and (if it require a Seal) be sealed by the Seal of the said Committee, then it shall be deemed to be sufficiently done, made, or executed, to all Intents and Purposes.

LXXIX. And be it enacted, That it shall be the Duty of the Registrar of Joint Stock Companies to make a Report annually to the said Committee of Privy Council for Trade, setting forth:

1. A List of Companies provisionally registered during the past Year:
2. A List of Companies completely registered during the past Year:
3. A List of Cases in which Application shall have been made for the Enforcement of Penalties for Failure to register, and the Proceedings, whether by Prosecution or otherwise, taken in consequence of such Applications, and the Results of such Proceedings:

4. A List of Companies which shall have been provisionally registered, but which have not obtained complete Registration:
5. A Return of the Regulations made by the said Committee with regard to the Returns required to be made by Companies:
6. A Return of Persons appointed to the Office of Registrar of Joint Stock Companies, and other Officers and Clerks, and of their Salaries or other Remuneration, and of the Rules made for the Regulation of the said Office:
7. A Return of the Amount of all Fees paid for Certificates of provisional or complete Registration, and for every other Purpose:
8. A Return of the Scale of Fees appointed by the Commissioners of Her Majesty's Treasury for the Services to be performed by the Registrar, and of the respective Amounts of such Fees:
9. A Return of the Cases in which the Companies had failed to appoint Auditors, and of the Proceedings taken thereon:
10. A Return of Prosecutions under this Act for any Offences not herein-before specified:
11. A Return of the Number of Bankruptcies of Joint Stock Companies, and of the Amount of the Debts and Assets of such Companies respectively:
12. A Return of Modifications made by the Committee of the Privy Council for Trade, in pursuance of this Act, in the Conditions and Regulations to be observed by Companies, whether existing or future:

And that, within Six Weeks after the Meeting of Parliament next after the First Day of *January* in every Year, such Report shall be laid before both Houses of Parliament.

LXXX. And be it enacted, That this Act may be amended or repealed by any Act to be passed in this present Session of Parliament.

Part 2

THE RAILWAY MANIA

10

THE RAILWAY SHAREHOLDER'S MANUAL

Henry Tuck

Source: Henry Tuck, *The Railway Shareholder's Manual; or Practical Guide to the Railways of Great Britain* (London: Effingham Wilson, 1845), pp. iii-v, 13–14, 16, 37.

EDITORIAL HEADNOTE

The large number of railway schemes and the explosion of statistical data proved difficult for potential investors to navigate. Henry Tuck provided guidance with his *Railway Shareholder's Manual,* which first appeared in March 1845 and quickly went through multiple editions. Tuck provided basic information about individual railway companies, including the extent of their lines, share prices, amount of paid-up capital, and dividends paid. Tuck also informed inexperienced investors about the deposits required when purchasing shares and the commissions charged by brokers. But, as recent scholarship points out, Tuck was not simply a "disinterested collector of data." He was financially interested in railway promotion, and "his manuals aimed to hype the railway share market, and – as the mania developed – to defend it from its many critics."[1]

Note

1 Paul Crosthwaite, Peter Knight, Nicky Marsh, Helen Paul, James Taylor, *Invested: How Three Centuries of Stock Market Advice Reshaped Our Money, Markets, and Minds* (Chicago: University of Chicago Press, 2022), pp. 54–56.

The astonishing number of projected Railways which have recently been brought before the public, and for which the sanction of the Legislature is sought to be obtained during the present Session of Parliament, will render the year 1845 unparalleled in the history of railway enterprise. The prominence that has been given to railway affairs by the newspaper press, and by discussions in Parliament – the

DOI: 10.4324/9781003713890-12

extension of the railway system throughout Great Britain, the Continent of Europe, and North America – have convinced even the most prejudiced, that railway communication is the most rapid, safe, and economical, that human ingenuity has yet devised. This species of enterprise no longer appears to the public as chimerical, or too much in advance of the age to be worthy of serious trial, but merchants, manufacturers, wholesale dealers, traders, and farmers, are all becoming supporters of railway locomotion, and shareholders in existing or projected lines. Nor is this change in opinion to be wondered at, when it is borne in mind that superabundant capital, naturally seeks investments in those undertakings, which develope the resources of the country, give employment to labour, extend trade, and promise a large and permanent interest. It is a known fact that millions of British capital have been lost to the country by investment in Foreign Loans and South American mining operations, on which, not one farthing either of interest or principal has ever been paid. But even when the interest is duly paid, all British capital sunk in such investments seriously injures the trade of the country. A poor foreign state, has only a limited quantity of produce (over and above what is required for the maintenance of its own people) for shipment to Great Britain, and if that be sold to pay the interest on loans contracted in England, there is nothing left to give in exchange for British manufactures; so that exactly in proportion, to the capital sent out of the country in loans to a foreign state, does our trade with that state narrow and contract. But in the construction of English railways, every shilling expended is a national advantage. Not only does no capital leave the country, but no money is locked up or sunk, as many foolish speakers and writers have asserted. At the worst it is only a transfer of capital that can be complained of; but that is not a national evil, for Lord Bacon[1] said truly, that "money was like muck, and did no good till it was spread." Seeing the large amount of capital required to construct the projected railways, many persons have said where is all the money to come from; but these and double the number, could be made with the greatest ease, without the least addition to the circulating medium of the country. When a Railway Act is obtained, the money is not all wanted immediately, and therefore a surplus capital of a few millions would suffice to intersect all Great Britain with railways, and to supersede every common road. A manufacturer, for instance, holds fifty shares in a new railway, and pays a call of £2 per share at intervals of three months. When the call is paid up by all the shareholders, the Directors disburse the amount for labour and construction, which is again expended by the labourers, for food and raiment, with the shopkeeper, who is thereby enabled to hand back the amount in payment to the manufacturer, probably in time for the next call; and thus it goes on till the entire line is completed, during which operation not one shilling of capital is abstracted or lost to the country.

That same idea may be formed of the immense stimulus the trade of the country would derive from the formation of these public works, it is only necessary to state, that were 2,000 miles of the projected railways to be constructed, it would give employment to *Five hundred thousand labourers* and *Forty thousand horses* for the next four years. The necessary buildings, sheds, and permanent way would cover *Twenty thousand acres of land*; and to lay a double line of rails would require *Four hundred thousand tons of iron.*

To give confidence to the numerous new holders of railway shares, in lines open for traffic, in progress, or projected, the following pages have been compiled, which furnish the necessary data to show that no temporary depression of shares have any effect in injuring the permanent prosperity of lines traversing populous districts of the kingdom; and although the great trunk lines have preoccupied the central portions of the country, yet by the diminution in the sums paid for land and compensation – by increased experience and improved methods of working – by the adoption of single lines of rail – and less expensive ornamental construction, it is fair to infer that many branch and connecting lines will prove very profitable undertakings. To all interested in railways, it is hoped this little Manual will be found useful.

Instructions to Shareholders:

Railways can borrow one-third of their capital at interest, on mortgage bonds, secured by the works, tolls, and traffic, but in no other way; and when paid off, it is by priority of date. The late Act has, however, legalized all *pending* contracts by loan notes, and admits of their renewal.

All proxy powers, to vote at general or special meetings, must be on a two-and-sixpenny stamp.

When Shares are allotted by a Railway Company, the deposit is paid, and the Parliamentary deed signed, by the party to whom the shares are allotted. Scrip is issued in exchange for the deposit-receipt, and becomes marketable till called in after the Act is obtained, when the holder becomes the registered Proprietor, and certificates are delivered to him. If the holder of the Scrip fails to register it at the time required, the signer of the deed is registered in the books of the Company, made liable as a partner, and can only be released from the obligation by a sale of the Shares so registered. If an Act be not obtained, the unexpended part of the deposit is paid back, and the partnership ceases.

Five per cent. only, instead of 10 per cent. deposit, is now required by the Standing Orders of the House of Commons, to be paid in money or Exchequer Bills, on all projected Railways, but no less than three-fourths of the subscribers must pay their deposit.

Rates of Commission Charged by London Brokers for Buying and Selling Shares:

Shares of 5*l.* and under 20*l.* value, 2s. 6d. per Share.
Ditto, of 20*l.* and under 50*l.* value, 5s. 0d. per Share.
Ditto, of 50*l.* and upwards, 10s. per cent. on the cost of the Shares.

When Shares are sold the money should be paid the vendor on the day the Broker receives the transfer deed.

When Shares are bought that require a stamped transfer, the money should be lodged with the Broker at the middle or end of the month, in time for settling day.

The Broker cannot always say when the Shares will be ready, as he may have to send the transfer into the country to be signed, and delay occurs over which he has no control.

The Stock Exchange allows fourteen days for a seller to deliver his Shares.

There are two settling days in each month, one in the middle, the other at the end.

When Shares are sold, and the money reinvested, in some other stock at once, it is not usual to charge a commission on both transactions. . . .

GREAT WESTERN RAILWAY

Length 118 miles 20 chains. 27 Passenger and Goods Stations. Terminates at Paddington, London, and at Temple Mead, Bristol; in junction with the Bristol and Exeter Railway. Passes through the counties of Middlesex, Bucks, Berks, Wilts, and Somerset. Has a branch to Oxford of 11 miles in length. Gauge of way 7 feet; ruling gradients 1 in 100; rise in feet per mile 52. Royal Assent given to Bill, 31st August, 1834. Partially opened, 31st May, 1838; opened throughout, 30th June, 1841. Branch to Oxford, opened 14th June, 1844. Half-yearly Meetings, February, in London; August, in Bristol. Cost per mile, 56,372*l.* Average time of performing the journey, including stoppages, 4 hours 30 minutes. Fares from London to Bristol, First Class 30s., Second Class 21s., Third Class 9s. 11d.

Capital Account

25,000 Shares, 100*l.* each; 80*l.* Paid. Whole Shares.
28,000 Shares, 50*l.* each; 50*l.* Paid. Half Shares.
*37,500 Shares, 20*l.* each; 12*l.* Paid. Fifth Shares.

Total sum authorized to be raised by Shares,	4,650,000*l.*
Ditto ditto by loan or mortgage	3,679,343*l.*
Total sum expended to December, 1844.	7,455,689*l.*

*On 6,550 of these shares only 4*l.* is paid.

Cost of Working and Earnings

Total earnings for the six months, ending December, 1844	440,046*l.*
Cost of working for the same period	143,279*l.*
Last half-yearly dividend, per share, 4*l.*; (per cent., per annum, 8*l.*)	

This Company are proprietors of the Cheltenham and Great Western Railway, and have a lease of the Bristol and Exeter line, 4 years of which is unexpired.

Table

Shewing the price of Great Western Railway Shares on 1st January and 1st July in each of the following Years.

Amount of Share	*Amount Paid up*	*Years*	*Period*	*Price*
100	65	1839	January	78
			July	72
100	65	1840	January	60
			July	107
100	65	1841	January	90
			July	93
100	65	1842	January	85
			July	87
100	65	1843	January	90
			July	90
100	65	1844	January	99
	75		July	125
100	80	1845	January	155

YORK AND NORTH MIDLAND RAILWAY

Length 23 miles 11 chains 5 Passenger and Goods Stations. Terminates in junction with Great North of England Railway at York, and in junction with North Midland Railway, 7 miles from Leeds. Passes through the county of York. Gauge of way 4 feet 8 ½ inches; ruling gradients 1 in 484; rise in feet per mile, 10. Royal Assent given to Bill, 21st June, 1836. Partially opened, 29th May, 1839; opened throughout, 30th June, 1840. Half-yearly Meetings, January and July, at York. Cost per mile, 23,960*l.* Average time of performing the journey, from London to York, including stoppages, 10 hours 30 minutes. Fares from London to York, First Class 59s. 6d., Second Class 41s.

Capital Account

6,700 Shares, 50*l.* each; 50*l.* Paid. Whole Shares.
6,700 Shares, 25*l.* each; 25*l.* Paid. Half Shares
10,400 Shares, 25*l.* each; 10*l.* paid. Scarborough Branch.

Total sum authorized to be raised by Shares	1,062,500*l.*
Ditto ditto by loan or mortgage	167,500*l.*
Total sum expended to December, 1844 . . .	1,107,146*l.*

Cost of Working and Earnings

Total earnings for the six months ending Decr.,	1844
(including Leeds and Selby)	75,474*l.*
Cost of working for the same period (ditto)	35,825*l.*

Last half-yearly dividend, per share, 2*l.* 10s. 0d.; (per cent., per annum, 10*l.*)

This Company, by an Act of Parliament passed May, 1844, purchased the Leeds and Selby Railway, and by another Act, are constructing a branch line to Scarborough, 48 miles in length, and have purchased the Whitby and Pickering Railway.

Table

Shewing the Price of North Midland Railway Shares on the 1st January and 1st July in each of the following Years.

Amount of Share	*Amount Paid up*	*Year*	*Period*	*Price*
50	20	1839	January	20
50	30		July	30
50	50	1840	January	40
50	50		July	73
50	50	1841	January	68
50	50		July	70
50	50	1842	January	90
50	50		July	90
50	50	1843	January	94
50	50		July	98
50	50	1844	January	120
50	50		July	106
50	50	1845	January	105

Editorial Endnote

1 Francis Bacon (1561–1626) English philosopher and statesman.

11

A LUCKY SPECULATOR; JEAMES'S DIARY

W.M. Thackeray

Source: W.M. Thackeray, 'A Lucky Speculator' and 'Jeames's Diary,' *Punch* 9 (1845), pp. 59, 207–8.

EDITORIAL HEADNOTE

These short, comic pieces, written in Cockney dialect, are part of a series from *Punch* magazine about a London footman's adventures as a railway speculator. They were later collected as "The Diary and Letters of C. Jeames de la Pluche." The Jeames stories play with the notion that sudden fortunes could be made and lost on the stock exchange. The protagonist is a domestic servant whose lucky investment in railway shares transforms him overnight into a wealthy man. His attempts to acquire gentlemanly polish and enter society give Thackeray ample scope to employ his comic gifts. Like much of Thackeray's work, the story satirizes a society obsessed with money and status. Thackeray had lost most of his inheritance in the Indian bank failures of the 1830s, which probably shaped his cynical view of financial matters.

William Makepeace Thackeray (1811–1863) was one of the great novelists of Victorian England. He was born in India, the son of a colonial official, and educated at Charterhouse and Trinity College, Cambridge. Thackeray studied law and worked as an artist and journalist before pursuing a career as a writer from the 1830s on. In addition to his celebrated novels, such as *Vanity Fair* (1848) and *Henry Esmond* (1852), Thackeray wrote many comic stories for popular periodicals like *Fraser's Magazine, Cornhill Magazine*, which he briefly edited, and *Punch*.

Punch, the humorous weekly, founded in 1841, quickly became the most popular Victorian comic periodical. Its longtime editor, Mark Lemon, established the magazine's successful format of cartoons, satirical poems, and short comic pieces.[1]

DOI: 10.4324/9781003713890-13

Note

1 "Thackeray, William Makepeace," in Ian Ousby, ed., *The Cambridge Guide to Literature in English* (Cambridge: Cambridge University Press, 1993), pp. 934–35, and John Sutherland, "*Punch*" and "Thackeray, William Makepeace," *The Stanford Guide to Victorian Fiction* (Stanford: Stanford University Press, 1989), pp. 515, 623–25.

"A LUCKY SPECULATOR"

Considerable sensation has been excited in the upper and lower circles in the West End by a startling piece of good fortune which has befallen James Plush, Esq., lately footman in a respected family in Berkeley Square.

One day last week, Mr. James waited upon his master, who is a banker in the City; and after a little blushing and hesitation, said he had saved a little money in service, was anxious to retire, and to invest his savings to advantage.

His master (we believe we may mention, without offending delicacy, the well-known name of Sir George Flimsy, of the House of Flimsy, Diddler, and Flash) smilingly asked Mr. James what was the amount of his savings, wondering considerably how, out of an income of thirty guineas – the main part of which he spent on bouquets, silk stockings, and perfumery – Mr. Plush could have managed to lay by anything.

Mr. Plush, with much hesitation, said he had been *speculating in railroads,* and stated his winnings to have been thirty thousand pounds. He had commenced his speculations with twenty, borrowed from a fellow-servant. He had dated his letters from the house in Berkeley Square, and humbly begged pardon of his master for not having instructed the Railway Secretaries who answered his applications to apply to the area-bell.

Sir George, who was at breakfast, instantly rose, and shook Mr. P. by the hand; Lady Flimsy begged him to be seated, and partake of the breakfast which he had laid on the table; and has subsequently invited him to her grand *déjeuner* at Richmond where it was observed that Miss Emily Flimsy, her beautiful and accomplished seventh daughter, paid the lucky gentleman *marked attention.*

We hear it stated that Mr. P. is of a very ancient family (Hugo de la Pluche came over with the Conqueror); and the new Brougham which he has started, bears the ancient coat of his race.

He has taken apartments at the Albany, and is a director of thirty-three railroads. He purposes to stand for Parliament at the next general election on decidedly conservative principles, which have always been the politics of his family.

Report says that, even in his humble capacity, Miss Emily Flimsy had remarked his high demeanour. Well, "none but the brave," say we, "deserve the fair." – *Morning Paper*.

This announcement will explain the following lines, which have been put into our box with a West-End post-mark. If, as we believe, they are written by the young woman from whom the Millionaire borrowed the sum on which he raised his fortune, what heart will not melt with sympathy at her tale, and pity the sorrows which she expresses in such artless language?

If it be not too late; if wealth have not rendered its possessor callous; if poor Maryanne *be still alive*; we trust, we trust, Mr. Plush will do her justice.

Jeames of Buckley Square
    A Heligy
Come all ye gents vot cleans the plate,
    Come all ye ladies'-maids so fair –

Vile I a story vil relate
    Of cruel Jeames of Buckley Square.
A tighter lad, it is confest,
    Neer valked vith powder in his air,
Or vore a nosegay in his breast,
    Than andsum Jeames of Buckley Square.

O Evns! It vas the best of sights,
    Behind his Master's coach and pair,
To see our Jeames in red plush tights,
    A driving hoff from Buckley Square.
He vel became his hagwiletts,
    He cocked his at with *such* a hair;
His calves and viskers *vas* such pets,
    That hall loved Jeames of Buckley Square.

He pleased the hup-stairs folks as vell,
    And O! I vithered vith despair,
Misses *vould* ring the parler bell,
    And call up Jeames in Buckley Square.
Both beer and sperrits he abhord,
    (Sperrits and beer I can't a bear),
You would have thought he vas a lord
    Down in our All in Buckley Square.

Last year, he visper'd, "Mary Hann,
    Ven I've an under'd pound to spare,
To take a public is my plan,
    And leave this hojous Buckley Square."
O how my gentle heart did bound,
    To think that I his name should bear,

"Dear Jeames," says I, "I've twenty pound,"
    And gev them him in Buckley Square.

Our master vas a City gent,
    His name's in railroads everywhere;
And lord, vot lots of letters vent
    Betwigst his brokers and Buckley Square!
My Jeames it was the letters took,
    And read 'em all, (I think it's fair),
And took a leaf from Master's book,
    As *hothers* do in Buckley Square.

Encouraged with my twenty pound,
    Of which poor *I* was unaware,
He wrote the Companies all round,
    And signed hisself from Buckley Square.
And how John Porter used to grin,
    As day by day, share after share,
Came railvay letters pouring in,
    "J. Plush, Esquire, in Buckley Square."

Our servants' All was in a rage –
    Scrip, stock, curves, gradients, bull and bear,
Vith butler, coachman, groom and page,
    Vas all the talk in Buckley Square.
But O! imagine vat I felt
    Last Vensday veek as ever were;
I gits a letter, which I spelt
    "Mis M.A. Hoggins, Buckley Square."

He sent me back my money true –
    He sent me back my lock of air,
And said, "My dear, I bid ajew
    To Mary Hann and Buckley Square.
Think not to marry, foolish Hann,
    With people who your betters are;
James Plush is now a gentleman,
    And you – a cook in Buckley Square.

"I've thirty thousand guineas won,
    In six short months by genus rare;
You little thought what Jeames was on,
    Poor Mary Hann, in Buckley Square.

I've thirty thousand guineas net,
Powder and plush I scorn to vear;
And so, Miss Mary Hann, forget
For hever Jeames, of Buckley Square."

The rest of the MS. is illegible, being literally washed away in a flood of tears.

"JEAMES'S DIARY"

One day in the panic week, our friend Jeames called at our Office, evidently in great perturbation of mind and disorder of dress. He had no flower in his button-hole; his yellow kid gloves were certainly two days old. He had not above three of the ten chains he usually sports, and his great coarse knotty-knuckled old hands were deprived of some dozen of the rubies, emeralds, and other cameos with which, since his elevation to fortune, the poor fellow has thought fit to adorn himself.

"How's scrip? Mr. Jeames," said we pleasantly, greeting our esteemed contributor.

"Scrip be ________," replied he, with an expression we cannot repeat, and a look of agony it is impossible to describe in print, and walked about the parlour whistling, humming, rattling his keys and coppers, and showing other signs of agitation. At last, "*Mr. Punch*," says he, after a moment's hesitation, "I wish to speak to you on a pint of businiss. I wish to be paid for my contribewtions to your paper. Suckmstances is haltered with me. I – I – in a word, *can* you lend me___£ for the account?"

He named the sum. It was one so great that we don't care to mention it here; but on receiving a cheque for the amount (on Messrs. Pump and Aldgate, bankers), tears came into the honest fellow's eyes. He squeezed our hand until he nearly wrung it off, and, shouting to a cab, he plunged into it at our office-door, and was off to the City.

Returning to our study, we found he had left on our table an open pocket-book; of the contents of which (for the sake of safety) we took an inventory. It contained: – three tavern-bills, paid; a tailor's ditto, unsettled; forty-nine allotments in different companies, twenty-six thousand seven hundred shares in all, of which the market value we take, on the average, to be ¼ discount; and an old bit of paper tied with a pink riband a lock of chestnut hair, with the initials M.A.H.

In the diary of the pocket-book was a Journal, jotted down by the proprietor from time to time. At first the entries are insignificant; as, for instance: – "*3rd January* – our beer in the Suvnts' Hall so *precious* small at this Christmas time that I reely *muss* give warning, & wood, but for my dear Mary Hann. *February 7* – That boot Screw, the Butler, wanted to kiss her, my dear Mary Hann boxt his hold hears, & served him right. I *datest* Screw" – and so forth. Then the diary relates to Stock Exchange operations, until we come to the time when, having achieved his successes, Mr. James quitted Berkeley Square and his livery, and began his life as a speculator and a gentleman upon town. It is from the latter part of his diary that we make the following

Extrax.

"Wen I anounced in the Servnts All my axeshn of forting, and that by the exasize of my own talince and ingianiuty I had reerlized a sum of 20,000lb. (it was only 5, but what's the use of a mann depreshiating the quality of his own mackyrel?) Wen I enounced my abrup intention to cut – you should have sean the sensation among hall the people! Cook wanted to know whether I woodn like a sweatbred, or the slice of the brest of a Cold Turkey. Screw, the butlet, (womb I always detested as a hinsalant hover-baring beest) begged me to walk into the *Hupper* Servnts All, and try a glass of Shuperior Shatto Margo. Heven Visp, the coachmin, eld out his and, & said, "Jeames, I hopes theres no quarraling betwigst you and me, and I'll stand a pot of beer with pleasure."

"The sickofnts! – that wery Cook had split on me to the Housekeeper only last week (catchin me prigging some cold tuttle soop, of which I'm remarkable fond). Has for the Butler, I always *ebomminated* him for his precious snears and imperence to all us Gents who woar livry, (he never would sit in our parlour, fasooth, nor drink out of our mugs); and in regard to Visp – why, it was only the day before the wulgar beest hoffered to fite me, and thretnd to give me a good iding if I refused. "Gentlemen and ladies," says I, as haughty as may be, "there's nothink that I want for that I can't go for to buy with my hown money, and take at my lodgins in Halbany, letter Hex; if I'm 'ungry I've no need to refresh myself in the *kitching*." And, so saying, I took a dignified ajew of these minnial domestics; and ascending to my epartment in the 4 pair back, brushed the powder out of my air, and, taking hoff those hojous livries for hever, put on a new soot, made for me by Cullin, of St. Jeames Street, and which fitted my manly figger as tight as whacks.

There was *one* pusson in the house with womb I was raything anxious to evoid a persnal leave-taking – Mary Hann Oggins, I mean – for my art is natural tender, and I can't abide seeing a pore gal in pane. I'd given her previous the infamation of my departure – doing the ansome thing by her at the same time – paying her back 20 lb., which she'd lent me 6 months before: and paying her back not ony the interest, but I gave her an andsome pair of scissors and a silver thimbil, by way of boanus. "Mary Hann," says I, "suckimstancies has haltered our rellatif positions in life. I quit the Servnts' Hall for hever, (for has for your marrying a person in my rank, that my dear is hall gammin), and so I wish you a good-by, my good gal, and if you want to better yourself, halways refer to me."

Mary Hann didn't hanser my speech (which I think was remarkable kind), but looked at me in the face quite wild like, and bust into something betwigst a laugh & cry, and fell down with her ed on the kitching dresser, where she lay until her young Missis rang the dressing-room bell. Would you bleave it? She left the thimbil & things, & my check for 20 lb. 10s. on the tabil, when she went to hanser the bell? And now I heard her sobbing and vimpering in her own room nex but one to mine, with the dore open, peraps expecting I should come in and say good-by. But, as soon as I was dressed, I cut down stairs, hony desiring Frederick, my fellow-servunt, to fetch me a cabb, requesting permission to take leaf of my lady & the family before my departure.

How Miss Hemly did hogle me to be sure! Her ladyship told me what a sweet gal she was – hamiable, fond of poetry, plays the gitter. Then she hasked me if I liked blond bewties and haubin hair. Haubin, indeed! I don't like carrits! as it must be confest Miss Hemly's his – and has for a *blond buty* she as pink I's like a Halbino, and her face looks as if it were dipt in a brann mash. How she squeeged my & as she went away!

Mary Hann now *has* haubin air, and a complexion like roses and hivory, and I's as blew as Evin.

I gev Frederick two and six for fetchin the cabb – been resolved to hact the gentleman in hall things. How he stared!

25th. – I am now the director of forty-seven hadvantageous lines, and have past hall day in the Citty. Although I've hate or nine new soots of close, and Mr. Cullin fitts me heligant, yet I fansy they hall reckonise me. Conshus wispers to me – "Jeams, you'r hony a footman in disguise hafter all."

28th. – Been to the Hopra. Music tol lol. That Lablash is a wopper at singing. I coodn make out why some people called out "Bravo," some "Bravar," and some "Bravee." "Bravee, Lablash," says I, at which hevery body laft.

I'm in my new stall. I've add new cushings put in, and my harms in goold on the back. I'm dressed hall in black excep a gold waistcoat and dimind studs in the embroidered busom of my shameese. I wear a Camallia Jiponiky in my button ole, and have a double-barreld opera glas, so big, that I make Timmins, my second man, bring it in the other cabb.

What an igstrony exabishn that Pawdy Carter is! If those four gals are faries, Tellioni is sutnly the fairy Queend. She can do all that they can do, and somethink they can't. There's an indiscrible grace about her, and Carlotty, my sweet Carlotty, she sets my art in flams.

Ow that Miss Hemly was noddin and winkin at me out of their box on the fourth tear!

What linx i's she must av. As if I could mount up there!

P.S. – Talking of *mounting hup!* The St. Helena's walked up 4 per cent this very day.

2nd July. – Rode my bay oss Desperation in the park. There was me, Lord George Ringwood (Lord Cinqbar's son), Lord Ballybunnion, Honorable Capting Trap, & sevral young swells. Sir John's carridge there in coarse. Miss Hemly lets fall her booky as I pass, and I'm obleged to get hoff and pick it hup, & get splashed up to the his. The getting on hoss back agin is halways the juice & hall. Just as I was hon, Desperation begins a-porring the hair with his 4 feet, and sinks down so on his anches, that I'm blest if I didn't slip off agin over his tail; at which Ballybunnion & the other chaps rord with lafter.

As Bally has istates in Queen's County, I've put him on the St. Helena direction. We call it the "Great St. Helena Napoleon Junction, from Jamestown to Longwood." The French are taking it hup heagerly.

6th July. – Dined to-day at the London Tavin with one of the Welsh bords of Direction I'm hon. The Cwrwmwrw & Plmwyddlywm, with tunnils through Snowding & Plinlimming.

Great nashnallity of coarse. Ap Shinkin in the chair, Ap Llwydd in the vice; Welsh mutton for dinner; Welsh iron knives & forks; Welsh rabbit after dinner; and a Welsh harper, be hanged to him; he went strummint on his hojous hinstrument, and played a toon piguliarly disagreeable to me.

It was *Pore Mary Hann.* The clarrit holmost choaked me as I tried it, and I very nearly wep myself as I thought of her bewtifle bue i's. Why *ham* I always thinkin about that gal? Sasiaty is sasiaty, it's lors is irresistable. Has a man of rank I can't marry a serving-made. What would Cinqbar and Ballybunnion say?

P.S. – I don't like the way that Cinqbars has of borrowing money, & halways making me pay the bill. Seven pound six at the Shipp, Grinnidge, which I don't grudge it, for Derbyshire's brown Ock is the best in Urup; nine pound three at the Trafflygar, and seventeen pound sixteen & nine at the Star and Garter, Richmond, with the Countess St. Emilion & the Baroness Frontignac. Not one word of French could I speak, and in consquince had nothink to do but to make myself halmost sick with heating hices and desert, while the hothers were chattering & parlyvooing.

Ha! I remember going to Grinnidge once with Mary Hann, when we were more happy (after a walk in the park, where we ad one gingy-beer betwigst us,) more appy with tea and a simple srimp than with hall this splender!

12

THE RAILWAY QUEEN

[John Sheehan]

Source: [John Sheehan], "The Railway Queen, by the Irish Whiskey Drinker," *Bentley's Miscellany* 18 (July 1845), pp. 386–91.

EDITORIAL HEADNOTE

During the 1840s, many observers noted that all classes of society were drawn in by the Railway Mania and that even women were not immune from the thrill of financial speculation. Like much of this commentary, the comic story "The Railway Queen" mocks those women who read the financial press and gambled in railway shares. Many Victorians were especially offended by women avidly pursuing gain on the stock market, as this was an affront to the greater modesty and spirituality expected of women.[1]

"Irish Whiskey Drinker" was a pseudonym frequently used by the Irish writer John Sheehan (1809–1882), the son of a prosperous farmer from County Kildare. Sheehan attended Clongowes Wood College, where he wrote articles for a radical student newspaper *The Comet*, which mocked the Irish establishment. Briefly imprisoned for libel, Sheehan afterwards moved to London. He worked as a journalist and editor and contributed comic articles to magazines.[2]

Bentley's Miscellany was an English literary magazine founded by Richard Bentley in 1836. Charles Dickens was the first editor, followed by William Ainsworth in 1839. Ainsworth managed the magazine until 1868, when it merged with *Temple Bar*.

Notes

1 George Robb, "Ladies of the Ticker: Women, Investment, and Fraud in England and America, 1850–1930," in Nancy Henry and Cannon Schmitt, eds., *Victorian Investments: New Perspectives on Finance and Culture* (Indiana University Press, 2009), pp. 131–34.

2 D.J. O'Donoghue, "Sheehan, John," *Oxford Dictionary of National Biography*, eds.

DOI: 10.4324/9781003713890-14

"Have you got any Spitzbergen and Patagonia?"
"I am sorry to say that I have."
"Why so? – they are at two premium."
"But I bought them at three-and-a-half."
"Don't be afraid: hold on."
"Hold on! I can't help myself. There is actually no business doing in them."
"The surest sign that they are to have a sudden and tremendous rise."
"When?"
"At the proper time. Hold on!"

This hint was given to me by a woman – one of consideration, – with a look and tone that would indicate a knowledge of things behind the curtain. I hope that she knows a move or two in the chequered game: if not, as far as I am concerned, it will not be of much consequence. I shall pay for my lesson; and that's all. Small men ought to stick to their trade of basket-making. And I shall profit by my lesson, you may depend on it. "Une fois philosophe; deux fois joueur determiné."[1]

Perhaps the men think they have the game all to themselves; that they alone are railway mad. If they do, they are grievously mistaken. What is it that makes London by far less dull just now than it usually is during the autumn? Numbers of the *beau sexe* have remained behind to look after the main point, for emphatically is railroad speculation considered the main point amongst, I am sorry to say, too many of them at this moment. Paris, for the same reason, has been scarcely more gay at any season of the year than the present. A certain fashionable and fascinating marchioness (an Englishwoman too), a resident of the gay capital of delights, won twenty-five thousand pounds there a few weeks back in one *belle* swoop. You would like to know how she did it. A brilliant company were assembled at the hotel of a Russian nobleman in the Faubourg St. Honoré; and between one of the pauses of the *danse*, a distinguished singer of the opera was entertaining the guests with a favorite air from "Norma," – it might be from "Il Barbiere" or "Don Giovanni," – or it might not. All was breathless attention, and intense delight. No! not all. The young and lovely Marchioness of________ occupied a *fauteuil* in a corner of the *salon.* The air was beautiful:

She heard it, but she heeded not – her eyes
Were with her heart, and that was far away,

Very far away – in the share-market! for even into such a gentle bosom, and amidst such a scene, the ruling passion of the age, – call it avarice, gambling, what you will, – could enter and assert its empire.

"I have got a better song for your Ladyship than even Mario's song," said a young and gallant cavalier, approaching her softly, seating himself on an unoccupied couch beside her.

"What is it?" said the Marchioness hastily.

"Within the last hour the King has expressed to the minister his approval of the Great Northern Line. Hush! Don't speak or appear agitated; we may be observed."

"Was R_______ there?"[2]

"Yes! – closeted for two hours with you know whom: and he left the palace about a minute or two before me with a joy in his face that I shall never forget. It spoke millions. You must see him to-morrow early; for the news will be over the town before the evening, and the applications will be innumerable."

"To-morrow! – to-night!" And in a few moments, her Ladyship's carriage having been ordered, she left for the house of the great financier.

It was in vain that porter and portress, valet and butler, major-domo and secretary, opposed the *entrée* of the fair besieger. Stop a woman, indeed, when she *will* go a-head! – stop a house on fire with a single bucket of water! She made her way to the sanctum sanctorum – the bureau of bureaux. It was not her first time. Plutus was not petrified: he knew the goddess well. He knew, too, that she must be obeyed; so, to save time, every moment of which was worth a diamond to him that night, he obeyed the commands of his fair tyrant. She arranged for a pretty considerable transaction, and departed to sleep happily on her pillow.

From the titled dame to the actress, even to the grisette, all the women are playing the railroad game in Paris. In London, if things are not going on *pari passu*, at the same mail-train pace, amongst the female speculators, they are going on fast enough, Heaven knows! considering the curves and inclines.

I called on a lady in St. John's Wood the other day. She was reading a morning newspaper. "Nothing in that, certainly," you'll say; but wait till you hear what part of it she was reading. Not the deaths, births, and marriages; not the court-circular; not the fashions of the month; not the column of advertisements, in which broken-hearted lovers address each other in monosyllables, and romantic runaways are told to come home directly to indignant and respectable fathers and virtuous and disconsolate mothers; nor was she diving into the delicate columns of law and police reports; nor discussing the moralities of the quacks; nor laughing at the quotations from *Punch*; no, not on any of these features of the daily romance of the world was my lady's attention fixed; but on the city article and the railway share list!!! Upon my conscience I'm not joking; and to make matters worse, she is one of the finest young women in England, although nearer to thirty than five-and-twenty. She has refused scores of good offers, fancying that her accumulating fortune will secure her some old marquis or duke at last.

"Namur and Liége – what's the news – Louvaine and Jemappe – how are they?" said she to me, the other day, as I called upon her towards the afternoon, and all this in the same breath as her "How d'you do?"

"Namur and Liége – Love and Jem!" exclaimed I in broken accents, and looking as stumped as a bee in a fallow.

"Do you know nothing about them?" said she sharply.

"Why, nothing particularly," I answered, "but that they are respectable places enough with regard to the picturesque and the population."

"No, no, that's not what I want to know, – how are the Belgians?" said she with a fidgety laugh that I did not relish.

"Is it how are the Belgians?" I inquired.

"Yes."

"Oh, bravely; *horum omnium fortissimi sunt Belgae,*"[3] said I, plucking up, "which means –"

"Nonsense," said Arabella; and she read the share list in the *Globe*, indulging in a running comment as she went along – "Direct Manchester – capital! South Midland – up again! Cambridge and Oxford – oh confound them! London and York – oh that abominable Hudson! London, Manchester, the Potteries and London – a good idea that about cheap crockery – three and a half premium – bravissimo! Northampton, Banbury, and – still going up – more sugar on the Banbury cakes – how nice! And let me see, here's another new line just out to connect the eastern and western coasts – what do they want to connect the coasts for, I wonder? But that's not my affair. Everybody and everything will be all connected together soon. I must write to Moonshine and Crash to purchase a hundred of the Cut-ahead-right-across-direct-eastern-and-westerns – one and a half premium tomorrow – two and a half next day – sell them –"

"A *cool* hundred that, Madam," I ventured to observe.

"Cool!" said she; "to be sure – in and out like a cold bath! – that's the new spirit of the age. It's only changing about the circulating medium more quickly after, all, as the nursery rhyme has it:

> Here we go up, up, up!
> Here we go down, down, down, oh!"

"And perhaps," I observed, "too many will have to chime in with:

> Directors, and brokers, and scrip,
> We're all done brown, brown, brown, oh!"

"Oh, not at all – none are to be done but the green. Are you not doing something in the railroad world yourself, Mr. O'Shaughnessy?" inquired the lovely speculatrix.

I answered, "A little."

"In foreign railroads?"

"No, thank you – I don't like spending one's capital out of the country." (I did not even whisper a word about the Spitzbergen and Patagonia.)

"But you get it back again three fold and more; even I as a woman am a better political economist. You sell it at a premium –"

"Or I don't."

"Well, then, what are you doing in shares?"

"Looking on –"

"Looking on; why *women* are not content to look on now-a-days," she observed contemptuously.

"So I perceive," said I, sending back the shuttlecock in the direction from whence it came.

"If I were a man," said Arabella with emphasis, "I should be secretary to a new railroad before a fortnight. I wish I were a man."

"Indeed!" I ejaculated, rather surprised.

"Yes; and should you like to know how I would go about it?"

"The secretaryship you mean?" said I.

"The company," said she: "you must get up the company before you can be secretary. Who is going to give you such a berth unless you prove your patent of invention?"

"That may be very true."

"Buy me a map of England," said she; "or, better still, a map of Ireland."

"First, catch your hare," was not an unnatural observation on my part.

"First catch your grandmother!" (how sordid pursuits make the most refined forget themselves!) – "run your finger up and down, and across through the length and breadth of the land. Hit upon some obscure uninitiated district, as yet not cut up."

"Rather a difficult matter to find that," said I.

"By no mean," she replied; "you'll find an opening somewhere."

"Talking of running your finger up and down a map, the French monarch, wishing to find fault with Marshal Turenne, put his finger on a line that marked a river, and said, 'Why did you not cross here?' –'Because your majesty's finger was not the bridge,' answered the marshal."

"Ah, but," said Arabella, "Marshal Turenne did not live in a railroad age. Nothing is impossible to steam."

"Well, say that I have hit upon an opening, what next?"

"Point your guns."

"Point my guns?"

"Yes, and then shot them to the muzzle."

"Guns and shot – muzzles – really"

"Well, then issue your prospectuses."

"Cramming them well with promises of public advantage is what you mean by shotting the guns?" said I, getting a slight glimpse of land.

"Exactly so. I shall make something of you at last. If the district be agricultural, talk about increasing its produce and population, about running up to the cattle-show in Baker Street, with a tup, or an ox, or an ass, or a newly-invented plough, in an hour or two. If the district be a manufacturing one –"

"Say we are on the map of Ireland."

"Well, be it so. Would you cut through one of your Irish bogs? Talk of it in El Dorado terms, praise its picturesque beauty and fertility, and the vast quantity of unexplored riches in the bowels of the earth. But perhaps you are chary of railroad speculation?"

I confessed that I was not over-enthusiastic.

"Well, try something else in the national line for Ireland. Irish improvement according to English notions will be all the rage when our 'own commissioner' returns from Ireland. You have seen what he has written about Lough Erne being only four miles from the sea, and that there is no outlet to it in that direction. Why not cut a canal through, and make Enniskillen a rival to Cork? Or, better still, for it will require more money, and consequently give rise to more speculation – drain it."

"Drain it!"

"Yes. A good board of directors ought to be able to lay a plan to drain anything. Talk about Holland, the draining of the Fens, and Whittlesea Mere in your prospectus."

"I am afraid that we have had already one or two many of those sort of companies connected with Ireland," I observed. "They were *drainage* companies in reality, which drained off more than the water, – to wit, the investments of the only moneyed persons connected with the undertaking. I know one in particular, which went to work on the Irish plan of 'leap before you look.' They drained off all the water; and, instead of the rich alluvial soil which was promised beneath, and over which the golden gifts of Ceres were to flourish in future years, they found *a sandy bottom*."

"Ah! It's just the way," said she; "whenever a new thing is started, there are plenty of growlers and grumblers like you, Mr. O'Shaughnessy, to bore us with your ponderous platitudes about the ancient ways and the slow coaches. The only part of the railroads with which you sympathise are the *sleepers*."

"And, what's the odds?"

"Ten to one against your getting on, unless you purchase into the Dublin and Galway."

"At five premium – eh?"

"Well, you might do worse." . . . "for, in spite of your sneering . . . the Dublin and Galway is one of the greatest favourites in the market."

"Well, I am rejoiced to hear as much, if you, madam, have your affections centered in it," said I, resuming my gossamer, and my little bit of timber, and bidding Miss Arabella a very good afternoon.

"Good evening!" said she, waving her hand, "you'll be a dreamer all your life!"

As I went down the stairs, an odd-looking fellow with a jaunty air, and his clothes built in spread-eagle fashion, passed up, three steps at a time, humming:

"Yankee Doodle borrows cash,
    Yankee Doodle spends it,
And then he snaps his fingers at
    The jolly flat that lends it."

"Could she have been mad enough to buy Pennsylvanians?" thought I to myself. I dare say she did; for the next day the news arrived that the drab-coloured people no longer repudiated, but were going to pay: although at a long date. Yes! They at length promised to pay. Now, if I had invested amongst them, not a penny should I, or the other creditors have got, although we lived a hundred years, and as long as we liked afterwards.

Whereupon, moralizing on the uncertainty of all things here below, and the folly of most of them, I rambled into the woods and fields.

"You'll be a dreamer all your life!" said the railway queen to me. Well, I'd rather be a dreamer or a lotus-eater, – ay, a "mild-eyed melancholy lotus-eater," – and have easy days and nights of it in the wilderness of "a *dissolute* island," as Paddy called Robin Crusoe's territory, than be obliged to lay my head upon a restless pillow stuffed with tormenting arithmetic, and turbid visions floating about me of Mammon and bankruptcy. . . .

Editorial Endnotes

1 "Once a philosopher, twice a confirmed gambler."
2 Probably a reference to Jacob Rothschild (1792–1868) who headed the Paris branch of the fabled international banking house.
3 "of all these people, the Belgians are the bravest," from Julius Caesar's *Gallic Wars*.

13

THE RAILWAY PANIC

Hints to Railroad Speculators

Henry Wilson

Source: Henry Wilson, *The Railway Panic: Hints to Railroad Speculators, Together with the Influence Railroads Will Have Upon Society* (London: Henry Wilson, 1845), pp. 3–7, 11–12.

EDITORIAL HEADNOTE

Surveyor and Valuer for the Royal Exchange Land and Estate Office, Henry Wilson envisioned utopian possibilities for railways to improve commerce, diffuse knowledge, and promote a more egalitarian society. Yet he also warned the British public about the dangers involved in stock market speculation in railway shares and the corrupt practices of some promoters who had no real intention of building a railroad, but who floated a company merely to collect share deposits.[1]

Note

1 Michael Wheeler, *The Year that Shaped the Victorian Age: Lives, Loves and Letters of 1845* (Cambridge: Cambridge University Press, 2022), Chapter 2: The Railway Juggernaut.

In this age of improvements and inventions, nothing perhaps, has interested public attention more than *Railways*. These modern wonders are now making rapid strides all over the kingdom, and their rise and progress are truly wonderful. It is difficult, in a country like England, in which public opinion bears a decided sway, to discuss any measure that is likely to have a wide influence upon society, with feelings altogether unbiased, or with a tone perfectly impartial:

> "Every white will have its black,
> And every sweet its sour."

DOI: 10.4324/9781003713890-15

But I will confess that my opinion is most favorable to *Railroads;* and I am sorry to see so few scientific men amongst the names of directors and promoters of these Herculean labours. I think it needs no spirit of prophesy to foresee that all foreign powers, without exception, will follow our example. The time is not far distant, when these modes of conveyance will become general all over the world: up to the present period there are:

74 Railways completed, or in the course of completion, with capital amounting to	£ 103,166,230
Branches projected by ditto	35,000,000
707 New Companies up to this period	464,698,656
	602,864,876

This is independent of Foreign and Colonial Lines.

Although in favour of Railroads, as a great national good, I would at once denounce the Railroads of modern schemers; for I have known many instances where new projects are brought into the market, with the names of some of our first-rate merchants and aldermen to them as Directors, followed up by a firm as Bankers of the Company, of whose respectability there cannot by a question, in order to delude the public: this is done without asking their consent or approbation, – therefore it behooves those gentlemen whose names have been used as *decoy ducks* by schemers, at once to insist upon their names being withdrawn, or cause advertisements to be inserted in the daily and railway papers, stating that they have no connection whatever with such Companies. If they do not, they become parties to the fraud. I know it has become the practice amongst a few to allow their names to continue until the scheme succeeds, and then to qualify as Directors; – this, no respectable man, who has any regard for his commercial character, would consent to do. Under all circumstances, therefore, it ought to be viewed with considerable suspicion, when new Companies change their Directors or Bankers soon after their formation, until due enquiries are made to know why the change has taken place.

Those who are rushing heedlessly into the mazes of RAILWAY SPECULATIONS can hardly be aware of the full extent of the responsibilities upon which they are entering. It is no doubt a very agreeable thing to be so fortunate as to become the original holder of a large number of Shares in a Line which to day command a favourable position in the market, and may be converted into cash at a high premium. But those to whom shares are allotted should be careful to count the cost, and it may not be amiss to remind them of the fallacy of supposing, that by Jobbing their Shares off at a profit, and pocketing a pound or two, or more, per share, for premium realized on the sale, all future liability is evaded. This however is not the case. Those who, in the first instance, obtain the allotment, and subscribe the Parliamentary Contract and Subscribers' agreement, (both of which is required to be done by every Shareholder at the time when the allotment is made to him) are bound to provide the money for the completion of the line, at whatever inconvenience, and at whatever loss. No matter to whom they may have sold their shares, or how often they may have subsequently changed hands; to the original holder the strong arm of the law will come for the necessary means to carry on the work, to their great loss and inconvenience.

To the Projectors of each Line, or rather, perhaps, to its Provisional Committee, is delegated the authority to select from the numerous applicants for shares those persons who either are, or are publicly reputed to be, men of property and substance. Those persons to whom the business of selection is confided, will take care, as far as they can, that allotments will only be made to proper responsible men, it behooves, therefore, all those who embark in these undertakings, to ascertain beforehand whether it will be quite convenient to spare the amount of money which the shares they propose to take, would, when fully paid up, require of them.

Supposing even a small number of the bills coming before Parliament next Session pass, it is evident, from the extensive speculation which now prevails, that when the panic overtakes them, (which must inevitably come) it will greatly exceed the memorable epochs of 1797, 1815, and 1825 and 1826, shares will be found in the hands of parties totally unable to pay the calls upon them. In therefore, many instances, the first proprietor will find himself suddenly called upon for contributions which will involve him in irretrievable ruin. Who can be so rash as to attempt to predict, for any Line, however desirable or promising it may be in the outset, that it will steer its course safely through all the shoals and quicksands of Standing Orders, and the destructive fire of persevering opposition, arising from local causes, and interested competition? Even, however, if these difficulties be overcome, and the Act be obtained, then comes the other important point to which I have before averted, that of providing the money.

It is really wonderful how people will go out of their ordinary course to traffic in these dangerous commodities. Railway speculations, however, like all other gambling, is a fascinating, but delusive passion. Its votaries only look at the bright side of the picture – at the prospect of winning – and having made one or two lucky hits, they go on in repeating their hazards, and extending their risks, until the last unfortunate throw strips them of their all, and reduces them to a state of distress and desperation.

It is with a view to save my readers from these disastrous consequences that I must repeat my caution, "*Beware of trafficking in New Railway Shares!*" brought out by mere schemers, without a prospect of being carried out.

Every succeeding session of Parliament adds new and increasing importance to the subject; and, as yet, the attention of the public in general has never been directed to it. Indeed, with the exception of the solicitors, parliamentary agents, and other individuals, whose business it is "*to get Bills through the House,*" few persons are acquainted with the mode in which these Railroad Companies are started.

TRANSACTIONS IN RAILWAY SCRIP

The question is what course Government will take to protect the country from the direful effects of gambling in railway scrip. It is advancing like a frightful avalanche, gathering as it proceeds; – Can Government erect a barrier? – They might have done so last session: – but what is to be done now?

The Government have acted wrong – they should have decreased the deposits: instead of which they took the worst course they could take, by passing a Standing Order that all deposits on new shares should be increased from 5 to 10 per cent. This was a very wide idea for checking speculation: it resembles the case of the goldsmith, who heard that thieves were coming to break into his premises, actually heaped up bags and bars of gold against the entrance to keep out the robbers. *The public required protection, and the Government doubled the bait to greedy adventurers: from the day that deposits were increased, the schemes multiplied.* The duty of the Government was at once to have prohibited the public from subscribing to any Railway scheme that the Board of Trade had not pronounced judgement upon, *all calls should be strictly forbidden under heavy penalties, until the Board of Trade had given its decision upon the merit of the Line.*

Were this system adopted, all gambling schemes would at once disappear, and the market would once more appear in a healthy state. Useful projects, based on sound calculations for public advantage, would receive the support of safe and practical men, and would be brought at once to a successful termination.

That clever writer, Mr. Charles Dickens, has admirably portrayed, (in his description of the *City of Eden*, in *Martin Chuzzlewit*,) the disastrous consequences of this "*Go-a-Head*" system of reckless enterprise and projects without the means of carrying them into execution. The panics which have prevailed in this country ought to be a *solemn warning* against all improvident speculation, but each age refuses the warning of its predecessor.

Is not the *Railway mania* gone far beyond safe limits? That will be at once perceived, when I tell my readers that 600 Railway Companies have issued their prospectuses, and registered the shares, during the year 1845. In a great many cases no survey has even been had, or equitable calculation made as to the probable amount of capital that would be required. Just for argument sake, suppose I estimate these 600 companies at £1,000,000 each, it certainly would not exceed the truth, that would produce £600,000,000! A vast majority of the shares will be found in the hands of mere speculators and gamblers, who have *all to gain and nothing to lose.*

The Legislature says that 10 per cent. upon the total capital of every Railroad Company shall be paid into the hands of the Accountant General before any Bill can be even received in the House: if from any cause whatever, the Company should not apply for the Act, the deposit remains in the hands of the Company, to be divided or applied as the promoters or directors think proper. In my opinion, a vast majority of these Companies have no serious intention of coming before Parliament, because the scrutinizing examination of their subscription deeds would lead to their downfall: their deposits will not be ready, and their ends will be better served by procrastination.

Suppose one fourth of these schemes fulfil the conditions that Parliament requires, I cannot possibly think how £20,000,000 of money can be abstracted at any given period, out of the existing currency, without the most disastrous consequences, as the cash must be paid in notes and specie.

Will any of my readers inform me how this great financial difficulty is to be overcome. Money must become scarce as the period approaches. The London bankers having a drain upon them by their customers, will be less able to assist with discounts; therefore, when this large amount of money is required, and prices decline, the loss upon the *bubble schemes* will be truly awful: *How many thousands will think themselves too happy if they get out of all responsibility by forfeiting their deposits.*

Persons unaccustomed to the peculiar tactics of the Stock Exchange become infected with the madness: – *Officials, farmers, and shop-keepers throw away their substance for the shadow!* This makes the panic more appalling, – a *nation like England cannot gamble with impunity.* I am morally certain a re-action will come, and then the *panic* of 1846 will be the result. I would recommend all parties who have hitherto not been inoculated with this Railroad disease, *to pause and reflect,* as it has proved fatal in many cases.

Look at the columns of the daily and weekly press. Does not this exhibit the absorbing influence of the mania? Every person you meet is inquiring the state of the market, as if their very existence depended upon the success of some favorite scheme. Alas! How many thousands will be reduced to poverty. Argument is of no avail; for the gambler is quite impervious to reason – he pursues his headlong course, regardless of consequences, until in one sad hour he finds himself without friends, and pennyless. The Directors of new schemes monopolize the scrip, which they hold fast; their next operation is to send out so many *stags* into the market to inquire for shares in these bubbles, – thus excitement is produced, and the shares of many hundreds have, by these *honest* means, reached a premium.

I know from my own experience that many of the schemes at present in the market, have never had even the land surveyed; so that nothing but a false estimate of the expenses can be given to the public; but *so mad are people to obtain scrip, that hundreds become the dupes of these railway swindlers.* The spring of 1846 will see the bubble burst! This, any one who takes an unprejudiced view of the present railway mania must perceive, and the consequences will be overwhelming.

Many local stock exchanges throughout the kingdom have restricted the dealing in unregistered scrip: I would recommend its general adoption, under penalties. By such a stringent regulation, it would impose no restraint upon wholesome speculation, and a portion of the mischief produced by the madness of the day would be redressed. This would be the means of excluding irresponsible persons, mere gamblers in stock, without funds to meet their liabilities.

I trust these abuses will be remedied as they produce all the mischief. I would recommend all respectable brokers to unite in some decided measures to repress this great evil, which is becoming daily more serious. The Legislature must be appealed to early next session as the present law bears a very doubtful construction.

RISE AND PROGRESS OF RAILROADS

It may not be considered uninteresting here to trace the Rise and Progress of Railroads, those great arteries by whose instrumentality the prices of manufactures, and the agricultural produce are to be reduced, and new supplies brought into use, particularly those of which the expense of fuel forms a constituent part, increasing the demand for them, and by this method enlarge greatly the circle of *British commerce*. . . .

The railways ought to receive from Englishmen extensive patronage, as they are English inventions, and therefore this astonishing undertaking claims also an additional support, as it will not interfere with existing interests, and will eventually greatly improve the isolated railways already introduced, or about to be introduced, by connecting the several branches all over the country into the grand duct of these several commercial veins in the kingdom, and calculating minutely all the several expenses incident to them, the proprietors will be able to transport heavy goods at the rate of rather less than one farthing per ton for each mile; the addition of dues, &c., I suppose will raise this to three half-pence for coal, lime, straw, &c., and perhaps to 2d. on grain and some other articles, and 3d. on general merchandise, while now the charges are from 5d. to 8d. including toll-dues. Even on our canals, with the addition of dues, are about 3 ½ d.; and if we consider the importance of these facts, and their wonderful influence on internal trade, for how great a portion of the several articles of daily consumption consists of heavy goods, it stands to reason that will reduce the price of articles so transported, and therefore will necessarily increase trade in those branches at this moderate rate of carriage. Suppose we take coal for an example; this important article of family expense, the charge of conveying it forms the chief part of the price. Coals you may purchase at the mouth of the pit; this article is sold at the rate of 5s. to 10s. per ton, and at the distance of fourteen miles we find it costs double that sum, so that in fact the natural resources of this country lie waste, and valuable stores of coals, as well as many other mineral treasures in different parts of this country are allowed to rest in the earth, as the sum they would fetch in the market would not be sufficient to defray the expenses. And that is a very excellent and unanswerable argument in favour of railways being established all over the kingdom, – this shews at one view the advantages in pounds, shillings, and pence.

Another good effect brought about by railways is, in conjunction with other influences, a visible breaking up of that exclusiveness, – a gradual thawing of that reserve, for which the people of Great Britain are celebrated. In former times, each class of persons had their modes of travelling. There was for the rich, the post chaise; for the country gentleman, the mail; for the tradesman, the stage coach; and for the poor, the wagon; a man's respectability was established by the mode in which he travelled. The difference between railway and stage coach travelling is nearly all the difference between civilization and barbarism. The railways will, ultimately, reverse the picture; and the rich will be brought in contact and converse with the poor, sympathies are engendered between the various classes, and manners of the higher class descend to the lower. In the year 1843, no fewer than 25 millions of passengers were conveyed 330 millions of miles. Railways are gigantic distributors of money while in operation, to say nothing of outlay, with cost of repairs, machinery, and servants.

This country has gained the start, of all others by this new mode of internal conveyance, by the assistance of the gigantic power of steam; whether we look to *Commerce* to *Agriculture* or to *Manufactures.*

The period is fast approaching when the remotest parts of this country and the continent will be brought into easy and rapid communication; and all foreign powers will follow our example in promoting this gigantic work of peace. The evils arising out of the differences of language and soil, and climate, all vanishing before the desire of mankind for commercial intercourse. The prejudices and mistaken interests which separate one district of the same nation from another, are broken down by such noble inventions as these; and the same spirit of civilization which results from that increase of our reason, which bestowed by a beneficent Providence, will eventually render all men as brethren, and children of one great Father. It will become a check to the alarming growth of cities and towns, especially in this modern Babylon in which I write; and will, there is no possible doubt, above all, spread knowledge and diffuse intelligence over towns and cities, and finally tend to "universal good."

14

THE BUBBLE OF THE AGE

Arthur Smith

Source: Arthur Smith, *The Bubble of the Age; or, The Fallacy of Railway Investment, Railway Accounts, and Railway Dividends* (London: Sherwood, Gilbert, and Piper, 1848), pp. 3–15.

EDITORIAL HEADNOTE

Little is known about Arthur Smith, though a contemporary of his claimed that he "was a young barrister, with little business." Smith, however, played a key role in stirring up investor doubts about the financial solvency of many railway schemes. In works such as *Railways as They Really Are* (1848) and *The Bubble of the Age* (1848), he suggested that most railway companies paid dividends out of capital rather than earnings, and he alerted the public about the lack of transparency in railway accounting.[1]

Note

1 Andrew Odlyzko, "The Collapse of the Railway Mania, the Development of Capital Markets, and Robert Lucas Nash, a Forgotten Pioneer of Accounting and Financial Analysis," *Accounting History Review* 21 (2011), pp. 309–45.

The interest of Directors and Shareholders, however much may be said in theory, are not always found in practice to be identical – the former are invariably too powerful for the latter, even from a superior knowledge of detail alone; and the real state of affairs is constantly kept back, misrepresented, or made unintelligible to the generality of the public. During the past few months, for instance, we have seen a large Joint Stock Bank stop payment, in one of our wealthiest and most commercial districts; the shares had stood at high premiums; at the previous half-yearly meeting the dividends declared were large, and the representations of the Directors most encouraging; yet, to the amazement of every one, this *flourishing concern* stops payment; and on investigation, it is discovered that some half a million had been lent to one firm without security; that the shares were held to

DOI: 10.4324/9781003713890-16

a considerable extent by parties who had never paid a farthing; that the capital had been lent to persons on unavailable securities; and that discounts had been effected with some who were not regular customers, and with others whose commercial standing did not justify advances.

The country has just received intelligence of the result of the Union Bank of Calcutta; a Company under the management of leading merchants in that City, many shares being held in England; the Company had enjoyed a high repute, chiefly from the enormous premiums of the shares; but it would now appear, that the Capital had for years been squandered in keeping up the value of the shares in the market; that they had issued and distributed notes and securities equal to 1,200,000*l.* without receiving consideration; and that the representations of the Directors were wholly without foundation in truth; and a large call is now absolutely necessary to pay even the debts due by the Company.

In the Metropolis of Great Britain we find that the Company of Copper Miners of England, which for some years had stood in high repute, (the principal of the Company being, not only the Chairman of the London, Brighton, and South Coast Company, but also a Director of the Bank of England.) The dividends declared had been large, and the representations most encouraging, and yet in the midst of all this the innocent proprietary are horrified by finding the Company in difficulties, and the Bank of England applied to for assistance. The Bank commences investigation, and for the *first time*, the proprietors learn their true position; instead of the flourishing dividends, the losses in the past few years had actually reached 350,000*l.*, and it is openly stated in the public prints, that the Company had actually borrowed large sums on debentures, without legal authority, the holders having no legal remedy against the Company, and that though the Chart of the Company only authorised dealings in copper, a trade had also been carried on in iron.

The injury inflicted on the Country, both in a moral and pecuniary point of view, by these small Companies, sinks into insignificance when compared to the Railway Companies. For it is not alone whether trade shall be stagnant and commerce paralysed, but it is also a question, whether by the grossest deception, a small number of the community shall be allowed to pilfer with impunity the remainder, give garbled statements, or decline to give any explanation at all to Shareholders, set Acts of Parliament at nought, trifle with, and deceive the Legislature, and give false information and deceptive returns to Government. Since the Legislature and Government have been so much misled, can we be surprised at the manner in which the public generally, and even Shareholders themselves have been betrayed into mistaken notions of the real nature of Railway investment? No apology need then be made on presenting these pages to the public, the deep distress which now pervades the Country, should arouse the attention of every one – it affects all. Integrity is one of the great internal safe-guards of a nation: whenever the parliament, or an influential portion of the people have been corrupt, commercial and mercantile pursuits have invariably languished, and trade and all monetary transactions placed in immense danger; chicanery, repudiation, and low cunning, soon sacrifice every thing that is honorable, noble, or great, on an altar of rapacity and ruin. In 1844 and 1845, the welfare of the country was compromised by an infusion from interested sources, of unhealthy hopes of speedy fortunes, or momentary aggrandizement – gold for the time was sought after with a recklessness and hazard equalled only by abandoned gamblers; and the successes of the leading individuals, were proportioned to their abandonment of principle. As with dice, he who has loaded them knows how to win, so with Railway shares, they who concocted allotments, amalgamations, and purchases, gained; while the confiding, misinformed, or ill-advised purchasers proportionately lost. A few years have since passed, honest men see their wealth fast dwindling to nothing; while the half ignorant and half cunning find they have been impoverished to enrich some Director, who was far more knowing and subtle; men of property find their fortunes reduced, and rent and interest unpaid; merchants are failing by the hundreds, and the minor tradesmen by thousands; manufacturers can get no orders; tradesmen have either no customers or no money paid them; and mechanics have no work and no resources; and the inevitable consequences follow: – namely, political meetings and threatened outbreaks. The working man feels something has been wrong, and attributes it to bad government; and, in effect, there is little difference between measures founded on corrupt motives, and legislation based on incorrect information. For, under the authority of these Acts, money has been obtained from tens of thousands, by a specious appearance of value, premiums having been fictitiously created in the market, and other deceptions have been resorted to, which concern not the respective persons interested or injured alone, but are matters of deepest import to the whole community: crimes affecting the whole nation, and should be strictly regarded as such. If a man is robbed, and the thief is discovered, the person whose property was taken is bound over under a heavy penalty to prosecute. If a man has been induced to part with his money or property under false representations, he has a remedy. Should not the Government and Legislature institute an inquiry, and should not powers corruptly obtained be at once withdrawn, before further sums are abstracted from the unfortunate proprietors, and further injury inflicted? No later than the year 1844, when it was discovered that Railway Companies had borrowed, without any legal authority, millions on loan notes; the Government at once took steps, and it being the opinion of the Law Officers of the Crown, that the holders of these (generally believed) securities had no legal remedy whatever for the recovery of their money, either against the Companies or the Directors. The inquiry was instituted, which now forms the fifth report from the select Committee on Railways; and Mr. Gladstone lost no time in bringing in a bill legalizing the notes then issued, and prohibiting them in future; and for this act of justice Sir Robert Peel and Mr. Gladstone were denounced at Railway Meetings, (the whole subject having been misrepresented) by Directors, as having used unconstitutional means for carrying the measure, while the interference of Government was characterised as most overbearing and tyrannical. Still, no one can deny that both the inquiry and the legislative enactment was most proper and constitutional; the legislature having delegated certain powers to a corporation, surely, at all times has the power of inquiring into, and correcting any abuse of the power so granted.

The fact now so much alarming Railway investors is, they begin to find that Railways have invariably required a constant outlay greater than the dividend declared, without reference to the expenditure on the branches or extensions. Can then the distrust now so predominant in the public mind on the real nature of Railway investment be wondered at. In the year 1845, Railway Directors enjoyed the confidence of a proprietary unbounded in its liberality. In 1848, instead of implicit trust, we see nothing but doubt, fear, and suspicion. Every good citizen rejoices at the honest success of his neighbour, and the welfare of the nation; he laments the prostration of trade, and the ruin of thousands: nay more, it is his duty to examine into the causes of distress, and to endeavor to eradicate evils.

For some years we have had the most flourishing descriptions of Railway Companies, and certainly, if one or two accounts are cursorily looked over, the impression left is most gratifying and encouraging; in many Companies, the dividends declared are large; in others, if the dividends are not large, it is confidently stated, that at no distant period they will be increased, and if a diminution of the dividend is recommended, the proprietary is congratulated on having so large a sum placed to a reserve fund. Unfortunately it is only by a careful retrospect of the general affairs and accounts of a Company that a correct opinion can be formed, and all must admit, that the almost unintelligible manner in which the accounts have been kept has proved most injurious; for an attentive and careful analysis of a series of the accounts, forms either a direct contradiction to the statements and predictions which have been from time to time put forth in Reports and Speeches, or clearly proved that Railways are only to be worked by a constant outlay of capital greater than the dividends declared, and that has been the case ever since the introduction of locomotive power.

Not more than two years have elapsed since an investment in London and Birmingham shares, or in the Shares of either of the amalgamated Companies now forming the London and North Western Railway Company, was generally considered by the bulk of society as safe as an investment in the Government stocks; since which, Directors have had their own way, there have been no legislative interference with the management, and no competition. The causes then of the extraordinary increase in the value of shares in the years 1844 and 1845, and the subsequent depreciation, is matter of interest, not alone to the Railway Proprietors, but it also deeply concerns the public at large, for not a person in the United Kingdom has escaped its effects; directly, by the depreciation of his property, or, indirectly, by the scarcity of money caused by such depreciation; the dullness of business proceeding from the losses among general consumers, or the absorption of capital in Railway construction, to the prejudice and neglect of mercantile and other pursuits.

In the year 1845, the period at which confidence in Directors stood at its highest point, – and it must be of the greatest importance to Railway Proprietors to know whether their confidence was misplaced – Railway Shares were selling in the London and Birmingham Company at 250*l.* each, that is the market value of 41,250 shares on which 4,125,000*l.* had been called up, was 10,312,500*l.;* the selling price of 42,968 shares on which 85,936*l.* had been paid, was 1,890,592*l.;* and the value of 55,000 shares, on which 110,000*l.* had been paid, stood at 1,815,000*l.*; the value then of the London and Birmingham Railway shares, on which 4,320,936*l.* had been paid, was 14,018,092*l.* The Grand Junction Shares on which 2,087,225*l.* had been paid, stood at 5,697,350*l.*, and the shares of all the leading Railway Companies stood proportionately high. What could have caused the present depreciation? – a depreciation in the shares of the one Company alone, now denominated the London and North Western, from 26,406,334*l.* with 8,656,631*l.* of share capital paid up, to 18,797,010*l.* with 13,091,066*l.* paid up; the same progressive increase in price in proportion to the sum paid, would make the present value 46,604,220*l.;* the depreciation, therefore, is equal to the difference between that sum and the present value, namely 23,809,210*l.*; and the aggregate depreciation in the value of the shares of all the English Railways, exceeds the enormous sum of 200,000,000*l.* in two years.

The Government has introduced no Bill to interfere with Railway Management – an Ex-chancellor of the Exchequer has certainly proposed a Bill for auditing Railway accounts; but if anything, that should have the effect of adding to the stability of Railway property as an official Government announcement, confirming the oft repeated declaration of the Directors, would be hailed with pleasure – one would suppose – by the Directors themselves; but the Directors opposed the measure in every possible manner, and succeeded in throwing it out, which is certainly most suspicious. There are no competitions between Railway Companies, and if there were, one Company's shares would certainly augment in value as the other depreciated, but all shares have fallen alike. The Government has done nothing prejudicial. Let us see what the Directors have been doing: – 1st, the Directors of the London and North Western Company have made a nominal increase of near a million; that is, they have paid dividend on the sum of 964,762*l.* not received, and have also issued (notwithstanding the prohibitory Act passed by the Government for the protection of the public, in 1844 and limiting dividends to 10 per cent) 68,750 shares, the proprietors of which have been receiving 10*l.* per cent on the sums called, and 5*l.* per cent on the sums not called. 2nd. The Directors of the Midland Company have agreed to guarantee 10*l.* per cent on the Leeds and Bradford Railway, and its extension – a line which had previously been promoted by themselves, and which had been by the most unaccountable means taken out of their hands, and at the time such guarantee was given, was under the control of their own Chairman and his friends, who together held nearly every share. 3rd. The Directors of the North Midland Company agreed to lease the Hull and Selby Railway (which had never professed in the returns made to Government, to have paid the expense of working) at a guarantee of 10*l.* per cent, and to redeem – as the Company chooses to denominate it – the Railway at 2,000,000*l.* when, just previously to such guarantee being given, the total market value of the shares was under 250,000*l.*, that is, the 8,000 50*l.* shares were selling for 35*l.* each, or 15*l.* discount;

and by similar means, the premiums on new shares issued to the proprietors of the former North Midland shares, have amounted to 250*l.* each, which proved a clear gain to those in the secret; who sold on the one hand, and a dead loss to the unfortunate purchaser on the other. 4th. The Directors of the Newcastle and Darlington Company (now York, Newcastle, and Berwick) agreed to lease the Great North of England Railway (the 100*l.* shares of which Company had, not long previously to such agreement, sold at 40*l.* discount,) until 1851, at a rent equal to 10*l.* per cent on the 100*l.* shares, and 52*l.* per cent on the 40*l.* shares; and to redeem (as it is termed) the Railway in the year 1851, at 250*l.* for each 100*l.* share; 100*l.* for each 40*l.* share, (on which 5*l.* only is to be called) 75*l.* for each 30*l.* share, and 37*l.* 10*s.* for each 10*l.* share; in other words 4,000,000*l.* has been agreed to be given for a Railway, the shares of which were selling a short time previously for 438,900*l.*: that is to say, Directors in one Company have purchased, guaranteed, and leased their own property in another. In 1844 and 1845, the only thought amongst Directors, was (to use their own terms,) how "*to calve,*" – that was, how to propose branches that would appear plausible – the real object being the creation of new shares, in which the Directors took good care of themselves by issuing largely to their nominees – generally brokers. These shares they puffed and rigged to large premiums, and immediately sold. In 1846, it was what low-priced railway or canal, could be purchased, amalgamated, or leased, and the shares raised in a few months to double and even treble the previous market value. In 1844 and 1845, everything was premium; in 1846 and 1847, the Directors termed it prize money. If, on investigation, it should be clear that the Railway Companies have in no case paid a fair and honest dividend, but on the contrary, the dividends have been paid by continually charging sums to capital, which should be charged against revenue, then it must be clear to every honest man – to every Englishman who is proud of having his country considered the first in honest dealings – that an inquiry should be instituted. Let us commence then a calm and unimpassioned examination of the affairs of the leading Companies, and see how far any premiums *have ever been justified by facts.* It was notorious in 1845, that shares were raised to very high premiums in the worst bubble Companies; so that, however gratifying it may be to sellers to receive large premiums, yet premiums alone cannot be taken as a test of value. The general speculations of 1845, arose from the ignorance of the public in Stock Exchange manoeuvres, they mistook the quoted prices for actual value; these market prices were only maintained as long as Directors, and Provisional Committee-men had shares to sell, and a High Sheriff (a broker) confessed, when in a witness-box, that he had been engaged by several Companies to rig their shares.

15

HUDSON'S STATUE

Thomas Carlyle

Source: Thomas Carlyle, 'Hudson's Statue,' *Latter-Day Pamphlets* (London: Chapman and Hall, 1850), pp. 307–11, 319–23.

EDITORIAL HEADNOTE

Thomas Carlyle (1795–1881) rose from a modest background in rural Scotland to become a dominant intellectual force in Victorian Britain as a historian, essayist, and social critic. Educated at Edinburgh University, he struggled for years as a teacher and writer before achieving fame in the 1830s for works such as *Sartor Resartus* (1834) and *The French Revolution* (1837). In an era experiencing profound economic and social upheavals, Carlyle emphasized the importance of work, duty, and personal responsibility as moral guideposts and sources of stability. He believed that heroic individuals could regenerate society.[1]

Thomas Carlyle was harshly critical of the materialism of his own society, believing that human relations had been reduced to a "cash nexus." For Carlyle, George Hudson, "the Railway King," was a false messiah, who stood for nothing more than the ruthless and relentless pursuit of wealth. Hudson had been the leading railway promoter of the age before losing much of his fortune, and his reputation, in the Financial Crisis of 1847–48. In the aftermath of the crash, shareholders' investigations uncovered a great number of unsavory business practices in Hudson's companies.

Note

1 "Carlyle, Thomas" in Ian Ousby, *The Cambridge Guide to Literature in English* (Cambridge University Press, 1993), pp. 154–55.

DOI: 10.4324/9781003713890-17

At St. Yves in Huntingdonshire, where Oliver Cromwell farmed and resided for some years, the people have determined to attempt some kind of memorial to that memorable character. Other persons in other quarters seem to be, more or less languidly, taking up the question; in Country Papers I have read emphatic leading-articles, recommending and urging that there should be a "People's Statue" of this great Oliver, – Statue furnished by universal contribution from the English People; and set up, if possible, in Lindon, in Huntingdon, or failing both these places, in St. Ives, or Naseby Field. Indeed a considerable notion seems to exist in the English mind, that some brass or stone acknowledgment is due to Cromwell, and ought to be paid him. So that the vexed question, "Shall Cromwell have a Statue?" appears to be resuscitating itself; and the weary Public must prepare to agitate it again.

Poor English Public, they really are exceedingly bewildered with Statues at present. They would fain do honour to somebody, if they did but know whom or how. Unfortunately they know neither whom nor how; they are, at present, the farthest in the world from knowing! They have raised a set of the ugliest Statues, and to the most extraordinary persons, ever seen under the sun before. Being myself questioned, in reference to the New Houses of Parliament some years ago, "Shall Cromwell have a Statue?" I had to answer, with sorrowful dubiety: "Cromwell? Side by side with the sacred Charleses, Jameses, Georges, and Defenders of the Faith, – I am afraid he wouldn't like it! Let us decide provisionally, No." And now again to St. Ives and the People's Statue, is it not to be asked in like manner: "Who are the 'People'? Are they a People worthy to build Statues to Cromwell; or worthy only of doing it to Hudson?" – This latter is a consideration that will lead us into far deeper and more momentous than sculptural inquiries; and I will request the reader's excellent company into these for a little.

The truth is, dear Reader, nowhere, to an impartial observant person, does the deep-sunk condition of the English mind, in these sad epochs; and how, in all spiritual or moral provinces, it has long quitted company with fact, and ceased to have veracity of heart, and clearness or sincerity of purpose, in regard to such matters, – more signally manifest itself, than in this affair of Public Statues. Whom doth the king delight to honour? That is the question of questions concerning the king's own honour. Show me the man you honour; I know by that symptom, better than by any other, what kind of man you yourself are. For you show me there what your ideal of manhood is; what kind of man you long inexpressibly to be, and would thank the gods, with your whole soul, for being if you could.

In this point of view, it was always matter of regret with me that Hudson's Statue, among the other wonders of the present age, was not completed. The 25,000*l.* subscribed, or offered as oblation, by the Hero-worshippers of England to their Ideal of a Man, awoke many questions as to what outward figure it could most profitably take, under the eternal canopy; questions never finally settled; nor ever now to be settled, now when the universal Hudson *ragnarok*, or "twilight of the gods," has arrived, and it is too clear no statue or cast-metal image of that Incarnation of the English Vishnu will ever be molten now! Why was it not set up; that the whole world might see it; that our "Religion" might be seen, mounted on some figure of a Locomotive, garnished with Scrip-rolls proper; and raised aloft in some conspicuous place, – for example, on the *other* arch at Hyde-Park Corner? By all opportunities, especially to all subscribers and pious sacrificers to the Hudson Testimonial, I have earnestly urged: Complete your Sin-Offering; buy, with the Five-and-twenty Thousand Pounds, what utmost amount of brazen metal and reasonable sculptural supervision it will cover, – say ten tons of brass, with a tolerable sculptor: model that, with what exactness Art can, into the enduring Brass Portrait and Express Image of King Hudson, as he receives the grandees of this country at his levees or soirees and couchees; mount him on the highest place you can discover in the most crowded thoroughfare, on what you consider the pinnacle of the English world: I assure you he will have beneficial effects there. To all men who are struggling for your approbation, and fretting their poor souls to fiddlestrings because you will not sufficiently give it, I will say, leading them to the foot of the Hudson mount of vision: "See, my worthy Mr. Rigmarole; consider this surprising Copper Pyramid, in partly human form: did the celestial value of men's approbation ever strike you so forcibly before? The *new* Apollo Belvidere this, or Ideal of the Scrip Ages. What do you think of it? *Allah Ilallah;* there is still one God, you see, in England; and this is his Prophet. Let it be a source of healing to you, my unhappy Mr. Rigmarole; draw from it 'uses of terror,' as the old divines said; uses of amazement, of new wisdom, unutterable reflection upon the present epoch of the world!"

For, in fact, there was more of real worship in the affair of Hudson than is usual in such. The practical English mind has its own notions as to the Supreme Excellence; knows the real from the spurious Avatar of Vishnu; and does not worship without its reasons. The practical English mind, contemplating its divine Hudson, says with what remainder of reverence is in it: "Yes, you are something like the Ideal of a Man; you are he I would give my right arm and leg, and accept a pot-belly, with gout, and an appetite for strong-waters, to be like! You out of nothing can make a world, or huge fortune of gold. A divine intellect is in you, which Earth and Heaven, and Capel Court itself acknowledge; at the word of which are done miracles. You find a dying railway; you say to it, Live, blossom anew with scrip; – and it lives, and blossoms into umbrageous flowery scrip, to enrich with golden apples, surpassing those of the Hesperides, the hungry souls of men. Diviner miracle what god ever did? Hudson, – though I mumble about my thirty-nine articles, and the service of *other* divinities, – Hudson is my god, and to him I will sacrifice the twenty-pound note: if perhaps he will be propitious to me!"

Object not that there was a mixed motive in this worship of Hudson; that perhaps it was not worship at all. Undoubtedly there were two motives mixed, but both of them sincere, – as often happens in worship. "Transcendent admiration" is defined as the origin of sacrifice; but also the hope of profit joins itself. If by sacrificing a goat, or the like trifle, to Supreme Jove, you can get Supreme Jove's favour, will not that, for one, be a good investment? Jove is sacrificed to, and worshipped, from transcendent admiration: but also, in part, men of practical nature worship him as pumps are primed, – give him a little water, that you may get from him a river. O god-like Hudson, O god-recognising England, why was not the partly anthropomorphous Pyramid of Copper cast, then, and set upon the pinnacle of England, that all men might have seen it, and the sooner got to understand these things! The twenty-five-thousand pound oblation lay upon the altar at the Bank; this monstrous Copper Vishnu of the Scrip Ages might have been revealed to men, and was not. Unexpected obstacles occurred. In fact, there rose from the general English soul, – lying dumb and infinitely bewildered, but not yet altogether dead, poor wretch, – such a growl of inarticulate amazement, at this unexpected Hudson Apotheosis, as alarmed the pious worshippers; and their Copper Pyramid remains unrealised; not to be realised to all eternity now, or at least not till Chaos come again, and the ancient mud-gods have dominion! The *Ne-plus-ultra* of State-building was within sight; but it was not attained, it was to be forever unattainable. . . .

Hudson the railway king, if Popular Election be the rule, seems to me by far the most authentic king extant in the world. Hudson has been "elected by the people" so as almost none other is or was. Hudson solicited no vote; his votes were silent voluntary ones, not liable to be false: he *did* a thing which men found, in their inarticulate hearts, to be worthy of paying money for; and they paid it. What the desire of every heart was, Hudson had or seemed to have produced: Scrip out of which profit could be made. They "voted" for him by purchasing his scrip with a profit to him. Every vote was the spontaneous product of those men's deepest insights and most practical convictions, about Hudson and themselves and this Universe: I say, it was incapable of being insincere. What their appetites, intelligences, stupidities, and pruriences had taught these men, they authentically told you there. I beg you to mark that well. Not by all the ballot-boxes in Nature could you have hoped to get, with such exactness, from these men, what the deepest inarticulate voice of the gods and of the demons in them was, as by this spontaneous purchase of scrip. It is the ultimate rectified quintessence of these men's "votes": the distillation of their very souls; the sincerest sincerity that was in them. Without gratitude to Hudson, or even without thought of him, they raised Hudson to his bad eminence, not by their voices given once at some hustings under the influence of balderdash and beer, but by the thought of their heart, by the inarticulate, indisputable dictate of their whole being. Hudson inquired of England: "What precious thing can I do for you, O enlightened Countrymen; what may be the value to you, by popular election, of this stroke of work that lies in me?" Popular election, with universal, with household and other suffrage, free as air, deep as life and death, free and deep as *spoken* suffrage never was or could be, has answered: "Pounds sterling to such and such amount; that is the apparent value of thy stroke of work to *us*, – blockheads as we are." Real value differs from apparent to a frightful extent in this world, try it by what suffrage you will!

Hudson's value as a demigod being what it was, his value as a maker of railways shall hardly concern us here. What Hudson's real worth to mankind in the matter of railways might be, I cannot pretend to say. Fact knows it to the uttermost fraction, and will pay him yet; but men differ widely in opinion, and in general do not in the least know. From my own private observations and conjecture, I should say, Trifling if any worth.

Much as we love railways, there is one thing undeniable: Railways are shifting all Towns of Britain into new places; no Town will stand where it did, and nobody can tell for a long while yet where it will stand. This is an unexpected, and indeed most disastrous result. I perceive, railways have set all the Towns of Britain a-dancing. Reading is coming up to London, Basingstoke is going down to Gosport or Southampton, Dumfries to Liverpool and Glasgow; while at Crewe, and other points, I see new ganglions of human population establishing themselves, and the prophecy of metallurgic cities which were not heard of before. Reading, Basingstoke and the rest, the unfortunate Towns, subscribed money to get railways; and it proves to be for cutting their own throats. Their business has gone elsewhither; and they – cannot stay behind their business! They are set a-dancing, as I said; confusedly waltzing, in a state of progressive dissolution, towards the four winds; and know not where the end of the death-dance will be for them, in what point of space will they be allowed to rebuild themselves. That is their sad case.

And what an affair it is in each of the shops and houses of those Towns, thus silently bleeding to death, or what we call dancing away to other points of the British territory: how Joplin of Reading, who had anchored himself in that pleasant place, and fondly hoping to live by upholstery and paperhanging, had wedded, and made friends there, – awakens some morning, and finds that his trade has flitted away! Here it is not any longer; it is gone to London, to Bristol: whither has it gone? Joplin knows not whither; knows and sees only that gone it is; and that he by preternatural sagacity must scent it out again, follow it over the world, and catch it again, or else die. Sad news for Joplin: – indeed I fear, should his sagacity be too inconsiderable, he is not unlikely to break his heart, or take to drinking, in these inextricable circumstances! And it is the history, more or less, in every town, house, shop and industrial dwelling-place of the British Empire at this moment; – and the cipher of afflicted Joplins; and the amount of private distress, uncertainty, discontent; and withal of "revolutionary movement," created hereby, is tragical to think of. This is "revolutionary movement" with a witness; revolution brought home to everybody's hearth and moneysafe and heart and stomach. – Which miserable result, with so many others from the same source, what method was there of avoiding or indefinitely mitigating? This surely, as the beginning of all: that you had made your railways *not* in haste; that, at least, you had spread the huge process, sure to alter all men's mutual position and relations, over a reasonable breadth of time!

For all manner of reasons, how much could one have wished that the making of our British railways had gone on with deliberation; that these great works had made themselves not in five years but in fifty-and-five! Hudson's "worth" to railways, I think, will mainly resolve itself into this, That he carried them to completion within the former short limit of time; that he got them made, – in extremely improper directions I am told, and surely with endless confusion to the innumerable passive Joplins, and likewise to the numerous active scrip-holders, a wide-spread class, once rich, now coinless, – hastily in five years, not deliberately in fifty-five. His worth to railways? His *worth*, I take it, to English railways, much more to English men, will turn out to be extremely inconsiderable; to be incalculable damage rather! Foolish railway people gave him two millions, and thought it not enough without a Statue to boot. But Fact thought, and is now audibly saying far otherwise! Rhadamanthus, had you been able to consult him, would in nowise have given this man twenty-five thousand pounds for a statue. What if Rhadamanthus doomed him rather, let us say, to ride in Express-trains, nowhither, for twenty-five aeons, or to hang in Heaven as a Locomotive Constellation, and be a sign forever!

Fact and Suffrage: what a discrepancy! Fact decided for some coalshaft such as we describe. Suffrage decides for such a column. Suffrage having money in its pocket, carries it hollow, for the moment. And so there is Rayless Majesty exalted far above the chimney-pots, with a potential Copper Likeness, twenty-five thousand pounds worth of copper over and above; and a King properly belonging only to *this* epoch. – That there are greedy blockheads in huge majority, in all epochs, is certain; but that any sane mortal should think of counting *their* heads to ascertain who or what is to be King, this is a little peculiar. All Democratic men, and members of the Suffrage Movement, it appears to me, are called upon to think seriously, with a seriousness approaching to despair, of these things.

16

THE LADDER OF GOLD

Robert Bell

Source: Robert Bell, *The Ladder of Gold: An English Story* (London: G. Routledge and Company, 1858), Book 3, pp. 199–206.

EDITORIAL HEADNOTE

Robert Bell (1800–67) was born in Ireland, the son of a magistrate. He was educated at Trinity College, Dublin, before pursuing a career as a writer. After moving to London in 1828, he achieved literary celebrity as an editor, essayist, and biographer. Later in life he turned to fiction, and his novel, *The Ladder of Gold*, was both a popular and critical success.[1]

Inspired by the Railway Mania of the 1840s, *The Ladder of Gold,* is a bildungsroman which charts the rise and fall of an ambitious young businessman, Richard Rawlings. After marrying a wealthy widow, Rawlings builds his fortune through railway speculation, and becomes an MP, before losing it all in the Financial Panic of 1847. In this excerpt, Rawlings employs disreputable agents who assist him in rigging the share market and overcoming principled opposition at a shareholders' meeting.

Note

1 John Sutherland, "Bell, Robert," *The Stanford Companion to Victorian Fiction* (Stanford: Stanford University Press, 1989), p. 56.

On the day in question there was to be a general meeting of the shareholders of the London and Yarlton Railway, on which occasion a turbulent discussion was expected touching the financial management. It had been remarked that every line with which Mr. Rawlings connected himself was up at a great premium; and as this uniform success invariably ensued upon his measures, it was naturally regarded as a test of the soundness of his judgment. Certainly such wonderful

DOI: 10.4324/9781003713890-18

results could have been accomplished only by a singularly sagacious policy, or by some necromancy in the art of drawing up balance-sheets. Now, as the bulk of the public did not believe in magic, they referred these results to the ability of Mr. Rawlings; but a captious minority, who had no faith even in the gains they pocketed, pretended to think that there must be a mystery somewhere, although they could not find it out.

At the head of this minority was Sir Peter Jinks, the bank director. Sir Peter was a man of considerable wealth, amassed as a merchant in the city of London. He belonged to that section of the mercantile community which stands as proudly and ostentatiously on the integrity and respectability of its transactions, as the aristocrat upon his quarterings. His position was in the fullest sense legitimate. No man could pick out a stain in his life. Sir Peter represented one of the great commercial cities in Parliament, and was a leading man in the House on all questions of trade and political economy. He set his face at the beginning against the railway mania, and predicted that it would end in convulsion. By nature a hard, just man, the habits of a counting-house, where business was conducted on the strictest principles, had rendered him distrustful of all speculations and speculators. From the outset of Richard Rawlings' parliamentary career, as a railway magnate, he had vigilantly observed his proceedings, taking upon himself, as a public duty, the task of tracing the rise, progress, and end of what he regarded as a national delusion. In order that he might be better enabled to pursue his investigations, he purchased shares in the Yarlton line and its dependencies, and narrowly scrutinized the manner in which the committee discharged their functions. It was clear to him that they were mere puppets in the hands of the chairman; but so consummate was the skill with which the affairs of the company were carried on, that, although he suspected the honesty of every item in the accounts, with all his experience and acuteness he could not detect a single flaw. His doubts, however, were not to be satisfied by a dexterous exhibition of figures, and he continued to hang on the track of Richard Rawlings like a bloodhound.

The eyes of this mercantile lynx had gleamed sometimes so piercingly upon Rawlings as to awaken him to the necessity of caution. That sagacious observer was always on his guard against men who, like himself, never take their spring until they are sure of their object.

A few more letters were opened and dispatched, when Crikey Snaggs came into the library, and announced Mr. Michael Costigan.

Before Mr. Michael Costigan makes his appearance, we must say two or three words about him.

You had only to look at him, or hear him speak, to be assured that Ireland had the honour of giving him birth. He had the mellifluous brogue which is native to the neighborhood of Limerick, a place where his ancestors flourished in stone castles long before the flood. The Costigans, descended from a line of kings, were rich in royal blood, but unfortunately in nothing else; and the present representative of that regal race was reduced to the necessity of living upon his wits. The railway mania brought up to the surface many gentlemen whose talents must otherwise have been buried in obscurity; and amongst them Mr. Michael, or as he was jocularly called, Mr. Mick Costigan, shone out conspicuously. He belonged to no profession whatever. He scorned professions. He existed entirely under "skyey influences," which spurned routine employment or business drudgery. But put him to any meteoric achievement, lying out of the ordinary system, and he carried everything before him. Being wholly irresponsible to himself, or to anybody else, he was the best man in the world for all kinds of eccentric negotiations and social forlorn hopes.

It would be difficult to convey to the uninitiated the exact nature of his connexion with the great railway movement; but as the railways entered largely into the history of the time, and Mr. Costigan represented a new class of industry which they called into existence, we must endeavour to describe his multifarious occupations.

Mr. Costigan had a large parliamentary acquaintance, selected chiefly out of that loose squadron of Irish members that used to skirmish so briskly on the outskirts of party questions. The grand thing in concocting the prospectus of a new railway was to get up a committee of apparent responsibility; and as the "promoters" were mostly scampish attorneys, who had no connexions amongst reputable people, the services of Mr. Costigan, who always walked about with a list in his pocket of intimate friends, having what he called "handles" to their names, were inestimable. He could make out a committee in a twinkling; such a committee, too, of M.P.'s, baronets, and honourables as came upon the innocent public like a blast of trumpets. To be sure it was only a nominal committee, after all, the few names that had any substance attached to them being used without authority, and the rest being little more than the labels of wasted patrimonies, fit only to make tails for kites. But like a gaudy sign over an ill-furnished hostelrie, it answered the temporary purpose of attracting flocks of customers. For the services thus rendered, Mr. Costigan was generally placed on the committee himself, with a batch of shares at his disposal, the payment for which was slurred over by a little private management. Sometimes when a bill was in progress he acted as a sort of flying parliamentary agent, an anomalous employment which we should deplore of rendering intelligible by the most minute account of the sundry and complex intrigues it involved. At other times he was engaged in "rigging" the market. This ingenious process consisted of putting out upon the Stock Exchange a quantity of shares in an incipient line, and buying them up himself at a large premium, so as to secure a dazzling quotation in the next day's papers, a bait which the *gobemouches*[1] were sure to swallow. Then he was of great value in the committees, for, although he never troubled his head about practical details, and knew nothing about local statistics or any of the other problems of geography and finance comprehended in a railway scheme, he had a gift of speech that bore down all opposition. Whenever a stormy meeting of shareholders was anticipated, Mr. Costigan was the whipper-in, with a leash of followers at his back and a bundle of proxies under his arm, prepared to beat down the clamour with a terrorizing majority. Such were the agencies by which the railway bubble was blown till it burst. The greatest statesmen have made use of worse instruments on weightier occasions, and Mr. Rawlings did not hesitate to avail himself of the many-sided dexterity of Mr. Michael Costigan.

When the door of the library opened, the visitor came in with a great noise and bustle. That was his way; and his large and ungainly figure gave additional impetus to his vigorous bearing. He had a wild shock head, with hair scattered and starting out at cross angles, bushy whiskers, and a broad face gleaming with an expression of headlong bacchanalian gaiety. His dress was so loose, that it was a wonder how he kept it together upon him. Everything he wore seemed detached, and ready to fly off: – his cravat streamed over his shoulders in a tie that looked as if it were dropping out; his coat was thrown open, and stood away from his body; his waistcoat wandered over his chest, restrained from total separation by only a single button; and his great trousers were crumpled all round his legs, with the flaps of the pockets hanging down at the sides. The daring negligence of his dress was the type of his character.

"It's done!" he said, as he roared into the room; "you may snap your fingers at them – done as clean as a whistle."

"Sit down, Mr. Costigan," replied Rawlings; "and tell me quietly what you have done."

"Done?" responded Mr. Costigan; "got a hundred and fifty proxies complete in my hat – *verbum sap.*[2] You don't understand Latin? No matter. We'll dispense with the Latin and stick to the aboriginal vernacular. Jinks is a cantankerous old reptile, and a mighty unpleasant object to look at."

"Is he coming to the meeting?"

"Of course he is – but I've made a hole in his pipes that'll spoil his music. The minute he pops up his wizened abortion of a dirty baked face, I've my body-guard ready to give him a shillaloo. We won't let him speak a word – that's the short cut to get rid of him."

"No, no, we mustn't do that. We must hear him, and answer him. Are we sure of a majority?"

"Are you sure it's pelting rain? Majority! Only order out your coach, and let us be off."

"What's the time?'

"I can't exactly answer for the punctuality of my kettle – somehow or other it's always out of order; but I've a sort of superstitious suspicion that we're late."

"Now understand, Mr. Costigan – the business of the meeting is simply to carry the resolutions of the committee. The less discussion, the better; and no uproar or hostility against Sir Peter."

"Not the least taste in life. Let him fire away and more power to him."

The meeting was to be held in the great room of the Freemason's Tavern, and thither Mr. Rawlings, accompanied by his robustious ally, hastened at a spanking pace. In the little ante-chamber where the committee assembled for preliminary arrangements, the murmur of the crowd could be distinctly heard, and surging above the general buzz might be detected the ominous coughs and haws! of Mr.

Costigan's adherents, who were evidently preparing their lungs for the approaching conflict. At length the committee made their appearance and Mr. Rawlings, in dumb show, was voted into the chair. You could see at once, from the aspect of the meeting, that there was angry work before them.

The business was opened in a few curt words, by which the shareholders were informed that the meeting was convened to receive the report, and re-elect the committee. The report was then read in due form, and when it was put to the vote, Sir Peter rose, and began with "Before the report is put to the vote, I beg –" he had scarcely delivered himself of half the sentence when an indescribable clamour broke out at the lower end of the room. Mr. Rawlings immediately interposed, and requested a hearing for Sir Peter; but succeeded only in obtaining a hearing for himself, the row increasing when Sir Peter rose a second time.

Mr. Costgan's body-guard were clearly over-doing their instructions, and the moment was come for that gentleman to bring his influence into play. Starting up, and running his hands through his hair, as if it were not horrent enough already, he addressed them with a stentorian humour that elicited rounds of laughter. "Readin' and writin'," he said, "was a wonderful invention, but spakin' had the whip-hand o' them. Now we've had the readin' and writin', let us have a little spakin'. Let the gentleman spake – maybe he has a trifle of a report of his own – he's a bank director, and you know there are quare reports sometimes from the Bank," finishing with a rolling wink of his eye, which drew down fresh demonstrations of applause from his adherents. It may be remarked, *en passant*, of Mr. Costigan, that like most of his countrymen, when he became animated and oratorical, he gave full vent to his rich brogue, which, in ordinary conversations, he kept somewhat under control.

Sir Peter, having obtained a brief silence, proceeded to state his objections to the report. He said that he acted entirely on public grounds – that he did not impugn the integrity or capacity of the committee, or of his honourable friend, the chairman; but that he wished for some information concerning certain items in the balance-sheet. There was a large reserve of shares unaccounted for. What did the committee do with them? He saw names on the committee of gentlemen who were never heard of in the mercantile world before – he wouldn't specify – but he would ask were they all properly qualified? (At this question, Dingle twisted his bamboo between his legs.) How was the dividend created? Where did it come from? It was impossible to get at it by any ordinary process. Was it fact or fiction? Did it come from profits, or was it only taken out of one pocket and put into another? Then there were negotiations of enormous magnitude with other lines. Who authorised them? Who conducted them? Had any member or members of the committee a personal interest in these transactions? These observations and interrogatories were delivered amidst many interruptions; but when Sir Peter touched upon the personal interest of the committee, it was no longer possible to restrain the zeal of Mr. Costigan's body-guard, who saluted Sir Peter with such a storm of hisses, as compelled him to sit down. Several members of the committee rose at once, but Mr. Costigan was again on his legs, and was heard above them all.

"What's the question?" demanded Mr. Costigan. "I told you you'd have a quare report from the Bank, and now you've had it can you make head or tail of it? I tell you what it is, if you were as strong as Samson, and as ould as Methuselah, and had as many curls in your wig as there are waves in the say, I defy you to unravel what the gentleman means. The Irish is a beautiful language, gentlemen, a powerful, prismatic language, and as full of words as an egg is of meat; but you have one word in your language that beats all the other words hollow, and that word is – *rigmarole*. Now, gentlemen, rigmarole may do very well in the Bank parlour – but this isn't the Bank parlour; this is an open meeting of free-born Saxons who are not to be mystified by that kind of jargon. What was it all about? He'd be a clever fellow that'd tell you that. All I could make out was, that the hon. Gentleman wants to know where the dividend comes from. Where does he think it comes from? Of course, I suppose he thinks it comes from the sky. Well, I've no objection to that. It's a celestial shower entirely, and it has my good wishes that it may continue to rain upon us till there isn't a drop left. If the gentleman's afraid of the wet, let him put up his umbrella, or get out o' the way. Question, Mr. Chairman! What's the question?"

This oration utterly overwhelmed the Bank director. The small party that supported him cried out in vain for a hearing; Mr. Costigan had effectually put an end to the possibility of any further speech-making on that side. Mr. Rawlings, chagrined at the ludicrous turn given to the debate, and anxious to sustain the formality of the proceedings, begged to say a few words; he was ready to give any explanations required – the accounts were printed, and in the hands of the shareholders – the committee had arduous and difficult duties to discharge – but it was impracticable on such occasions to go into every insignificant item of expenditure – some confidence must be reposed in the discretion of the committee, or no man would undertake such onerous labours – for his part, he had worked day and night, and all the recompence he asked was the continuance of their confidence – was it not enough that their affairs were prosperous? – a large dividend was the best test of ability and prudence in the management – he gave his honourable friend full credit for the excellence of his intentions, and he wished they had the advantages of his experience and high character in the committee; but he felt at the same time that it would be a flagrant injustice to the gentlemen who had served them with such zeal, not to re-elect them – he was aware of only two questions before the meeting – the adoption of the report, and the re-election of the committee, and without trespassing further on their patience, he would at once put them to the vote.

This clear and satisfactory statement was received with loud acclamations; whereupon Sir Peter Jinks' minority made another effort to protest against the proceedings; and intermittent exclamations of "Subterfuge!" and "Packed meeting!" and other charges of unfairness assailed the ears of the committee. The confusion became general – everybody was standing up and shouting – the body of the room presented a scene of indescribable uproar, in the midst of which a brief pantomime was enacted on the platform, the purport of which was revealed only to the newspaper reporters, who informed the public the next morning that the resolutions were carried by acclamation, and that the unanimous thanks of the meeting were voted to Richard Rawlings, Esq., M.P., for his able conduct of the chair, and for the valuable services he had rendered the company in the management of their affairs.

Editorial Endnotes

1 Credulous people.
2 "A word to the wise."

17

RAILWAY MORALS AND RAILWAY POLICY

Herbert Spencer

Source: Herbert Spencer, 'Railway Morals and Railway Policy,' *Edinburgh Review* 100 (October 1854), pp. 216–26.

EDITORIAL HEADNOTE

Herbert Spencer (1820–1903) was a philosopher and social scientist who exerted a profound intellectual influence during the Victorian era. In works such as *Social Statics* (1851) and *Principles of Biology* (1864), he posited that all phenomena can be explained through evolutionary progress. According to Spencer, human societies and individuals, as well as biological species, were subject to natural selection in which the "survival of the fittest" prevailed. (This doctrine is popularly known as "Social Darwinism.") A prolific writer, Spencer not only published dozens of books, but also many articles, in which he frequently commented on important political, social, and economic topics of the day.[1]

The *Edinburgh Review,* a literary and political magazine founded in 1802, was one of the most influential British periodicals of the nineteenth century. It was a strong advocate of Liberal principles and reform.

In this essay, influenced by the 1853 Parliamentary Select Committee on Railway and Canal Bills, Spencer concludes that there was "some deep-seated vice ramifying throughout our system of railway government." He attributed much of this corruption to a "corporate conscience" which allowed company directors to distance themselves from wrongful acts by spreading the responsibility widely among numerous actors.

Note

1 Jose Harris, "Spencer, Herbert," *Oxford Dictionary of National Biography*, eds. H.C.G. Matthew and Brian Harrison (Oxford: Oxford University Press, 2004), Vol. 51, pp. 851–61.

DOI: 10.4324/9781003713890-19

Believers in the intrinsic virtues of political forms might draw an instructive lesson from the politics of our railways. If there is a conclusive proof that the most carefully framed constitutions are worthless, unless they be embodiments of the popular character, – if there needs a conclusive proof that governmental arrangements in advance of the time will inevitably lapse back into congruity with the time; such proof may be found over and over again repeated in the current history of joint-stock enterprises. As devised by Act of Parliament, the administrations of our public companies are almost purely democratic. The representative system is carried out in them with scarcely a check. Shareholders elect their directors, directors their chairman; there is an annual retirement of a certain proportion of the board, giving facilities for superseding them; and, by this means, the whole ruling body may be changed in periods varying from three to five years. Yet, not only are the characteristic vices of our political state reproduced in each of these mercantile corporations – some even in an intenser degree, – but the very form of government, whilst remaining nominally democratic, is substantially so remodeled as to become a miniature of our national constitution. The direction, ceasing to fulfil its theory as a deliberative body whose members possess like powers, falls under the control of some one member of superior cunning, will, or wealth, to whom the majority become so subordinate, that the decision on every question depends on the course he takes. Proprietors, instead of constantly exercising their franchise, allow it to become on all ordinary occasions a dead letter; retiring directors are so habitually re-elected without opposition, and have so great a power of insuring their own re-election when opposed, that the board becomes practically a close body; and it is only when the misgovernment grows extreme enough to produce a revolutionary agitation among the shareholders that any change can be effected. Thus, a mixture of the monarchic, the aristocratic, and the democratic elements is repeated with such modifications only as the circumstances involve. The modes of action, too, are substantially the same; save in this, that the copy outruns the original. Threats of resignation, which ministries hold out in extreme cases, are commonly made by railway boards to stave-off a disagreeable inquiry. By no means regarding themselves as servants of the shareholders, directors rebel against dictation from them; and frequently construe any amendment they may urge into a vote of want of confidence. At half-yearly meetings, disagreeable criticism and objections are met by the chairman with the remark, that if the shareholders cannot trust his colleagues and himself, they had better choose others. With most, this assumption of offended dignity tells; and, under the fear that the company's interests may suffer from any disturbance, measures quite at variance with the wishes of the proprietary are allowed to be carried. The parallel holds yet further. If it be true of national administrations, that those in office count on the support of all public *employés*, it is not less true of incorporated companies, that the directors are greatly aided by their officials in their struggles with shareholders. If, in times past, there have been ministries who spent public money to secure party ends, there are, in times present, railway boards who use the funds of the shareholders to defeat the shareholders. Nay, even in detail, the similarity is maintained. Like their prototype, joint-stock companies have their expensive election contests, managed by election committees, employing election agents; they have their canvassing with its sundry illegitimate accompaniments; they have their occasional manufacture of fraudulent votes. And, as a general result, that class-legislation, which, until of late, was habitually charged against statesmen, is now habitually displayed in the proceedings of these trading associations; constituted though they are on purely representative principles.

These last assertions will probably surprise not a few. The general public who have little or no direct interest in railway matters, – who never see a railway journal, and who skip the reports of half-yearly meetings that appear in the daily papers – are under the impression that dishonesties akin to those gigantic ones so notorious during the mania, are no longer committed. They do not forget the doings of stags and stock-jobbers and runaway directors; they remember how men of straw held shares amounting to 100,000l. and even 200,000l; how numerous directorates were filled by the same persons – one having a seat at twenty-three boards; how subscription contracts were made up with signatures bought at 10s. and 4s. each, and porters and errand-boys made themselves liable for 30,000l. and 40,000l. apiece. They can narrate how boards kept their books in cypher; made false registries, and refrained from recording their proceedings in minute books; how in one company half a million of capital was down to unreal names; how in another, directors bought for account more shares than they issued, and so forced up the price; and how in many others, they repurchased for the company their own shares, paying themselves with the depositors' money. But, though more or less aware of the iniquities that have been practiced, the generality think of them solely as the accompaniments of bubble schemes. More recent enterprises they know to have been *bona fide* ones, mostly carried out by old-established companies; and knowing this, they do not suspect that in the getting up of branch lines and extensions, there are chicaneries near akin to those of Capel Court, and quite as disastrous in their ultimate results. Associating the ideas of wealth and respectability, and habitually using respectability as synonymous with morality, it seems to them incredible, that many of the large capitalists and men of station who administer railway affairs should be guilty of indirectly enriching themselves at the expense of their constituents. True, they occasionally meet with a law report, disclosing some enormous fraud, or read a 'Times' leader, characterizing directorial acts in terms that are held libelous; but they regard the cases thus brought to light as entirely exceptional: and under that feeling of loyalty which ever idealises men in authority, they constantly tend towards the conviction, if not that directors can do no wrong, yet that they are very unlikely to do wrong.

A history of railway management and railway intrigue, however, would quickly undeceive them. In such a history, the doings of projectors and the mysteries of the share-market would occupy less space than the analysis of the multiform dishonesties that have been committed since 1845, and the genesis of that elaborate system of tactics by which companies are betrayed into ruinous undertakings that benefit the few at the cost of the many. Such a history would not only have to detail the doings of the personage famed 'for making things pleasant'; nor would it have merely to add the misdeeds of his colleagues; but it would have to describe the kindred corruptness of other railway administrations. From the published report of an investigation committee it would be shown how, not many years since, the directors of one of our lines allotted among themselves 15,000 new shares then at a premium in the market, – how to pay the deposits on these shares they used the company's funds, – how one of their number thus accommodated himself in meeting both deposits and calls to the extent of more than 80,000l. We should also read in it of directors who made loans to themselves out of the company's floating balances at a low rate of interest when the market rate was high; and who paid themselves larger salaries than those assigned; entering the difference in an obscure corner of the ledger under the head of 'petty disbursements'. There would be documents showing that the proxies enabling boards to carry contested measures have in some cases been obtained by garbled statements; and, again, that proxies given for a specific purpose have been used for other purposes. One of our companies would be proved to have projected a line, serving as a feeder, for which it obtained shareholders by offering a guaranteed dividend, which, though understood by the public to be unconditional, was really contingent upon a condition not likely to be fulfilled. The managers of another company would be convicted of having carried party measures by the aid of preference shares standing in the names of station masters; and of being aided by the proxies of the secretary's children too young to write.

That the corruptions here glanced at are not mere exceptional evils, but result from some deep-seated vice ramifying throughout our system of railway government, is sufficiently proved by the simple fact that notwithstanding the depreciation of railway dividends produced by the extension policy, that policy has been year after year continued. Does any tradesman, who, having enlarged his shop, finds a proportionate diminution in his rate of profit, go on, even under the stimulus of competition, making further enlargements at the cost of further diminutions? Does any merchant, however strong his desire to take away an opponent's markets, make successive mortgages on his capital, and pay for each sum thus raised a higher interest than he gains by trading with it? Yet this course, so absurd that no one would insult a private individual by asking him to follow it, is the course which railway boards at meeting after meeting persuade their clients to pursue. Since 1845, when the dividends of our leading lines ranged from 8 to 10 per cent, they have, notwithstanding an ever growing traffic, fallen from 10 per cent to 5, from 8 to 4, from 9 to 3 ¼; and yet the system of extensions, leases, and guarantees, notoriously the cause of this, has been year by year persevered in. Is there not something needing explanation here – something more than the world is allowed to see? If there be any one to whom the broad fact of obstinate persistence in unprofitable expenditure does not alone carry the conviction that sinister influences are at work, let him read the seductive statements by which shareholders are led to authorise new projects, and then compare these with the proved results. Let him look at the estimated cost, anticipated traffic, and calculated dividend on some proposed branch line; let him observe how the proprietary, before whom the scheme is laid, are induced to approve it as promising a fair return; and then let him contemplate, in the resulting depreciation of stock, the extent of their loss. Is there any avoiding the inference? Clearly, railway shareholders can never have habitually voted for new undertakings which they knew would be injurious to them. Every one knows, however, that these new undertakings have almost uniformly proved injurious to them. Obviously, therefore, railway shareholders have been continually deluded by false representations. The only possible escape from this conclusion is in the belief that boards and their officers have been themselves deceived; and were the discrepancies between promises and results occasional only, there would be grounds for this lenient interpretation. But to suppose that a railway government should repeatedly make such mistakes, and yet gain no wisdom from disastrous experiences – should after a dozen disappointments again mislead half-yearly meetings by bright anticipations into dark realities, and all in good faith – taxes credulity somewhat too far. Even then were there no demonstrated iniquities to rouse suspicion, we think that the continuous depreciation in the value of railway stock, the determined perseverance of boards in the policy that has produced this depreciation, and the proved untruth of the statements by which they have induced shareholders to sanction this policy, would of themselves suffice to show the essential viciousness of railway administration.

That the existing evils, and the causes conspiring to produce them, may be the better understood, it will be needful briefly to glance at the mode in which the system of extensions grew up. Earliest among the incentives to it was a feeling of rivalry. Even whilst yet their main lines were unmade, a contest for supremacy arose between our two greatest companies. This presently generated a confirmed antagonism; and the same impulse which in election contests and the like has frequently led to the squandering of a fortune to gain a victory, has largely aided to make each of these great rivals submit to repeated sacrifices rather than be beaten. Feuds of like nature are in other cases perpetually prompting boards to make aggressions on each other's territory – every attack on the one side leading to a reprisal on the other; and so violent is the hostility occasionally produced, that directors might be pointed out whose votes are wholly determined by the desire to be revenged on their opponents. Among the first methods by which leading companies sought to strengthen themselves and weaken their competitors, was the leasing or purchase of subordinate neighboring lines. Of course, those to whom overtures were made, obtained bids from both sides; and it naturally resulted that the first sales thus effected, being at prices far above the real values, brought great profits to the sellers. What resulted? After a few recurrences of this proceeding, it was clearly perceived by quick-witted speculators that the making of lines so circumstanced as to be bid for by competing companies, would be a lucrative policy. Shareholders who had once pocketed these large and easily-made gains, were eager to repeat the process; and cast about for districts in which it might be done. Even the directors of the companies by whom these high prices were given, were under the temptation to aid in this; for it was manifest to them that by obtaining a larger interest in any such new undertaking than they possessed in the purchasing company, and by using their influence in the purchasing company to obtain a good price or guarantee for the new undertaking, a great advantage would be gained; and that this motive has been largely operative, railway history abundantly proves. Once commenced, sundry other influences conspired to stimulate this making of feeders and extensions. The non-closure of capital accounts rendered possible the 'cooking' of dividends, which was at one point carried to a great extent. Under various incentives, speculative and other, expenditure that should have been charged against revenue was charged against capital; works and rolling stock were allowed to go unrepaired, or insufficient additions made to them, by which means the current expenses were rendered delusively small; long-credit agreements with contractors permitted sundry disbursements that had been virtually made to be kept out of the accounts; and thus the net returns were made to appear much greater than they really were. Naturally the new undertakings put before the monied world by companies whose stock and dividends had been thus artificially raised, were received with proportionate favour. Under the prestige of their parentage their shares come out at high premiums, bringing large profits to the projectors. The hint was soon taken; and it presently became an established policy, under the auspices of a prosperity either real or mock, to get up these subsidiary lines – 'calves' as they were called in the slang of the initiated – and to traffic in the premiums their shares commanded. Meanwhile had been developing a secondary set of influences which also contributed to foster unwise enterprises; namely, the business interests of the lawyers, engineers, contractors, and others directly or indirectly employed in railway construction. The methods of projecting and carrying new schemes could not fail, in the course of years, to become familiar to all persons concerned; and there could not fail to grow up amongst them a concerted system of tactics calculated to achieve their common end. Thus partly from jealousy of rival boards, partly form avarice of shareholders in purchased lines, partly form the dishonest schemings of directors, partly from the manoeuvers of those whose business it is to carry out the projects legally authorized, partly, and perhaps mainly, from the delusive appearance of prosperity maintained by many established companies, there came the wild speculations of 1844 and 1845. The consequent disasters, whilst they pretty well destroyed the last of these incentives, left the rest much as they were. Though the painfully-undeceived public have ceased to aid as they once did, the various private interests that had grown up, have since been working together as before; have developed their system of co-operation into still more complex and subtle forms; and are even now daily thrusting unfortunate shareholders into losing undertakings.

Before proceeding to analyse the existing state of things, however, we would have it clearly understood that we do not suppose those implicated to be *on the average* morally lower than the community at large. Men taken at random from any class would, in all probability, behave much in the same way when placed in like positions. There are unquestionably directors grossly dishonest: unquestionably also there are others whose standard of honour is far higher than that of most persons: and for the remainder, they are, we doubt not, as good as the mass. Of the engineers, parliamentary agents, lawyers, contractors, and various others concerned, it may be admitted that though daily custom has induced laxity of principle, yet they would be harshly judged were the transactions that may be recorded against them used as measures. Those who do not see how, in these involved affairs, the most inequitable results may be wrought out by men not correspondingly flagitious, will readily do so on considering all the conditions. In the first place there is the familiar fact that the corporate conscience is ever inferior to the individual conscience – that a body of men will commit as a joint act, that which every individual of them would shrink from did he feel personally responsible. And it may be remarked that not only is the conduct *of* a corporate body thus comparatively lax, but also the conduct *towards* one. There is even a more or less distinct perception that a broad-backed company scarcely feels what would be ruinous to a private person; and this perception is in constant operation on all railway administrators and their *employés* – on all contractors, landowners, and others concerned; leading them to show a graspingness and want of principle foreign to their general behavior. Again, the indirectness and remoteness of the evils produced greatly weaken the restraints on wrong doing. Men's actions are proximately produced by mental representations of the results to be anticipated; and the decisions come to largely depend on the vividness with which these results can be imagined. A consequence, good or bad, that is immediate, and clearly apprehended, influences conduct far more potently than a consequence that has to be traced through a long chain of causation, and as eventually reached, is not a particular and readily conceivable one, but a general and vaguely conceivable one. Hence in railway affairs a questionable share transaction, an exorbitant charge, a proceeding which brings great individual advantage without apparently injuring any one, but which, even if analysed in its ultimate results, can but very circuitously affect unknown persons living no one know where, may be brought home to men who, could the results be embodied before them, would be shocked at the cruel injustices they had committed – men who in their private business where the results *can* be thus embodied, are sufficiently equitable. Further, it requires to be noted that most of these great delinquencies are wrought out, not by the extreme dishonesty of any one man or group of men, but by the combined self-interest of many men and groups of men, whose minor delinquencies are cumulative. Much as a story which, passing from mouth to mouth, and receiving a slight exaggeration at each repetition, comes round to the original narrator in a form scarcely to be recognized; so, by a little improper influence on the part of landowners, a little favouritism on the part of members of Parliament, a little intriguing of lawyers, a little manoeuvering by contractors and engineers, a little self-seeking on the part of directors, a little understatement of estimates and over-statement of traffic, a little magnifying of the evils to be avoided and the benefits to be gained – it happens that shareholders are betrayed into ruinous undertakings by grossly untrue representations, without any one being guilty of more than a small portion of the fraud. Bearing in mind, then, the comparative laxity of the corporate conscience; the diffusion and remoteness of the evils which malpractices produce; and the composite origin of these malpractices; it becomes possible to understand how, in railway affairs, gigantic dishonesties can be perpetrated by men, who, on the average, are little if at all below the generality in moral character.

With this preliminary mitigation we proceed to detail the various illegitimate agencies by which these seemingly insane extensions and this continual squandering of shareholders' property are brought about.

Conspicuous amongst these is the self-interest of landowners. Once the greatest obstacles to railway enterprise, owners of estates have of late years been amongst its chief promoters. Since the Liverpool and Manchester line was first defeated by landed opposition, and succeeded with its second bill only by keeping out of sight of all mansions, and avoiding the game preserves – since the time when the London and Birmingham company, after seeing their project thrown out by a committee of peers who ignored the evidence, had to 'conciliate' their antagonists by raising the estimate for land from £250,000 to £750,000 – since the time when Parliamentary counsel bolstered up a groundless resistance by the flimsiest and absurdist excuses, even to reproaching engineers with having 'trodden down the corn of widows' and 'destroyed the strawberry beds of gardeners' – since then, a marked change of policy has taken place. Nor was it in human nature that it should be otherwise. When it became known that railway companies commonly paid for 'land and compensation,' sums varying from £4,000 to £8,000 per mile; that men were indemnified for supposed injury to their property by sums so inordinate that the greater part has been known to be returned by the heir as conscience money; that in one case, £120,000 was given for land said to be worth but £5,000 – when it was bruited abroad that large bonuses in the shape of preference shares and the like were granted to buy off opposition – when it came to be an established fact that estates are greatly enhanced in value by the proximity of railways – it is not surprising that country gentlemen should have become active supporters of schemes to which they were once the bitterest enemies. On considering the many temptations, we shall see nothing wonderful in the fact, that in 1845 they were zealous provisional committeemen; nor in the fact, that their influence as promoters enabled them to get good terms for their own acres; nor in the fact that they committed various acts sufficiently reprehensible from any but their own point of view. If we are told of squires soliciting interviews with the engineer of a projected railway; prompting him to take their side of the country; promising support if he did, and threatening opposition if he did not; dictating the course to be followed through their domains; and hinting that a fair price would be expected; we are simply told of the special modes in which certain private interests show themselves. If we hear of an extensive landowner using his influence as chairman of a board of directors to project a branch running for many miles through his own estate, and putting his company to the cost of a parliamentary contest to carry this line; we hear only of that which was likely to occur under such circumstances. If we find now before the public, a line proposed by a large capitalist, serving amongst other ends to effect desirable communications with his property; and the estimates for which line, though considered by the engineering world insufficient, are alleged by him to be ample; we have but a marked case of the distorted representation which under such conditions self-interest is sure to engender. If we discover of this or that scheme that it was got up by the local nobility and gentry – that they employed to make the survey, a third-rate engineer, who was ready, in anticipation of future benefit, to do this for his bare expenses – that principals and agent wearied the directors of an adjacent trunk line to take up their project; threatened that if they did not their great rival would; alarmed them into concession; asked for a contribution to their expenses; and would have gained all these points but for shareholders' resistance – we do but discover the organised tactics which in process of time naturally grow up under such stimuli. It is not that these facts are particularly remarkable. From the gross instance of the landowner who asked for 8,000l. for that which he eventually accepted 80l. for, down to the every day instances of influence used to get railway accommodation for the neighborhood, the acts of the landed class are simply manifestations of the average character acting under special conditions. All that it now behooves us to notice is that we have here a large and powerful body whose interests are very pressing on railway extension irrespective of its intrinsic propriety.

The great change in the attitude of the Legislature towards railways from 'the extreme of determined rejection or dilatory acquiescence to the opposite extreme of unlimited concession,' was simultaneous with the change above described. It could not well fail to be so. Supplying as the landowning community does so large a portion of both Houses of Parliament, it necessarily follows that the play of private interests seen in the first, repeats itself in the last under modified forms, and complicated by other influences. Remembering the extent to which legislators were themselves involved in the speculations of the mania, it is scarcely probable that they should since have been free from personal bias. A return proved, that in 1845 there were 157 members of Parliament, whose names were on the registers of new companies for sums varying from 291,000l. downward. The supporters of new projects boasted of the number of votes they could command in the House. Members were personally canvassed, and peers were solicited. It was publicly complained in the upper chamber that 'it was nearly impossible to bring together a jury, some members of which were not interested in the railway they were about to assess.' Doubtless this state of things was in a great degree exceptional; and there has since been not only a diminution of the temptations, but a marked increase of equitable feeling. Still it is not to be expected that private interests should cease to act. It is not to be expected that a landowner who, out of Parliament, exerts himself to get a railway for his district, should, when in Parliament, not employ the power his new position gives him to the same end. It is not to be expected that the accumulation of such individual actions should leave the legislative policy unchanged. Hence the fact, that the influence once used to throw out railway bills is now used to carry them. Hence the fact, that railway committees no longer require a good traffic case to be made out in justification of the powers asked.

Hence the fact, that the directors and chairmen of boards, with seats in the House of Commons, are induced to pledge their companies to carry out extensions. But it is not only, nor indeed mainly, from directly personal motives that legislators have of late years unduly fostered railway enterprise. Indirect motives of various kinds have been largely operative. The wish to satisfy constituents has been one. Inhabitants of unaccommodated districts are naturally urgent with their representatives to help them to a line. Such representatives are not unfrequently conscious that their next elections may possible turn upon their successful response to this appeal. Even when there is no popular pressure, there is the pressure of their leading political supporters; of large landholders whom it will not do to neglect; of the magistracy with whom it is needful to be on good terms; of local lawyers, important as electioneering friends, to whom a railway always brings business. Thus, without having any immediately private ends, members of Parliament are often almost coerced into pressing forward schemes which from a national, or from the shareholders' point of view, are very unwise ones. Moreover, it requires in fairness to be said, that possessed as most members of Parliament are with the belief that all railway making is nationally beneficial, there exist in their minds few or no reasons for resisting the influences brought to bear on them. True, shareholders may be injured; but that it their own affair: – the public will be better served; constituents will be satisfied; friends will be pleased; perhaps personal ends gained; and under some or all of these incentives affirmative votes are readily given. Thus from the Legislature also there has of late years proceeded a factitious stimulus to railway extensions.

From Parliament to Parliamentary agents, and the general body of lawyers concerned in railway enterprise, is a ready transition. With these, the getting up and carrying of new lines and branches is a matter of business, Whoever studies the process of obtaining a railway act; or considers the number of legal transactions involved in the execution of railway works; or notes the large sums that figure in half-yearly reports under the head of 'law charges'; will at once see how strong are the temptations which a new project holds out to solicitors, conveyancers, and counsel. It has been shown that in past years Parliamentary expenses have varied from 650l. to 3,000l. per mile; of which a large proportion has gone into the pockets of the profession. In one contest 57,000l. was spent amongst six counsel and twenty solicitors. At a late meeting of one of our companies it was pointed out that the sum expended in legal and parliamentary expenses during nine years had reached 480,000l.; or had averaged 53,000l. a year. With these and scores of like facts before them, it would indeed be strange did not so acute a body of men as lawyers use vigorous efforts and sagacious devices to promote fresh enterprises. Indeed, if we look back at the proceedings of 1845 we shall suspect not only that lawyers are still the active promoters of fresh enterprises, but often the originators of them. Most persons have heard how in those excited times the projects daily announced were very frequently set afloat by local solicitors – how these looked over maps to see where plausible lines could be sketched out – how they canvassed the local gentry to obtain provisional committeemen – how they agreed with engineers to make trial surveys – how, under the wild hopes of the day, they found little difficulty in forming companies – and how most of them managed to get as far as the Committee on Standing Orders, if no farther. Remembering all this, and remembering that those who were successful are not likely to have forgotten their cunning, but rather to have yearly exercised and increased it, we may naturally expect to find railway lawyers amongst the most influential of the many parties conspiring to urge railway proprietaries into disastrous undertakings: and we shall not be deceived. To a great extent they are in league with engineers. From the proposal to the completion of a new line the lawyer and the engineer work together; and their interests are throughout identical. Whilst the one makes the survey, the other prepares the book of reference. The parish plans which the one gets ready, the other deposits. The notices to owners and occupiers which the one fills in, the other serves upon those concerned. Throughout there is continual consultation between them as to the dealing with local opposition and the obtainment of local support. In the getting up of their case for Parliament they necessarily act in concert. Whilst before committees the one gets his ten guineas per day for attending to give evidence, the other makes profits on all the complicated transactions which the carrying a bill involves. During the execution of the works they are in frequent correspondence; and alike profit by any expansion of the undertaking. Thus there naturally arises in each the perception that in aiding the other he is aiding himself; and gradually, as in course of years, the proceedings come to be often repeated, and a perfect familiarity with railway politics gained, there naturally grows up a well-organized system of co-operation between them – a system rendered the more efficient by the wealth and influence which each has year by year accumulated.

Amongst the manoeuvers employed by railway solicitors thus established and thus helped, not the least remarkable is that of getting their own nominees elected as directors. Startling though it may seem, it is yet a fact, which we state on good authority, that there are puppet-directors who vote for this or that at the instigation of the company's lawyers, whose creatures they are. The obtainment of such tools is by no means difficult. Vacancies are about to occur in the directorate. Almost always there are sundry men over whom a solicitor, conducting the extensive law business of a railway, has considerable power; not only connections and friends, but clients and persons to whom, in his legal capacity, he can do great benefit or great injury. He selects the most suitable of these; giving preference, if other things are equal, to one living in the country near the line. On opening the matter to him, he points out the sundry advantages attendant on a director's position – the free pass and the many facilities it gives; the annual 100l. or so which the office brings; the honour and influence accruing; the opportunities for profitable investment that are likely to occur; and so forth. Should ignorance of railway affairs be raised as an objection, the tempter, in whose eyes the ignorance is a chief recommendation, replies that he shall always be at hand to guide his votes. Should non-possession of a due amount of the company's stock be pleaded, the tempter readily meets the difficulty by offering himself to furnish the needful qualification.

Thus incited and flattered, and, perhaps, conscious that it would be dangerous to refuse, the intended puppet allows himself to be put in nomination; and as it is the general habit of half-yearly meetings, unless under great indignation, to elect any one proposed to them by those in authority, the nomination is successful. On subsequent occasions this proceeding can, of course, be repeated; and thus the company's legal agent and those leagued with him may command sufficient votes to turn the sale in their own favour.

Then to the personal interest and power of the head solicitor have to be added those of the local ones, with whom he is in constant business intercourse. They, too, profit by new undertakings; they, therefore, are commonly urgent in pressing them forwards. Acting in co-operation with their chief, they form a local staff of great influence. They are active canvassers; they stimulate and concentrate the feeling of their districts; they encourage rivalry with other lines; they alarm local shareholders with rumours of threatened competition. When the question of extension or non-extension comes to a division, they collect proxies for the extension party. They bring pressure to bear on their shareholding clients and relatives. Nay, so deep an interest do they feel in the decision as occasionally to manufacture votes with the view of influencing it. We have before us the case of a local solicitor, who, before the special meeting called to adopt or reject a contemplated branch, transferred portions of his own shares into the names of sundry members of his family, and so multiplied his seventeen votes into forty-one; all of which he recorded for the adoption of the new scheme.

Greatly as engineers are interested in railway enterprise, it is to be expected that they should be active, and not very scrupulous promoters of it. To illustrate the vigour and skill with which they further new undertakings, a few facts may be cited. Not far from London, and lying between two lines of railway, is an estate that has been purchased by one of our engineers. He has since obtained Acts for branches to both of the adjacent lines. One of these branches he has leased to the company whose line it joins; and he has tried to do the like with the other, but as yet without success. Even as it is, however, he is considered to have doubled the value of his property. To press forward extensions by the companies with which they are connected, they occasionally go to great lengths. Not long since, at a half-yearly meeting, certain projects which the proprietary had already once rejected, were again brought forward by two engineers who attended in their capacity of shareholders. Though known to be personally interested, one of them moved and the other seconded, that certain proposals from the promoters of these schemes be considered without delay by the directors. The motion was carried; the directors approved the proposals; and again, the proprietors negatived them. A third time a like effort was made; a third time a conflict arose; and within a few days of the special meeting at which the division was to take place, one of these engineers circulated amongst the shareholders a pamphlet denying the allegations of the dissentient party and making counter-statements, which it was then too late to meet – nay, he did more; he employed agents to canvass the shareholders for proxies in support of the new undertaking, and was obliged to confess as much when charged with it at the meeting.

Turn we now to contractors. Railway enterprise has given to this class of men a gigantic development, not only in respect of numbers, but in respect of the vast wealth to which some of them have attained. Originally, half a dozen miles of earthwork, fencing, and bridges, was as much as any single contractor undertook. Of late years, however, it has become common for one man to engage to construct an entire railway and deliver it over to the company in a fit condition for opening. Great capital is necessarily required for this; great profits are made by it; and the fortunes accumulated, in course of time, have been such that sundry contractors are described as being each able to make a railway at his own expense. But they are insatiate as millionaires in general; and so long as they continue in business at all, are, in some sort, forced to provide new undertakings to keep their plant employed. As may be imagined, enormous stocks of working materials are needed; many hundreds of earth-wagons, and of horses; many miles of temporary rails and sleepers; some half dozen locomotive engines, and several fixed ones; innumerable tools; beside vast stores of timber, bricks, stone, rails, and other constituents of permanent works, that have been bought on speculation. To keep the capital thus invested, and also a large staff of *employés*, standing idle, entails loss, partly negative, partly positive. The great contractor, therefore, is alike under a pressing stimulus to get fresh work, and enabled by his wealth to do this. Hence the not unfrequent inversion of the old arrangement under which companies and engineers employed contactors, into an arrangement under which contractors employ engineers and form companies. Many recent undertaking have been thus set on foot. The most gigantic project which private enterprise has yet dared – a project, of which, unfortunately, there is now no hope – originated with a distinguished contracting firm. In some cases, as in this chief one, this mode of procedure may be considered as advantageous; but in a far greater proportion of cases its results are disastrous. Interested in promoting railway extensions even in a greater degree than engineers and lawyers, contractors frequently co-operate with these either as agents or as coadjutors. Lines are fostered into being, which it is known from the very beginning, will not pay. Of late it has become common for landowners, merchants, and others personally interested, who, under the belief that their indirect gains will compensate for their meagre dividends, have themselves raised part of the capital for a local railway, but who cannot raise the rest – it has become common for such to make an agreement with a wealthy contractor to construct the line, taking in part payment a portion of the shares, amounting to, perhaps, a third of the whole, and to charge for his work according to a schedule of prices to be thereafter settled between himself and the engineer. By this last clause the contractor renders himself secure. It would never answer his purpose to take part payment in shares likely to return some 2*l.* per cent, unless he compensated himself by unusually high profits; and this subsequent settlement of prices with one whose interests, like his own, are wrapped up in the prosecution of the undertaking, insures him high profits. Meanwhile, the facts that all the capital has been subscribed and the line contracted for, unduly raise the public estimate of the scheme; the shares are quoted at much above their true worth; unwary persons buy; the contractor from time to time parts with his moiety at fair prices; and the new shareholders ultimately find themselves part owners of a railway which, unprofitable as it originally promised to be, has been made yet more unprofitable by expensiveness of construction. Nor are these the only cases in which contractors gain after this fashion. They do the like with undertakings of their own projecting. To obtain acts for these, they sign the subscription contracts for large accounts; knowing, that in the way above described, they can always make it answer to do this. So general had the practice latterly become as to attract the attention of committees. As was remarked by a personage noted for his complicity in these transactions; 'Committees are getting too knowing; they won't stand that dodge now'. Nevertheless, the thing is still done under a disguised form. Though contractors no longer enter their own names on subscription lists for thousands of shares, yet they effect the same end by making nominal holders of their foremen and others; themselves being the real ones.

Of directorial misdoings some samples have already been referred to; and more might be added. Besides those arising from directly personal aims are sundry others. One of these is, the still increasing community between railway boards and the House of Commons. There are eighty-one directors sitting in Parliament; and though many of them take little or no part in the affairs of their respective railways, many of them are the most active members of the boards to which they belong. We have but to look back a few years and mark the unanimity with which companies adopted the policy of getting themselves represented in the Legislature, to see that the furtherance of their respective interests – especially in case of competition – was the incentive. How well this policy is understood amongst the initiated may be judged from the fact that gentlemen are now in some cases elected on boards simply because they are members of Parliament. Of course this implies that railway legislation is affected by a complicated play of private influences; and that these influences generally work towards the facilitation of new enterprises is tolerably obvious. It naturally happens that directors whose companies are not opposed, exchange good offices. It naturally happened that they can more or less smooth the way of their annual batch of new bills through committees. Moreover, directors sitting in the House of Commons not only facilitate the passing of the schemes in which they are interested, but are solicited to undertake further schemes by those around them. It is a very common sense conclusion that representatives of small towns and country districts needing railway accommodation, who are daily thrown in contact with the chairman of a company capable of giving this accommodation, will not neglect the opportunity of furthering their ends. It is a very common sense conclusion that by hospitalities, by favours, by flattery, by the many means used to bias men, they will seek to obtain his good offices. And it is an equally common sense conclusion that in many cases they will succeed – that by some complication of persuasions and temptations they will swerve him from his calmer judgment; and so introduce into the company he represents, influences at variance with its welfare.

Under some motives, however – whether those of direct self-interest, or private favour, or of antagonistic feeling, need not here be discussed – it is certain that directors are constantly committing their constituents to unwise enterprises; and that they frequently employ unjustifiable means for either eluding or overcoming their opposition, Shareholders occasionally find that their directors have given to Parliament, pledges of extension much exceeding what they were authorized to give; and are then persuaded that they are bound to endorse the promises made for them by their agents. In some cases, among the misleading statements laid before shareholders to obtain their consent to a new project, will be found an abstract of the earnings of a previously executed branch or feeder to which the proposed one bears some analogy. These earnings are shown (not always without 'cooking') to be tolerably good and improving; and it is argued that the new project having like prospects offers a fair investment. Meanwhile, it is not stated that the capital for this previously executed branch or feeder was raised on debentures or by guaranteed shares, at a higher rate of interest than the dividend pays; it is not stated that as the capital for this further undertaking will be raised on like terms the annual interest on debt will swallow up more than the annual revenue; and thus unsuspecting shareholders – some unacquainted with the company's antecedents, some unable to understand its complicated accounts – give their proxies or raise their hands for new works which will tell with disastrous effect on their future dividends.

To complete the sketch, it requires to say something on the management of board meetings and meetings of the shareholders. For the first – their decisions are affected by various manoeuvres. Of course, on the fit occasions there is a whipping up of those favourable to any project which it is desired to carry. Were this all, there would be little to complain of; but something more than this is done. There are boards in which it is the practice to defeat opposition by stratagem. The extension party having summoned their forces for the occasion, and having entered on the minutes of business a notice worded with the requisite vagueness, shape their proceedings according to the character of the meeting. Should their antagonists muster more strongly than was expected, this vaguely-worded notice serves simply to introduce some general statement or further information concerning the project named in it; and the matter is passed over as though nothing more had been meant. On the contrary, should the proportion of the two sides be more favourable, the notice becomes the basis of a definite motion committing the board to some important procedure. If due precautions have been taken the motion is passed; and once passed, those who, if present, would have resisted it have no remedy; for in railway government there is no 'second reading', much less a third. So determined and so unscrupulous are the efforts sometimes made by the stronger party to overcome and silence their antagonists, that when a contested measure, carried by them at the board, has to go before a general meeting for confirmation, they have even been known to pass a resolution that their dissentient colleagues shall not address the proprietary!

How, at half-yearly and special meetings, shareholders should be so readily led by boards, even after repeated experience of their untrustworthiness, seems at first sight difficult to understand. The mystery disappears, however, on inquiry. Very frequently contested measures are carried quite against the sense of the meetings before which they are laid, by means of the large number of proxies previously collected by the directors. These proxies are obtained mostly from proprietors scattered everywhere throughout the kingdom, who are very generally weak enough to sign the first document sent to them. Then of those present when the question is brought to an issue, not many dare attempt a speech; of those who dare, but few are clearheaded enough to see the full bearings of the measure they are about to vote upon; and such as can see it are often prevented by nervousness from doing justice to the views they hold. Moreover, it must be borne in mind that the party displaying antagonism to the board are apt to be regarded by their brother proprietors with more or less reprobation. Unless the misconduct of the governing body has been very glaring or very recent, there ever arises in the mass a prejudice against all playing the part of an opposition. They are condemned as noisy, and factious, and obstructive; and often only by very determined courage avoid being put down. Besides these negative reasons for the general inefficiency of shareholders' resistance, there are sundry positive ones. As writes a Member of Parliament who has been an extensive holder of stock in many Companies from the first days of railway enterprise: – 'My large and long acquaintance with Railway Companies' affairs enables me to say that a large majority of shareholders trust wholly to their directors, having little or no information, nor caring to have any opinion of their own: . . . some others, better informed but timid, are afraid, by opposing the directors, of causing a depreciation of the value of their stock in the market, and are more alarmed at the prospect of this temporary depreciation than at the permanent loss entailed on the company by the useless and therefore unprofitable outlay of additional capital: . . . others again, believing that the impending permanent evil is inevitable, resolve on the spot to sell out immediately, and to keep up the prices of their shares, also give their support to the directors.' Thus, from the lack of organization and efficiency amongst those who express their opposition, and from the timidity and double-facedness of those who do not, it happens that extremely unwise projects are carried by large majorities. Nor it this all. The tactics of the aggressive party are commonly as skillful as those of their antagonists are bungling. In the first place the chairman, who is very generally the chief promoter of the contested scheme, has it in his power to favour those who take his own side, and to throw difficulties in the way of opponents; and this he not unfrequently does to a great extent – refusing to hear, putting down on some plea of breach or order, browbeating, even using threats. It generally turns out too, that whether intentionally or not, some of the most important motions are postponed until nearly the close of the meeting, when the greater proportion of the shareholders are gone: large money-votes, extensive powers, unlimited permits to directors to take, in certain matters, 'such steps as in their judgment they may deem most expedient,' – these and the like are left to be hurried over during the last half-hour, when the tired and impatient remnant will no longer listen to objectors; and when those who have personal ends to serve by outstaying the rest carry everything their own way. Indeed, in some instances, the arrangements are such as almost to insure the meeting becoming a pro-extension one towards the end. The result is brought about thus: – A certain portion of the general body of proprietors are also proprietors of some subordinate work – some branch line, or steam-boats, or canal, which the Company has purchased or leased; and as holders of guaranteed stock, probably having capital to take up further such stock if they can get it, they are naturally favourable to projects that are to be executed on the preference-share system. These hold their meeting for the declaration of dividend, &c, as soon as the meeting of the Company at large has been dissolved, and in the same room. Hence it happens that being kept together by prospect of subsequent business they gradually, toward the close of the general meeting, come to form the majority of those present; and the ordinary shareholders who have been patient enough to stay, are outvoted by those having interests quite distinct form their own – quite at variance with the welfare of the Company.

And here this allusion to the preference-share system introduces us to a *fact* which may fitly close this detail of private interests and questionable practices – a fact serving at once to illustrate the subtlety and concert of railway officialism, and the power it can exert. That this fact can be fully appreciated it must be premised that though preference-shares do not usually carry votes they are sometimes specially endowed with them; and further, that they occasionally remain unpaid up until the expiration of a time after which no further calls can be legally made. In the case in question a large number of £50 preference-shares had thus long stood with but £5 paid. Those desirous of promoting extensions, &c, had here a fine opportunity of getting great power in the Company at small cost; and as we shall see they duly availed themselves of it. Already had their party twice tried to thrust the proprietary into a new undertaking of great magnitude. Twice had they entailed on them an expensive and harassing contest. A third time, notwithstanding a professed relinquishment of it, they brought forward substantially the same scheme, and were defeated only by a small majority.

Part 3

THE COMING OF LIMITED LIABILITY

18

THE PENNY SAVED

Henry Morley

Source: Henry Morley, 'The Penny Saved; A Blue-Book Catechism,' *Household Words* 2 (October 19, 1850), pp. 81–84.

EDITORIAL HEADNOTE

Henry Morley (1822–1894) was the son of an apothecary. He studied at King's College, London before qualifying as an apothecary himself. Morley later established a school in Manchester and began writing in his spare time. He published some satirical articles that attracted the attention of Charles Dickens, who in 1850 invited Morley to become a contributor to *Household Words*. "The Penny Saved" is an example of this work. Morley later became Professor of English Literature at University College, London. He is best remembered for his ten-volume literary history, *English Writers* (1864–1894).[1]

"The Penny Saved," written as a dialog between a working-class father and son, advocated for an extension of limited liability to Industrial Associations, allowing working men to pool their resources for business purposes. Morley saw this as a modest alternative to the "rich man's law" that required an expensive incorporation or a royal charter of limited liability.

Note

1 Fred Hunter, "Morley, Henry," *Oxford Dictionary of National Biography*, eds. H.C.G. Matthew and Brian Harrison (Oxford: Oxford University Press, 2004), Vol. 39, pp. 222–23.

Rising Young Operative. "Please, father, what is a blue-book?"

Paternal Operative. "A blue-book is a thick heavy catechism done up in blue covers."

"What is it for?"

DOI: 10.4324/9781003713890-21

"Why, when Parliament sets some of its Members to inquire about a subject, and hear evidence quietly in a room for to get at facts, they print the evidence and so on, and send it to all the other Members, so that they may read and know the facts."

"What is that blue-book you have borrowed to read?"

"It is all about Savings Banks."

"But do not the Parliament men know all about Savings Banks already?"

"Not a bit. That's why they have to make these huge blue-books to tell 'em. This one is on the 'Savings of the Middle and Working Classes.' As secretary to our shop-savings club, I was examined as one of the witnesses."

Inquisitive Shop-mate. "Don't you think it is a blest hardship that if a man saves enough to buy a bit of land he is not able by law to do so?"

"Why, for sums between one hundred and five hundred pounds it's shockingly difficult to get good and safe investments of any sort from the present state of the law."

"If you want to buy a bit of land you can't – especially if it is mortgaged, – can you?"

"Not by no means. Why it costs more than the land is worth to what they call 'investigate the title.'"

"Then people can't club small sums and be partners in an enterprise, can they?"

"Oh, bless you, no! If they do so without a Charter or an Act of Parliament, every one of them is responsible to no end of money."

"And people who know what they're about, don't eh?"

"No, indeed. If a man has fifty pounds, he can't say he'll subscribe five to a concern and loose so much if it fail. He must be ready to lose all his fifty if it fails. People with five hundred pounds to invest, can't invest fifty as a share in such an enterprise and go no further. They must risk all their five hundred on the venture, though they are sure of only getting profit on the five. So they don't invest in that way, when they're prudent; but the reckless do."

"What is the cause of that?"

"The Law of Partnership."

"But does not that affect the rich as well?"

"Yes, but a larger enterprise, with money at command, affords to buy an Act of Parliament or Charter, but that luxury is too expensive for a little undertaking."

"What do you call a little undertaking?"

"A Society for the Improvement of Dwellings of the Poor; or a Society for Building Baths and Washhouses, or anything of that sort – any local improvement of a humble character is too small to afford a Charter."

"Why, what then does a Charter cost?"

"Some hundreds. The Charter of the Metropolitan Association for Improving the Dwellings of the Industrious Classes cost one thousand one hundred and thirty-nine pounds, seven shillings, and eightpence; out of which seven hundred and twenty-four pounds, ten shillings, and eightpence went in pure fees to Crown officers. Here it is all down in the blue-book."

"Indeed! Well, well, what next?"

"Why the next thing was that six or a dozen similar societies in different parts of the country, finding the cost of a Charter, abandoned their benevolent designs."

"What good would a Charter have done them? Why couldn't they go on without it?"

"A Charter would have placed them out of the law of partnership, and enabled the projectors and supporters of the charity to contribute to it according to their means. Without it they would be responsible for its success with all their property."

"Is that the law of partnership?"

"Yes. By the English law of partnership, all partners are answerable with their whole substance for the acts of any one."

"You say by the English law; but does not the same law exist in other countries?"

"Certainly not. All civilized countries differ from England in the law of partnership. They have either partnerships in which responsibility is altogether limited, the limit being in each case known; or they have a kind of partnership called *commandite*."

"And what is the *commandite* partnership?"

"Here you have it: The partnership *en commandite* allows any number of men to subscribe money to an undertaking in a limited amount; they are the *commanditaires*, and they are not allowed to perform any act of management; the managers of any partnership *en commandite* become responsible with all their property."

"Is not that the same as if the managers of an English partnership borrowed the money supplied elsewhere by *commanditaires*?"

"No, it is not. The lender is a creditor with the other creditors, but the *commanditaire* can have no claim until all the creditors are paid. A firm that borrows, multiplies its liabilities; monies advanced *en commandite* multiplies strength."

"Does English law deter people from speculation?"

"Quite the contrary, it perverts wholesome enterprise into a gambler's risk, and converts numerous undertakings into speculations which would otherwise be fit for prudent men to patronise, to an extent suited to their means. It filters out sensible people, and lets the reckless pass through into the management of valuable projects."

"How does this act upon us handicraftsmen and operatives?"

"Not directly, in this latter point of view. His labour is his capital. It is not much to him to lose his all of cash. But it deters people of the middle class – people with three hundred pounds or four hundred pounds capital, and others of a higher class than that – from sharing in a great number of small undertakings which are of true value to the poor. The law of partnership in England needs revision, and will be revised; but the direct wants of the poor man can be met without revising it."

"How does it act directly on the poor?"

"It is a rich man's law. If working-men combine for any purpose of industry, one may defraud the rest of all the common stock, or any part of it, and there is no redress for the defrauded parties – no redress of any certain kind, or of a kind cheaply attainable."

"What sort of law ought we to have, then?"

"An extension of an Act that they already have to protect Friendly Societies, which should protect also Industrial Associations; make them legal under a law all their own, enable them to bring disputes before a magistrate, and summarily punish any one among them who should act dishonestly toward the rest."

"And these Industrial Associations, what do the workmen want with them?"

"Well, I'll tell you. Look at my case. Once I worked as journeyman to a rich man, who established with his capital a large shop, and bought for himself a country-house. He lives in his country-house, and seldom sees his shop; he pays wages to a large number of workmen, receives their work, and sells it to the public at a price which enables him to pay a manager for overlooking us, and live at ease upon the surplus, doing nothing. That made us think that if some of us, who were steady, clubbed together to maintain a shop, we might sell our work in it ourselves, and so divide among ourselves the profit of our labour; it goes now to a master who does nothing, and whose sole advantage over us is that of having capital."

"But your Association might not answer?"

"Perhaps not; but what we say is, that the law gives a rich man power to use us, and compels us to be used. It is at our own peril if we club our work together and try to get the entire value of our labour for ourselves; no law protects us against one cheat among a hundred companions. We say that we are not free men, if we have not a right to earn our bread in any honest way we can. It's very likely most of us would still prefer to work for certain wages; and we'd be well content to do so if we did so by our own free choice; but we are not content because we have not liberty of action."

"What do you want, then?"

"Why we cannot now associate without making ourselves a Joint-Stock Company, and coming under a parcel of laws made for people who can wrap up every penny we have in a five-pound note. We want extended reading of the Friendly Societies Act, so that we may have liberty to combine our labours if we please, and cheap protection, when we do so, against one another. We want no special advantages. We only want our arms untied; free-trade in labour. Let us find out for ourselves what is good for us; don't hinder us from any fair attempt to turn our money to advantage; don't compel us to work for a master and put our money in the Savings Banks, or Three per Cents. It may be some of you are right in saying that it is best for us. Perhaps it is. If it is, we shall find it out also, never fear. But let us find it out; don't dictate to us, leave us free to act; and then, if we go wrong, we shall know it's our own fault, or a thing that can't be helped; and not put down a part of it to your denial of our honest wishes. Fustian doesn't envy

Broadcloth; each lives best in the society to which he has been born; but fettered men envy the free. The way to spread content among the working-classes, is to show them that you look on them as men and not as children, and to give them choice to earn their bread on any path they like, that is an honest one.

"Do you think we ought to have what we want?"

"Of course, I do. Whether the plan of Industrial Associations would succeed is, of course, yet uncertain, but it well deserves a trial. More than that, – we ought to have the right of trying it. Then, if we fail, we should know who is to blame; and those few (for there would not, at first, be a large number probably) who commenced with the experiment would go back to the old plan of wages."

"But if they succeeded and this system spread?"

"Then that would be a blessing to this country. The class of middlemen who live upon the work of others is now very large; that would decrease, and the country would be enriched by a far larger number of producers. The loss of intermediate profit-takers would also cheapen produce, and a more extended sense throughout the country that each man was working for himself would impart to the whole body of the people a free manly tone, and give to all a greater interest in peace and order. I think, that although the result may possibly not realise a sanguine vision, yet, that it is unjust to forbid attempts which point in a right direction. If we neglect these wishes of the working-classes, we cannot wonder if they say that rich men make rights for themselves which do not fit the uses of the poor, and give the poor man no equivalent."

"What are they going to do about Savings Banks?"

"Government says, it intends to be responsible for their security, and that will take away a prevalent impression that they are unsafe. Possibly, as they are the safest, so they are the best investment for the savings of the working-classes, but we have no right to drive them to this kind of hoarding. The mere sense of so much money being kept for them by other people, out of their sight, has not so great a moral hold upon their minds as would be had by something which they every day could see and use. If they invested savings in their daily work, in cottages, or, better still, a piece of ground, which they could call their own, man is so constituted as to be more usefully acted upon by that visible fruit of his exertion than by the abstract idea of possessing its equivalent in money. That is truer of a man the more you find him unsophisticated. I would, therefore, have the workman's labour and the money, or the fruit of it, to be his own, and remove all removable impediments to his free use of either."

"You think much of investment in a cottage or a piece of land?"

"Yes, all experience abroad, and all we know of history, and all we see doing about us, show how beneficial such investments are."

"All this being the case, what do you mean to say at the next meeting of our Shop Savings Bank?"

"Why, I mean to make a speech. I mean to say, that both the middle and the working-classes of men desire to invest money in land. That the uncertainty and complexity of titles, the length and expenses of conveyances, together with the cost of stamps, place such investments beyond common reach. ('Hear, hear!' from the Rising Young Operative and the Shop-mate). That simplifying titles, shortening conveyances, would be a good thing for the landowners themselves, by increasing the available value of their property. And then I shall wind up by saying, that I know, from what I was told by a lawyer, yesterday, that it would be easy enough to simplify the present law."

19

REMARKS ON THE LAW OF PARTNERSHIP

Lord Hobart

Source: Lord Hobart, *Remarks on the Law of Partnership Liability* (London: John W. Parker and Son, 1853), pp. 9–15.

EDITORIAL HEADNOTE

Vere Henry Hobart, Lord Hobart (1818–1875) was the son of the sixth Earl of Buckinghamshire. He studied at Trinity College, Oxford and worked at the Board of Trade and the Home Office. He was appointed Governor of Madras in 1872 and held this office until his death in India from typhoid fever in 1875. Hobart published numerous essays and pamphlets on economic and political issues of the day.[1]

Hobart advocated for an extension of limited liability to create new investment outlets in Britain for the estimated £40 million of capital added to national wealth annually. He believed that unlimited liability imposed "a severe check upon the associative employment of capital in this country" and led to Britons investing their money abroad.

Note

1 N.D.F. Pearce, "Hobart, Vere Henry," *Oxford Dictionary of National Biography*, eds. H.C.G. Matthew and Brian Harrison (Oxford: Oxford University Press, 2004), Vol. 27, p. 384.

We now proceed to deal with the question as one of expediency – or, in other words, to inquire what is the economic effect of the present law of partnership liability, and whether that law might be altered with advantage to the material interests of the community.

It is a fact of which there can be no reasonable doubt, that the present law of partnership liability acts as a formidable obstacle to the associative investment of

DOI: 10.4324/9781003713890-22

capital, 1, – In the most common form which such investment assumes, viz., that of contribution to a company composed of shareholders, who elect from time to time some of their number to act as directors; and 2, – In the form which it may also take of an alliance between capital on the one hand, and skill on the other; as, for instance, where a person has made a discovery, or projected an undertaking, which he proposes to carry on by means of loans obtained from other persons, at an interest varying with the profits of his enterprise.

Under the present law, it is very rarely that capital is associated in either of these forms, because the contributors of capital, whether as shareholders or lenders of money, would each of them be liable to the full extent of his property for the debts incurred in respect of the undertaking for the purposes of which the capital was raised.

By those who advocate the continuance of the present law the assertion that it forms a bar to the associative employment of capital is sometimes met by a simple denial; and it is urged, in the way of illustration, that no person in this country who may be desirous of investing money in any associative undertaking, has any difficulty whatever in doing so.

Now, in the first place, it is to be observed that, so far as this proposition is true, it is true only because the Legislature and the Crown has, to a not inconsiderable extent, relaxed the law affecting partnership liability. Were it not that all railway companies, gas companies, water companies, some steam-boat companies requiring very large capital, and a few other associations, have been incorporated by the Crown, or by Act of Parliament, and have thus obtained the exceptional privilege of limited liability, there would be the greatest possible difficulty in making investments of the nature referred to. To persons desirous of investing money in associative concerns in this country none would have presented themselves but the Government funds, or such associations as might be formed in spite of the law of liability. As regards the latter, their number has always been very small in proportion to the national wealth. The Government funds, therefore, would have been the only popular investment; and it is sufficiently obvious, that loans to the government, occurring at intervals of many years, could not have afforded full employment to the continually increasing capital of the country.

In the next place, although the law has been relaxed to the extent above mentioned, it certainly cannot be said that, thus relaxed, it no longer imposes any serious restriction on the associative employment of the capital of the country; or, in other words, that by such relaxation provision has been made for the associative employment of the whole or the greater portion of that capital. The increase of the capital of this country has been estimated at 40,000,000*l.* annually; and this sum is probably below its real amount. Supposing, then, for the purposes of argument, that the whole of the capital which possessors are desirous of investing associatively, is at present invested in the Government funds, and in the undertakings above mentioned, as, namely, railway, gas, and other companies, and in the few companies acting without limited liability – is it to be imagined that, under the present law, there will be an increase in the number of these investments sufficient to keep pace with an increase of capital proceeding at the rate of 40,000,000*l.* annually? There is no prospect of any large addition to our national debt; the number of our railway companies is not likely materially to increase; most of our towns are provided with gas and water companies: and with regard to companies acting without limited liability, there seems no disposition on the part of the public to add to their number or importance, which are both very inconsiderable.

It seems sufficiently clear, then, that the law of partnership liability imposes a severe check upon the associative employment of capital in this country; and so far as it produces this effect, it must, even on the favourable supposition that the capital which fails to obtain such employment at home does not seek for it abroad, be the occasion of serious national loss. This is sufficiently evident in cases where the employment of capital which the law prevents is the alliance before referred to of capital with skill. As respects the more ordinary form of commercial association, – there are many undertakings of such magnitude, that they cannot be carried on by what may be termed individual capital, and this is of course the class of undertakings from which the largest amount of national profit is to be derived; – and there are others which, though they may be carried on with *some* profit by means of a small capital, cannot be carried on so profitably by a small capital as by a large one. In preventing therefore the association of capital in this form, the law occasions the neglect of many undertakings which would be productive of great profit to the nation, and is the cause of other undertakings being conducted less productively than might otherwise have been the case.

The opponents of any change in the law have indeed gone so far as to deny that there are any undertakings presenting a reasonable prospect of profit, for the prosecution of which capital is not forthcoming in this country, notwithstanding the present state of the law. Thus Lord Overstone (then Mr. Jones Loyd) in his paper appended to Mr. B. Ker's Report of 1837 to the House of Commons, on the Law of Partnership, expresses himself as follows: –

"I am not aware of any facts from which it can be inferred that the employment of capital is unduly checked, or that undertakings presenting a fair prospect of profit are neglected in consequence of the present state of the Law of Partnership."

Now, it must in the first place be remarked, that the chief reason given by Lord Overstone for his opinion that the fact must be as he states, is this: "That the abundance of capital and active spirit of enterprise and commercial emulation which exist in England, are found to be practically sufficient to secure the prosecution of any undertaking of reasonable promise." It is clear, however, that this spirit must have existed before the incorporation of railway and other companies; yet it will hardly be contended that if the Legislature had refused to incorporate such companies, and so to confer upon them limited liability, they would have been established to anything like their present extent; – at least, if we are to suppose that such would have been the case, the legislative incorporation of such companies was a useless measure, a proposition which (it is believed) has never yet been advanced.

In the next place, it is a fact of which the whole mercantile community is well aware – that schemes are daily presenting themselves, of the success of which there is a reasonable probability, but from the prosecution of which men are deterred from a consideration of the law of liability. If evidence were wanting of this, it would be supplied by the Records of the Board of Trade, to which notwithstanding the expense attendant upon a royal charter conferring limited liability, a great number of applications are now and have for a long time been made, for the purpose of obtaining such charters. Many of these have probably no other object than to obtain a premium on allotted shares; but very many also unquestionably relate to projects of whose success there is a "fair prospect," but for which sufficient capital cannot be raised unless limited liability is granted to the shareholders. To most of these the Board of Trade is compelled to give a refusal; for there are only a very few special cases in which that department considers itself at liberty to advise the Crown to grant privileges which are at variance with the common law of the country.

The loss to the nation will be still more serious, supposing that the capital which in vain seeks associative investment at home, seeks and finds it in foreign countries; and unfortunately this supposition, while it is the most unfavourable to national wealth, seems also to be that which is most in accordance with fact. Greater facilities of intercourse between nations, and more cosmopolitan habits both physical and mental have of late years rendered the transfer of capital from one country to another a matter of comparative ease and frequency; and it is now scarcely to be expected that capital will remain at home which can be employed more productively, by being employed associatively, abroad. It is accordingly notorious that a large and increasing amount of British capital is employed in foreign countries. There are no means of ascertaining the amount with anything like accuracy; but it is certainly very large, and probably much larger than is generally supposed.

20

OBSERVATIONS ON UNLIMITED AND LIMITED LIABILITY

William Hawes

Source: William Hawes, *Observations on Unlimited and Limited Liability; and Suggestions for the Improvement of the Law of Partnership* (London: W. Clowes and Sons, 1854), pp. 17–30.

EDITORIAL HEADNOTE

William Hawes (1805–1885) was an English businessman and reformer. The son of a wealthy London soap manufacturer, he worked in the family business and later served as chairman on the London and County Bank and director of the Wallingford and Watlington Railway. Hawes was an active member of several learned societies, including the Geological Society, the Royal Institution, and the Statistical Society. In 1857 he became a founding member of the Social Science Association. Hawes was especially interested in the reform of commercial law.

In this work, Hawes insists that the dangers of unlimited liability have been greatly exaggerated. "There is no risk, if ordinary care and prudence be exercised, that the last shilling or the last acre will ever be called for." He believed that limited liability posed far greater risks to national wealth as it would encourage reckless speculation and relieve investors of their obligation to exercise "prudence, foresight, and care" in the employment of their capital.[1]

Note

1 James Taylor, *Creating Capitalism* (London: Royal Historical Society, 2006), p. 75.

DOI: 10.4324/9781003713890-23

Does the Law of Unlimited Liability Exclude Capital from Commerce?

The advocates of limited liability assert –

1. That the law of unlimited liability interferes with the employment of capital in a manner quite inconsistent with the principles of Free Trade.
2. That it excludes, what they are pleased to call, cheap capital from trade; and
3. They dwell at great length, and with great emphasis, on the injury done to the commerce of the country by the retention of monopoly, as they term it, of the employment of capital in trade by those engaged in business, for they assert that no prudent person not actually engaged in trade can be so infatuated as to risk his last shilling and his last acre, by embarking his capital in partnerships with unlimited liability; or in the words of the *Westminster Review*, "that ruin threatens all who may embark a shilling in (unlimited) partnership."

I will first consider whether capital is excluded from commerce by this law; and then whether its cost is raised thereby to the borrower.

The first and best answer to this absurd proposition is the enormous amount of capital now invested in Joint Stock Banks and other Companies, and in private partnerships with unlimited liability, and the security of which depends entirely upon the skillful management of well-selected Directors and Managers, and the judgment and honesty of partners.

In the vast majority of cases the reliance upon this skillful management, and upon the integrity and judgment of partners, is well placed and is not attended with ruin to the lender; in some cases, however, it cannot be denied that misfortune and loss follow such reliance. But before we condemn the system which obliges partners who can do so, to liquidate the liabilities they have incurred, or which have been incurred with their sanction by the agents they have employed, by whose means, and perhaps by whose previously rash speculations they have received large profits, we must enquire whether the fault and loss originate with the law, or result from the want of prudence, foresight, and care, of those who have entrusted their capital to improper persons.

There are no data respecting the number of, or the amount of capital invested in, private partnerships upon which we can reason; but the number of Dissolutions published in the *Gazette*, amounting to above 3,000 per annum, and not including those terminated by death or by bankruptcy, may afford some idea of the number formed annually. It is impossible to form any estimate of the amount of capital employed in private partnerships but few will dispute that it exceeds by many times that invested in chartered companies, for we find by the Parliamentary return just published, that the number of Joint Stock Companies fully registered during the past year, has been only 122. That friends out of business lend money to those who are engaged in business, and occasionally suffer loss, is too notorious to be disputed; but that such friends are frequently, or indeed but very rarely, brought in as partners, and obliged to pay as far as they are able the partnership debts is, I believe, entirely untrue. I am sure, were the annals of our

Court of Bankruptcy to be consulted, the number of such cases, and the amount so contributed, would be absolutely insignificant; and it surely cannot be considered a bad consequence of our present law, that many who might otherwise run the risk of losing part of their property are saved from doing so by the fear of losing all.

The failure of Joint Stock Companies, Banks, and other trading associations, have, however, in a few instances, caused such severe distress to individuals, by the claims which have been made upon them to satisfy the partnership debts, that those whose duty it has been to extricate their clients, if possible, from a ruinous liability, have attributed, in my opinion very hastily and unjustly, the cause of such disasters to the law of unlimited liability, rather than to cause perfectly within the control of all those shareholders whose indolence, or whose credulity, or whose unreasonable reliance upon friends, or upon statements published in conformity with Parliamentary forms, have been the main cause of the disaster, from the consequences of which they afterwards try to relieve themselves.

I will first refer to the failures of Joint Stock Banks. – The establishment of most of these institutions between 1830 and 1840, after the very numerous failures of private Banks which had previously occurred is within the recollection of most men of business. The public, eager to guard themselves against the recurrence of the losses they then suffered through over reliance on private individuals, threw themselves into the system of Joint Stock Banks, which spread rapidly over the country, and for a time they erred as much in giving a sudden and unreasonable amount of confidence to a new, and then untried system, as they had before erred by over confidence in the old establishments of Private Bankers. Unknown and untried men were elected Directors and Managers; the public, falsely relying on the checks imposed upon them by Parliament, neglected their duty as much as the Managers of the few which have failed abused the confidence reposed in them. Of the very large number of Joint Stock Banks established between 1830 and 1836, and again from that time to 1841, it is not surprising that a few should have been badly managed and failed.

Manchester, Liverpool, and Newcastle-on-Tyne (the great foci of speculation), were the seats of the worst disasters. In London, with but one contemptible exception, most perfect success has attended them; and, since 1841, the same result has almost as entirely followed Joint Stock Banking in the country; so that nearly 30,000 shareholders, with £35,000,000 of paid-up capital, and an aggregate reserveed fund of nearly £3,000,000 more, whose dividends are regularly paid, and as regularly increasing in amounts as the management becomes consolidated, attest publicly to the extent of their business, and the skill and safety of their management; and thereby, in the most practical and convincing manner possible, disprove the bold, but entirely unfounded assertions of the advocates of limited liability, that "these Banks sow the seeds of extravagant speculation, and carry with them the elements of dissolution," – that "ruin threatens all who invest a shilling in such partnerships" – that "the prejudice against Joint Stock Banks is increasing daily," and "that those who do enroll themselves in partnerships, must fall under the category of fools who think they can lose nothing, rogues who know they have nothing to lose and may gain all, and gamblers who will stake everything upon the cast of a die." Very far, indeed, from deserving any such stigma must be those, who in a few years, under very great difficulties, besides the payment of good dividends, have accumulated a reserve fund equal to one-tenth of their paid-up capital, – conclusive evidence that the shareholders are neither fools nor gamblers.

Can any one be surprised, however, seeing what false ideas of Joint Stock Banks still exist, that institutions so novel – placing an almost unlimited command of capital in the hands of new and untried parties – having to form a trade against powerful rivals, perfectly acquainted with their respective localities – and tempted sometimes in order to obtain trade, to make advances not justified by the resources of their customers, should, in a few instances, at an early period in their history, have overstepped the bounds of prudence, and involved themselves and their shareholders in difficulty and loss?

Nor must it be forgotten that these institutions, now so important – supported by the property of the country and managed by its best men of business, were at first unpopular with those who are now their main support, and that this, in many cases, threw their management for a time into less experienced hands: but notwithstanding all these disadvantages – and the still more unfavourable state of the law of partnership as it affected Joint Stock Companies which then existed, and the prejudice which was excited against them by the practical operation of unlimited liability not being understood – the profit attending investments in Joint Stock Banks, ascertained by the dividends paid and the reserved funds accumulated, has been far greater than that derived from railways, docks, and other undertakings in which shareholders, being under the paternal care, as it is called, of the Legislature, are relieved by the limitation of their loss, from that vigilant superintendence of the management, without which good profits and great success cannot be obtained.

Their utility and intrinsic value, and the influence their management gave to the Directors, soon attracted the attention of capitalists, and rules for their government were introduced, which will, I believe, except in the grossest cases of fraud, prevent for the future the repetition of the few, though disastrous failures, which have been stereotyped in the recollection of some of the advocates of limited partnerships.

In the best Joint Stock Banks, a portion only of the subscribed capital is called for; in many instances it is only one-fifth, and an annually increasing reserved fund is accumulating, as an additional security to the shareholders.

Any shareholder, by attention to the half-yearly or annual accounts, and by the careful selection of Directors and Auditors, can secure a management which will never involve him in a loss that can exceed the subscribed capital, or the liability which he voluntarily undertakes when he becomes a shareholder.

This is a security which it is in the power of every one to obtain; it only requires the exercise of that prudence in the selection of an investment for his capital, without which no law can relieve him from liability to loss.

There is no risk, if ordinary care and prudence be exercised, that the last shilling or the last acre will ever be called for, though, if neither care nor prudence be exercised, ruin may follow such an investment, as it may follow one made with equal want of caution in any other description of security. In fact, whether we look at the Joint Stock Banks in Scotland, Ireland, or England, we find Mercantile Institutions of the first class, conducted by able and intelligent men practical as well as scientific, which have grown up with the trade and commerce of their respective districts, to the vitality of which they are essentially necessary; and also, that strong in the public confidence, they have earned, in the comparatively short time they have been established, they are now equally safe to the shareholder and depositor.

A few words will be sufficient to dispose of the arguments based upon Insurance Companies. Proprietary Life-Offices only require a subscribed capital to give confidence to insurers at their first formation. There is scarcely an instance of any important portion of this being called for; there is no trading, and the business of a successful office soon finds itself in capital: and as regards Mutual Insurance Offices, each insurer is responsible for the payment of his fellow insurer's policy, and can only feel himself secure from loss by watching carefully the accumulation of premiums, and their prudent investment by the Directors of his choice, and in both cases a special contract is made with every insurer or creditor.

There is no analogy between Life-Insurance Offices and ordinary trading companies – they are, in fact, Savings Banks, subject, of course, to imprudent management and loss, but entirely free from the ordinary trading risks of Joint Stock Banks or other Joint Stock Companies. But it is said, to be consistent, you ought to object to limited liability being granted to Railway Companies, Steam-Boat Companies, and other large associations to which Parliament or the Board of Trade have granted this privilege. On principle, I should object, for I believe, were the public sufficiently self-reliant, and depended on its own good sense and vigilance for security, rather than upon the protection afforded by Acts of Parliament, not only would this privilege be unnecessary, but the companies would be better managed without it.

I cannot see on what principle a partner in one company is to be relieved from a liability which attaches to him in another; though I can understand why Parliament, fully acknowledging the soundness of, and the necessity of maintaining the principle that every man should be responsible for his own or his Agent's acts, should admit a few special exceptions, where the extent of the undertaking, and its great public importance, alike appear to demand the particular encouragement of the Legislature.

There is also another feature of great importance which must not be omitted in the consideration of the question, whether Parliament should allow any, and if any, what exceptions to the general rule of unlimited liability, and that is the nature of the operations of the proposed company.

I am not aware of any recent instance of limited liability being granted to a purely trading and commercial company – a company in which all or nearly all its capital is engaged in floating securities – in produce or manufactures at home or abroad; and it is to this distinction between limited and unlimited liability, when applied to Railway Companies, &c., and when applied to ordinary trading partnerships, that great attention should be directed.

In Railways, Steam Navigation Companies, Dock Companies, Electric Telegraph Companies, and other enterprises of a similar character, eight-tenths of the capital is absolutely invested in land, works, and machinery, and the remainder only, a large portion of which is generally required to meet the daily demands of a large company, is subject to speculative losses. Here then it is almost impossible that debts can be incurred, which by any accident can materially injure the creditors. Not so, however, in purely trading and commercial partnerships, whose profit in many cases depends upon the result of the balance of fluctuations in prices of produce at different seasons of the year, and in the management of which one error in judgment, or one unsound speculation, may cause the entire loss of the original capital, as well as that of the Creditors, unless another portion of the property of the Partners were liable to meet their claims. Such a partnership, on Commandite principles, would wind up, and leave the Creditors to shift for themselves, whilst the Partners making another advance of capital, and placing it under the management of a new Gerant, would re-commence business as before. I cannot conceive that there is any analogy between the limited liability of those great Joint Stock Companies, the appropriation of whose capital is restricted to a particular object, the greater part of whose capital is permanently invested, and whose affairs are conducted by responsible Board of Directors, subject to the control of their Shareholders, and that of a private partnership, under no control, and whose capital is of necessity available for any speculative purpose, and therefore subject to sudden loss.

Can any one believe, who has watched the periodical recurrence of speculation in this country, that its results would not have been infinitely more disastrous, had all the speculations in 1844–5 and 6, been relieved from that check upon their proceedings which unlimited liability afforded, and had been free to risk anything, knowing that their losses would be limited, whilst that of their Creditors might have been unlimited?

In all the discussions I have heard upon this subject, this great distinction between Private Partnerships and those of Joint Stock Companies is overlooked. Upon this distinction the whole case turns. What may be right applied to a partnership, formed and managed under certain conditions, whose capital is fixed, and not available for speculative purposes, may not be right where none of those conditions exist or can be enforced.

But it is argued by another distinguished advocate of limited liability (Lord Hotham,) that whilst creditors have a joint claim upon the entire property of every person taking part in the management of any company or business, whether as a director of a company, a partner in a firm, or a borrower of money at an interest, varying with the success of the concern they have no such claim against a contributor of money for business purposes, whether a shareholder, a partner, or a lender of money at a varying rate of interest, not taking a part in the management in the business.

To these definitions there is little to object, but their practical application is the difficulty. I would observe upon them, first, that the neglect by a partner if so obvious a public and private duty as looking after a business in which his capital is invested, ought not to injure the creditors; and, secondly, that the shareholder in a company who attends a meeting duly convened, and votes for a large expenditure of the Company's funds, who sanctions a loan, and concurs in the appointment of officers, and agrees to the balance sheet, must be a partner taking an active part in the management of the business.

A shareholder also having duly received notice of a meeting, called to authorize the same expenditure, to raise the same loan, &c. &c. &c., and who sends his proxy to support the propositions of the directors also becomes a partner taking an active part in the management. In both cases, the shareholder present and the shareholder absent, ought to have obtained sufficient knowledge of the business to enable them to decide how to vote; and having voted, their credit is pledged, and the contract is complete, to which they are bound.

A lender of money also, at profit rates of interest, whose name and capital in a business is published in the *Gazette*, and in the local papers, and posted up in the shop, or place of business, according to the law of partnership "en Commandite," is a person taking an active part in the business; for without this use of his name, the credit required to conduct the affairs of the partnership could not be obtained. He becomes, perhaps, the most important, and as regards the business, the most active partner, though he may never enter the countinghouse or place of business. *Every* contract is with him, and his credit is pledged to every creditor; for no creditor can know whether his own transaction is a solitary one, or one of a hundred. He cannot tell whether it be provident or improvident.

How then can this question of interference be defined? I venture to say but in one way only, and that is, by the present law of unlimited liability, which practically declares that he who ostensibly shares the profit must also share the loss, be it what it may.

But if the lender of capital, at a fixed rate of interest – be it high or low, never appears or acts in the business, is never held forth to the public as a partner, never enters into any contract with the creditors, directly or indirectly, then there can be no claim upon his property, not invested in the trade, if the business be ever so unsuccessful.

I hope then I have shown that the state of insolvency in those countries where limited liability for common Partnerships exists, is greater than in England; that the evils, if any, arising from the application of the principle of unlimited liability to Joint Stock Banks and Insurance Offices, and other Joint Stock Companies, have been exaggerated; that these institutions, as now conducted, are essentially safe and popular; that their dividends are higher and their accumulations greater than those of Companies with limited liability, and that the reasoning upon the success of Chartered Companies, and those incorporated by Parliament, where the liability is limited is fallacious, such success, if success there be, having arisen from other causes rather than from the limitation of the liability of the Partners.

But it may be said, that without this limitation the capital for such companies would not have been subscribed; to which I reply, that the capital embarked in Joint Stock Companies, Insurance Offices, and Joint Stock Banks, where the liability is unlimited, is scarcely, if at all, inferior to that embarked in Railways and other Chartered Companies all the powers and privileges contained in their Acts of Incorporation, without the limitation of liability, and could the promoters have shewn a good prima facie case for profitable investment, the necessary capital would have been supplied to them, as it has been by millions, to other Companies without any such limitation to the liability of the shareholders. I am obliged then to believe that the law of unlimited liability does not exclude capital from trade, and that the contrary assertion cannot be proved by any data, within our reach.

I will now proceed to shew that the charge that Unlimited Liability excludes cheap Capital from Commerce, is as groundless as that it excludes capital at all.

It is stated that no prudent person will join a Joint Stock Company with unlimited liability, and therefore that the money of all prudent capitalists is either excluded altogether from commercial investment, or invested in such companies as pay so a high rate of interest as to overcome the prudential principles of the capitalist.

I cannot find any where a tittle of evidence upon which this assertion rests.

We are told that it is so, and must be so; prudent people it is said, will not invest capital in partnerships, public or private, with unlimited liability, but remove this difficulty, and you will have an influx of capital, which will materially affect the economical production of our manufactures; but I have already shewn that capitalists do invest very large amounts in such companies, and with safety.

It is also stated by one very ardent advocate of limited liability,[1] that all capital now embarked in Joint Stock Companies passes through *many middle men*, who take their profits from its distribution; and that this profit, as well as the enormous risk which he persuades himself is involved in these companies, has to be paid by the public in the price of the article produced.

These middle men, he says, are Bankers, Bill Brokers, Merchants, and others, who live on diffusing capital, from the cautious lender to the most wildly speculative borrower. It is unnecessary to say to a man of business, that this is extracted from the writings of a lawyer.

The Bankers of London, he says, live by lending the capital of the cautious lender to the most wildly speculative borrower.

Never was a greater amount of ignorance of their habits and of the mode of conducting business by our Bankers displayed, than in this sentence; and this by one who enters most dogmatically upon the subject, and attributes to all who oppose his views, personally interested motives. Remark upon it is unnecessary: it is only needful to say it is absolutely incorrect. The Banker does not in the proper sense of the term borrow money from his customer – his customers deposit their money not by way of loan to him, but for the sake of placing it in safety and yet of accessibility at a moment's notice; and the business of a Banker would very soon be alienated, were it known that he lent his customers' money – money deposited with him because they know the entire property of the firm with whom they bank is responsible for its payment when required – to the most wildly speculative borrower.

Bill Brokers and Merchants are equally obnoxious to this charge; and it is a singular evidence of how little some writers on this subject know of the actual operations of capitalists, that these middle men, whose losses and rash speculations, they say, oblige them to make such heavy charges as to raise the market price of capital, are in almost all cases those who lend money at the lowest rates; but it is not necessary to shew, by any further remark, the rashness of this statement.

Again, it is said, that as large capitals are rare, and that as few of those who have them will embark them in trade, it is necessary, when large capitals are required for companies, that they should be gathered together from many sources; and that the law of unlimited liability interposes obstacles to this successful gathering of capital for important undertakings, and thus excludes the public from the benefit of cheap capital.

It would be difficult for the writer to name any enterprise, supported by the opinion of competent authority, which failed simply and exclusively from the impossibility of obtaining capital to conduct it. Indeed, in lieu of enterprises wanting the support of capital, the normal state of England for many years previously to the introduction of free trade, and even now to a great extent, has been capital seeking occupation, and encouraging rash speculation by its very cheapness and abundance; and this difficulty of obtaining its prudent and safe employment, has generally been followed by one of those outbreaks of rash and wild speculation which spreads desolation, not only over the commercial world, but among a large class of persons out of trade, who, misled by the reported profits of trade, have been induced, to their ultimate loss, to embark their small capitals in ventures they did not understand, and after which, years of extra caution and prudence have been required to restore the mercantile atmosphere to its ordinarily safe and wholesome condition. Indeed, in the words of Mr. Lalor, a "general glut" has, until recently, been the habitual state of our mercantile system – a state in entire antagonism to that which requires the interference of Parliament to entice, by special exemption from the natural law of unlimited liability, the investment of capital in trade.

That it is the habit of many persons to attribute the difficulty which is found in forming a new company to the want of limitation of the liability of partners, and thus to throw the failure of an unsound project with which they have identified themselves, upon the state of the law, is notorious; and that this state of the law enables many to give an excuse for not joining this or that undertaking, and thereby to conceal their real reason, be it want of spare capital at the time, distrust of the scheme, or distrust of the promoters.

Whilst then it is difficult, if not impossible, to prove, that any sound and well-considered enterprise has been stopped for want of the capital withheld in consequence of the liability of the partners being unlimited, I have already shewn that a very large amount of capital has been advanced, and is prudently and well invested in companies and partnerships, with unlimited liability notwithstanding this dreadful state of the law.

I believe, then, that the effect of the law of unlimited liability, in withholding capital from commerce, is small, and that its operation, is most beneficial to commerce; but at the same time I believe that the operation of other parts of our law of partnership upon the investment of capital, is most mischievous, and tends to produce the results which are attributed to unlimited liability alone.

In France and America, where these partnerships exist, capital is very much dearer than in England; whether it would be dearer still did the law of unlimited liability exist in those countries, no one will pretend to say. But it cannot be denied, that in England, where that law exists, capital is cheaper than in any other country in the world, and that, until quite recently, capital was always available for commercial purposes for fixed periods, at a lower rate of interest than was obtained by that class, whom the writer I have referred to considers the only prudent capitalists, and who invest their capital in the funds or on the security of land.

Whilst then we have the great fact before us, that capital for commercial purposes is cheaper in England than elsewhere, and that in other countries, our competitors in commerce, laws exist which enable any trader failing, either from fair and legitimate causes, or from the result of undue speculation, to throw such losses, without any redress, upon his creditors, whatever may be the debtor's means to pay, may we not fairly conclude, that to the lessened risk of loss which our law of unlimited liability affords to those embarked in trade, the cheaper rate at which money is lent is this country for commercial purposes may be attributed; instead of arriving at the contrary conclusion, that the increased safety of the lender induces him to ask a higher rate of interest upon his capital.

It is always stated, in arguing this question, that the advocates of unlimited liability desire the interference of the Government to check speculation – to direct and to protect the investment of capital – to encourage good and to discourage bad investments, and that such interference tends to preserve the monopoly of capital to traders; but the writer in the *Westminster Review* who makes these assertions, knows full well that the supporters of unlimited liability are as zealous advocates of non-interference by the State, in all matters relating to the employment of capital, as himself. They quite agree with Mr. Mill, that every one should be allowed to employ his labour and his capital on any terms he pleases, and to deal with others on any terms that they please, but not on the condition he imposes upon this freedom, viz.: – provided *"the terms are known,"* and that they do not give themselves out for what they are not.

The terms here referred to are the registration of the Gerants, and of the amount subscribed by each Commanditaire; but this is a registration of the Credit side of the account only, and is calculated to enable a Commandite Partnership to give itself out for what it is not, which Mr. Mill so properly condemns. If we have any publication we must have the Debtor side of the account also, and this is impossible.

The whole question – the necessity of publicity – upon which the advocates of limited liability rest their case, is involved in this *condition* of Mr. Mill. To make *'the terms known,"* we must not only know the assets of a Commandite firm, but the liabilities; every speculation which may be at once published – every untoward loss declared, otherwise the notices of the names of the partners and the capital advanced, proposed by the advocates of this system, to be posted over the doors, counters, and desks, would be but a delusion and a snare for the ignorant and unwary, and specially dangerous and delusive, because countenanced by Act of Parliament. What possible Act of Parliament guardianship, could prevent a partnership, with a liability of £10,000, from giving by the same post twenty orders, to the amount of £5,000 each, or enable any one of the persons to whom the orders were sent to know whether he could safely accept it? All that the advocates of unlimited liability ask is the maintenance of the law which makes every one responsible for his own or his Agent's acts, whether profitable or unprofitable; whereas the writer in the *Westminster Review* asks for the active interference of Parliament, to enact a law which shall afford means whereby traders en Commandite may incur losses and throw the risks of them upon innocent parties, leaving those by whose acts the losses were incurred, and who would have received the profit had one arisen, in the possession of their wealth, lessened only by the amount they chose to gamble with, and not by the loss arising from such gambling.

All that the advocates of unlimited liability require is, that the loss attending reckless speculation, misfortune, or want of success, from whatever cause it may arise, should be borne, as far as they are able, by those whose speculations, trading, call it by what name you please, caused the loss.

Editorial Endnote

1 Hawes is arguing against a recent article in favor of limited liability: "Partnerships with Limited Liability," *Westminster Review* 60 (October 1853), pp. 375–416.

21

PARLIAMENTARY DEBATE ON LIMITED LIABILITY

Source: U.K. Parliament, House of Commons, Debate on the Law of Partnership, 27 June 1854, *Hansard,* vol. 134, pp. 754–800.

EDITORIAL HEADNOTE

During the 1850s there was a vigorous public debate over the desirability of making limited liability more easily obtainable by joint-stock companies. The debate played out in newspapers, journals, pamphlets, books, and parliamentary investigations. In 1854 a Royal Commission on the Law of Partnership solicited testimony from sixty-nine legal and commercial experts, thirty-seven of whom recommended an alteration of company law in favor of limited liability.[1]

In June 1854, the Commons debated the Royal Commission's Report, with most speakers strongly in favor of limited liability for investors. Parliamentary advocates of limited liability argued that it would stimulate commercial and industrial expansion and increase competition. They noted that limited liability prevailed in most of Europe and the United States with few ill effects. At the conclusion of the debate, the House endorsed a resolution permitting persons to invest in trading concerns and share the profits, "without incurring liability beyond a limited amount." A Limited Liability Act, embodying the spirit of this resolution, followed in 1855.

Note

1 James Taylor, *Creating Capitalism* (London: Royal Historical Society, 2006), pp. 149–54.

Mr. Collier moved the following Resolution:

> "That the Law of Partnership, which renders every person who, though not an ostensible partner, shares the profits of a trading concern, liable to the whole of its debts, is unsatisfactory, and should be so far modified as to permit persons to contribute to the capital of such concerns on

DOI: 10.4324/9781003713890-24

> terms of sharing their profits, without incurring liability beyond a limited amount."

The hon. and learned Member said, he entreated the attention of the House for a short time to a question of great importance to the mercantile classes of this country. He was anxious that it should not be considered a lawyer's question, dependent upon mere technical knowledge; there were no legal difficulties surrounding it that could in the least embarrass its consideration by any Member of that House: indeed it was a matter of regret that questions involving law reforms should have been left so much in the hands of lawyers as they had been; he believed the cause of law reform was most effectively promoted by the co-operation of legal and non-legal minds. The law of partnership, as it now stands in this country, presumed that every partner could bind each one of his co-partners to an unlimited extent; and this unlimited liability extended to all persons who received any share in the profits of the concern, although they might not be ostensible partners, or have been dealt with or trusted. For instance, the widow of a deceased partner who received a certain proportion of the profits was regarded as a partner, subject to unlimited liability, as was also the clerk who was paid a salary regulated according to the amount of the profits. It is true that the liability of a partner might be limited by express notice proved to have been conveyed to every creditor of the concern, but this was scarcely possible in practice. Practically the law prohibited limited liability, and there was no escape from the principle of unlimited liability, unless by an Act of Parliament specially obtained for the purpose, or a charter granted by the Crown through the Board of Trade. The law of this country, in this respect, was peculiar, and at variance with the civil law; this rule of law had not, however, been settled for more than sixty years, when a decision was given, in the case of Waugh v. Carver, the propriety of which had been frequently doubted by eminent lawyers. In foreign countries the state of the law was different; for limited partnerships had existed for centuries on the Continent of Europe, called partnerships *en commandite.* These partnerships consisted of certain partners called *gerants* or managers, and certain others called *commanditaires* or contributors of Capital. The managing portion, or *gerants,* were unlimitedly liable; but they had a subscribed capital, to which other persons contributed, who were only liable for the amounts they respectively contributed, the amounts being registered; – so that everybody knew the extent of each man's liability. The *commanditaires* were entitled to be repaid what they had advanced to the *gerants,* but their claim was postponed to the claims of the other creditors. That description was sufficient for his (Mr. Collier's) argument upon this question. The principle of partnership *en commandite* had been early adopted in Italy, and under its operation the great Italian republics, Florence, Genoa, Venice, attained a commercial prosperity which, considering the circumstances surrounding them, may be considered unprecedented in the history of the world. It thence spreads to France; it was adopted in Holland; and by its operation many of the great works by which the Dutch had rescued large tracts of land from the sea had been executed. It extended to

Germany – to Russia also – and to most of the European States, and finally, our transatlantic brethren in the United States, with all their prejudices in favour of English laws, adopted the principle; and the report of the Commission which had been appointed to inquire into this subject, distinctly showed that both in Europe and in America the *commandite* partnership system had, with very trifling exceptions, worked, beyond all doubt, beneficially. This question had been investigated by two Committees of that House; and the second Committee reported, in the year 1852, in favour of his present Resolution, but they recommended that the matter should be further referred to a Commission. Well, that Commission was appointed, and it had reported.

The Commissioners were divided in opinion. Five of the Commissioners reported against any change in the law; but Mr. Bramwell, one of the Commissioners, and a distinguished member of the common law bar, reported most strongly in favour of a change; Mr. Kirkman Hodgson, an eminent merchant, reported likewise in favour of his (Mr. Collier's) proposition; and Mr. Anderson, a third Commissioner, expressed views substantially the same. With this difference of opinion among the Commissioners, thinking it impossible to carry a Bill on the subject in this Session, he (Mr. Collier) had considered it most desirable to elicit the opinion of the House upon it by a resolution.

Now, in the first place, he said that the *onus probandi* was thrown upon those who maintained that restrictions ought to be imposed upon contracts. If any number of persons, such as A, B, and C, chose, by means of a public register, to announce to the world that they were willing to deal with those who would deal with them upon the terms that each should be liable to a certain amount, or if A, and B, announced that they would hold themselves liable unlimitedly, but that they had a certain amount of capital subscribed by others who would not be liable beyond a certain extent, those who held that they ought not to be allowed to enter into such an arrangement were bound to make out a case that they should not be so allowed. But it was objected *in limine* to such an arrangement, that the principle of unlimited liability was founded upon an unalterable rule of natural justice, viz., that a man who shared in the profits of a concern should bear its losses. Now, if any such rule of natural justice existed, he answered that that rule was violated annually by that House in the case of every railway Bill which it passed, and was violated also every time the Crown, by the advice of the President of the Board of Trade, granted a charter of incorporation to a trading company. But on examination they would find, that all semblance of natural justice vanished from this rule if accurately stated. The doctrine of the present law was, that any person who obtained a share, however small, of the profits of a concern, must be liable to pay all its debts, however large, whether or not he had any hand in contracting them. Suppose he made a contract with A, and B, and nobody else dealt with them, and trusted them, but found out subsequently that W., the widow of a deceased partner, received an annuity proportioned to the profits, without any share in the management of the concern – was there any principle of natural justice by which he could make her pay a debt which she never contracted, and which he had contracted with others? Again, the same principle of unlimited liability on a ground of a share in the profits, would apply to any person who advanced money to a partnership on terms of receiving a fixed interest, for that interest must come out of the profits; but the law attached no such liability to such a fixed interest, but only to a remuneration varying according to the profits – a distinction in which there was no justice whatever.

The true principle applicable to the matter was this, that no man ought to be liable to pay a debt contracted by another, unless he either authorized that other to make the contract, or represented him as so authorised. But it was said, that the commercial greatness of this country had grown under the principle of unlimited liability, and it would therefore be unwise to interfere with it. The truth, however, was just the reverse of this; to what did we owe our railways, canals, docks, fleets of steamers, and all our greatest works? Not to the observance, but to the breach of the law of unlimited liability. But for the violation of that law, we should still have travelled in stage coaches, and voyaged in sailing packets. But for the violation of that law, that greatest work of modern art and science, the Crystal Palace, would never have been witnessed. All our noblest monuments, which would attest our national greatness when our race has passed away, attested the working of the principle of limited, and not of unlimited liability.

Again, he asked, could a state of things which gave a preference to a certain class of companies, by Act of Parliament or by charter, and denied the same advantage to all other classes of companies, be defended, and whether it was not desirable to place all on the same footing or at least to give all the power as a matter of right, of limiting their liability by means of a public registry? There was a general concurrence of opinion that the present practice of granting charters of limited liability was unsatisfactory. He would read to the House what was said upon this subject by the Secretary to the India Board (Mr. Lowe). The hon. Gentleman, in his reply to the question issued by the Commission, said: "I view the terms on which the persons choose to associate in business as a matter which they should settle for themselves, and not one which Parliament or the Board of Trade should settle for them. But of all systems, the very worst is surely to forbid limited liability, and then vest in a Minister holding his seat by a Parliamentary majority the power of suspending the law in favour of such associations as he thinks fit. If a law be right, it ought to be enforced; if wrong, to be repealed. I should as soon think of allowing the Secretary of the Treasury to grant dispensation for smuggling, or the Attorney General licenses to commit murder."

The operation of the present law was further attended with this effect, that, practically, there were no safe investments for persons of small capital except in these incorporated partnerships, and the consequences had been an unnatural diversion of capital into this channel of chartered and incorporated companies. To this cause might in a great measure be attributed the railway mania; for people who were not engaged in trade had now no safe and profitable investment of their capital, except in these undertakings. Mr. Porter had given as his opinion, that from this cause a great deal of money had been invested in foreign railways, which would otherwise have been beneficially employed in the trade of this country. Mr. Hodgson, one of the Commissioners, said: "This country is now, I believe, almost the only one in which this law of limited liability does not exist. It prevails in all of those with which we have the most extended and important intercourse, and this isolation acts very injuriously in many cases to the English merchant. I could mention whole trades which, thirty years ago, were entirely carried on by English houses, in which at the present moment scarcely one is to be found; their places have been entirely supplied by foreigners, who establish branches of their houses here and in the manufacturing districts, while the main establishments (almost all under the *commandite* principle) are abroad."

A great many enterprises of beneficial character in this country – such as local improvement of the dwellings of the poor, and undertakings of that description – were prevented by the operation of the law. He might refer, also, to the effect of the law on mining companies in Cornwall and Devonshire, and would venture to say that scarcely any prudent man would take a share in a mining company, because, by the law of unlimited liability, he might have to pay all the debts of the concern. If a man were only to be liable for a certain amount, important additions would be made to the capital of these companies, and the mineral resources of the country would be developed to an extent that was scarcely supposed to be possible at the present moment; but the result of the present state of the law was to leave such companies mainly in the hands of adventurers who had nothing to lose, and encourage speculation of the worst and most ruinous description. A law such as was recommended by the Resolution would also have the effect of enabling men of capital to assist men without capital, but possessing ability, honesty, and industry, to set up in trade, and, in process of time, to become capitalists. He had been informed by more than one Member of the House engaged in commercial transactions, that, but for this rule of unlimited liability, he would be glad to assist many an enterprising workman, but he was deterred by the present state of the law; all the capitalist could do was to advance money at a certain fixed rate of interest, which very often the workmen could not pay. It was desirable that a retiring partner might be at liberty to leave a certain amount of money in the business from which he was retiring without being haunted by the fear of unlimited liability, and that women, and other persons, not capable of actively engaging in trade should possess safe channels of investment, which were at that moment closed against them.

It was said, by way of objection, that great injury would arise from the proposed change to various classes of society. Now, if any one were to be injured, it must be either the partners themselves, their creditors, or the public. As to the effect on the partners – if he were to enter into partnership with AB on the terms of advancing 1,000*l.*, and participating in the profits, he wanted to know who would be injured by that? He could not be injured in the first place, for his liability would be limited; and AB was not injured, to whom he lent the money, because it was more to the advantage of AB to pay him out of the profits, when he could afford it, than to pay him a fixed interest, whether he could afford it or not. In the next place, the creditor did not require to be protected, because it was more for his advantage that the money should be advanced by a partner, than that it should be lent at a fixed rate of interest; in the former case it was assets of the firm, in case of their failing, in which he shared: in the latter it was a debt of the firm subtracted from their assets; moreover, he was not bound to trust parties trading under limited liability, unless he liked. He might either confine his dealings to those who traded under unlimited liability, or he might charge an additional profit to cover the increased risk. With regard to the interests of the public, the Commissioners stated, that it appeared to them that the benefit to be acquired by the system of limited partners would be at the expense of a more than countervailing amount of injury to the trader bearing the burden of unlimited liability, and who would have to enter into competition with those who were enjoying the benefits of limited liability. But, with the greatest respect for the Commissioners, they had in that paragraph shown, he would not say ignorance, but a total disregard of the first principles of political economy, it was the old anti-free trade argument over again, that one class was entitled to be protected against the rest of the community, but he knew no reason why capitalists should be protected more than the landholder, or any other class of the community. If concerns trading under limited liability succeeded, it would be because they could supply the public more cheaply than at present; if they failed, no injury could be done to the fair trader as he was called. There would be nothing to prevent persons from carrying on their business with unlimited liability. Limited liability would be adopted by some, and unlimited liability by others; the latter had certain advantages in their favour, and there would be a fair competition in the open market between the two.

Every one of these arguments of justice, of convenience, and of protection, entirely failed when they came to be investigated. It was said, that a change in the law would be injurious to the commercial credit of this country, but he did not see why this result should follow; – it was a confusion of ideas to think that the operations of a limited company would affect the credit of an unlimited company. The last argument which the supporters of the present law could resort to, was that, probably, in a poor country with little capital, the principle of limited liability ought to be adopted; but this country, was rich enough, and the principle did not apply here. He would venture to say that the hon. Member for Meath (Mr. Lucas), who had given notice of moving an addition to the Resolution, would not say such an argument was applicable to Ireland; but, if applicable at all, it was one applicable to this country also; and he wanted to know when we were considered rich enough to render the application of such a principle unnecessary? He did not understand that it was possible for a country, in an economical point of view, to be too rich; and why a principle, which in one state of its progress would have the effect of developing its resources, should have an opposite effect in another, he was unable to discover. It devolved on the opponents of the principle to show why this change of effects should be produced. That was not the opinion of that high authority on political economy, Mr. John Stewart Mill, who was strongly in favour of the *commandite* principle, and who stated that no man could consistently condemn that principle without being prepared to maintain that it was desirable that no one should carry on business on borrowed capital, confining business to those who had already accumulated capital or inherited it, which was manifestly absurd. He (Mr. Collier) believed that the effect of this proposed change in the law would be to cheapen capital; in fact, he looked upon it as tending to an increased capital, which could not by any possibility injure any one but the very great capitalists who had an interest in a monopoly. No doubt, if such a change were made, it would be desirable to have a public registration, and various provisions for protection against fraud, but these were matters of detail which he would not now discuss. He had endeavoured, as briefly as possible, to state the law of this county as compared with that of other countries, and he might venture to say, in conclusion, that he had great faith in the operation of the principle of unrestricted competition, a principle not less clearly demonstrated in theory than it had been verified by experience. On every application of this principle, prophesies of the most gloomy character had been falsified, while anticipated benefits had been realised beyond the most sanguine expectations; on the removal of each restriction, our commerce had bounded forward with an elasticity apparently immeasurable and infinite. In conclusion, he believed that the change proposed would have important social bearings, tending materially to diminish the distance between capital and labour, interests sometimes apparently opposed but in reality always identical; and that it would be socially, politically, and economically beneficial.

Viscount Goderich seconded the motion with pleasure, because he believed the principle involved in it was one which, if adopted by the Legislature, was calculated to confer great benefit upon the country, and especially because he believed it would be consistent with the whole course of their recent commercial legislation. Under the present state of the law there existed a double system of monopoly, enjoyed on the one hand by the great capitalists, who were alone able, in consequence of the system of unlimited liability, to enter into trading companies; and, on the other hand, a smaller description of monopoly which of recent years had been devised by the Legislature in order in some degree to correct the evils engendered by the former monopoly, and which consisted in the power possessed by the Board of Trade virtually, though nominally it rested in the Crown, of granting charters to such companies as it chose, which charters were accompanied by special privileges which the law refused to other companies engaged in the same branch of industry. He confessed he was at a loss to understand how hon. Gentlemen could stand up in that House and support the existing condition of the law in that respect who had been the consistent opponents of all other monopolies, who in former days were consistent freetraders, and who had passed a large portion of their lives in advocating the right of persons engaged in commerce and industrial pursuits to conduct their own affairs in the manner they chose.

He knew that those who most objected to the proposition of the hon. Member for Plymouth (Mr. Collier) also objected to the powers which were now vested in the Board of Trade; but while he agreed with them that these powers were most objectionable, he could see no means by which the necessity of the existence of those powers could be got rid of, except by the adoption of that system recommended by the hon. and learned Member. No one could deny that certain undertakings would be altogether impossible if it were not that means were found for altering in their favour the law of unlimited liability. The cases alluded to of railway and other great commercial and industrial companies, the objects of which were so gigantic that they could not be carried out at all without such an alteration, required special consideration; but then arose the question of whether it was right or just to grant privileges to companies formed for the accomplishments of these great undertakings which they denied others of a smaller character, but which were framed on commercial principles as well as the larger ones. He knew it might be said the great companies were formed to carry out works of great public utility; but it appeared to him that there were other persons to be considered in this question besides the public, and the House ought to judge how far it was consistent with sound principles or with common fairness that they should deny to any body of men in this country, because the objects of which they wished to unite were not of a vast, transcendent, and important character, the right to combine together for commercial and industrial enterprises in any manner that might appear to them fit, provided sufficient guarantees were taken against fraud on their part. In the present day and under the existing circumstances of the country every opportunity ought to be offered for the combination of the three elements of skill, labour, and capital that could be devised. It was a great evil to retain upon the Statute book any law that tended to keep these elements separate from one another, and the object of our legislation should be to facilitate their union and bind them together by the ties of a common interest. But this, it would not be denied, the existing law of partnership effectually prevented.

He could instance this by a circumstance that came within his own particular knowledge. A friend of his, of great scientific attainments, after considerable labour and much thought, made a discovery by which he believed he should be able greatly to cheapen an article in large and general consumption. In the experiments required for the perfection of his discovery he expended all his little capital, and by the time he had convinced himself, and was able to produce the fruit of his labours to others, and demonstrate the truth and accuracy of his discovery, he had no further means to proceed with it so as to bring it into general notice. In his anxiety to obtain the means of coupling his skill, knowledge, and industry, with the capital of other persons, he applied to several capitalists, when he was invariably met with an answer of this nature – "If I enter into partnership with you under the existing state of the law, in the first place you will be able to bind me and all the members of that partnership in any manner you please; and, in the next place, I shall be liable for the debts of the concern, to use a common expression, to my last acre and my last shilling. I cannot, therefore, enter into partnership with you on those terms, and the law will not permit me to advance a small portion of my capital to carry out the discovery on the condition of appropriating the profits – half to your skill and half to my capital. The only alternative, therefore, would be to lend you the money, but, as I am not certain your discovery will be attended with success, I could not afford, on account of the risk, to lend it, except at a very high rate of interest." The result in this case was, that the invention had been rendered useless, the discoverer lost all benefit to himself, and the public lost the benefit which might have accrued from the discovery. It might be well conceived that a succession of such cases must prove a great evil.

The present system tended to lock up capital by preventing persons retired from business investing any portion of their money in the concerns of trade in which other parties participated, and thus to impoverish the country by withdrawing from it a portion of its circulation. The only resource was to put it into banks or the public funds, where it was not so actively employed in the production of wealth. His hon. and learned friend (Mr. Collier) had drawn attention to the case of foreign countries; but he did not mention the fact, that all the foreign firms whom the Commissioners had written to had, with one exception, given their testimony in favour of the working of the system of limited liability in their own country. Some of them might have said they were unable to judge what might be the effect of an alteration of the law in this country, but, with the exception of Messrs. Hope and Co., of Amsterdam, they had all expressed their approval of the system. He was quite sensible of the many advantages conferred by large capitalists and monopolists upon the country; but surely they, of all persons in the world, were the least entitled to the protection of the House, where commercial, industrial, and social advantages were to be derived from an alteration in the law of this nature. Not only were these great commercial and industrial advantages to be derived from the alteration advocated by the hon. and learned Member for Plymouth, but he was also strongly inclined to think that great social benefits would spring out of it, because the alteration of the law would tend to remove an obstacle that now existed to carrying out and exemplifying that community of interests which ought to bind together all classes, but of the advantages of which, unhappily, those classes were not sufficiently aware.

Not long since a person largely engaged in commercial affairs, who was well known to the House, while speaking on the subject, expressed a fear that, if such a change should take place, workmen might save up their money, enter into partnership, and compete with the manufacturers, and he wondered that Mr. Cobden and Mr. Bright did not move in the matter. However that might be, he was sure the hon. Members for the West Riding and for Manchester would be the last to object to the measure on such grounds as that, believing that they were willing to extend to every class, and especially to the operative manufacturers, a fair stage and no favour. But, if Gentlemen of commercial experience entertained that opinion, there could be no doubt it extended among the working classes themselves, and that they looked with little favour upon those laws which prevented them from combining for industrial purposes, although, probably, in some cases, if they did they would meet with results they very little expected.

He considered it was unwise on every ground – social, political, and economical – that the House should maintain restrictions which were felt by them to be obnoxious, unless there were grounds of overwhelming public necessity in favour of their maintenance. On a former occasion, when the question was before the House, the hon. Member for South Lancashire (Mr. W. Brown) spoke of the higher character of our commercial firms, and of the greater credit that was afforded to them in the market of the world, than was afforded to those of France; and he said that the reason was, that in England we had a law of unlimited liability, whilst in France they had a law of limited liability. Surely the hon. Gentleman must have forgotten or purposely overlooked many other important differences – differences which affected far more than any law of partnership the respective credit of the two countries. Did he forget that France had had, within the last seventy years, no less than six revolutions, whilst we had had none? Did he forget the security of property which must exist in a country so subject to political change, and that which existed in a country such as this? Did he forget the difference, of which we might justly be proud, between the industrial character of Englishmen and the industrial character of Frenchmen?

He (Viscount Goderich) hoped Her Majesty's Government would, therefore, consent to the Resolution, or that the President of the Board of Trade would at least state that, if he could not agree to it at this moment, he had not made up his mind upon the question irrevocably, and that he would be prepared to consider it, and give due weight to the great authorities in favour of a change. The Commissioners stated that they had taken the opinions of sixty-nine persons in England, Ireland, and Scotland, thirty-seven of whom expressed themselves decidedly in favour of a law of limited liability, while some of the remaining thirty-two were of opinion that a considerable change should be made in the existing law. He thought, therefore, that the House would do well to review their legislation upon this subject, and to adopt a system which had worked satisfactorily in those countries in which it had been established, and which he believed would tend to bind together the various classes of the trading and commercial community. Motion made, and Question proposed –

> "That the Law of Partnership, which renders every person who, though not an ostensible partner, shares the profits of a trading concern, liable to the whole of its debts, is unsatisfactory, and should be so far modified as to permit persons to contribute to the capital of such concerns on terms of sharing their profits, without incurring liability beyond a limited amount."

Mr. Cardwell [President of the Board of Trade], said, his hon. and learned friend the Member for Plymouth (Mr. Collier) had brought before the House, with his usual ability, a subject which certainly excited great interest in this country; and therefore he (Mr. Cardwell) would readily answer the appeal which had been made to him by his noble friend (Viscount Goderich), and would state that he was willing and anxious to consider fully all the arguments which were presented to the House in the report that had recently been laid upon the table. The Committee which had sat to consider this question for two successive years had abstained from reporting any positive opinion to the House, but had recommended the appointment of a Commission, composed of men possessing great legal and commercial knowledge, in order to pursue an inquiry into the details of the subject. He certainly understood that it was the bounden duty of those to whom the report of that Commission was made, most carefully and most respectfully to consider it in all its bearings and in its fullest application; and of this he was quite sure – that when full time had been given for the consideration of the report, and when it should be right to take any course with regard to the alteration of the law of partnership, no objection would be made to a change in the law on grounds antagonistic to the principles of unrestricted competition. He was sure, if any proposal were submitted to the House with the view of improving the law of partnership, they would not be told that it was necessary for the protection of great capitalists that restrictions should be imposed upon the application of small capital. He was sure it would not be argued, that any system which impeded the welfare of industrious young men should be continued for the protection of those who, having been more fortunate in life, had greater advantages at command. When the subject was ripe for consideration, the only question would be, what was the mode by which free competition might be most effectually promoted, by which social improvement might most advantageously be advanced, and by which the rights and interests of scientific and ingenious men who effected improvements might best be secured? He thought that upon this, which he might call the free-trade ground of the argument, they might be assured no objection would ever be made to an alteration of the law, but the only question would be how the law ought to be framed with the view of accomplishing the important objects to which he had referred.

He would, in the first place, ask the House to consider what the law of the country actually was upon the subject under discussion – he doubted whether the true bearing of the existing law was distinctly known to those who were most anxious that is should be altered. It was quite true that with regard to partnerships, as at present regulated, there was a general presumption of agency – in other words, the general presumption was, that when persons were engaged in partnership in trade, every one of those partners was instructed by his colleagues with a power to bind the others in their commercial transactions. That was a general presumption as a matter of evidence; but were persons therefore prohibited by the present law from entering into engagements by which they might limit their liability? The law did not prevent them from doing so, but permitted individuals to enter into arrangements, as between themselves, regulating their liabilities precisely in such proportions as they thought right. The present law also permitted a partnership to make contracts with other persons, restricting their liability as a partnership by contract with the persons who become their creditors to a limited object. This was not a mere inoperative power, but one constantly carried into practice by many of the large companies in the City of London.

The point in which the law of this country differed from that of many foreign States was this – that we had not established by legal enactment those modes of creating a presumptive notice of partnership and liability which existed in foreign countries. In many of the United States of America there were laws, commonly known as the laws of *commandite* partnership, the effect of which was that, by complying with certain regulations, persons were deemed to have given notice to all the world of the nature and limitation of their liabilities. In France a system existed, similar in its general principles, but differing in its details. With regard to Ireland, there was an Act of the Irish Parliament which enabled persons engaged in trade in that country to limit their liabilities. The object of the Commission had been, by obtaining evidence from America, from France, and from other countries, and the opinions of those persons in this country who were best qualified to form a judgment upon such a question, to ascertain whether or not it was desirable to establish in this country, by legislative enactment, a mode by which a presumption of limitation of liability should be created.

The question for the House to consider, in dealing with this subject, would therefore be this – what would be the effect of certain specific provisions for this purpose, and would they be calculated to operate for the advantage of the community or not? It would be necessary to consider what the operation of such a law would be upon persons who had not received actual notice of the limitation of liability. They had been told by the hon. and learned Gentleman that the evidence from America was altogether in favour of an enactment which would establish a presumptive limitation of liability. He must admit that as the Report which was a document of considerable magnitude, had only been in his hands for a week, he had not, been enabled, in consequence of his other engagements, to make himself acquainted with its contents so far as to justify him in pronouncing an opinion upon them.

The Committee of 1851 obtained remarkable evidence of the value of this law of limited liability in the United States of America. They had before them the American Secretary of Legation, who was then resident in this country, and who gave strong evidence in favour of the existing law in America. He observed, however, that that Gentleman appended to his printed evidence, as a note, the following statement which he had not an opportunity of making to the Committee: "Since my examination I have seen a Statute enacted since I left America, by which stock-holders in a bank stopping payment are made liable individually to redeem all unpaid bills issued by the bank, in proportion to the stock they respectively held at the time when the bank stopped." He (Mr. Cardwell) was not going to attempt to draw from this statement any conclusion adverse to the proposition before the House; but he had thought it right to call their attention to the note appended by Mr. Davis to his evidence.

The hon. Member for Meath (Mr. Lucas) had given notice of his intention to move a rider to the Resolution before the House, calling attention to the particular demands of Ireland with regard to the limitation of liability. As he (Mr. Cardwell) had previously stated, a law had for many years been in force in Ireland of which persons might avail themselves, if they pleased, for the purpose of limiting their liabilities, but that it had not been made use of to any extent. He might be told that persons had not availed themselves of that law in consequence of the manner in which it was framed; but, so far as he was aware, no one had ever come forward with any specific proposal for the amendment of the law. He thought the inquiry of the Commissioners might furnish the House with information which they had not hitherto possessed with respect to this Irish law; and they might depend upon it that, in order to legislate satisfactorily upon such a question, to confirm the credit and to expand the industry of the country, the best course was, not to approach the subject until all the materials were so fully before them that they would be enabled to guard the community against any dangers which might be involved in a change of the law.

He had read the opinions of the different Commissioners, and among them the elaborate argument addressed to them by one of their own body, Lord Curriehill, who thought that neither on the ground of convenience to persons engaged in partnerships *en commandite*, or to others, nor on the free trade ground, could the change in the law proposed by the hon. and learned Member for Plymouth be recommended for adoption. With regard to the argument, that natural justice was involved in this question, the great authority of Mr. Mill had been cited; but he (Mr. Cardwell) thought he could show that persons who were well known as high authorities upon free-trade questions were entirely divided in opinion upon this subject. Mr. Tooke stated, in his evidence before the Committee of 1837, that a notion seemed to prevail that something like a right existed on the part of persons to circumscribe their liabilities as the condition of their embarking a certain sum in trade, and that it was only by the special interference of the law of partnership that they were prevented from exercising that right; but he said it must be obvious that partnership *en commandite* was a privilege, and had not the shadow of foundation in natural right; indeed, not only eminent lawyers, but also eminent political economists, viewed the question altogether apart from free trade, and only as to its effects upon contracts and dealings with persons having no knowledge of the arrangements of partnerships.

The Report of the Commission had been for so short a time before the House that it was scarcely possible any hon. Members could have made themselves conversant with the contents of the volume. He had only had time to ascertain the general nature of the Report, and he observed that there was considerable differences of opinion among the witnesses examined by the Commissioners. They had been informed by the noble Viscount that sixty-nine witnesses were examined, of whom thirty-seven were in favour of a change in the law, while the remaining thirty-two did not entertain the same opinion. He (Mr. Cardwell) considered that, before the House resolved to alter the law, they should know what was the nature of the changes to be proposed, in order that they might not assent to enactments which might be prejudicial to the community. He did not think any hon. Gentlemen in that House who were favourable to a change in the law had come to a conclusion as to whether it was desirable to adopt the law existing in America, or that which was established in France, or an amendment of the law in force in Ireland. He might say, however, he thought it was clear that the Irish law would not prove acceptable to those who were desirous of a change.

It would be necessary, in dealing with this subject, to consider many cases which involved great difficulties. Suppose a person with a limited capital embarked in a speculative concern, in which the gains might be very great, but in which the losses might be very disastrous to himself or to others – if such a concern became insolvent, who was to bear the loss? Was it proposed to say that the liability of such a person should be limited to the small capital he had embarked in the undertaking, and that, if he obtained large credit, the disastrous consequence of his failure should fall upon his creditor? Suppose that during four or five years the parties had derived very large profits from their speculation, and that, when the concern was wound up, it appeared that such profits ought to be brought into account, what course was to be pursued? By the American law, in such a case the profits would be brought into account, but it had been a moot question among those in this country who desired a change in the law of partnership, whether such profits should be brought into account or not. He found a difference of opinion prevailed upon this point among the thirty-seven witnesses examined before the Commission who, it was said, were favourable to an alteration of the law. Another question was, whether the names of the shareholders in a concern ought to be registered in order to afford security to the creditors. He found that some of the witnesses thought there should be an open register, while others entertained a contrary opinion. Another question was, supposing a concern was unprosperous, and 25 or 50 or 75 per cent of the capital had already been lost, ought the undertaking at such a juncture to be wound up for the protection of the creditors? This was a question of great importance and difficulty, and he found that the witnesses differed materially upon the subject. In short, among these thirty-seven witnesses there was every difference imaginable as to the nature and extent of the security to be taken for the protection of the public. He submitted, then, that it was the duty of the House of Commons to master these difficulties, and to have a definite opinion on these questions before they came to a final decision on the subject.

When he turned to the other class of witnesses – those who had given an opinion against any change in the law – he found they were persons of the very highest authority in such matters, and whose views, therefore, must be regarded with the most respectful consideration. The House would admit that such evidence as that of the Commercial Association of Glasgow, of Lord Overstone, of the hon. Member for South Lancashire (Mr. W. Brown), was of very great weight. This was by no means a new subject, for it had been considered by Committees of the House in 1837, in 1844, in 1850, and again in 1851. Up to the latter year the Committees had come to no decision on the point now in question, and the only specific suggestion made by the Committee of 1851 had reference to a system of loans in the nature of limited partnership, the interest receivable upon which should be in proportion to the prosperity of the concern. That Committee, however, recommended the appointment of a Commission, of adequate legal and commercial knowledge, to consider not only a consolidation of the existing law, but also to suggest such changes in the law as the altered condition of the country might require, especial attention being paid to the important and much controverted question of limited and unlimited liability.

The Commission appointed in pursuance of that recommendation exactly fulfilled the conditions required of adequate legal and commercial knowledge, for it was composed of the Master of Rolls in Ireland, of Mr. Justice Crosswell, of Lord Curriehill, of Mr. G. Bramwell, Q.C., of Mr. J. Anderson, Q.C., of Mr. Kirkman Hodgson, a director of the bank, of Mr. Thomas Bazley, President of the Manchester Chamber of Commerce, and of Mr. Robert Slater. These most eminent persons, after elaborate inquiry into the subject entrusted to them, had reported that they had: "Been much embarrassed by the great contrariety of opinion entertained by those who have favoured them with answers to their questions. Gentlemen of great experience and talent have arrived at conclusions diametrically opposite; and, in supporting those conclusions, have displayed reasoning power of the highest order." As a result of their deliberations upon these so various views, the Commissioners, by a majority of five out of eight, reported: "In considering this subject, the question which appeared to Your Majesty's Commissioners of paramount importance was, whether the proposed alteration of the law would operate beneficially on the general trading interests of the country? And they have arrived at the conclusion that it would not. They have not been able to discover any evidence of the want of a sufficient amount of capital for the requirements of trade; and the annually increasing wealth of the country and the difficulty of finding profitable investments for it, seem to them sufficient guarantees that an adequate amount will always be devoted to any mercantile enterprise that holds out a reasonable prospect of gain, without any forced action upon capital to determine it in that direction; while any such forced action would have a great tendency to induce men to embark in speculative adventures to an extent that would be dangerous to the interests of the general commerce of the country." The Commissioners thus summed up: "In concluding their brief Report, Your Majesty's Commissioners feel that, although the details of our mercantile laws may require correction, yet while there is on every side such abundant evidence of satisfactory progress and national prosperity, it would be unwise to interfere with principles which, in their judgment, have proved beneficial to the general industry of the country." A sixth Commissioner (Mr. Anderson), though not joining in the Report, separately records his opinion in favour of unlimited liability. Two of the Commissioners, on the other hand, were in favour of *commandite* partnerships. This variance of opinion on the part of the Commissioners was quite within the precedent of one of the earlier Committees, as appeared from their Report: "The opinions of those who must be considered as best able to form an opinion on this difficult and important question are at variance; by far the greater number of those who have been examined are decidedly unfavourable to its adoption under any circumstances whatever. Among those opposed to the measure will be found Mr. Samuel Jones Loyd, Mr. Thomas Tooke, Mr. Larpent,

Mr. Horsley Palmer, Mr. Kirkman Finlay, and Mr. Gladstone; while Lord Ashburton, Mr. J.W. Norman, the Hon. F. Baring, and Mr. Senior have expressed opinions favourable to its adoption."

When on the part of persons so eminently qualified to form opinions, and who had sought the opinions of others of high authority, there was such difficulty and such diversity, the House should take the utmost care thoroughly to master all the information which had been procured for its guidance ere it proceeded to take any decisive measure upon so important and so intricate a subject. With regard to the recommendation made by the Commissioners, that a change should be effected in the manner of granting privileges of limited liability by means of a charter, he quite concurred that some such change was expedient. He hoped the House would be of opinion that he was but discharging his duty in abstaining from arguing the question on either side. He had on all occasions, since in office, endeavoured to exercise the invidious power vested in him of granting such charters as to keep the subject clear for the deliberation of Parliament, when it should come under discussion. It was unquestionable, as the Commissioners suggested, that natural justice demanded that where these charters were sought persons who conceived they might be injured by the grant should have the opportunity, at a reasonable cost, of stating their objections. The whole question of joint-stock companies required the grave consideration of Parliament, and this question of limited liability would occupy an important feature in such an inquiry. The recommendation of the Commissioners that the usury laws should be revised had been adopted by the Chancellor of the Exchequer, who had a notice of a Bill on the subject on that day's paper. There was no doubt, as his hon. and learned friend had so eloquently pointed out, foreign States had prospered under a system in the particular respect under consideration different from our own, but at the same time it must be borne in mind that under the system which prevailed here our own country had attained a degree of commercial prosperity, of commercial credit, and of commercial stability wholly unexampled in the history of the world. When the House should have maturely considered the opinions which, in their Report, had been procured for its use, it would be in a position to take a decisive course upon the subject; then, should that course involve a change in the present system, the change, he should hope, would be presented to their notice, not in the desultory form of an abstract Resolution, but in the definite and authoritative form of a Bill so cautiously, so carefully, and so conclusively framed that, once adopted as a Parliamentary Act, it would tend to enhance our commercial prosperity, and to consolidate our commercial credit, on the bases of, if possible, increased security and increased confidence.

Mr. Lucas said, he was desirous of submitting to the House the Amendment of which he had given notice, specially extending the effect of the Resolution to Ireland, because he was anxious to draw the attention of Government and the House to the circumstances which made the application of this principle peculiarly expedient in Ireland; and whatever weight there might be in the right hon. Gentleman's (Mr. Cardwell's) opinion that the matter was not ripe for decision as to Great

Britain, there was certainly no occasion for any delay in applying the principle of limited liability to Ireland, where it was eminently required by the industrial and social condition of that country. The result of the inquiries of the Commission whose Report was now before them was most favourable to the principle now contended for; for it appeared that in every quarter of the globe where the principle of limited liability was known, it had been established by the sanction of the law, with the exception of the United Kingdom and its dependencies. Lord Curriehill in his evidence stated that the principle of limited liability had been tried in Ireland, and had failed there; now, it could not possibly have failed there, for it had not been tried – and it was finding such a preposterous statement in the Report of one of the Commissioners that had in part induced him to give notice of an addition to Mr. Collier's Motion. The Commissioners, hostile as they are to the principle of limited liability, have collected a great deal of evidence, and the result of it is decidedly favourable to the principle which they condemn. They admit that the evidence from foreign countries is unmistakably favourable to limited liability wherever it has been tried. In Great Britain a numerous majority of witnesses is on the same side; and the Irish witnesses are all but unanimous in favour of limited liability. Out of the six Irish witnesses who had expressed their opinions on the subject, five were in favour of the law of limited liability. All of these declared their opinion that if the change were adopted, capital would find advantageous means of investment which were at present not open to it, and would thereby add materially to the prosperity and well-being of the country. Mr. Bristow, of Belfast, was the only adverse witness, and the legitimate deduction from his evidence was, that he thought the principle of limited liability was a proper one to be adopted in three of the four provinces, of Ireland.

Lord Curriehill said the experiment had been already established in Ireland by an Act of the Irish Parliament of 1782, and that it had failed. So it had, but why? Here was a paragraph on the subject from the evidence of Mr. Kennedy, of Belfast, who said: "The Irish Act, passed in 1782, is a dead letter; its provisions are so loose, and have been interpreted so illiberally by our courts of law, that no lawyer would advise his client to take advantage of the Act. One of these provisions is, that the anonymous partner can only withdraw the half of his profits, no matter whether or not the concern is in debt. This entails a serious loss on the acting partners, as it is usual in a firm for each member to receive interest upon the sum he has paid up; and, besides, the firm may not require this additional capital in its business. Another provision is, that it cannot discount bills with its surplus capital; and, if the concern sells by retail, or breaks hulk in any way, the limited partners become accountable and lose all the advantages of their position. Traders should be left free to deal in whatever way their interest may dictate." What, then, was the meaning of the assertion that the experiment had been tried in Ireland, when it had only been tried by an Act so badly drawn by the Legislature, or so badly interpreted by the courts of law, that it could not be made available without considerable risk?

In arguing this case as regards Ireland his course had to be somewhat different from that of the hon. and learned Gentleman who moved, and the noble

Lord who seconded, the Motion with such ability. They had to reply to the arguments and overturn the authority of the witnesses who oppose limited liability. He (Mr. Lucas) had no such opposition to deal with. Not only the friends, but the opponents of limited liability are in favour of that principle as regards Ireland; and what he had to do – putting aside the logic and the authority of the friends of limited liability – was to bring before the House the admissions of its opponents. The Commissioners had to find a reason why a law which had succeeded everywhere else should not succeed in Great Britain; and their argument uniformly was, that there existed in this country sufficient capital and sufficient enterprise under the present system, and that the law of limited liability would apply an improper and unnecessary stimulus to speculation. The first and main reason stated by the Commissioners in their Report was: "They have not been able to discover any evidence of a want of a sufficient amount of capital for the requirements of trade." Was this, however, the case with regard to Ireland? Most unquestionably not.

No one could say there was a sufficient amount of capital or of speculative spirit in Ireland. Lord Curriehill, in his Report, said: "The circumstances of this country in reference to commercial matters are in some respects very different from those of these other countries. In France and other European countries where *commandite* partnerships have been introduced, capital is less abundant, and the spirit of commercial speculation is far less active than is the case in this country; and therefore a factitious attraction of capital to commerce may be sound policy there." Mr. Slater, another Commissioner, gave testimony of the same effect. He said: "Partnerships *en commandite* are doubtless well adapted for countries where capital is not abundant, and where it is of importance to call into action the dominant energies of a people whose industry has been laid prostrate by means of political events." With very slight change of phrase, did not this apply to Ireland?

But the adverse witnesses are not less clear upon this point than the adverse Commissioners; and he (Mr. Lucas) was happy to have to select particularly those adverse witnesses whose authority the President of the Board of Trade rated so very highly. Thus Lord Overstone and Mr. W.G. Prescott have given a very elaborate joint opinion hostile to limited liability. But what do they think of it applied to such a country as Ireland? These are their words:

> "Some caution, we think, may be requisite in applying to the legislature of this country lessons derived from the experience of other countries differently circumstanced."
>
> "There may be a great difference between the effects of a law introduced in the early stages of a community – when its transactions are few and simple, and the trading habits of the people not firmly settled, and therefore capable of easy adaptation to the law, whatever it may be – and the effects of the same law, when introduced into a community at a later period, under exactly the opposite circumstances."

If Lord Overstone and Mr. Prescott had had Ireland in their view at the moment of writing this, it was impossible that they could have used language more applicable to the case of that country. Then, again, Mr. S. Gurney said: "In those countries where commerce is in its infancy, and capital scarce, a law limiting responsibility to capital actually advanced may be expedient. Under such circumstances it may attract capital and foster commerce. In this country, where there is abundant capital and abundant commercial talent and energy, such limitation is not called for."

The Chamber of Commerce at Glasgow declared that they considered the circumstances of Great Britain to be so materially different as to destroy any analogy between them and other countries, and they went on to say: "With an 'exuberance' of capital, and a tendency to speculative investment, which is not deterred by the present law of unlimited responsibility for embarking in all sorts of hazardous schemes – when noblemen, and professional gentlemen, and tradesmen, and farmers, and ladies engage in mines and ironworks, and marine insurance, and banks, and exchange companies, and shipowners, assuredly the disposition to invest capital in business requires no additional stimulus." Similar opinions were expressed by many of the other gentlemen who had forwarded their views to the Commission. Other witnesses are these – Mr. James Freshfield, jun., solicitor:

> "Other exceptions may exist in a state of society, or in countries where capital is scarce and cannot be easily procured. Banks could hardly be established in the Colonies without a limit of liability, and associations for other trading purposes will be found to need encouragement in the Colonies on this ground; but in England capital for all legitimate purposes is over abundant."

Laurence Robinson, cashier of the Royal Bank of Scotland, Glasgow:

> "I am not acquainted with the operation in Ireland of the Act of Parliament here quoted; but I can easily conceive how the poverty and insecurity of property in that country may, in the year 1782, have created a necessity for limited liability in certain undertakings for the accomplishment of which sufficient enterprise and capital could not then be found, but which, at the same time, could form no precedent for the application of similar measures in Great Britain, especially during the present era of superabundant capital for all legitimate purposes."

Mr. Bellenden Ker has been quoted by the right hon. Gentleman – and is esteemed, I believe, by every succeeding Board of Trade – as a great authority. His elaborate Report changed Lord Brougham's opinion some years ago, and it therefore deserves particular attention. In his reply to the Commissioners, Mr. Ker reasserts, though with diminished confidence, the opinions hostile to limited liability which he gave before the Committee of 1850. He (Mr. Lucas) was, therefore, justified in quoting his opinion given in writing to the Partnership Committee of 1851. This is the first paragraph of his reply to the queries circulated by that Committee:

"Reply to Queries by H.B. Ker, Esq., Lincoln's Inn, 27th June 1851

My dear Sir – With reference to the question you have sent to me, I beg to observe that I venture to think that the limited liability, as regards ordinary trading partnerships, or even as regards 'the aiding of useful local enterprises,' is inexpedient, as I am led to believe there is always a sufficiency of capital for all commercial enterprises, and for the carrying out what I suppose to be meant by local enterprises – namely, canals, roads, mills, &c. In a country where there is not a sufficiency of capital for such purposes, the introduction of this would be beneficial, and it is mortifying to see that no one will bring the matter before Parliament, as regards Ireland." Lord Brougham, whose opinion was modified by Mr. Ker, drew precisely the same conclusion in writing to the same Committee. He says: "The *commandite* appears better adopted to a community which has moderate mercantile capital and concerns than to ours, and would be more wanted as well as more safe in such a community." And, lastly, he must quote Mr. Bristow, of Belfast, the only Irish witness hostile to the principle, but who yet admits that to three-fourths of Ireland it may be suitable: "In a new country whose resources are undeveloped, and where capital is scarce among trading people, it may be expedient to modify, for a time, this principle; but in an old country, with a wealthy and enterprising class of merchants, such modification should be unnecessary." Thus of all the adverse witnesses those entitled to most weight agreed that to a country like Ireland limited liability may apply.

There was only one witness who distinctly stated an objection fatal, if it were sound, to this principle in Ireland as well as in Great Britain. This objection was alluded to by one or two other witnesses, but it was distinctly stated by Mr. Clarke, of the house of Finlay in Glasgow, and he (Mr. Lucas) gave it in its own words. Mr. Clarke is of opinion that in point of fact capital is not "hoarded" or "locked up," and that, therefore, there is no capital either in Ireland or in England which a law of limited liability could set free: "It seems to me that a general fallacy lurks in the argument on the other side, which assumed that capital remains unemployed, deterred by the apprehension of its owners, in respect of unlimited responsibility; whereas I am of opinion that no more capital than is necessary as a reserve remains on the average idle, but is loaned out productively for industrial undertakings or mercantile operations, and is thereby effectually engaged in the business of society as if every man were directly devoting his own quota of it to individual effort. In my answer to the first question, while giving my reason for the conclusion at which I had arrived, I stated my conviction that it is fallacious to suppose that capital remains unemployed. What is true of the employment of capital in this country is true also as respects the colonies of England because it is only in countries and places where property and life are insecure, where war and rapine are normal conditions, that hoarding is prevalent – a state of things happily unknown here for many generations."

This is an argument which, though weak and unsound, deserves an answer, and the first answer he (Mr. Lucas) gave is the words of Mr. Kennedy: "I am satisfied, if we had a proper limited partnership law, a large amount of capital that is now invested in continental stock and railway shares would be invested in this country, and that it would make the increase of our imports from Britain as important as her exports are at present to the Continent, and likewise enable us to add largely to the revenue of the empire." This was his first answer to Mr. Clarke. It was no satisfaction to him that Irish capital was not hoarded if its employment was in England and on the Continent, and not at home, where it was most needed. But there was another and a more conclusive answer. The best capital of every country is not money capital, but the skill and industry of its inhabitants; and if your laws are such as to dissuade from industry, to put a check on the energies of the people, to take from them the proper stimulus to exertion, and thus to encourage indolence – then it might with strict logical accuracy be said that the capital of the country is "hoarded," is "locked up," and is restrained from a full and profitable application. This really was the state of the case as regarded Ireland, and they had a right to ask from the Imperial Legislature, considering the state of poverty and exhaustion to which Ireland had been reduced, her want of commercial resources, and the fact that her population was flying at every outlet from her shores, that laws should be passed enabling Irish capital to be spent in Ireland in the most profitable way in which it could be spent for the interests of Irish industry and trade; and he asked them to give to the industry of the country that protection which would enable every man to apply his best exertions to develop the industrial resources within his reach, and suitable to the locality in which he resided.

From his own personal experience he could testify that the existence of the present law prevented industrious persons from being as industrious as they would be – prevented prudent persons possessed of a little capital from applying it prudently and profitably to the encouragement of commercial enterprises of various kinds in their own localities – prevented one class from being industrious and others from being prudently enterprising in commercial matters. Nobody could deny that the case was complete as regarded Ireland, and he did not see the slightest difficulty in laying down the main branches of alteration which were required in the Irish law. In the first place repeal the absurd proviso which compels a partner to be content with half his profits during the continuance of the partnership. Then repeal the clause which forbids limited partnerships to have retail as well as wholesale transactions. Then withdraw the obstacle which the Act places in the way of discounting bills where the ordinary course of trade requires and sanctions such accommodation. Abolish the limitation of 1,000*l.* which is fixed as the minimum of capital for such partnerships. Such changes as were necessary for making this law productive of the greatest possible benefit to Ireland were very simple, and he hoped this debate would not end without some one on the part of the Government giving the industrious people of Ireland reason to hope that the law on this subject would be so amended that it would no longer interpose between the desire for honest industry and commercial wealth and the possibility of attaining these ends. Amendment proposed, at the end of the Question, to add the words:

> "And such modification is especially necessary in Ireland, regard being had to the peculiar social and industrial condition of that part of the United Kingdom."

Mr. Cobden agreed with the right hon. Gentleman the President of the Board of Trade, that the subject of limited liability was one which had not been thoroughly discussed, and which deserved to be debated in that House. But it was a subject which there would be great difficulty discussing unless they heard both sides; and all he could learn of the views of the right hon. Gentleman was, that he told them when he began he would not offer an opinion, and he contrived very ingeniously to keep his word. With reference to the observations of the hon. Gentleman who addressed the House specially in reference to Ireland as regards this question, he thought the case for Ireland was, after all, much the case of England. There was no law of England which forbade commercial transactions taking place under a contract of limited liability; on the contrary, the law would enforce contracts made on that principle, provided only certain conditions were observed; but then the particulars necessary to be observed had the effect of clogging the entering into such transactions, and of rendering it impossible to carry on business upon that system. It was admitted there was nothing in the system of limited liability that was contrary to public morality; for if there were, the law would refuse to enforce such contracts altogether; and as the law enforced those contracts, he took it for granted that the spirit of the law was favourable to limited liability, and what they had to do in that House, whether with regard to Ireland or to England, was to address themselves to consider in what manner the restrictions which the law imposed upon commercial transactions conducted on the system of limited liability, and rendered therein impracticable in the working, might best be remedied.

He would put the case of two persons, A and B, who entered into partnership. A was the moneyed, and what was called the sleeping partner, and he put 10,000*l.* into the hands of B, who was the manager and working partner. Now, if the partnership, in giving orders for goods, or in the different mercantile transactions in which they were engaged, were to give a written notice that A was responsible to the extent of 10,000*l.*, and for no more – if that written notice were repeated in every transaction, then no creditor could have a claim upon A for more than that amount. But under such a condition as that every transaction of the partnership must be accompanied by a written notice; it would be impossible that the firm could carry on their business, and they would be involved in the pitfalls of the law at every turn. The object of the law was, apparently, to take care that the creditors of A and B – that was to say, of the man who sold the goods – should know exactly that A was responsible for only 10,000*l.* It was, in fact, the same in principle with an ancient law which existed among their Saxon forefathers in the kingdom of Kent, which provided, for the sake of their being witnesses to the sale, that no bargain should take place in the market unless in the presence of the bailiff, the mass priest, or the lord of the manor. The law of unlimited liability was an act of precisely the same supererogatory character, and he believed that at no distant time the law of unlimited liability would appear as absurd to their descendants as the law of Kent did to them.

What was the ground on which it was required that they should maintain this restrictive law? It was said to be necessary for the protection of the capitalist and trader. But were hon. Gentlemen afraid that such persons would give credit indiscriminately, and without first ascertaining the circumstances of the persons with whom they had transactions. Now did they require as much publicity in the case of professions? Take the case of a barrister. His hon. and learned friend who introduced the Motion had been admitted to practice as a barrister, by having his name enrolled in one of the inns of court. Now did the law require that he should carry the certificates of his enrolment about with him, that he might thrust it in the face of everybody who might want his services? Did not everybody know that by going to the inns of court, and inspecting the register, they could satisfy themselves whether he had been properly enrolled or not? And did not the House think that they might, with just as much safety, alter the law to this convenient extent, that there should be one general registry, where every case of partnership should be bound to register the fact that, while B was the acting partner, and was responsible for his dealings to the extent of all that he possessed, A was responsible for only 10,000*l.*

For his part, he thought that the argument against a law of limited liability was founded on this fallacy – that people possessed of capital were to be easily induced to give credit, and that the law must therefore take care of their interests. Why, the capitalists, the men who had money at their disposal, were the shrewdest people in the world – men whose intellects were stimulated and sharpened by that conservative principle which attached to the possession of property. Were they to be supposed to be in a condition where they could not be trusted with the management of their own property? Why, in proposing to provide for their safety by fixing the principle on which they should give credit, this House never was engaged in a greater supererogation. Take the case of a large house with extensive dealings. Everybody knew that it was one of the most delicate, one of the most responsible, and one of the most incessant occupations of the most trusted partners or managing men of the firm to ascertain the trustworthiness of everybody with whom they opened an account, and to keep watch upon their solvency from month to month, as indicated by the regularity of their payments and by other symptoms, to note all down in a book kept for the special purpose, and to do all this with the ingenuity and the art, he was going to say, of an officer of the detective police. If these men trusted their affairs to Acts of Parliament in these days of competition, they would not be long in a condition to trust anybody.

There was another fallacy which seemed prominent upon this subject, for the question was often argued as if the persons who were in favour of a system of limited liability were about to pass a law which would force people to trust those firms established on that principle of partnership. Nothing of the kind was contemplated. They never intended, by any Act of Parliament, to force the creditor to do business with the firm of A and B. They would leave to all parties their right of free action, to trust the firm or to pass it by as they chose. But then they were told, in some of the arguments in the blue books, that partnerships established on the principle of limited liability would not obtain credit. Well, then, the law would be inoperative, and would do no harm. It was also argued, and, he believed, universally maintained, that the credit of such partnerships would be inferior to that of others. He did not admit that; he believed that credit depended upon skill and industry, and the known amount of capital in the business. He did not mean to say that a house with only 10,000*l.* of capital would have the same amount of credit as a house with a capital of 100,000*l.*; but he believed that for the same amount of capital there would be the same extent of credit as under the present system.

In reading the evidence contained in the blue book – and he could conscientiously say that he had read every word of it – he was forcibly struck with one feature it presented. He found that the questions proposed by the Commissioners were generally addressed to men in business who were of the large capitalist class – men of weight on 'Change – leading men in mercantile associations and chambers of commerce; and yet of such men not above half were unfavourable to the principle of limited liability. But he would be bound to say that if they took another class – the class of young men who were engaged as clerks or shopmen in houses of business – of whom there were, he believed, in London alone, no fewer than 100,000 – he doubted if they would not find in them a unanimous feeling in favour of the principle of limited liability, which was the principle that afforded them the best chance of entering into business on their own account, and of making their way in the world. If they went to the class of mechanics and artisans, they would find them all but unanimous in favour of an alteration of the law. He confessed that it was in that point of view, which had been so eloquently and so feelingly dwelt upon by his noble friend the Member for Huddersfield (Viscount Goderich) – it was in that point of view that he took the greatest interest in the question. It was stated before the Committee of 1851, by Mr. Wynn Ellis, formerly a Member of this House, and who had a large wholesale warehouse in London, that there were several occasions when he would have liked to enter into limited partnership with young men who were standing behind the counter – young men of talent and promise, but without capital – but that he was deterred from doing so as that would involve the risk of his whole fortune in the undertaking, but that he would have done so if he could have limited his liability; and he (Mr. Cobden) had no doubt that it was a matter of every-day occurrence in London, Manchester, Leeds, and elsewhere, where capitalists would like to assist young men who showed aptitude for business – who ingratiated themselves with their employers' customers – who made themselves, in fact, almost indispensable in the houses in whose business they were concerned – where capitalists would like to join themselves to these young men, and give them the chance of a start in life, provided they could do so without involving their whole fortune in the risk. It was the same with the persons employed for wages in the manufacturing concerns in the north of England. But the law of unlimited liability was an insurmountable obstacle which prevented this from taking place; and therefore, if the system were to be continued, there should be some cogent reason shown for its continuance.

What were those reasons? In reading this blue book, he had been surprised to find men with whom he formerly acted in advocating sound economical opinions, now giving utterance to the most erroneous sentiments, and urging them with so much feebleness of argument. He found in these persons a constant tendency to embark in predictions, which, in his opinion, was the invariable sign of a weak cause. Whenever men began to argue in the future tense – when they talked of what would, could, should, or might be – he was certain to find that this was because there was a total want of support from existing facts. Then they were told that this system of limited liability might do very well in painstaking France, in frugal Holland, and in moral Germany, but that it would never do in this country, where there was an abundance of capital. Now he could not understand this. Political economy was not a plant that flowered only in certain climates and latitudes. If there was truth in the principle, it was applicable to all countries and to all times. But the obvious answer was this – if the system did not suit this country, it would not be adopted. All he asked for was a permissive, not a compulsory law. If it did not suit England after the trial had been fairly made, then everybody would be satisfied, and no harm would be done.

Neither could he subscribe to the doctrine which was sometimes laid down, that this country was doing very well, and that they ought to let well alone. Such a doctrine was adverse to all progress and to all reform for the future; – he could not understand such an argument coming from the mouths of men who were the champions of economical and social reform. He must say, once for all, that this was not a question to be referred to the arbitrement of any one class; – he did not think that any class could be trusted to legislate in favour of its own interest, for it generally mistook its own interest. Take the case of the shipowners, and the repeal of the Navigation Laws: – when was navigation in a more prosperous state? When were ships better employed than at present? Take the case of the Corn Laws: land was never higher – farmers were never more prosperous. And yet if these parties had had their way, there would have been no repeal of the Corn or of the Navigation Laws. And so it was with the capitalists, many of whom were afraid that a law of limited liability would injure capital. He could not understand this feeling at all, because a law of limited liability could not benefit any one if it did not benefit the capitalist. He could not imagine anything more suicidal on the part of the capitalists than to oppose this proposition, which would afford new and hitherto unthought-of openings for their capital. It was no answer to say that capital was already easy enough of access. Men of genius and invention did not find capital easily obtained. The law interposed difficulties in the way; it would not allow of the free marriage of capital and skill; it forbade the banns by the law of unlimited liability. It was because he thought it one of the social blots in this country that capital had such a tendency to accumulate in great masses and in few hands – because he believed that the removal of the present law would tend to remove that blot, and tend to diffuse capital – because he thought it would tend to bridge over the gulf which now divided different classes, and to diminish that spirit of alienation between employers and employed which they all deplored – that he hoped that the Government would, either to-night or on some future occasion, give their sanction to the change proposed in the Resolution of his hon. and learned friend.

Mr. Malins said, that on the present occasion he had the satisfaction of concurring in almost every expression that had fallen from the hon. Member for the West Riding, and thanked the hon. and learned Member for Plymouth for having brought the subject forward. A question of greater importance than the present, affecting the commercial well-being of the country, he believed it would be difficult to bring under the consideration of the House; and he ventured to predict that the period was not distant when the principle of the present proposition would be carried into effect. He quite agreed with the President of the Board of Trade that every Member ought duly to weigh the evidence laid upon the table of the House before pledging himself one way or the other; but he regretted to perceive that the bent of the right hon. Gentleman's mind was adverse to the alteration in the law. He (Mr. Malins) had formed his opinions on the subject, not from theory, but from extensive observation of the great mischief arising from the present state of the law, which was not creditable to the country.

No one objected that two parties ostensibly carrying on business should both be liable for all their undertakings; but the law was in an anomalous state if one of the partners was a secret one, though with ever so small an interest, for if a person gave credit to one partner only, and if, after having delivered his goods, he found that there was another, he might call upon him to pay the utmost farthing of his means, though he had trusted the firm not knowing that such person was a partner. The legislature day after day gave the protection of limited liability to railway and dock companies by particular Acts of Parliament; and he thought no one could object to give the same facilities to private partnerships which they were every day giving to public partnerships.

Some advance had been made in the matter, for they had passed the Joint Stock Registration Act. When that Act was passed many persons thought that a limited liability was created; but it had been decided upon an appeal in the Court of Chancery, that that Act had not established the principle of limited liability. He would ask the House, if with reference to great undertakings the principle of limited liability were permitted to be applied, upon what ground was it that the Legislature should hesitate to enable all persons – not under an absolute, but under a discretionary law – to establish limited liability for themselves, care being taken that due notice should be given to the public of the terms upon which the partnerships had been framed?

Let them consider for a moment the calamities which had resulted from the operation of the law with respect to partnership as it at present stood. Frequently persons of genius had been unable from want of capital to render their inventive talents serviceable to the country. Really, the anomalies of the existing state of things were such as to make one blush for the state of our law on this subject. Let them look at the numerous instances in which persons were induced to join particular companies upon the understanding that the principle of limited liability existed with respect to the transactions in which those companies happened to be engaged, and yet afterwards found out to their cost that no such principle prevailed. The general provision of the law upon the subject was, that any persons who were associated together for any commercial purposes, and participated in the advantages of the business in which they were engaged, became liable to the debts in which, in the pursuit of that business, that firm might become involved.

But the question was one with respect to which many and great anomalies existed. Take the case of a number of gentlemen associated together in a club. One would suppose that, according to the general principle of the law with reference to the subject of limited liability, the members of the club generally would be held responsible for the debts incurred by the committee of the club for the supply of provisions. [An Hon. Member: Such is the case.] He did not wonder that the hon. Member would be of that opinion, inasmuch as it was one entirely in accordance with the general principle of the law upon the subject. He could, however, inform the hon. Member that it had been decided that it was only the members of the committee of a club who were held to be liable for debts which they might have incurred with tradesmen on behalf of the members generally. Now, in order to induce a fact in proof of what he had just been saying, he should state, that in the case of a club in St. James's Street, in which establishment a nobleman who was well known to the public had been an active member of the committee, it was found that debts to the amount of 40,000*l.* had been contracted on behalf of its members. It had been supposed that the members generally were liable to the payment of their proportion of the debt, and an application had accordingly been made to Vice Chancellor Bruce for an order to wind up the affairs of the club. That order had been made; but it had afterwards been reversed upon appeal to the Lord Chancellor, and ten or fifteen members of the committee had been made liable for the whole amount. Now, he would ask if that were a proper state of the law?

It was well known to the profession to which he belonged – and it was probably equally well known to the House – that day after day cases occurred in which utter ruin was the consequence of the investments made by parties in commercial transactions, supposing those transactions to be carried under the operation of a principle of limited liability; when suddenly, perhaps, through the reckless conduct of the directors, the concern broke down and involved all engaged in it in ruin. In the town of Newcastle-upon-Tyne there had been in existence some time since a company, denominated "The Newcastle-upon-Tyne Banking Company," with whom large sums of money had been invested upon the faith of the principle of the existence of the law of limited liability, and the consequence had been that an order for winding up having been made, all parties engaged in the transaction had been to a great extent ruined. A still more recent case was that of the Monmouth and Glamorganshire Bank, where the people believed their money was as safe as in the public funds when it was invested in a joint-stock bank, and only found out their mistake when the bank broke down and involved them in ruin.

Was this a state of things that ought to last? For whose benefit was it? Some said it was necessary for the protection of the creditor; but it was rather for the destruction of the creditor. Business was never well conducted unless it was conducted with prudence and foresight; and a man ought to be induced to give credit only where he saw the likelihood of repayment from a business being well and prudently managed. But under the present system credit was given to a company, because the creditor, after scanning the list of shareholders, was able to pick out 50 or 100 men from whom he knew he could extract every farthing of his debt, whether the undertaking flourished or fell. Was that, he would ask, a state of things which, in a national point of view, it was desirable should exist?

They all knew that there were numbers of reckless creditors, and that the system which they adopted could not fail to be a national injury. In the discussion upon the Oxford University Bill – the arguments which had been put forward to prevent expense from being incurred by the student, because of his being *in statu pupillari,* went to the extent that it was desirable to place more restriction upon the principle upon which credit generally was given. His own opinion was, that the system of recklessly giving credit was most injurious, and that considerable advantage would result from the adoption, upon the part of tradesmen, of trusting with their money those persons only whom they deemed to be in possession of the means of meeting their demands.

He must say that he thought the whole argument that evening against the principle of limited liability had failed. He was satisfied the period had passed when such a system as the present could be maintained, and he, therefore, entertained the most sanguine hope that the state of the law would speedily be altered. The right hon. Gentleman (Mr. Cardwell) had shown considerable hesitation on this occasion; but why should there be any hesitation in advancing upon a question like the present? If there had always been this backwardness, how much slower would have been our progress in those commercial changes which had been effected by the House! He trusted, therefore, that during the recess they were approaching the right hon. Gentleman would apply the powers of his mind to the question, so as to be able at the commencement of the next Session to give them an assurance that he was prepared to introduce a change. If he did so, he was certain that, in that House at least, he would have no difficulties to contend with. In conclusion, he trusted that the House would, on the present occasion, accede to the Motion of the hon. and learned Member for Plymouth, and show its willingness to remove the existing absurdities of the law, leaving the public in their own way to settle all these matters for themselves.

Mr. Glyn said, that as he had been a Member of a Committee which was appointed in the year 1851 to inquire into this subject, he was anxious to address a few words to the House before the discussion should be brought to a close. He was not one of those described by the noble Lord (Viscount Goderich) at the commencement of the debate, who desired to maintain the monopoly which was supposed to exist under the operation of the present law, and he had for some time considered the whole system of commercial jurisprudence in this country to be in a most anomalous and unsatisfactory condition. But although he had attended that Committee with an eager desire to find, if it should be possible, some remedy for a system which he thought required amendment, he should confess that neither in the evidence produced at the time, nor in the Report lately laid before the House, had he met with anything which could lead him to believe that, however desirable it might be that certain changes should take place, they were as yet in a position to decide how these changes ought to be effected. It appeared to him that the Report presented to the House was deficient in many respects, and was not, in point of fact, one which could form the basis of legislation upon the subject.

He would remind the hon. Gentleman the Member for the West Riding of Yorkshire (Mr. Cobden), who had also served upon the Committee, that although he (Mr. Glyn) agreed with him in most of the views he had laid down, he had omitted, and the Report had also omitted to touch upon that particular point which had been the source of the greatest difficulty to the Committee, namely the possibility of preventing that fraud which, under a system of limited liability, would inevitably occur. He said inevitably, because, from the evidence taken before the Committee given by those most favourable to the system of limited liability, and by foreigners well acquainted with its working, that that system afforded great facilities for fraud. The consequence had been that in those countries where the principle of partnerships *en commandite* had been carried to the greatest extent, and particularly in France, it had been found necessary to give the bankruptcy laws an extremely penal character. Now, our bankruptcy laws were of a much less rigorous description. In the year 1849 certain changes had been made in those laws, which gave to them a more penal character than they had before possessed; and the result had been that since this period the laws had become so odious that the Bankruptcy Court was at present almost entirely deserted. What, then, would be the case if they were to render the bankrupt laws still more stringent, as every foreigner who had given an opinion on the subject said that they must do in the event of their adopting the system of limited liability? He believed that the only remedy against fraud which had been suggested by the witnesses could not, in that case, be carried into practical operation. The Report, however, did not even notice that circumstance. He appealed to the hon. and learned Gentleman who had last addressed the House, whether the state of the bankruptcy laws was not a most material ingredient in the discussion of that question, and whether, before they had received evidence upon it, the President of the Board of Trade could venture to introduce a measure for the alteration of the law of partnership, as was urged by hon. Members? He felt persuaded that until they should have further considered the only remedy against fraud which had been suggested under the proposal before the House, it would be worse than folly on their part to accede to that proposal.

There were other points connected with the question which would also, as he thought, require very attentive consideration before any decided step should be taken in the matter. It was all very well to argue the question merely as it affected partnerships in trade and joint-stock companies; but it should be borne in mind that in this country the system of credit was unlike that which prevailed in any other country. A large portion of the business in the manufacturing districts was conducted by means of bills of exchange, circulated from hand to hand, with endorsements bearing an unlimited liability; and the fact was, that if the change in question were adopted a material alteration must be effected in the whole of our commercial jurisprudence. He did not throw out these observations for the purpose of defending the present law of partnership, for he believed that the law required considerable alteration. But as one who had largely engaged in commercial pursuits, and who knew by experience the frauds daily practiced in those pursuits, he was anxious that they should enter into the discussion of that question with the fullest knowledge of all the facts connected with it, and with a desire to obviate the difficulties by which it was surrounded. He had certainly no wish to delay any longer than necessary those alterations in our present commercial system, which, if they could be safely made, would prove of decided benefit to the commercial relations of this country.

Mr. J.G. Phillimore hoped the House would not be led away by the plausible speech of the right hon. Gentleman the President of the Board of Trade, or by the ingenious arguments of the hon. Gentleman who had last addressed them. The right hon. Gentleman had told them in the language, or rather, he might say, the cant which was so often adopted in a certain portion of the House, that the subject was not yet ripe for decision. Not ripe! As if they were dealing with a law that had not been incorporated into the mercantile code of every other country in Europe, from the earliest period down to the *Code Napoléon.* That law had raised the old Italian Republics to the height of prosperity which they had once enjoyed; it had covered the Atlantic with ships, and New England with monuments of industry, and yet they were told by the right hon. Gentleman to go and study the blue book. He (Mr. J.G. Phillimore) knew, from the very constitution of the Commission, that its Report would be as flimsy and self-contradictory as they had been told that it had proved; and, therefore, when he was asked to attend as a witness he had merely sent word that he had seen no reason to alter his former opinion.

All parties must see the great importance of showing the working classes that they really took a deep interest in their welfare, and were ready to afford them the means of raising themselves in the scale of society by the force of their own moral energies. For what would the working classes think if they saw the advantages possessed by men of their own rank in America continue to be denied them in this country? With the results of this principle in America, and with ancient experience, confirmed by modern, as to the benefit to be derived from it, had not the lower classes a right to ask the House to carry out the principle which would effect for them such important changes? When the hon. Member (Mr. Glyn) said that the bankruptcy laws in foreign countries, especially in France, had been made more penal and stringent, in consequence of the adoption of the principle proposed, he had forgotten that in France these laws were rendered necessary, not by the *société en commandite,* but by the *société anonyme,* which was of a far more speculative and dangerous character. Every application that was made to the right hon. Gentleman to get rid of the necessity for unlimited liability in exceptional cases proved the present unsatisfactory state of the law, which deprived the poor man of those opportunities of benefiting himself which every one must desire to have, and which it was most desirable that every one should have. Adam Smith had said that a joint-stock company was an excellent thing, because it enabled men of small capital to take part in great enterprises; but he said it had one fault, for it did not make the persons of large capital take a sufficient interest in its affairs. But the *société en commandite* possessed all the advantages of a stock company, and avoided that fault; for, while the non-active members were liable only to the extent of their capital, the people at the head of the concern were responsible to the last shilling they possessed. They had thus the same means of associating men of small capital, and they had also a sufficient guarantee for the integrity of the managers.

Mr. F. Leveson Gower said, he would not venture to trespass long on their patience, but he trusted to receive the indulgence the House always extended to a new Member, while he made a few observations upon this subject, which was one in which he felt the deepest possible interest. He agreed in the main with nearly every speech which had been delivered this evening with the exception of that of the President of the Board of Trade, which he might call a neutral speech, and that of the Gentleman near him (Mr. Glyn), which, however, he was gratified to observe, was not characterised by that spirit of hostility which was displayed by some of the opponents of any change in the law of partnership. He admitted that, if machinery could not be devised that would secure societies established on the principle of limited liability from being tainted with fraud, such societies could never prosper in this country; but he was not of opinion that such machinery could not be introduced. He believed that the interest which the country took in this question was spreading and growing every day; and that not only would the Report which had been just published be read with attention, but also the arguments which accompanied it – the two, as it struck him, pointing at a very different conclusion.

He was somewhat astonished at the conclusion at which the Commissioners had arrived – it was founded neither on the principle of protection nor upon the principle that the Government was a better judge of the interests of private individuals than those individuals themselves, but their chief argument seemed to be, that there was no evidence to prove the want of a sufficient amount of capital for the requirements of trade. Now, he believed that trade was always varying, that it varied according to the capital of a country, and that the proposed change was calculated to increase that capital. He had read the opinion of Lord Overstone that limited liability could not possibly increase the capital of the country. He (Mr. F.L. Gower) asked the House with diffidence, whether they could agree with such an opinion? Surely, if a law of limited liability held out inducements to men to lay by, instead of spending their incomes, it must thereby increase the capital of the country; and it was likewise notorious that a great amount of capital was now invested abroad because limited liability did not exist in this country. A short time ago he was anxious to invest a small sum of money, and he was advised to invest it in a foreign society, so as to have the benefit of limited liability. He had no doubt that similar advice was frequently given, and, therefore, the introduction of limited liability would materially increase the capital of the country. It must also be considered that limited liability made the capital of the country more effective, which would be tantamount to increasing it, and he could not therefore understand the view which was taken by Lord Overstone. If it increased capital, it would, of course, increase the trade of the country.

The only other practical objection that had been made to the change was the encouragement it would give to speculation. He believed that the present age was tending toward association – that the great things which might be effected by means of association were now, for the first time, being appreciated – and he therefore thought it was the duty of every legislator to endeavour, to the utmost of his ability, to have the principle of association carried out by prudent, instead of inconsiderate men; but by the present law prudent men were driven away from association. Lord Overstone, in his evidence, said that a man would now look twice before joining an undertaking, the failure of which would cause his entire destruction. He went further than Lord Overstone, for he contended that that man was no better than a madman or a gambler who would risk his whole fortune or means of existence in an undertaking in the management of which he could not have a share; and therefore, notwithstanding an association might hold out the greatest prospect of success, no prudent, cautious man would wish to join it in the present state of the law; this was one of the principle reasons which rendered a change desirable. The question which the right hon. Gentleman had put to the proposers of the measure was rather an unfair one, because, although it was easy for those who wished things to remain as they were to be unanimous, unanimity in those who proposed an alteration was difficult to be obtained. He thought that, if two or more persons joined themselves in partnership upon any conditions they thought fit, the only thing the law had to do was to secure the publicity of those conditions, and no partnerships would succeed unless they were such that credit would be given the undertaking. Having now stated his opinions upon this subject, he would assure the hon. and learned Gentleman who had brought it forward that, if he persevered in advocating a change in the law, he would always find in him a zealous supporter.

Mr. Digby Seymour thought that in three very material points the President of the Board of Control had made great and important concessions – namely, with regard to the questions of notice, of special loans, and of charters – for which the advocates of limited liability ought to feel grateful. Upon the general question, he would call the attention of the House to the opinion which had been expressed by Mr. Whitworth in his Report upon the Industrial Exhibition of New York. Mr. Whitworth said that limited liability produced very beneficial results in facilitating the introduction of new inventions and manufactures, and of causing the investment of capital by educated artisans, and thereby regulating the relations between employers and employed. It seemed to him that in these times, when we were ready to encourage every work tending to improve the condition of the working classes – such as model lodging-houses, baths, and wash-houses, and the like – it was important that the humbler classes should be enabled to invest their earnings in works of a nature that did not involve the risk of ruining themselves and families. On these grounds he supported the Motion; and he thought this discussion would, at least, have the good effect of showing that it was admitted that our present partnership laws were a disgrace to the jurisprudence of the country.

Mr. Kendall observed, in reference to a remark which had been made by the hon. and learned Member for Plymouth, that Cornish mining was subject to certain stannary laws, by which a man could at any time, without consulting his partners, withdraw from the partnership and release himself from liability. He, therefore, denied that prudent persons would not be willing to risk their money in Cornish mines.

Mr. W. Brown said, he had always been ready to adopt any measure which could be advantageous to the middle classes, and therefore wished to state his reasons for the course he should take on the present occasion. He should be exceedingly sorry to see anything done to impair the credit of the country, believing that such a course would inflict great injury upon the humbler as well as the higher classes. This very question had been debated for three days in the Liverpool Chamber of Commerce, and the result was a vote of 107 in favour of limited liability, and 209 against it; being pretty much the same conclusion as that come to by the Royal Commissioners in their Report. When money was lent to railroads, banks, and large establishments of that kind, there was a visible security in the shape of the property belonging to the company; but in other descriptions of partnership there was nothing to look to at all but the individual partners themselves. His conviction was decided that it would be injurious to the interests of the country to adopt, in the present state of information upon the subject, a system of limited liability in partnerships.

Mr. Sotheron regretted that the hon. and learned Member for Plymouth had not brought the subject under consideration in such a form that the result of the debate might have been in some measure of a practical nature. It seemed rather to degrade the character of a legislative assembly to discuss abstract propositions of this kind as if they were a mere debating society. If the hon. and learned Gentleman, instead of inviting the House to discuss an abstract proposition, had asked for leave to bring in a Bill for the purpose of giving a legislative sanction to loans of money on the principle of *commandite,* a really practical and desirable object might have been attained, and a great deal of apprehension which the Motion in its present state excited would have been saved.

The Attorney General [Alexander Cockburn] appealed to the hon. and learned Member for Plymouth not to press the Resolution to a division, and said, he felt that he made the appeal with greater force when he fully and frankly admitted that he was a decided friend to the principle the hon. and learned Gentleman was desirous of laying down. This was not the first time it had been under consideration in that House, a Report having been recently made which was founded on a considerable body of evidence upon the subject. There was no object, however, to be effected in carrying an abstract Resolution, and if a measure were to be introduced upon the question, it would require great consideration, in order to afford safeguards for the prevention of fraud. He put it to his hon. and learned friend whether his object was not fully answered by the discussion which had already taken place, and which had served to elicit the opinion of so many hon. Members? It would be really useless to carry this abstract Resolution, and it must now be clear to the hon. and learned Gentleman, that the question was not only deserving the serious consideration of the House and of Her Majesty's Government, but that it would receive their most serious consideration.

Mr. Napier said, he had been much instructed by the discussion which had taken place on this important subject, and he thought it had served a very good purpose. His opinion had been throughout in favour of limited liability. His chief motive for rising was to express his astonishment at the terms in which the hon. and learned Gentleman (Mr. J.G. Phillimore) had spoken of the Report of the Commissioners on this subject. Remembering who were the learned persons composing that Commission – that included among them were the Master of the Rolls for Ireland and Mr. Justice Crosswell – he must say he could not remain silent when he heard the hon. and learned Gentleman characterize the Report of these gentlemen as a flimsy production.

Mr. J.G. Phillimore explained that he had said it was a one-sided Report, and that he did not call it a flimsy Report.

Mr. Napier said, the Commissioners, of all persons in the world, representing as they did England, Scotland, and Ireland, were the last to be suspected of making a one-sided Report. Considering the vast importance of the question, and that it came now rather prematurely before the House, he thought that more could hardly be expected than that it should be ventilated by a full discussion. Under these circumstances, he entirely concurred with what had been said by the Attorney General, and hoped the hon. and learned Member for Plymouth would not press his Motion to a division.

Viscount Palmerston wished to add his request to the hon. and learned Member for Plymouth not to press his Motion to a division. He thought, with the right hon. and learned Gentleman who spoke last, that he ought to be satisfied with the expression of opinion in favour of his proposition which had been elicited, and which had certainly been more general than often happened. Nobody could deny the importance of the question brought under the consideration of the House. It was one on which, no doubt, great differences of opinion existed, and as this division of opinion existed, a Commission was appointed upon the recommendation of a Committee of the House to inquire into the matter. That Commission had only recently reported, and he was sure the House would feel that Her Majesty's Government would not be acting properly if they were at once to rush to a conclusion without giving to the Report of the Commissioners that consideration to which it was undoubtedly entitled. It could not be expected that the Government should be prepared at the present moment to declare the result to which they had come, or were likely to come on the question at issue; and he thought it would be hardly fair to tie the hands of Government, or to induce the House to come to an abstract Resolution on a matter of so much importance, without maturely considering not only the recommendation of the Commissioners, but the evidence given before them, and enabling the Government to prepare the opinion which they might think it right to submit to the House on the subject. He was quite sure, at all events, that the House would give Her Majesty's Government credit for great anxiety to correct those defects which it was admitted by everybody existed in the law as it now stood; and he trusted that credit would be allowed them for a sincere desire to propose any change in the law which might assist in the development of national industry, and give to the humbler classes of society a better means of investing their savings as well as a greater inducement to make savings in the course of their limited transactions. There was also another matter which should be taken into consideration. It had been generally understood that the hon. and learned Member for Plymouth wanted merely to elicit the opinion of individual Members, and not to call on the House to announce its opinion in a division. In consequence, many hon. Members were absent, and it was unfair, therefore, when there had been an impression that no division would take place, to take advantage of the general concurrence, which he certainly could not deny existed, for the purpose of pledging the House to an abstract Resolution.

Mr. J.L. Ricardo differed from the noble Lord, and from the two speakers who had immediately preceded him. He had never seen the House so unanimous upon any question as it had upon this, and he could not understand what reason could exist why they should not place their unanimity upon record, so that the country might be aware of it as well as they were aware of it themselves. He had never seen a more straightforward Resolution, or one more directly to the purpose, than that which the hon. and learned Member had proposed. It was one which no one could misunderstand, for it went straight to the point, and not all the mystification of the right hon. Gentleman the President of the Board of Trade could envelop it in any degree of difficulty whatever. There had been only one champion on the other side, and even he did not affect to be ignorant of what the Resolution meant. There might have been some strength in the argument of the Attorney General if they had not previously heard the speech of the President of the Board of Trade, because the hon. and learned Gentleman had come forward in the most straightforward manner, and had expressed his entire concurrence in the views of the hon. and learned Gentleman who had proposed this Resolution. The President of the Board of Trade, upon the other hand, had appeared carefully to avoid expressing any opinion at all; but if anything could be gathered from his speech, it was that he differed entirely from the opinion which the learned Attorney General had expressed. The question had been before the country more than twenty years, and there was no reason why the House should delay expressing its opinion upon it.

Mr. Cairns said, he also saw no reason why the House should not express their unanimous opinion on the question. It was true it was an abstract Resolution, but it was enough to embody the opinion of the House. The effect would be to strengthen the hands of the Government, and would enable them to feel confident in the support of the House when they brought in a Bill to carry out the Resolution – a confidence of success they did not often feel.

Mr. Horsfall had carefully abstained from expressing an opinion upon the question until he should have had an opportunity of considering it in connection with the Report of the Commission. He had not had that opportunity yet; it had been impossible to do it in the few days that had elapsed since the Report had been in the hands of Members, and if he were obliged to give a vote now it would not be upon the merits, but against the House pledging itself at this moment to an abstract Resolution. He hoped, therefore, the Motion would not be pressed.

Mr. Thomson Hankey regretted that any Member of the Government should have entreated the hon. and learned Member not to press his Motion; and hoped that those who took a deep interest, as he did, in the question, would not be deprived of the opportunity of showing that they were a strong and united body in pressing upon Her Majesty's Government a measure which they believed to be of great importance to the commercial community.

Mr. Crossley thought that the hon. and learned Member for Plymouth was right in the main, but hoped he would not go to a division. He should divide with him if he did; but as the matter was of great importance, and one upon which there was a good deal of difference of opinion, he thought there ought to be an opportunity for further discussion.

Mr. Spooner said, he was not prepared to vote for an abstract Resolution, in opposition to the conclusion of a majority of the Commissioners. If the Motion were passed, he should move the previous question.

Mr. Speaker intimated that this could not be done with an Amendment before the House.

Mr. Warner said, the Commissioners were equally divided upon the question of allowing "special loans," which practically embodied the whole question.

Mr. Collier having expressed his gratification at the manner in which the Resolution had been received, and the unanimity of opinion which had been expressed in the course of the debate, said it appeared to him to be immaterial whether he divided the House or not. The feeling of the House had been unmistakably expressed; and, as he felt the force of the appeals made to him by the Home Secretary and the Attorney General, who had intimated the readiness of the Government to take the question into its consideration, and as his own object had been answered by what had taken place, he would, if the House would allow him, withdraw his Motion. The House, however, by loud cries, having expressed its wish that the Motion should not be withdrawn, Question, "That those words be there added," put, and *agreed to*: – Main Question, as amended, put, and *agreed to.*

22

1855 LIMITED LIABILITY ACT

Source: Act for Limiting the Liability of Members of Certain Joint Stock Companies, 1855, 18/19 Victoria, Cap. CXXXIII.

EDITORIAL HEADNOTE

Several parliamentary hearings considered the extension of limited liability, culminating in the Royal Commission on the Mercantile Laws and the Laws of Partnership in 1854. Although no clear consensus emerged from these hearings, and mercantile and financial opinion remained deeply divided over limited liability, parliament passed a Limited Liability Act in 1855 with strong support from both Liberals and Conservatives. This official endorsement of limited liability probably reflected the growing influence of free trade principles as well as a practical desire by the government to divest itself of the onerous responsibility of granting or denying limited liability to joint-stock companies on a case-by-case basis. Henceforth the investing public rather than the state would decide which businesses were most worthy of support.[1]

Note

1 James Taylor, *Creating Capitalism: Joint-Stock Enterprise in British Politics and Culture, 1800–1870* (Royal Historical Society, 2006), pp. 148–75.

Whereas it is expedient to enable Members of Joint Stock Companies to limit the Liability for the Debts and Engagements of such Companies to which they are now subject: Be it therefore enacted by the Queen's most Excellent Majesty, by and with the Advice and Consent of the Lords Spiritual and Temporal, and Commons, in this present Parliament assembled, and by the Authority of the same, as follows:

I. Any Joint Stock Company to be formed under the Act of the Eighth Year of Her Majesty, Chapter One hundred and ten, (other than an Assurance Company,) with a Capital to be divided into Shares of a nominal Value not less than Ten Pounds each, may obtain a Certificate of Complete Registration with Limited Liability upon complying with the Conditions following, in

DOI: 10.4324/9781003713890-25

addition to doing all other Matters and Things now required in order to obtain a Certificate of Complete Registration; that is to say,

1. The Promoters shall state on their Returns to the Office for Provisional Registration that such Company is proposed to be formed with Limited Liability:
2. The Word "Limited" shall be the last Word of the Name of the Company:
3. The Deed of Settlement shall contain a Statement to the Effect that the Company is formed with Limited Liability:
4. The Deed of Settlement shall be executed by the Shareholders, not less than Twenty-five in Number, holding Shares to the Amount in the aggregate of at least Three Fourths of the nominal Capital of the Company, and there shall have been paid up by each of the Shareholders on account of his Shares not less than Twenty Pounds *per Centum*:
5. The Payment of the above Per-centage shall be acknowledged in or endorsed on the Deed of Settlement, and the Fact of the same having been *bona fide* so paid shall be verified by a Declaration of the Promoters, or any Two of them, made in pursuance of the Act made in the Sixth Year of the Reign of His late Majesty King *William* the Fourth, Chapter Sixty-two:

And upon such Conditions being complied with, and such other Matters and Things done, the Registrar of Joint Stock Companies shall grant a Certificate of Complete Registration with Limited Liability to such Company.

II. Any Joint Stock Company, except as aforesaid, now or hereafter completely registered under the said Act of the Eighth Year of Her Majesty, may obtain a Certificate of Complete Registration with Limited Liability, in manner and subject to the Condition following; that is to say,

The Directors of such Company may, with the Consent of at least Three Fourths in Number and Value of its Shareholders who may be present, personally or by Proxy, at any General Meeting summoned for that Purpose, make such Alteration in the Name, nominal Value of Shares, and Deed of Settlement of the Company as may be necessary for enabling it to comply with the Conditions herein-before mentioned with respect to Joint Stock Companies seeking to obtain Certificates of Complete Registration with Limited Liability; and upon Compliance with such Conditions the Registrar, after the Affairs of the Company shall at the Expense of the Company have been audited by some Person appointed by the Board of Trade, and on Certificate from the said Board that the complete Solvency thereof has been established on such Audit to its Satisfaction, shall grant to such Company, by its new Name, a Certificate of Complete Registration with Limited Liability, and thereupon all Privileges and Obligations hereby attached to Companies with Limited Liability, their Shareholders, Directors, and Officers, shall attach to the Company named in such Certificate, its Shareholders, Directors, and Officers.

III. Any Joint Stock Company, except as aforesaid, constituted under any Private Act of Parliament, whereof it shall be proved to the Satisfaction of the Board of Trade, after the Affairs of the Company shall, at the Expense of the Company, have been audited by some Person appointed by the Board of Trade, that the said Company is perfectly solvent, and that not less than Twenty *per Centum* of Three Fourths of the nominal Capital of such Company has been paid up, may obtain a Certificate of Complete Registration with Limited Liability, in manner and subject to the Condition following; that is to say,

The Directors of such Company may, with the Consent of at least Three Fourths in Number and Value of its Shareholders who may be present, personally or by Proxy, at any General Meeting summoned for that Purpose, make such Alteration in the Name and nominal Value of Shares as may be necessary for enabling it to comply with the Condition in that Behalf herein-before mentioned with respect to Joint Stock Companies seeking to obtain Certificates of Complete Registration with Limited Liability; and upon Compliance with such Condition the Registrar, on Receipt of a Certificate of the Solvency of the Company, and of the Payment of Capital as before mentioned, shall grant to such Company, by its new Name, a Certificate of Complete Registration with Limited Liability; and thereupon all Privileges and Obligations hereby attached to Companies with Limited Liability, their Shareholders, Directors, and Officers, shall attach to the Company named in such Certificate, its Shareholders, Directors, and Officers.

IV. Every Company that has obtained a Certificate of Complete Registration with Limited Liability shall paint or affix, and shall keep painted or affixed, its Name on the Outside of every Office or Place in which the Business of the Company is carried on, in a conspicuous Position, in Letters easily legible, and shall have its Name engraven in legible Characters on its Seal, and shall have its Name mentioned in legible Characters in all Notices, Advertisements, and other official Publications of such Company, and in all Bills of Exchange, Promissory Notes, Cheques, Orders for Money, Bills of Parcels, Invoices, Receipts, Letters, and other Writings used in the Transaction of the Business of the Company.

V. If such Company do not paint or affix, and keep painted or affixed, its Name, in the manner aforesaid, each of the Directors thereof shall be liable to a Penalty not exceeding Five Pounds for not so painting or affixing its Name, and for every Day during which such Name is not kept painted or affixed: and if any Director or other Officer of the Company, or any Person on its Behalf, use any Seal purporting to be a Seal of the Company whereon its Name is not so engraven as aforesaid, or issue or authorize the Issue of any Notice, Advertisement, or other official Publication of such Company, or of any Bill of Exchange, Promissory Note, Cheque, Order for Money, Bill of Parcels, Invoice, Receipt, Letter, and other Writing used in the Transaction of the Business of the Company, wherein its Name is not mentioned in the Manner aforesaid, he shall be liable to a Penalty of Fifty Pounds, and shall further be personally liable to the Holder of any such Bill of Exchange, Promissory Note, Cheque, or Order for Money, for Amount thereof, unless the same shall be duly paid by the Company.

VI. No Increase to be made in the nominal Capital of any Company that has obtained a Certificate of Complete Registration with Limited Liability shall be advertised or otherwise treated as Part of the Capital of such Company, until it has been registered with the Registrar of Joint Stock Companies; and no such Registration shall be made unless a Deed is produced to the Registrar, executed by Shareholders holding Shares of the nominal Value of not less than Ten Pounds to the Amount in the aggregate of at least Three Fourths of the proposed increased Capital of the Company, nor unless it is proved to the Registrar, by such Acknowledgment and Declaration as herein-after mentioned, that upon each of such Shares there has been paid up by the Holder thereof an Amount of not less than Twenty Pounds *per Centum*; and if any such Increase of Capital as aforesaid is advertised or otherwise treated as Part of the Capital of the Company before the same has been so registered, every Director of such Company shall incur a Penalty of Fifty Pounds; and the Payment of the above Percentage shall be acknowledged in or endorsed on the Deed so produced, and the Fact of the same having been bona fide so paid shall be verified by a Declaration of the Directors, or any Two of them, made in pursuance of the said Act made in the Sixth Year of the Reign of His late Majesty King *William* the Fourth, Chapter Sixty-two.

VII. The Members of a Joint Stock Company which has so obtained a Certificate of Complete Registration with Limited Liability, after such Certificate is granted, notwithstanding the Provisions contained in the said Act of the Eighth Year of Her present Majesty, shall not be liable, under any Judgment, Decree, or Order which shall be obtained against such Company, or for any Debt or Engagement of such Company, further or otherwise than in herein-after provided.

VIII. If any Execution, Sequestration, or other Process in the Nature of Execution, either at Law or in Equity, shall have been issued against the Property or Effects of the Company, and if there cannot be found sufficient whereon to levy or enforce the Execution, Sequestration, or other Process, then such Execution, Sequestration, or other Process may be issued against any of the Shareholders to the Extent of the Portions of their Shares respectively in the Capital of the Company not then paid up, but no Shareholder shall be liable to pay in satisfaction of any One or more such Execution, Sequestration, or other Process a greater Sum than shall be equal to the Portion of his Shares not paid up: Provided always, that no such Execution shall issue against any Shareholder except upon an Order of the Court, or of a Judge of the Court, in which the Action, Suit, or other Proceeding shall have been brought or instituted, and such Court or Judge may order Execution to issue accordingly, with such reasonable Costs of such Application, and Execution to be taxed by a Master of the said Court; and for the Purpose of ascertaining the Names of the Shareholders, and the Amount of Capital remaining to be paid upon their respective Shares, it shall be lawful for any

Person entitled to any such Execution, at all reasonable Times, to inspect the Register of Shareholders without Fee.

IX. If the Directors of any such Company shall declare and pay any Dividend when the Company is known by them to be insolvent, or any Dividend the Payment of which would to their Knowledge render it insolvent, they shall be jointly and severally liable for all the Debts of the Company then existing, and for all that shall be thereafter contracted, so long as they shall respectively continue in Office; provided that the Amount for which they shall all be so liable shall not exceed the Amount of such Dividend, and that if any of the Directors shall be absent at the Time of making the Dividend, or shall object thereto, and shall file their Objection in Writing with the Clerk of the Company, they shall be exempted from the said Liability.

X. No Note or Obligation given by any Shareholder to the Company whereof he is a Shareholder, whether secured by any Pledge or otherwise, shall be considered as Payment of any Money due from him on any Share held by him, and no Loan of Money shall be made by any such Company to any Shareholder therein; and if any such Loan shall be made to a Shareholder, the Directors who shall make it, or who shall assent thereto, shall be jointly and severally liable to the Extent of such Loan, and Interest for all the Debts of the Company contracted before the Repayment of the Sum so lent.

XI. Where any Company completely registered under the said Act of the Eighth Year of Her present Majesty, or any Company constituted under any Act of Parliament, shall obtain a Certificate of Complete Registration with Limited Liability, the Grant of such Certificate shall not prejudice or affect any Right which previously to the Grant of such Certificate has accrued to any Creditor or other Person against the Company in its Corporate Capacity, or against any Person then being or having been a Member of such Company, but every such Creditor or other Person shall be entitled to all such Remedies against the Company in its Corporate Capacity, and against every Person then being or having been a Member of such Company, as he would have been entitled to in case such Certificate had not been obtained.

XII. No Alteration made by virtue of this Act in the Name of any Company shall prejudice or affect any Right which previously to such Alteration has accrued to such Company as against any other Company or Person, or which has accrued to any other Company or Person as against such Company, but every such Company as against any other Company or Person, and every other Company or Person as against such Company and the Members thereof, shall be entitled to all such Remedies as they or he would have been entitled to if no such Alteration had been made; and no such Alteration shall abate or render defective any legal Proceeding pending at the Time when such Alteration is made.

XIII. In the Case of any Company which has obtained a Certificate of Limited Liability, whenever, on taking the yearly Accounts of such Company, or by any Report of the Auditors thereof, it appears that Three Fourths of the subscribed Capital Stock of the Company has been lost, or has become unavailable in the Course of Trade, from the Insolvency of Shareholders, or from any other Cause, the Trading and Business of such Company shall forthwith cease, or shall be carried on for the sole Purpose of winding up its Affairs; and the Directors of such Company shall forthwith take proper Steps for the Dissolution of such Company, and for the winding up of its Affairs, either by Petition to the Court of Chancery, or by Exercise of the Powers of the Deed of Settlement, or by such other lawful Course as they may think most fit.

XIV. In Cases where a Certificate of Registration with Limited Liability has been obtained, when One Auditor only shall have been appointed by the thirty-eighth Section of the Act of the Eighth of *Victoria,* Chapter One hundred and ten, that single Auditor, and when Two or more such Auditors shall have been so appointed then One of such Auditors, shall be subject to the Approval of the Board of Trade, and such Board in case the Auditor submitted to them for Approval shall for any Reason appear unfit or objectionable shall appoint another in his Place.

XV. Every pecuniary Penalty imposed in pursuance of this Act shall be deemed a Debt due to the Crown, and shall be recoverable accordingly.

XVI. This Act shall, so far as is consistent with the Contents and Subject Matter thereof, be taken as Part of and construed with the said Act of the Eighth Year of Her present Majesty, Chapter One hundred and ten, and the Act of the Eleventh Year of Her Majesty, Chapter Seventy-eight, and all the Provisions of the said Acts, save in so far as they are varied by this Act, shall apply to Persons and Companies applying for or obtaining a Certificate of Complete Registration with Limited Liability.

XVII. The Provisions of the Act of the Eighth Year of Her present Majesty, Chapter One hundred and eleven, and of the Joint Stock Companies Winding-up Act, 1848, and the Joint Stock Companies Winding-up Amendment Act, 1849, shall apply to Persons and Companies obtaining a Certificate of Complete Registration with Limited Liability, subject only to such Variations as may be occasioned by the Provisions of this Act.

XVIII. This Act shall not apply to *Scotland.*

XIX. This Act may be cited for all Purposes as "The Limited Liability Act, 1855."

23

WHITHER IS LIMITED LIABILITY LEADING US?

David Morier Evans

Source: David Morier Evans, 'Whither is Limited Liability Leading Us?', *Speculative Notes and Notes on Speculation, Ideal and Real* (London: Groombridge and Sons, 1864), pp. 228–36.

EDITORIAL HEADNOTE

David Morier Evans (1819–1874) was one of the leading financial journalists and writers of his time. He began his career working for the *Times* of London and later wrote the money articles for the *Morning Herald* and *Standard.* He was also a frequent contributor to the *Bankers' Magazine* and the *Stock Exchange Gazette*. Evans wrote a series of popular books detailing the financial crises, failures, and frauds of the Victorian era, including *The Commercial Crisis, 1847–48* (1848), *City Men and City Manners* (1852), and *Facts, Failures, and Frauds: Revelations Financial, Mercantile, and Criminal* (1859). Ironically, Evans' own career ended in bankruptcy, brought on by the failure of a newspaper, the *Hour,* into which he had sunk his life savings.[1]

In this essay, Evans evaluates the impact of limited liability over the eight years since it became freely available to joint-stock companies. Although he notes some problems, he realizes that there is no turning back. What was once "considered an experiment and an experiment of a very dangerous character . . . has at length become so popular, that it bids fair to over-ride antecedent interests, joint-stock and private, and throw them wholly into the shade."

Note

1 A.R. Vian, "Evans, David Morier," *Oxford Dictionary of National Biography*, eds. H.C.G. Matthew and Brian Harrison (Oxford: Oxford University Press, 2004), Vol. 18, p. 679.

DOI: 10.4324/9781003713890-26

Significant indeed is the fact, that limited liability has become "a power among men." It was not supposed that the Act, in its general acceptation, would have been received with such favour, when first it obtained the sanction of the Legislature. Vaunting, as were its authors, of its adaptability to the wants of the mercantile and financial community, it was several years before its privileges were made available; and when they were originally brought into operation, they did not shadow forth its advantages in the most encouraging light.

The early attempts to introduce its privileges – much as they were spoken of – eventuated, as it might be supposed they would, in the most lamentable failures; and then it was distinctly asseverated that so little were they suited to English taste, and English convenience, that they fell still-born, leaving the public dissatisfied with the experiment, and willing to abandon the new system for the old and better-working machinery of the general Joint-Stock Act. For a somewhat lengthened period "limited liability" was, so to speak, a dead letter, and notwithstanding provincial experience was rather more favourable to the development of the principle, it was difficult to get a metropolitan proprietary to organize undertakings, which should give it a proper or extensive trial.

Disheartening as were the prospects which were associated with the progress of the movement, a few companies with small capitals were started, which essayed to give vitality to the Act; and though these could not be looked upon as more than additional crude experiments, they made progress, and finally rendered the public familiar with what was before considered a partially impracticable dogma.

Although appeals were made to transatlantic knowledge, where the elements of success were so unmistakably apparent, like every new notion based upon theory rather than practice, our countrymen were most slow to take the initiative. Into operation, however, the principle came at last, and notwithstanding it was by steady and sure degrees, the multitude, when it was fairly recognized, were only too ready and eager to adopt it. The earlier undertakings that acknowledged its influence, and made its provisions subservient to their purposes, were those of a manufacturing description; and though even after the first great break-down there were occasional difficulties through mismanagement, they were ultimately counterbalanced by the more legitimate results arising in other channels from this kind of co-partnery.

Nevertheless, doubts were still entertained if "limited liability" would turn out the great boon that had been predicted by its most ardent admirers, and none were more averse to the new form of arrangement than the Joint-Stock Banks and Private banking interests. Strange to say, as is very frequently the case, and as if some foreshadowing of such change were approaching, the Joint-Stock and the Private Banks have probably more than any other class, been affected by the revolution. The "limited liability" rage made its first step in Manchester, and there attacked the financial community in its stronghold, by converting an old and influential bank to the tenets of the bill. Liverpool followed, and, with a prescience acknowledged in the locality, it was not long before Birmingham, refusing to be behindhand, did not wait for old banks to recognize the principle, but started one on this basis, which has since, although a creation of only a few years, proved one of the most thriving in the neighborhood.

But people shook their heads, looked sombre, and were not then prepared to admit that there was the slightest prospect of the Act taking substantial root in London, or even becoming thoroughly acknowledged. A short time, however, only elapsed before the plethora of money, occasioned by the curtailment of trade through the American war, opened a new field for the inventive genius of those, who considered themselves specially adapted to promote joint-stock enterprise, and they at once sought to make its principles subservient to their plans.

The dividends of the half-yearly meetings in 1861 and 1862 had been very favourable; capital was seeking an outlet for employment; and though the supply of banking accommodation was large, it was nevertheless believed that it might be extended. The effects of unlimited responsibility were discussed, but notwithstanding they were considered the best applicable to banking, both as giving confidence to the public and customers, promoters themselves found that "limited liability" was more suited to their prospects and arrangements, and at a very opportune moment the vessel with the new name, showing new colours, was launched, not without, however, a little fear and trembling.

The period, it was soon ascertained, was propitious, the current ran smoothly; and though occasional cries of breakers ahead were heard, they never in reality appeared. Two banks were originally started, but the names of the directors in either case being scarcely, in City parlance, strong enough to float such institutions, arrangements were made for effecting an amalgamation. Before this one bank, under its altered appearance, and with a strengthened board, could make its preliminaries perfect for commencing business, the prospectuses of two others appeared for public support – not, it is true, simultaneously, but following closely on each other's heels. One, in the shape of share subscriptions, was a most decided success; the other speedily secured its capital, but measuring its worth by the market price, it was not so great a favourite, either with the speculative, or the investing public as its competitor.

Previously to this, it should be mentioned, Discount Companies had been started, with the same inscription on their business banners, but in more prosaic terms, and they were regarded for a period as banks in disguise, though events subsequently showed the contrary. But it was a partial struggle for them to succeed, and when the great failures in the leather trade took place, predictions fatal to the lengthened existence of these institutions, were freely uttered. Their losses, it was certain, were large, in common with the various banks and discounting establishments, which suffered through the enormous mass of accommodation paper, put into circulation through the agency of Lawrence, Streatfield, and Co., and accruing when they were least able to bear them, caused their balance-sheets, when printed, to exhibit a discouraging appearance.

The principal company stood their ground bravely, the managers worked well and vigorously, and in the space of two half years re-established their position, much to the satisfaction of the proprietors, who manifested throughout, complete confidence in their directors. The other unfortunate company, guided by a timid board, and assaulted by shareholders who, purchasing stock at a depreciated value, found on investigating the accounts, a profitable amount of assets to divide, failed to recover its *status,* and it was not long before it was determined to liquidate its affairs, which was gradually and successfully accomplished. This was a blow to the development of the principle of "limited liability" in the financial circles of the Metropolis; and until the inauguration of the new banking movement, was the great argument always employed by the anti-limited liability party.

But when it was so readily perceived that, with a decided plethora in the money market, a revived taste among the public for speculation, and encouraging prices for shares, that limited liability would be accepted even among the banking community, and that the experiment would not be adopted on an unimportant scale, scarcely any bounds were placed to the animation which now ensued, and "limited liability" soon became not only patronized by banks, but by every other conceivable kind of financial and industrial undertaking.

Not only, however, was the principle rendered applicable to banking in London and the provinces, but organizations were formed for extending its usefulness to the more distant quarters of the globe. Hindustan and China, Brazil and Portugal, Austria and Italy, the Cape of Good Hope, Australia and New Zealand, were very speedily accommodated, and in several of the more important instances with every prospect of success. Even the nearer relations of the United Kingdom were not neglected: France, Belgium, and the Netherlands being at the same time completely supplied. The effect, as might be supposed, was also to introduce those large and important finance credit companies which have since been raised, with capitals more extended than those of the banks. These again, striking into new paths and new channels, have been accompanied by those exchange establishments, which are entering upon domains in the territory of finance, before occupied alone by the leviathan capitalists, whose names have been passwords throughout Europe and the world, for wealth and resources, almost defying competition.

It will be several years ere the true success of these institutes will be established; but, regarding them as agents working in circles, where they must come in contact with the connections and operations of their great predecessors, they will doubtless attempt to wrest from their grasp, a portion of the enormous returns and profits, they have hitherto exclusively appropriated to their own benefit. Whether these private leviathan houses will have to succumb in the open hostilities, which may now be considered to have been declared between themselves and the limited liability undertakings, cannot immediately be determined; but it is reasonable to suppose that they will have to encounter strong competition – stronger probably than was originally imagined.

But it is not in this direction solely that limited liability is putting forth claims for universal support. Everywhere now the adoption of the principle is encouraged, and from the highest to the lowest enterprise, no other kind of foundation is permitted. Bold would be the individual who dared in these days to propose to start an undertaking on the unlimited system, holding the shareholders, as in the case of many existing institutions, responsible "to his last shilling, and his last acre." That which seven or eight years ago was considered an experiment – and an experiment of a very dangerous character, even as applied to the most ordinary adventures, has at length become so popular, that it bids fair to over-ride antecedent interests, joint-stock and private, and throw them wholly into the shade. Indeed, it may be said to be an analogous expansion to that experienced in the period of railway history, when every route, every highway, or every canal, was to become auxiliary to the new interest, and be finally absorbed.

In the present instance the adaptation of the principle to the whole class of projects seeking popular support, leaves no chance for any other system to be developed, and when we see that vested interests, which were previously furious against the alleged innovation, ready to recognize its value, it may be fairly considered that limited liability possesses claims which cannot be altogether ignored. It would be all very well to say that the new principle might be regarded as an experiment, if its application were strictly confined to undertakings which were ushered into existence during the last two or three years; but when we discover, apart from this, that old and wealthy establishments – several of undoubted reputation and position – are making arrangements to dissolve their private partnership character, and array themselves in the apparel of the Hon. Mr. Lowe's Act,[1] it must be allowed that either we are again in the midst of a most speculative epoch, or that the privileges offered, deserve to be fully tested.

Of course "limited liability" may in its extended form be carried beyond due bounds; it may, like the railway system, be so expanded that the recoil from the shock may be felt detrimentally in some quarters when a collapse takes place; but although this may occur sooner or later, it does not follow that "limited liability" as a principle will not turn out a success, and stamp encouraging traces of its handiwork upon many of the recently established financial and commercial institutions. The very excess of the prepondering influence, which has brought forward the late large crop of industrial enterprise, must at no distant date be relieved by reaction; but although this will come, and its effect will be exhibited in a variety of localities, the result will not for ever prejudice the vitality of the principle.

Limited liability has at length made itself a name, and a position in the land; and though there may still be failures, and mischances in individual cases associated with its working, it will not be an easy task to divert it from its recognized channels. Limited liability, it has been jocosely remarked, has become our banker, our credit and finance purveyor, our armourer, our hotel-keeper, our brewer, our baker – not as yet out butcher, though there is no great reason why eventually this may not be the case – our bootmaker, our dairy supplier, and caterer for our most ordinary wants.

With this dominant tendency the power of the Act, now it has been so fully brought into play, must be severely felt, particularly by those who have hitherto endeavoured to stem the tide of its operation, and disinclined, as they even now may be, to receive its proffered assistance, they will not eventually escape its gradually absorbing powers. Limited liability is therefore, established as a great principle; it may have its weak points, and defective arrangements will, in all probability, occasionally bring its development into disgrace; but, as a principle, it will outlive any such drawbacks as these, and finally extend its influence, if possible, even more widely than at present.

Editorial Endnote

1 1856 Companies Act, 19/20 Vict. c.47, championed in the Commons by Liberal MP Robert Lowe (1811–1892).

Part 4

COMPANY PROMOTION AND COMPANY PROMOTERS

24

GUINNESS BREWERY PROSPECTUS

Source: Prospectus for Arthur Guinness Son and Company, Limited (1886).

EDITORIAL HEADNOTE

The prospectus was an important marketing tool for new companies, or, as in the case of Guinness, an established business offering shares to the public for the first time. Prospectuses were widely circulated: printed in newspapers, distributed to brokers, and mailed to prospective investors.

Before the Companies Act, 1900, the legal requirements for prospectuses were vague. At the very least, prospectuses detailed the total amount of capital being raised, the number and denominations of shares, the names of the company's directors, and directions on how to apply for shares. Prospectuses for newly created businesses, like a railway or mine, made an optimistic case for the promotion, often predicting success based on recent promotions of a similar kind. Prospectuses for existing private companies going public, such as Guinness in 1886, provided additional information about the business's assets, goodwill, and track record of profits.[1]

The 1886 flotation of the Guinness Brewery by Baring's Bank was one of the most successful company promotions of the era. The rush for shares necessitated police cordons to control the crowds, with some people wrapping their share applications around stones and throwing them through the bank's windows. It later transpired that Baring's had held back almost £1 million of shares for itself, reserved many more for allied City firms, and only released about 25% of Guinness shares to the general public.[2]

Notes

1 Janette Rutterford, " 'Propositions put forward by quite honest men': Company Prospectuses and Their Contents, 1856 to 1940," *Business History* 53 (October 2011), pp. 866–99.
2 David Kynaston, *The City of London, Vol. 1: A World of Its Own, 1815–1890* (London: Chatto and Windus, 1994), pp. 405–7.

DOI: 10.4324/9781003713890-28

PROSPECTUS

Messrs. BARING BROTHERS & CO. offer for Subscription the Capital undermentioned.
The Subscription List will open on Monday, the 25th instant, and will close on or before
Tuesday, the 26th at 4pm.
Arthur Guinness Son & Co., Limited.
(Incorporated Under the Companies' Acts, 1862 to 1886.)
SHARE CAPITAL, £4,500,000,
Debenture Stock, £1,500,000,
To Be Issued As Follows:

Ordinary Shares (of £10 each)	. . . £2,500,000
Preference Six per Cent. Shares (of £10 each)	. . . £2,000,000
Total Share Capital	. . . £4,500,000
Debenture Stock, bearing Interest at Five per Cent.	. . . £1,500,000
(Redeemable at the Company's option after the expiration of 20 years from 1st January, 1887, at 110 per Cent.)	. . . £6,000,000

Interest on the Debenture Stock will be payable 1st May and 1st November, the first payment on 1st May, 1887. The Company will receive the profits of the business from 1st October, 1886.

One-third of the present issue of Ordinary Share Capital (being about £800,000) is reserved for the Vendor, who agrees to hold this amount for not less than five years, and the remainder, together with the Preference Shares and the Debenture Stock, are now offered severally for public subscription at par.

The payments for each class of security will be as follows:

£5 per Cent.	on Application.
£20 per Cent.	on Allotment.
£25 per Cent.	on 14th December, 1886.
£25 per Cent.	on 10th January, 1887.
£25 per Cent.	on 8th February, 1887.
£100 per Cent.	

The instalments may be paid up under discount at the rate of 4 per cent. per annum on Allotment, or on any subsequent Tuesday or Friday.

The Allotment will be made as early as possible after the Subscription is closed, and in cases where it is not practicable to make any allotment, the amount deposited on application will be returned as soon as possible.

The failure to pay any instalment when due forfeits all previous payments.

Provisional Certificates will be issued as early as possible after Allotment, and the Definitive Certificates when the payments have been completed.

The Debenture Stock will be secured by a Mortgage over the whole of the undertaking.

Trustees for Debenture Stockholders:

The Right Honble. LORD REVELSTOKE. The Right Honble. LORD HILLINGTON.

The Right Honble. D.R. PLUNKET, Q.C., M.P.

The Preference Shares will be entitled to a cumulative preferential dividend of 6 per cent., payable out of the profits of the Company, and will also be entitled to rank on the property and assets of the Company, in preference to the ordinary shares.

DIRECTORS

*SIR EDWARD CECIL GUINNESS, BART., *Chairman.*
CLAUDE GUINNESS, ESQ., *Managing Director*
REGINALD B. GUINNESS, ESQ., Dublin.
VISCOUNT CASTLEROSSE, Killarney House, Ireland.
HENRY R. GLYN, ESQ., 67, Lombard Street, E.C.
HERMAN HOSKIER, ESQ., *Director of the Union Bank of London, Limited.*
JAMES R. STEWART, JUN., ESQ., (Messrs. Stewart & Kincaid), Dublin.

*Will join Board after Allotment.

BANKERS.

Messrs. GLYN, MILLS, CURRIE & CO.

SOLICITORS.

Messrs. MARKBY, STEWART & CO., 57, Coleman Street, London, E.C.

AUDITORS.

Messrs. TURQUAND, YOUNGS & CO., 41, Coleman Street, London, E.C.

SECRETARY.

C. THEOBALD, ESQ.

TEMPORARY OFFICES.

8 BISHOPSGATE STREET WITHIN, LONDON.

The business was founded in 1759, and, having from that time forward steadily increased, it is now the largest Brewery in the world. It has, hitherto, been conducted as a private business, but the enormous proportions which it has attained, and its probable further growth, have determined the present proprietor to seek some relief from the constant attention and strain which his position as sole owner unavoidably entails.

Sir Edward Cecil Guinness will, however, accept the Chairmanship of the Company, retaining a large pecuniary interest in it, and Mr. Claude Guinness, who now holds an important position in the practical management of the business, will act as Managing Director.

The proportions of the business and the progress made, are attested by the following figures for successive quinquennial periods:

Quinquennial Period.	Average Sales Per annum, Hogsheads.	Net Average Profit per annum. £
1862–1866	196, 125	122,119
1867–1871	263,562	130,340
1872–1876	436,691	178,571
1877–1881	589,499	308,033
1882–1886	755,235	452,294

In the above figures the net profit of the year 1886 is estimated as the same as that of 1885, an estimate which is more than justified by the actual sales of the first nine months, and is confirmed by the following figures.

The sales for 1885 amounted to 818,984 hogsheads, and the profits to £554,327. The first quarter's profits for 1885 amounted to £113,108 14s. The second quarter's profits of 1885 amounted to £167,000 8s. 10d. In the present year, the first quarter's profits amounted to £122,832 10s. 5d.; and the second quarter's profits amounted to £172,496 1s. The accounts of the third quarter are not yet closed.

The annual interest on £1,500,000 Debenture Stock at 5 per cent is	£75,000
The annual dividend on £2,000,000 Preference Shares at 6 per cent.	120,000
A Dividend of, say, 10 per cent. on £2,500,000 Ordinary Shares would be	250,000
	£445,000

If the profits in the future are the same as those of the year 1885 (and judging from the results of the first half of 1886 as above stated they give promise of being larger), this would leave a surplus of £109,327 to be carried forward, or would raise the dividend on the ordinary stock to over 14 per cent.

The following comparative statement of the business done by the four leading Brewery Firms is taken from Parliamentary Returns for each financial year:

Quarters of Malt Used.

	1881	1882	1883	1884	1885
Guinness & Co.	254,648	294,349	270,936	310,930	334,170
The next	228,330	248,644	238,718	239,602	230,701
Ditto	208,059	202647	207,026	213,547	189,312
Ditto	110,060	109,202	100,963	126,387	131,549

Barrels of Beer Brewed.

	1881	1882	1883	1884	1885
Guinness & Co.	1,027,764	1,198,347	1,088,762	1,253,900	1,357,592
The next	945,322	998,915	965,405	968,566	928,216
Ditto	814,327	795,975	813,580	824,607	737,621
Ditto	450,078	468,871	475,837	502,562	515,115

Amount of Duty Paid.

	1881	1882	1883	1884	1885
Guinness & Co.	£321,176	£374,483	£340,238	£391,843	£424,247
The next	295,413	312,161	301,689	302,677	290,067
Ditto	254,477	248,742	254,243	257,689	230,506
Ditto	140,649	146,522	148,698	157,050	160,973

The following were the principal gross receipts for the year 1885:

For porter	£2,165,765
Grains	29,224
Yeast and Malt Dust	10,177

The business is conducted at the St. James' Gate Brewery in Dublin. The Brewery premises and property cover an area of 42 acres, and are either freehold or (with small and unimportant exceptions) long leasehold, unburdened by mortgage, and will be conveyed to the Company along with the whole of the assets of whatsoever description belonging to the present firm.

During the past 20 years (1866–1885) a sum of £1,106,554 has been spent on extensions, permanent improvements, and maintenance of buildings and machinery. Of this sum £358,405 has been spent on maintenance and deducted from profits, and £748,149 upon permanent improvements. The premises at present are in perfect repair, and are sufficient in all respects for the existing or an increased business. New Malt Stores are in course of erection, and will be completed within a few months. The total cost of these will be about £65,000, of which £26,000 has already been expended in addition to the above figure of £748,149.

The business consists exclusively of the production of Porter, and is not subject to competition from the great Ale Brewers who rank next in the magnitude of their outturn; it has also this special feature, which it is believed is possessed by no other large Brewery, namely, that there are no tied houses, and no advances are made to Publicans or others. There is, therefore, no capital outlay beyond the mere cost of production. All sales, except to well known and old established customers, are for cash; consequently there are practically no bad debts. During the year 1885 the sales exceeded £2,165,000 sterling, whilst on this sum the bad debts amounted to less than £3,000.

In addition to the goodwill of the business, and the freehold and leasehold premises above mentioned, and machinery and fixed plant, the stocks and miscellaneous balances at 30th September, 1886, comprised the following items, the whole of which will be transferred to the Company:

Malt, Roasted Malt and Barley	£33,129
Hops	111,224
Porter	365,621
*Miscellaneous Balance including, Casks, Staves, Hoops, Locomotives, Wagons, Boats, Horses, Drays, Miscellaneous Stocks, and amounts due from Customers after deducting current trade liabilities, say	390,026
	£900,000

*This account is not yet closed.

The Vendor guarantees that the above items shall not amount to less than £900,000 as a minimum.

The business will be transferred to the Company as from 30th September, 1886.

The price to be paid to Sir Edward Cecil Guinness, the vendor, for the premises, goodwill, and entire assets of the business is £6,000,000. Of this sum £800,000 is payable in ordinary Shares which the vendor agrees to hold for a period of not less than five years.

The business will be taken over subject to all existing contracts. These (with the exception of the contracts for completion of the Malt Stores above mentioned) are of the ordinary trade character, but are too numerous to specify. Subscribers will be held to have notice thereof and to have waived their rights to be supplied with particulars.

The Agreement for the purchase of the business is dated 21st October, 1886, and is executed by Sir Edward Cecil Guinness, Bart., the Vendor, of the one part, and C. Theobald, Esq., on behalf of the Company, of the other part. Copies can be seen at the office either of Messrs. Travers Smith & Braithwaite, 25, Throgmartin Street, or Messrs. Markby, Stewart & Co., 57, Coleman Street, E.C. The only other agreement entered into by the Vendor (who is the Promoter) is one dated 20th October, 1886, between Sir Edward Cecil Guinness, of the one part, and Messrs. Baring Brothers & Co., on the other part, concerning the expenses of issuing the capital now offered for subscription, which expenses are born by the Vendor personally.

Copies of the Memorandum of Association can be obtained at the Offices of the Solicitors to the Company, or of Messrs. Travers Smith & Braithwaite, No. 25, Throgmorton Street, E.C.

London, 21st *October*, 1886.

25

HOW TO SCAN A PROSPECTUS

Hartley Withers

Source: Hartley Withers, 'How to Scan a Prospectus,' *Cornhill Magazine* 76 (July 1897), pp. 105–13.

EDITORIAL HEADNOTE

Hartley Withers (1867–1950) was a financial journalist and writer. He was the son of a bank manager and stockbroker and was educated at Westminster School and Christ Church College, Oxford. After working as a stockbroker, he joined the London *Times* in 1894, eventually becoming the city editor. In 1910 he joined the *Morning Post* and from 1916 to 1921 was editor of *The Economist.* In addition to his journalism, Withers wrote several books on financial topics, such as *The Meaning of Money* (1909), *The Business of Finance* (1918), and *The Case for Capitalism* (1920).[1]

The *Cornhill Magazine* was a monthly literary journal founded in 1860 by George Murray Smith. Its first editor was the novelist W.M. Thackeray. The *Cornhill* included serialized fiction as well as articles on a wide range of contemporary issues.[2]

In this article, Withers cautions potential investors to beware prospectuses that attempt to dazzle them with the names of aristocratic directors or fantastic predictions of future profits. The devil is in the details. Information must be provided about net profits, not gross profits, and earnings should be listed separately for several years running, not averaged together. Statements of profit should not be taken on faith, but must be accompanied by a signed statement by an independent accountant.

Notes

1 Dilwyn Porter, "Withers, Hartley," *Oxford Dictionary of National Biography*, eds. H.C.G. Matthew and Brian Harrison (Oxford: Oxford University Press, 2004), Vol. 59, pp. 885–86.
2 John Sutherland, "The Cornhill Magazine," *The Stanford Companion to Victorian Fiction* (Stanford: Stanford University Press, 1989), p. 150.

DOI: 10.4324/9781003713890-29

The application of the joint-stock system to industrial enterprise ought to be carrying out a silent but momentous reform by merging the worker and the capitalist, and permitting any thrifty labourer who has saved a few pounds to become an employer, and learn to look at both sides of the labour question. So far, however, the movement has chiefly benefited the company-promoter at the expense of the rest of society, and the joint-stock failures have been so numerous in proportion to the successes that many men say in their haste that all new companies are swindles. Nevertheless, there is no reason for despair, seeing that it is only since the introduction of limited liability that joint-stock enterprise can be said to have come within the reach of the smallest capitalists, and the investing democracy has hardly had time to learn to handle its new powers. It was natural enough that astute financiers should take advantage of the youthful blindness of the new investing public, and should consider that the public either knew how to take care of itself, or else wanted a lesson from experience. The law stood by complacently and said *Caveat emptor*; the public paid cheerfully any price that was asked for a new business, and then was surprised and hurt because results were not always on all fours with anticipations. The stage of the development was inevitable, but it has now lasted an altogether unreasonable time, and those who wish to believe in public discretion as a trustworthy actuality must almost despair when they examine the prospectuses which appeal for public subscriptions to new joint-stock concerns. The large majority of them are interesting only as examples of audacious impudence, and as giving lamentably emphatic evidence of public gullibility: they seldom give one-half of the information which anyone in his senses would require before investing in a new company, and yet it must be inferred that they do not display, or conceal, their charms in vain; unless they succeeded in attracting subscriptions why should promoters waste money in covering the pages of the Press with advertisements? If the public would only give a little attention to the matter of prospectuses, and decide as to what they ought to state and in what manner, and resolve never to be beguiled by one which did not fulfil all the canons of an irreducible standard, there would be a change for the better at once. But instead of doing so the public prefers to dub all company-promoters thieves, and then to encourage them to be so by its own laziness. It looks at the estimated yield to shareholders without troubling about the basis on which the estimate is founded, and perhaps reads the names of the directors, and if these are sufficiently ornamental it is enough. Anyone who bought a house, and even a pair shoes, on such terms would be considered a fit subject for medical examination, and yet one would have thought that such a matter as buying an interest in a new company required no less care and consideration. Prospectuses that appeal to the investor, as such, are those of established businesses which are converting themselves into limited liability companies. Those which appeal for subscriptions for the purpose of exploiting some new patent, or starting an entirely new business can only tempt the speculator or the adventurer. However rosy the prospects, however fat the profits that may be pictured by the imaginative promoter, the prudent investor will refuse to be lured by mere flights of fancy. The only excuse for entering into ventures of this sort is special knowledge of the process or patent to be worked, or – what come to the same thing – first-hand information from an expert in the subject, who may be relied on as not only knowing its technical side, but also understanding its financial possibilities. It is not, however, usual for a prospectus to appeal for subscriptions for an absolutely untried venture. More commonly a small syndicate takes this preliminary risk, when its efficacy and chances of remunerative working have been proved: this profit is perfectly legitimate as long as the original adventurers do not ask too much from the public, and are prepared to give full and sufficient information concerning the venture.

In the more common case of a business, already a going concern, which is to be sold to the public as a limited company, the first subject on which enlightenment is necessary is the past history of the venture, from an uncompromisingly money-making point of view. Statements that the company's soaps, or beers, or tyres, or whatever it may be, have acquired a world-wide reputation for purity and excellence, and have won gold medals at such and such exhibitions, and are used by so many crowned heads of Europe are perhaps inducements to buy the product, but have to be supplemented by sordid details of profit and loss before one feels inclined to buy the organisation which produces the product. For however perfect be the result of a company's work, it may be unsuccessful from the point of view of the shareholder. As examples of this melancholy fact we need not go beyond the Cunard Steamship Company, which is in the very front rank as far as the comfort of its passengers and the speed of its vessels are concerned, and yet has paid nothing to its shareholders since 1894, and the Maxim Nordenfelt Company, which turns out an admirably destructive engine of war, but during some years of its existence did not succeed in showing a divisible profit. So that we must insist on finding in a prospectus a statement showing that the business to be joint-stocked has had not only a *success d'estime*, but success in the matter of *£ s. d.* It is not enough to be told what the turnover was, or what was the amount of the gross profits, though many prospectuses consider such figures more than sufficient; we must know that were the net profits, after making all allowances for depreciation and upkeep of the plant, and we must demand to see these profits separately stated year by year for a period of at least half a dozen years, if the business has existed so long. In dealing with a prospectus we are always justified in assuming that there is a reason for the suppression of any relevant information that is withheld; and if, for instance, a business that boasts the fact that it has been established for twenty years only shows us the profits of the last two years, the vendor can only expect us to assume that its profits have been dwindling and are less than they were six years ago, and that this is the reason why the company is being sold to the public before its profits have dwindled altogether out of sight. A very common mark of the beast on prospectuses is the appearance of an averaged rate of profit for a term of years: that is to say, the promoter has doubtless some excellent reason for not wishing to show the public how the working of each separate year resulted, but rather to put the profits together and strike an average. This should always be taken as a sign that a clearer statement would have been unattractive to the investor, who is justified in any suspicion for which the prospectus affords any reasonable ground. Again, we ought not to be asked to take statements concerning profits on the faith of the vendor; a certificate signed by an independent accountant must always be insisted on. When a prospectus gives the figures of the trade turnover, and yet is reticent as to the resulting profits on the ground that commercial rivalry makes it inexpedient to reveal them, it need not be examined further, for publicity is an essential of the existence of public joint-stock companies, and if it is inadvisable to give full details of the financial working of a business before it is joint-stocked, it will hardly be able to prosper when it is publishing yearly and half-yearly balance sheets and profit and loss accounts.

If the statement of profits is found to be clearly drawn up in separate years by an independent auditor, the investor should proceed to consider whether there is any point in connection with the trade of business in question which should be taken into consideration as modifying the effect of the figures. An apposite example is afforded by the large number of cycle-making companies which have latterly appealed for subscriptions. Everybody knows that during the last two years there has been a general rush, on the part of all classes of the community, almost all over the world, to buy bicycles, that the supply has with difficulty coped with the demand, and that manufacturers have accordingly made very fine profits. On the basis of these profits they are now hastily capitalising their businesses and disposing of them to the public, which has therefore to consider whether this basis of valuation is altogether fair. There are certainly two opinions on the subject of the durability of the demand for bicycles, but on the whole it is perhaps fair to assume that it will continue, since, apart from the mere fashionable craze, this very convenient method of locomotion is not likely to be superseded in an hurry. But, on the other hand, it is safe to bet – though perhaps we had better not, since the pages of this magazine may be a 'place' – that the supply of bicycles will increase by leaps and bounds, and that the present rate of profit cannot be sustained in the face of the ever increasing competition that threatens the trade. It has been frequently stated that the actual cost to the makers of turning out a first-class machine is not more than five to six pounds. The statement is hardly credible, and is merely given for what it is worth, but it is at any rate clear that the present margin is large enough to allow the Americans, with their high wages and other disadvantages, to sell machines in Europe, so that there must be a good deal of room for cutting prices when competition becomes severe. In examining a cycle-making prospectus, therefore, the investor must take these probabilities into consideration, and should modify the prospects of the company according to his opinion of the future course of the trade. And all prospectuses should be subjected to a similar scrutiny, since every industry has its ups and downs, and whenever there is a friend at hand who has special knowledge of the trade in question his opinion should be consulted before the application form is filled up.

If our prospectus has come triumphantly through the profits test, we must proceed to scan with still greater severity the statement and valuation of the assets to be acquired by the budding company. It is not enough to know that the business has in the past yielded so much profit, we must also make sure that it is sufficiently well equipped to be able to continue to do so, and that the new shareholders will get some tangible and realizable assets in return for the purchase money that they pay. It need hardly be said that the valuation of the assets must be signed by a professional valuer: an airy statement guaranteed by the good faith of the vendor should always be treated as worthless. The statement must give each item of the assets separately, and great care must be taken by the investor to see that the valuation is a categorical assertion of fact and not a conditional prophecy. A very large number of prospectuses nowadays contain valuations which do not deal with the properties as they stand and as they are to be acquired by the company, but as they may be expected to be after the company has out of its own pocket altered, rebuilt, added fresh capital, or otherwise resuscitated the concern. This, of course, is a piece of barefaced misrepresentation, and is much the same thing as asking the investor to pay for his own money. It is like saying, 'This umbrella, now worth a guinea, will be worth thirty-one shillings after you have paid half a sovereign to have a silver knob put on to it. I will trouble you, therefore, for thirty-one shillings for it as it stands, and then you can hand over the half-sovereign and we'll see about the knob.' Suspicion should at once be aroused by a statement such as – 'The freehold and leasehold property, plant and machinery, stock-in-trade, book debts, each in hand, &c., and the valuable goodwill of the business have been valued at' so and so. That is not the way in which these things are set forth, unless there is some reason to hoodwink the investor by jumbling all the items together into a chaotic aggregate. We must know at what figure each item is priced, so that we may be sure that book debts are not too heavy and that the stock-in-trade is not so large that the vendor is evidently compelled by the reluctance of his customers to dispose of his goods *en bloc* to the shareholders whom he invites to subscribe. It is a *sine quâ non* that the investor should know the exact price that he pays for 'goodwill'; if this item is smothered in a cloud of others, the prospectus should be consigned to the waste-paper basket without further parley. But if the goodwill is not stated at all, and the assets are said to be valued without including it, then we can get at it by subtracting the rest of the assets from the purchase price. For instance, if the leasehold and other property, plant &c. come to 200,000 *l.* and the price to be paid to the vendor for the whole property is 300,000 *l.*, it is evident that he is asking 100,000 *l.* for his goodwill. It is impossible to lay down any hard and fast rule as to the amount which may be safely allowed for goodwill; it is said that the more Draconian auditors never allow more than two years' purchase – that is to say, they multiply the last year's profit by two to arrive at it. This test would be so severe, that hardly any new-born companies would survive it, and it is obvious that the value of a goodwill differs very materially according to the age and reputation of the business. Such a concern as an English brewery with a world-wide fame and connection, built up during half a century, might value its goodwill at eight or ten years' purchase without demanding too much; whereas a soap, with a vogue as evanescent as its fragrance, or a patent in bicycle-gearing, liable to be suspended in a week, might overreach itself in pricing its goodwill at one year's purchase. Perhaps we may take about three or four years as a fair average, leaving the investor to work a sliding scale at his own discretion.

As to the 'waiver clause,' the appearance of which many critics consider to be sufficient in itself to make a prospectus worthless, it is often merely an evasion of a clumsy failure on the part of the law to protect shareholders. A well-meant legislative attempt to make promoters and vendors disclose the contracts incident to the formation of a company, so that the new shareholders might know through the hands of how many middlemen the concern had passed, and how much each of them had made through the transfer, was so stupidly worded, that companies, if they complied with it strictly, would be obliged to disclose all the contracts to which the business was a party. This process would require so voluminous a document that all companies which take over a widely extended business must perforce shelter themselves behind the waiver clause, which provides that subscribers shall waive compliance with this enactment. Behind the custom that has thus grown up vendors who buy companies from middlemen and resell at immoderate profits are enabled to shelter themselves, though it is still doubtful whether the insertion of a waiver clause would hold good in the eyes of the law as a mask for fraud which was so obvious as to come within the ken of criminal justice. The manner in which intermediate profits are piled up was exemplified recently by the winding-up of a syndicate which had been formed to buy an option for the purchase of a large number of retail grocery businesses. After the formation of the syndicate, a company was formed to buy the option from the syndicate and exercise it by purchasing the businesses. Its appeal for subscriptions came at an inopportune moment and fell flat, and hence the liquidation of the syndicate, which thus lifted the veil which generally shrouds these intermediate proceedings.

But though the waiver clause thus often conceals transactions which ought, in the interests of the public, to be made known, it is not safe to infer that it is always so, and if investors are careful to see that they buy genuine assets with their money, and that the goodwill is not too highly priced, they may fairly reckon on defeating the wiles of the middleman. An Indian Railway not long ago made a new issue of shares, and inserted the waiver clause in the prospectus. Letters at once appeared in the monetary columns of the daily papers pointing out that this was a very objectionable proceeding on the part of a company of such standing and position. Whereupon the secretary of the company promptly pointed out that, since it was obviously out of the question to disclose all the contracts to which the railway was a party, the directors were advised that they had no choice in the matter. In this case – as it is in many others – the waiver clause was merely a *reductio ad absurdius* of the law, and did not by any means impair the value of the securities offered. In the case of an entirely new company, which does not take over the business of a going concern, there is, of course, no excuse whatever for the presence of the waiver clause; but these we have already decided to be out of court as far as the prudent investor is concerned. If this exclusion is accepted as a safe principle, it is hardly necessary to discuss the question of mining prospectuses. From the nature of the case we cannot expect from them a clear and succinct statement of past profits, much less a trustworthy valuation of the assets to be acquired, since, so far from there being any past profit to chronicle, promoters are generally satisfied that they have done something like a work of supererogation in the interests of the public if they have sunk a couple of boreholes in the property, and assayed half a dozen tons of likely-looking stone. In short, a new mine is generally a matter in which chance has a free hand, though it is not quite an even toss up, since the mere fact that the property is sold by the astute prospector on the spot, and after passing through many hands, is offered finally to the investing public at home, is against its probable success for two reasons: firstly, because the best properties are generally reserved for local consumption and do not find their way to London; and secondly, because the intermediate profits of middlemen vendors and promoters – all of which come ultimately out of the pocket of the shareholder – are so much deadweight to strangle the concern in its over-capitalised cradle.

Nevertheless, the mining prospectus is useful sometimes as showing what should be avoided. Most of them contain little but the glorification of the properties which adjoin the mine that is to be acquired by a privileged public. The regularity of the reefs, the consistently high grade of the ore, and the low rate of working expenses in the next-door neighbour, are brought forward as incontestable arguments that the same satisfactory conditions will be found to prevail on the new company's side of the boundary. Thus crudely stated, the contention is exposed in all its illogical absurdity; but variations of the same week syllogism in a more insidious form are often to be found in industrial prospectuses. For instance, it is common to see a list of the prices of similar companies' shares, and of the dividends that they pay, as an inducement to subscribe to a concern that may or may not follow in their footsteps. The argument is practically as follows: –

> Some hotel companies (say) are prosperous.
> This is an hotel company.
> This will be a prosperous company.

Hazy recollections of logic text-books studied in the distant past incite me to state that this is an instance of the fallacy of the 'undistributed middle,' but without the help of the science of formal ratiocination it is evident, at a glance, that the conclusion is hopelessly invalid. And the argument is often still further strained, as, for instance, when the success of the leading London music-halls was appealed to as a proof that the shares of a variety theatre in a dead-alive provincial town would be an equally profitable investment. In scanning a prospectus we must always be on the alert for ticks of this sort. Any specious considerations that are not strictly relevant and to the point should not only be flouted as inducements to subscribe, but regarded as deterrents, since a mass of illogical and irrelevant blarney is generally used to cover the absence of any sounder arguments in favour of the company. Again, statements to the effect that the vendor shows his faith in the future of the company by taking all the ordinary shares himself should be tested severely in the light of the other *data*. Instances have been known in which the vendor not only took all the ordinary shares, but also more cash – from the proceeds of the debenture stock and preference shares subscribed for by the public – than the business was worth. So that such a statement should not blind the investor to the necessity of examining carefully the assets that the company acquires, and especially keeping his eye on the valuation of the goodwill. If he cannot trace its exact amount he should throw the prospectus to the dogs, and if he has any suspicion that it is too highly priced he should refrain from applying. And lastly, let him note carefully that the goodwill is not valued twice over – in prospectuses which depict the beauties of a new amalgamation of several old businesses it is common enough for the valuation to price the several enterprises 'as established and going concerns,' which means to say that their respective goodwill is considered, and for the vendor then to require a further payment for the goodwill of the new business as an aggregate entity. In short, if the investor will suspect snares in every sentence, and insist on knowing what ought to be told and in disregarding what is irrelevant, he will not only avoid many of the pitfalls that beset his footsteps, but will even find prospectuses an interesting study from a purely platonic point of view.

26

JOHN SKEEME, THE PROMOTER

[Anon.]

Source: [Anon.], 'John Skeeme, the Promoter,' *All the Year Round* 24 (October 5 and 12, 1867), pp. 342–46, 376–81.

EDITORIAL HEADNOTE

All the Year Round was a weekly literary magazine founded by Charles Dickens in 1859 as a successor to *Household Words*. After Dickens' death in 1870, the magazine was edited by his oldest son, Charles Dickens, Jr.[1]

In this fantastical short story, John Skeeme, the cockney valet to an Army officer, re-invents himself as a company promoter. He enriches himself through a whole series of dubious financial operations before retiring to a mansion in South Kensington. Tellingly, Skeeme invests his own money in government securities, not in his questionable promotions.

Note

1 John Sutherland, "All the Year Round," *The Stanford Companion to Victorian Fiction* (Stanford: Stanford University Press, 1989), p. 19.

PART I

My first acquaintance with Mr. Skeeme – he was in those days simply called Skeeme, without the prefix of Mr. – was about the year 1838 or '39. I had then a near relative, a bachelor, who was very well off, and was living in a very comfortable – an almost luxurious – small house in South Audley-street. He had an income of about three thousand pounds a year, was captain and lieutenant-colonel in a battalion of the Guards stationed in London, kept his brougham as well as a couple of riding-horses, and was, on the whole, what at the present day would be called a decided "swell." To this gentleman John Skeeme was valet and factotum; and as I – then a schoolboy – used to spend a portion of my holidays with my relative,

DOI: 10.4324/9781003713890-30

I of course got to know his right-hand man. My cousin was very kind to me, and often took or sent me to the different theatres. When he could not go himself, he always told Skeeme to take me, and desired him to give me anything I wanted in the shape of supper afterwards, but to take care that I fell into no bad company. No man could be more trustworthy than Skeeme. He always took charge of me with the greatest readiness, although I have no doubt his doing so often interfered with his own evening amusements. Nothing could be more kind, and yet at the same time respectful, than he was. His dress and manner gave him more the appearance of a semi-clerical private tutor than a valet, and had it not been for a trick he had of dropping his H's, and an incurable habit he had of adding an R to the end of every word ending with a vowel, he might very well have passed as a somewhat dandyfied curate – that is, according to the coats, neckties, and waistcoats, which were worn by gentlemen who had "taken orders" in the days when ritualism was as yet unheard of in the land. I have no doubt that Skeeme made altogether a very nice thing out of my cousin: who, though not an extravagant man, left everything to his valet, and merely looked at the total of the latter's account-book when he presented it every month: giving him a cheque for the amount without asking a question. In fact, it always appeared to me that Skeeme appeared to have more ready money than his master. Every week or so my cousin would ask me, laughingly, whether I wanted pocket-money? And, as like all schoolboys, I invariably did want pocket-money, he always said, "Tell Skeeme to give you a couple of sovereigns;" which request the valet at once complied with, not even asking my cousin whether it was correct or not.

I remember on one occasion my cousin – "The Colonel," as Skeeme used to call him, though he was but a captain in the Guards, and a lieutenant-colonel in the army – making up his mind very late the night before the race that he would go down to see the Derby run next day, and would take me with him. A brother-officer of his was going to drive a party down by the road – in those days, rail to Epsom was unheard of – and was to call for my cousin and myself about eight A.M. Suddenly my cousin remembered that he only had a couple of sovereigns in his purse, and that it was long after banking hours, and that he would start next morning before the banks were open. "Let us see what Skeeme can do for me," said he, ringing the bell, which was at once answered by that most respectfully grave valet. "Skeeme," said my relation, "can you let me have any money? I want to start before the banks will be open tomorrow; I will give you a cheque which you can get cashed any time after nine." "How much do you require, colonel?" was the reply. "Well," said my cousin, "if you could get me twenty or thirty pounds it would be enough; if I want more, I can borrow it from some friend on the course." "Better make it fifty, colonel," said Skeeme: "Epsom is not a place to go without plenty of money in your pocket. I'll get you what you want at once." In five minutes he returned and handed over ten five-pound notes to his master, who sat down at once to write him a cheque. "No occasion for that, colonel," said the valet; "I'll put it down in the book, and you can give me a cheque for the whole at the end of the month." What Skeeme called "the book," was a thin account-book, in which every item of my cousin's expenditure was put down. And what with certain quiet dinner-parties, with whist to follow, which "the colonel" was rather celebrated for among his acquaintance, to say nothing of his wine-merchant's account, Fortnum and Mason's ditto, stable expenses, travelling expenses – for my cousin went about a great deal to various race meetings, and always took Skeeme with him, the latter paying everything, as his master was a man who hated trouble of all kinds – the various outlays were pretty heavy. Skeeme himself was a married man, but "without incumbrances," as the advertisements say. His wife – quite as respectable looking, and almost as grave as her husband – lived in my cousin's house as his cook and housekeeper, so that between them they had to pay no rent. Their united wages – with everything found – were (as Skeeme used to say with an air of a Chancellor of the Exchequer when stating the accounts of the kingdom) "a consolidated hundred pounds per annum." Besides this, there were, of course, certain perquisites.

The colonel, though by no means a "dressy man," or a loud "dresser," used to get tired of his clothes, and with the exception of his uniform and hunting-coats, very seldom wore any garment very long. What he got tired of was, as a matter of course, handed over to Skeeme. Then the butcher, baker, grocer, greengrocer, coal-merchant, and other tradesmen, of course supplied what was ordered by Mrs. Skeeme in her capacity of housekeeper, and the accounts were made up, submitted to and paid by, Mr. Skeeme, in his capacity of steward or butler. The average total of "the book," at the end of the month, was from one hundred and twenty to one hundred and fifty pounds. Was it to be wondered at if the family of Skeeme managed to make something exceedingly comfortable for themselves, and that after some six or eight years' service with the same master they were able to invest money in Consols, and even complained that the interest on government securities was so small?

About a couple of years after I first knew Skeeme – I think it was in 1841 – my cousin, who was also my guardian, and, indeed, the only near relative I had in the world, procured me a commission in the army. Having barely enough money of my own to purchase my various steps even in a line-regiment, it was deemed advisable that I should go out to India, and I accordingly asked for and obtained an ensigncy in a regiment stationed in that country. I was absent from England some four years, during which time I often heard from my cousin, and once or twice from his valet. The last letter I received from Skeeme, while I was still out in the East, informed me that "the colonel" was going to leave the Guards – to sell out of the service – and get married. "Of course," continued the writer, "I shall remain with my master until his marriage takes place, but both I and my wife will then leave him, for it would not suit us to keep in service with a married gentleman." A letter from my cousin confirmed what his servant had written, and at the same time expressed a hope that I would come home in time to be present at the wedding, which was to take place in about eight or nine months. Being able to obtain leave of absence, I very soon started for Europe, and in thirty-five days or so after leaving Bombay found myself in a Hansom cab bowling away from the

London-bridge station to South Audley-street, where the colonel gave me a very kind reception. Skeeme was as grave and respectable looking as ever. My cousin was dining out with the family of his intended, on the night of my arrival, and so I took my dinner alone, conversing all the time with Skeeme, who waited upon me, and upon whom I looked in the light of an old friend. He did not appear at all annoyed at the prospective change in my cousin's state of life, but said that in any case he and his wife would very soon have retired from service, as they had been able to "save a little money," and it was time they should enjoy themselves. I asked Skeeme if he intended to take a public-house or an inn? He replied that neither was at all in his line, and that he thought he would take an office in the City, and commence doing a little for himself in the way of speculating. At this I laughed, and said he must have put by something exceedingly comfortable. He replied in his own grave way that he *had* a few pounds more than was actually necessary for a couple without incumbrances, and, upon my cross-questioning him, acknowledged that he had a couple of houses "down Brompton way," which he had bought for a mere trifle at the sale of a bankrupt builder, and which now, between them, gave him an income of eighty pounds a year net. In addition to this property, he had two thousand five hundred in the Consols, and about as much more, which he kept floating in good bills at from sixty to eighty per cent – money lent through a discounter to gentlemen of property, Guardsmen, and others, who were hard up.

"Lord bless you, sir," said Skeeme, who became excited with the subject, and was warmed up with a couple of glasses of wine I had invited him to drink: "Lord bless you, sir, if you knew how often I have waited in this very room upon gentlemen dining with my master, whose bills for one hundred, two hundred, three hundred, pounds I had in my pocket, you would be surprised. Why, no longer ago than last Friday, there was Sir James Cofden, of the Blues, sitting at this table, and as the dinner was finished he pulled out his note-case, and handed ten ten-pound notes to my master, saying 'There you are, old fellow; there's the hundred I lost to you at Ascot. I only got my rents this morning from Yorkshire, or you should have had it before.' *I* knew well enough what 'rents' had been paid to Sir James the night before. *I* knew that he had done a bill with old Malden, of Clifford-street, the bill being drawn by himself, and accepted by Foster Crib, of the Ninth Hussars, and that for a three months' 'I promise to pay a hundred and fifty pounds,' on stamped paper, he had received Malden's cheque for one hundred and twenty pounds. *I* knew all this, and, indeed, I had his bill in my pocket at that very moment, for Malden had done the little business with *my* money, and *I* was the party to whom reference had to made 'in the City' before the transaction was completed. You seem surprised, sir," he continued, "but I assure you I have had in my time the acceptances of half the Household Brigade in my hands, to say nothing of the brigade of Foot Guards, and nearly all the crack cavalry regiments. But the game is too risky. I have now got very little money afloat in bills and even that little I intend to call in as soon as I possibly can."

At my cousin's marriage, I saw and spoke to Skeeme, who that day gave up his situation with "the colonel," and went down, as he told me, for a week's holiday to Brighton. The time I write of was the time of the railway mania, and those who remember the advertising columns of the *Times* in those days will not easily forget the prodigious schemes which, day by day, were put forth to the world, in the shape of new railway plans. I recollect one day in particular. It was about the middle of July, 1845. That morning there were no fewer than twenty-seven new railways – or rather say plans of impossible railway schemes – offered to the public; and a stockbroker told me that in forty-eight hours every one of the twenty-seven schemes was at a considerable premium. I was seized with the mania of speculation. It was easy to ask for, but by no means so easy to obtain, shares in those days, unless you knew some of the directors. I wrote to four or five of the newest lines, but obtained no favourable reply, and was one day lamenting my misfortune to Coxon of the Seventy-first, at the "Rag," knowing how well that youthful captain had increased his modest wealth by having had shares in new lines allotted to him, and invariably selling them the moment they commanded a premium, which was generally the very next day.

"Look here, old fellow," said my friend, as we sat at dinner one very hot evening; "for the last two months I have, on an average, had a hundred shares a day allotted me in one or more railway lines, and the average premium I have sold them at, has been a pound a share. That makes, at a hundred pounds a day for sixty days, six thousand pounds; if you come round to my lodgings to-morrow, I'll show you my banker's book with five thousand six hundred pounds to my credit, which will just make the balance right when I deduct the money I have spent."

This made my mouth water, for my ill luck had been as unceasing as my friend's good fortune had been great. I therefore asked him how it was he had succeeded in having so many shares allotted him, and whether he would, for old acquaintance' sake, "put me up to a good thing or two."

"I'll tell you what," said Coxon: "I'll tell you what I'll do. I'll take you into the City to-morrow and introduce you to a capital fellow, who is a director upon three or four of the best new lines that have come out, and who is to be a director of the 'Edinburgh and Cornwall Direct Line,' which will be out in the course of a few days. You ask him to allot you five or six hundred shares in that line, and you will sell them next day for at least a couple pounds premium."

"Where did you make the acquaintance of so estimable a character?" I asked.

"At the office of Malden, the bill-discounter, in Clifford-street," said Coxon. "I went there one day about a bit of stamped paper on which I had written my name, and which was considerably over-due. Malden either could, or would, do nothing to help me, but introduced me to 'the party from the City,' with whose money the bill had been 'done.' With this 'party' I got into conversation, and he very kindly renewed the document. I kept my word, in paying him when the fresh bill became due, and since that we have been very good friends indeed. He has more than once melted some valuable stamp paper for me, and when the railway mania broke out,

I got him to allot me shares in some of the very best things going; for he is very much sought after as a director."

"Pray, may I ask the name of your friend?" said I, little thinking what Coxon's reply would be.

"His name?" said the captain; "his name is Skeeme."

"What!" said I, "John Skeeme?"

"Yes," said Coxon; "do you know him?"

"Of course I do," was my reply; "he was valet to a cousin of mine in the Guards."

"Impossible, my dear fellow," said Coxon. "I have known Mr. Skeeme for three years and more, and have often met him at his office in the City, where he keeps two clerks, and has long done a considerable stroke of business in money-lending."

To make a long story short, I went next day with Coxon into the City, and in a court somewhere behind the Mansion House, up two pair of stairs, we came to a door, upon which was painted the name "Mr. Skeeme." Inside were two clerks, one of whom seemed to be copying very long and complicated accounts which the other read off from a ledger. On asking for Mr. Skeeme, we were told that he was within, but very busy indeed with two gentlemen, and would not be disengaged for an hour. We therefore went away; and, taking me to a stationer's, Coxon wrote a note of introduction for me, as he was pressed for time, and could not remain any longer at the east-end of town.

Armed with this document, I returned to Mr. Skeeme's office, and was at once shown into his sanctuary. As I had imagined, this great railway director was no other than my old friend.

I neither presented Coxon's letter of introduction, nor mentioned his name, for I did not want Skeeme to feel humiliated by the other's knowing he had been a valet. I pretended that I had seen his name down as a director of the new "Edinburgh and Cornwall Direct" line, and begged he would do his best to allot me a couple of hundred shares. This he not only agreed to do, but even offered, and I accepted, to put my name down for a hundred extra shares: all of which I sold as soon as the prospectus was published in the *Times,* at a premium, of two pounds ten shillings each.

As soon as our conversation about shares was over, Skeeme entered into a long explanation with me.

"I have had this office," said he, "for about four years, although, when valet to the colonel, I could not visit it every day. For a long time I did nothing except in the private bill discounting line; but when all the new railways began to be projected, I was asked by people, who only knew me in my business capacity, to become a director. After a great deal of hesitation I agreed to join the Chatham and Portsmouth board. Being a director, I allotted myself a thousand shares, and then sold them next day at two pounds premium. This was a very short time before my old master married. I knew I should have to leave him, and thought I might as well turn railway director as take to any other trade. I am, or I have been, on the direction of seven lines, and by these I have netted at least fourteen thousand pounds. But I think these fine days won't last very long, and so I intend this line to be my last venture. If it succeeds, as we believe it will, and I can get three pounds premium on the three thousand shares I have taken, I shall retire from the business, for I feel pretty certain that a crash will soon come."

After this, so long as my leave of absence lasted, hardly a couple of days passed without my going to Skeeme's office. The rage for railway shares lasted a little longer than he had prophesied, and I managed to make some four or five thousand pounds. My friend Skeeme would have done better if he had kept to his first resolution. After selling all his shares, he was induced, by love of gain, to recommence speculation again, and when the crash came it found him still mixed up as a director with four or five schemes, any one of which was itself enough to eat up all his profits, and more. When the evil day arrived, he was sued by two or three railway shareholders, and judgments were given against him. Little by little he had to part with nearly every pound he had; for being known to be a rich man, every shareholder in every company he had been connected with at any time, began to issue writs against him. He tried to get away to France, but some of his creditors were too sharp for him, and he was arrested upon a "capias" at Dover. He went to jail, and offered to compound with his creditors. His offer was refused, and so he filed his petition and went through the Bankruptcy Court, coming out at the end of three months without a shilling. My cousin, who liked poor Skeeme very much, settled one hundred pounds a year upon him, and the ex-valet retired to the country, where he and his wife lived on the annuity which their old master "the colonel" allowed him.

Some fifteen years passed by, and I saw or heard nothing of Skeeme. I had been out to India again; had come back once more; had then gone through a period of home service; after which I had embarked for Canada, and had come back to England after selling out. Happening to go into the City one morning, I ran against a gentleman who was coming out of a bank as I was going in. He turned to apologise, and before I could call to mind where I had seen his face before, he recognised me, called me by my name, and shook hands with me very heartily. The man was no other than my old acquaintance Skeeme. Not being able to talk in the noisy streets of the City, we went together to a luncheon-bar, and there he told me that he had remained some four or five years in the country, but that the old rage for speculation had come upon him so strongly that he had returned again to London; some friends had lent him a few hundred pounds on which to recommence, and though his life had at first been but a hand to mouth existence, he had been happier in London than in the country. Latterly, he had been doing very well indeed, and now that the mania for joint-stock companies of all kinds had set in, he hoped to make a good thing out of it. "I leave the directorships alone, now-a-days," he said; "my business is to 'promote' companies. Here, now, is a capital thing safe to come out at from one and a half to two premium;" saying which he unfolded the prospectus of "The Deep Sea Copper Mining Company (Limited), capital £500,000, in 100,000 shares of £5 each, of which £1 will be paid on application, £1 on allotment, and £1 not sooner than twelve months after allotment." "If you can get me one or two good directors for this company," said Skeeme, "I am quite willing to allow you three hundred pounds of my share of the promotion money."

It was evident that Skeeme, having money of his own to speculate with, had taken to the profession of a promoter with all the forethought and carefulness which his previous misfortunes had taught him. I did not much admire his "Deep Sea Copper Mining Company," although, to do him justice, he brought it out at three pounds premium, and a hundred shares which he had managed to get allotted to me I sold at that very respectable figure.

But a better and far more profitable project was put into shape by my old friend. Having felt severely the want of capital himself, he often considered whether a sort of unlimited credit upon bills, or other documents, could not be set on foot; and one day, by inspiration as it were, he solved the problem. His idea – not altogether new, for it had been worked to some extent on the Continent – was to establish a joint-stock company ("limited," of course), with, nominally, an immense capital, very little of which was to be paid up, but the operations of the concern were to be carried on altogether upon acceptances, or bills of the company. If it succeeded, the profits upon the paid-up capital would be immense. For instance, let us suppose that a certain railway wanted money – say a trifle of five hundred thousand pounds or so. To borrow such a sum at any bank would be an impossibility. In the first place, the line was only half constructed, and never could be finished unless the loan were obtained. Security, beyond the works already completed, it had none to offer; all its capital, to say nothing of the money obtained from debentures, having long ago been used up. Well; the railway directors would get the contractor to draw upon them for six hundred thousand or seven hundred thousand in bills, which the said board would accept. These the contractor would deposit with the new-fashioned finance company, and upon the security – if such a name can be given it – he would obtain the money he required to finish the works. This would not be given in cash. The contractor would have to draw another set of bills upon the board of directors of the finance company, these would be accepted, and then taken elsewhere to discount. For this transaction the finance company would, perhaps, charge as high as ten per cent – for merely giving its acceptance to the railway contractor – and ten per cent upon mere paper very soon makes the interest of the capital something exceedingly respectable. My friend Skeeme was quite full of this new plan. "Others charge interest for money," said he, "but we shall charge interest upon paper; being all the time as secure as if we had the guarantee of the Bank of England."

For a long time the plan seemed to work wonderfully well. I should have mentioned that Skeeme's company, "The General and Universal Confidence Company, Limited," took immensely in the City. The idea was thought so good, and there was something so new in it, that a regular rush was made to obtain shares. On the very first day that the concern was advertised, it rose to four premium. I managed to realise a nice little sum out of the fifty shares I obtained through the influence of Skeeme. In a very short time it was known in the City who had first planned the Confidence Company; and when middle-aged or old men knew that it was the Mr. Skeeme well known in old days, they were proud of the genius of their old friend. The promotion money that Skeeme obtained for bringing out the "General and Universal Confidence Company, Limited," was a very handsome sum: no less than ten thousand pounds. The reputation he achieved in the financial world was still greater. On every side, offers were made him to become a director of this, vice-chairman of that, or chairman of the other, company. For a long time he resisted the temptation, but it proved too strong at last. One morning, in the money article of the *Times*, I read that Mr. John Skeeme, the well-known authority on financial matters, had consented to become chairman of the "Universal Discount Company" (a new affair), and that, in consequence of this announcement, the shares of the company had risen from two pounds fifteen shillings, to four pounds two shillings and sixpence premium, in a single afternoon.

PART II

Some few months after Mr. Skeeme had become chairman of the Universal Discount Company, things went very badly with me in a pecuniary way. After leaving the army I had tried my hand at speculation in shares, and had lost two-thirds of what little money I had. I then set up in business as a foreign commission agent, and lost the remainder. My cousin – the Guardsman to whom John Skeeme was formerly valet – used to keep me a little, but he had his own responsibilities, and could not of course do very much for one who really had no claim upon him. Moreover, I disliked the idea of living upon charity. I could not bet, and did not understand the art of living at the rate of twelve or fifteen hundred pounds a year without any visible means of existence. In short, I wanted to turn my hand to something that would earn me an honest livelihood, and it struck me that I could not do better than look out my old friend the Promoter, and ask him to give me a helping hand.

To find the offices of the Universal Discount Company was not difficult. In the centre and soul of business London – the district bounded by Bishopsgate-street on the east, the Mansion House on the west, the end of Moorgate-street on the north, and King William-street on the south – every one knew the whereabouts of that celebrated undertaking. Towards it I bent my steps, and of the wealthy-looking burly porter – that man who at a glance could tell the monetary condition of all who addressed him – I asked for Mr. Skeeme. The question seemed to astonish the highly respectable servant. I had been too abrupt. It was as if I had driven to Marlborough House, and asked the sentinel on duty to show me up to the Prince of Wales. "Mr. Skeeme does come here," was the reply, in a supercilious tone which made me feel very small, "but he ain't here now, and what might you please to want?" The janitor evidently thought that I must be after no good, and that I perhaps had the intention of getting some of the vast funds of the "Universal Discount Company" by force from the chairman. "Was I a friend of Mr. Skeeme's, or did I come on business?"

"Yes, a very old friend."

"Well, that was board-day, Mr. Skeeme would be there about two o'clock, and if I would come about three, perhaps he would see me."

I did come about three, and having sent up my card, the porter came back most respectfully, begging I would follow him, and that "Mr. Skeeme would see me in five minutes."

The five minutes lengthened into ten, fifteen, twenty. But when the great man made his appearance, his manner assured me that no slight whatever was meant by the delay, and that if the City magnate earned money, he certainly worked for it, and worked hard too. He was "very glad indeed," he said, "to see me," but "if I wanted to speak to him beyond three minutes, I must come out to his house, for he had not now a moment to spare. It was half-past three, and he had an appointment" (here he rang a hand-bell, and ordered a Hansom immediately) "at the 'Great Southern Railway' at 3:45; and another at the 'Deep Sea Mining Company' at 4:30. But would I come the next day but one, Sunday, and dine at his house in Kensington Palace Gardens, at six sharp? Always dine early on Sunday; servants go to church; day long. Come, and we'll talk over anything you want." Saying this, Skeeme took my arm, to the amazement of the hall porter, who had the cab ready, and was pompously opening the half doors of the same, so that the great man might enter without trouble. We had just got to the street, when Skeeme said, "If you are going my way, I can give you a lift; jump in, for I forgot to say something to you;" and so off we bundled together.

Once the cab in movement, Skeeme began to speak. "Don't be annoyed," he said, "but if between this and tomorrow you want money, tell me frankly. Don't stand on ceremony. I have some blank cheques in my pocket-book, and can fill you in one for twenty, thirty, or forty pounds, only tell me exactly what and we'll talk over details to-morrow." But I hastened to assure Skeeme that, although very much in want of something to do, I was in no immediate necessity for money.

To Kensington Palace Gardens I betook myself the next Sunday. The house in which Skeeme lived was one of the best in that haven of millionaires. I had never been in a mansion of the kind before. Everything in it seemed so new, so fresh, so expensive, and so good of its kind, that you felt lost whether to summarise your opinion as to whether the evident lately acquired wealth was offensive, or the number of modern contrivances were to be praised. The hall was covered with pictures – game pieces, fruit pieces, fish pieces, the irrepressible replica of the abbot receiving the stag and the salmon at the porch of the monastery, the oil portrait of the favourite horse, the oil copy of two or three of Landseer's dogs – in short, the actual ornamentation was, on a small scale, what Belvoir or Raby Castle, might be on a large scale. But there was a newness about everything. The pictures seemed to have been painted to order, of a size to suit certain places or spare parts of the wall. There were stags' heads (from Wardour-street) upon which riding and hunting whips hung, that had the fault of everything else about the place – they were much too new. My hat was taken by a butler in a new suit of black, my great-coat by a footman in a still newer suit of livery, and I was ushered through a boudoir hung in pale yellow satin that was newer still, into a drawing-room ornamented with a pale blue material which was newest of all. Nothing could be finer nor in better taste than each particular article of furniture, but, as a whole, it had the fault which pervaded the whole house – every chair, table, picture, statuette, mirror, frame, fire-iron, writing ornament, the very grates – expressed that they had all gotten there by contract from their respective makers' hands at one and the same moment.

Not so Mrs. Skeeme – formerly housekeeper and cook at my cousin's. She, poor woman, had certainly not got younger since the days when she lived in South Audley-street. She was the only old looking object in the room, and was none the less pleasant to look at for that reason. The poor old soul did not appear to have risen either in spirits or in education with her rise in life. She was in constant dread that all the finery round her would vanish as quickly as it came. She welcomed me in a half-kind, half-diffident manner, as if she wanted to be cordial to me, and yet did not like me to think that she had forgotten how in the old times I had known her as a servant. At dinner, however, Mrs. Skeme was in her own element. The dinner was excellent; not a dish too much, nor a thing badly cooked. The mistress of the house evidently understood what to order, how to order it; nor had her lord and master forgotten his cunning as to the wine. Of the latter there was plenty without profusion. Very soon after dinner was finished Mrs. Skeeme left us to ourselves, and then commenced the conversation which I had sought for.

"And so you want something to do," said Skeeme. "I have been thinking over what little you told me, and have hit upon a plan which I think will assist you, only you must not be offended if I offer you what might appear strange with reference to the former position in which you knew me."

I replied that I would be only too glad if anything I could get to do would give me bread and cheese.

"Would you mind," said Skeeme, "serving under me? I ask you this before going further or saying more, as I will not make you the offer I am going to unless I see clearly that you do not object to being nominally, as it were, in my service."

"Not in the very least," I answered. "I would much rather serve you than any man I don't know, and very much rather than with many whom I do know. What is it you propose?"

"My idea is that you should become my private secretary – that is, nominally. You will have to attend every day at the Great Southern Railway, of which I am chairman, and work there in my private room. Your salary will be two hundred pounds a year, which will be nominally paid you by me, but really by the company." (This, I afterwards found out, was a pious fraud of my worthy old friend's, who really paid me out of his own pocket.) "You will have a good deal to do, for as (this between ourselves) I fully expect to get into parliament in a few weeks, I shall have much less time than at present to attend to my own business. My private correspondence, and all that, will be in your hands. The salary is small, but if you pay attention to what is passing around you in the railway and finance world, you will very soon be able to pick up wrinkles by which a few pounds can be turned, and I need hardly say that any way I can help you in this, I will gladly do so. And now we'll go to coffee."

Nothing connected with Skeeme and his rise, fall, and rise again in fortune, surprised me more than the way in which his manners had kept pace with his advancement in life. With the exception of certain liberties he still took with the poor letter H, there was hardly anything about him that reminded me of the old times when he was a lacquey. That he should dress well and quietly, or that he should behave at table as if he had moved in the best society from the day he left school, were acquirements which a keen, quick-witted man, could hardly have failed to pick up during his years of valetdom. But what did astonish me was the total change in his manners. Formerly he was at all times and in all places the same, staid, steady, slow-speaking upper-servant – perfectly civil, knowing his own place, and yet having a due quantity of self-respect, but still a servant in looks and in speech. In the City he was the hurried, bustling man of business, who either never has, or never allows that he has, time enough to get through all his work But at home he had all the ways of a well-to-do gentleman, whose greatest labour was to shoot partridges, ride to hounds, go over his agent's accounts, or, if in London, walk to White's, and there pass away an hour with the *Times* or *Post*.

Mr. Skeeme had, however, one great advantage, or "pull," as it is vulgarly called, over others who had risen from the lower ranks to a place in "society," which was, that so many years had elapsed since he was a valet, hardly anyone remembered him in that capacity. London has this, if it has no other, advantage over the rest of the world, namely, few people know, and still fewer care, who their neighbor is, where he is going, or whence he came. Twenty years ago in London! Who cares to ask or to know what you or I were doing half that time past? Skeeme had the advantage of this. In Liverpool, or Manchester, or Bristol, he would have been spoken of to the day of his death, if he had lived to fourscore, as the rich man who was once a gentleman's valet. In London, few ask what a man has been, all they care to know is what he is, especially if he be a director of several companies, a great authority on finance and railways, and spoken of as likely to be soon in parliament, promoter of some "General and Universal Confidence Company, Limited," or chairman of a "Universal Discount," or "Great Southern Railway Company." If by chance any one asked the questions as to where or how he had taken his rise, the answer was that he had been many years "something in the City; – a discount agent, they believed, but were not sure."

About a week after dining at Mr. Skeeme's, I took up my appointment as private secretary to that gentleman. My duties consisted in being at the office of the Great Southern Railway every morning soon after ten, when I had to open each letter received for the great Mr. Skeeme, mark down in a book from whom it came, draw up a précis of the contents of each, and be ready to take my chief's directions as to what reply was to be sent to each communication. Some letters I answered in my own name, others I took to Mr. Skeeme to sign, and the more particular ones – from bankers, great City men, lords, members of parliament, and other persons of standing – my chief would reply to in his own hand; although I generally drafted even the commonest notes. There was one thing in which Skeeme had not risen with his circumstances: he wrote, as he always had done, a very good hand, but his mode of expressing himself was anything but clear, and his spelling was eccentric. The few letters or notes that he penned himself, were written in a room next to the one in which I sat, and I have known him – when I did not draft the letter – ask perhaps how to spell a dozen words whilst writing as many lines. There were some errors in orthography which he seemed never to get over. Thus he had apparently an invincible dislike to double letters, especially the double *p*; so that he would aprize his correspondent to make an apointment to apropriate shares.

But at accounts few men could equal Skeeme. Let the cleverest of accountants jumble together, so as to make them unintelligible, the capital account of a line, the debentures, the preference stock and the rolling stock, he saw through the dodge in ten minutes, and having separated the wheat from the chaff, very soon showed how matters ought to be, and where was truth and where falsehood. As chairman of the Great Southern he had a somewhat difficult task to perform. The line was not paying, and the shareholders were every year grumbling more and more because it did not do so. Some of the directors wished to keep things quiet, "to make matters pleasant," by fabricating little dividends, and out of the capital paying a certain interest so as to prevent the grumbling becoming too loud. They were not actually dishonest men – they thought of their line as Mr. Micawber did of his fortunes, that some day, sooner or later, "something would turn up," which would enable them to repay to the capital what they had borrowed in order to expend as interest. And, after all, was not the capital the property of the shareholders? If you borrowed a few thousands from it every year, did not these moneys go into the pockets of these same shareholders? And what was the use of telling everything to the great body of shareholders? Some of them were lawyers, these were chiefly rogues; others – many – were women, these were mostly fools; was it not better to keep things smooth and quiet, and wait with patience until that something which they so earnestly expected should turn up?

I don't say that these were altogether the opinions of Skeeme, but they were those of most of his colleagues, and as he was a very large shareholder in the concern, he wished as much as possible to keep up the value of his property. Railway stock was just then commencing to look very bad indeed. On some lines the one hundred pounds stock was selling as low as fifty pounds, forty pounds, and even thirty pounds. In other companies even the debenture-holders could get no interest for their money, and in one or two instances the preference shareholders were in the same predicament. Before I had been long in the office, I saw very clearly what was the end and aim of Mr. Skeeme's working; in fact, he acknowledged it to me one day. He held a very large amount of shares in the Great Southern, and foreseeing that the system of railway account cooking could not last forever, he wanted by degrees – little by little, so as not to attract observation – to sell out, if not all, the greater part of his stock, so that when the evil day came his loss would be comparatively small. But to do this at the prices which then ruled would be folly, therefore he was working his utmost to raise the value of the shares before he threw his own on the market. He had promised, when I first joined him, to let me into any "real good thing" that turned up, and it was in showing me how he would befriend me that I discovered the plan he had of working the oracle to his own advantage.

The shares stood at sixty, and to increase their value in the market an increase of traffic or a decrease of expenses must be shown. To do the latter was impossible – or next to it – for the reason that every official on the line, from the traffic manager and secretary to the policemen and porters, were more or less the friends – and all the nominees – of the directors. I remember an instance in which it was attempted to reduce by five per cent the salaries of all officers who received more than one hundred pounds a year, and I shall never forget the storm it raised. Long before it could be carried out the secretary of the company was inundated with letters, petitions, remonstrances, and I know not what, from all, or nearly all, the shareholders of the line. Mr. Jones of Stoke Newington asked whether it was just that his son (who was deputy-assistant sub-secretary, and received one hundred and fifty pounds a year for hindering the work of the office) should have his salary reduced by seven pounds ten shillings, at a time when beef was elevenpence, and the best mutton thirteenpence a pound? Mr. Williamson of Swansea wrote to say that he considered it most infamous that his nephew should, after working hard for three years in the accountant's office, be reduced from two hundred pounds to one hundred and ninety pounds; and Mrs. James, a large shareholder and extensive philanthropist, came herself to see the Chairman, and told him that she would at once throw all the stock she held upon the market, if the two Station-masters down the country for whom she had got places, had their salaries reduced by five pounds a year each. What could be done with such people? To reduce the expenses of the line appeared to be impossible, and therefore all that could be done was to increase the receipts: but how?

There was a small fishing village about twenty miles from our line of railway, of which few people had ever heard, but which it was said by Mr. Skeeme and others could easily be turned into a very fashionable bathing-place. The local medical men were asked for Statistics about the health of the place, and such returns were given that the only wonder is every old person in the three kingdoms did not immediately flock there. The place was perfection; all it wanted was a few streets, and some people to inhabit them; but, above all things it required, was a line of railway, and this the Great Southern Railway Company proposed at once to construct. An act of parliament authorizing a line between Seaville and a certain station on the Great Southern, was very easily obtained, the more so as there was really no one to oppose it. Skeeme, having got into parliament, worked it through himself. The shares on this new branch line were not offered to the public; they were all taken up by Mr. Skeeme himself, his friends, brother-directors and their friends – the balance, or unappropriated shares, being put down to the Great Southern Railway Company. The way in which the capital for the undertaking was provided was simple in the extreme. The amount required was something considerable – I mean considerable to the minds of those persons who had not had a financial training – something over a million and a half. About a third was wanted at once, and this Mr. Skeeme, being also chairman of the "Universal Discount Company," as also a director of the "General and Universal Confidence Company," very easily managed. Having got me to lend my name as nominal contractor for the line – for it was not, perhaps, quite the thing that his name should appear in *that* transaction – I drew bills for the five hundred thousand pounds upon the Great Southern Railway Company, and these Mr. Skeeme, in his capacity as chairman of the company, accepted. The accepted bills were then taken, some to the "Universal Discount Company," of which Mr. Skeeme was chairman, others to the "General and Universal Confidence Company," of which he was a director, and they were discounted at a very respectable figure.

With this money, the line was commenced, and when a certain portion of it was finished, debentures were offered to the public at something like thirty-eight pounds in cash for one hundred pounds worth of stock. Thus from one hundred and fifty thousand to two hundred thousand pounds was raised in addition to the five hundred thousand pounds previously obtained; and as the traffic on the line had commenced over that part that was finished, the receipts were made to swell the credit side of the Great Southern Railway account. In the next session of parliament a bill for another extension line – this time towards a part of a great coal district – was carried through, and the same process was repeated with respect to the borrowing transactions. In all these little financial feats Skeeme invariably allowed me my little pickings, which in course of time amounted to something very respectable, and I began not only to acquire wealth, but actually to get a taste for a business in which, as it appeared to me, it was always certain winning for those behind the scenes. In my army days, when I knew nothing of business, I should have compared my new gains to playing with loaded dice.

We had, in the course of three years, two branch lines at work, both of which were so made to show a profit in the accounts, and to swell the traffic receipts, that our shares soon began to move upwards. Thus we carefully published every month in the newspapers that our traffic receipts, for instance, in July, were nine thousand four hundred and eighty-seven pounds four shillings and twopence, which, as compared with those in July in the previous year, being eight thousand one hundred and ten pounds six shillings and fourpence, or in the July of the year before that again, being six thousand and nine pounds nineteen shillings and a penny – facts which no one could dispute. The figures thus shown were quite correct, and the comparison made was perfectly true. But what we did not think it worth while to enlighten the public upon, was the fact that for every ten pounds of increased receipts we had – what with discount paid for bills, premiums upon debentures, and all the various losses incidental upon raising money at ruinous rates – sunk for ever at least two thousand pounds of capital, which had gone where last year's snow was.

In this way the shares in the Great Southern rose higher and higher, and as I had invested money – lent me by Skeeme – in purchasing the shares at forty, which

I now sold for fifty-five, fifty-eight, and sixty, the speculation turned out by no means a bad one.

All this time Skeeme must have been rolling up money very fast. From holding many thousand pounds-worth of Great Southern scrip, he had now reduced the amount he held to a mere trifle, and all he sold were parted with at a premium. His property in the Seaville and Coaltown Junction lines he quietly "obliged" the Great Southern with. The process was not difficult. At a board meeting he and three or four other directors who were shareholders in those branch undertakings, would ask their own leave that the shares should be bought, and upon their own consent being given, they entered the transaction in the minute-book, and ratified the proceedings at the next board meeting. That is what the inventor of the process named "making things pleasant."

Mr. Skeeme is no longer chairman of the Great Southern Railway. Soon after the little transactions I have noted in this paper, his health compelled him to retire from business, although he still retains his seat upon the "Universal Discount Company." He is now a very wealthy man. He owned one night lately to me, after a second bottle of the most unexceptional '20 port I ever tasted, that he would not take a hundred and fifty thousand pounds for the money he had invested in India Bonds, Consuls, and Bank of England Stock, and I believe him. He has sold his house in Kensington Palace Gardens, and bought a very splendid "mansion" in the New South Kensington district. His dinners are much thought of, and some of the best people in London are to be met with at his table.

As for myself, I have long given up the situation I held as private secretary to Mr. Skeeme, and have set up in business as a Financial Agent. There is very little doing at present in my line, but I dare say "a good time" is "coming," when people return to town after the holidays.

27

THE AUTOBIOGRAPHY OF A JOINT-STOCK COMPANY (LIMITED)

Laurence Oliphant

Source: Laurence Oliphant, 'The Autobiography of a Joint-Stock Company (Limited),' *Blackwood's Edinburgh Magazine* 120 (July 1876), pp. 96–122.

EDITORIAL HEADNOTE

Laurence Oliphant (1829–1888) was a popular travel writer and journalist. He was born in Capetown, South Africa, the son of a colonial official. In 1849 he qualified as a barrister in Ceylon, where his father was Chief Justice. During the 1860s Oliphant was employed by the Foreign Office and took part in diplomatic missions around the world, which became the basis for many of his travel books. For a time, he joined a utopian community in the United States, the Brotherhood of the New Life, and he later became a strong advocate of Zionism. Oliphant had a longstanding association with *Blackwood's*, which serialized several of his books and to which he frequently contributed articles.[1]

Blackwood's Edinburgh Magazine was founded by William Blackwood in 1817 as a Tory rival to the Whig *Edinburgh Review*. The magazine soon established itself as an important vehicle for creative writing.

"The Autobiography of a Joint-Stock Company (Limited)" is a type of literature known as an "it narrative," in which an inanimate object speaks for itself, in this case the XYZ Company, a fraudulent stock market promotion. The story provides a detailed account of the rise and fall of a limited company as a means of illustrating "all the refined forms of swindling which our advanced civilization makes possible." Among the numerous kinds of financial chicanery sometimes employed by company promoters, the story describes guinea-pig directors, deceptive prospectuses, false accounting, share rigging, and watered stock.

Note

1 John Sutherland, "Oliphant, Laurence," *The Stanford Companion to Victorian Fiction* (Stanford: Stanford University Press, 1989), pp. 474–76.

DOI: 10.4324/9781003713890-31

In a few days my brief and stormy career will finally close. I can calmly, and even thankfully, contemplate this premature extinction of an existence which has ruined reputations, shattered fortunes, and carried want and misery into hundreds of humble homes; for I am wearied and worn out with the effort it has caused me to achieve these deplorable results, and utterly disgusted with the advanced state of civilisation which has made me the victim of its immoral tendencies. As far as my exhausted and feeble condition will allow me to feel anything, I think I can honestly say I am conscious of being in a repentant frame of mind.

What philosopher can explain to me the nature of the causes of which I am the vile effect? It was not my own fault that, like those who first hatched me, I was conceived in sin and shapen in iniquity, and became immediately the means of demoralising every one who came into contact with me, of deceiving those who trusted in me, and of crushing those who opposed me, until my own turn came, and I fizzed out in a gutter of fraud like a bad squib. Depraved though I am, I regret to say that, knowing as much as I do of the merits of the other members of my fraternity who still exist and flourish, I may yet hope that a process of natural selection is in progress, and that joint-stock companies, like the human race, are to rise into new and better conditions through the "survival of the fittest." At the same time, I know that I am not altogether bad; for I always found myself in sympathy with the few honest men upon my board. Now and then I experienced the novel and delightful sensation of awakening conscience, forming good resolutions – which at one time I intended to keep; and I looked forward to a calm and serene old age, soothed by the reflection that thousands would be rendered happier by my existence, and that my own health and well-being would be a source of amiable anxiety to numbers of respectable shareholders.

How the moral element thus temporarily infused into my system was afterwards expelled, and my whole nature became even worse at the end than it was at the beginning, is part of the thrilling story of my life to which I invite the attention of the reader; and I address myself to all without distinction, for all will be the wiser by the perusal of this most timely and instructive warning. I address myself to you, my innocent clerical friends in remote country parishes – for I know of no more ignorant and confiding class of investors – and though you may not think that the life and fortunes of a joint-stock company (limited) can interest you whose vocation lies is such a very different direction, as long as you have little earnings which you blindly invest on the faith of neatly-addressed circulars and prospectuses, you are interested, deeply interested, in the story I have to tell. I address myself to you, fair readers, especially widows and spinsters; for however capable you may think yourselves of enjoying the franchise, I am able from my own knowledge to declare that you are utterly unfit to manage your own money-matters, and I should never have been able to enter upon my fraudulent career had it not been for the powerful support I derived from the trusting contributions of confiding or speculative female investors; and now, in such solemn tones as I find it possible to command, reclining as I am at this moment in the arms of my official liquidator, with but a feeble spark of vitality still left, I warn you to read carefully this melancholy history. Believe me, it concerns you deeply. Such of you as have invested in me, I shall endeavour to remind of my gay and misspent youth, by providing you, by means of the officer legally appointed for that purpose, with infinitesimal dividends, extracted at long intervals from my miserable and shrunken remains – Bless you!

I address myself to you, rich landed proprietors, who never meddle with City matters, or investments, or "that sort of thing," but leave it all to your men of business, and I ask you whether you have had reason to be satisfied with the results of their advice this year? Don't you think you had better try and understand a little where your money is, and where it is not? And you men of business, who advise your clients, no doubt with the best intentions, have you had reason always to be satisfied with the advice you have given them? Clever though you are, and honest though you may be, it will do you no harm to read my narrative. And you, impecunious connections of the aristocracy, who have neither brains nor experience, but think you know enough to combine West-end fashion with East-end financing, if you ever read anything, read me, that you may avoid having your purses, – which, indeed, at best are trash – stolen, and your good names filched. Alas! I fear that those I seek to reach are just those who will think I don't concern them. The parsons, the widows, the orphans, the officers on half pay, the rich squires, the titled dupes – the sponges, in fact, whom I want to warn against the squeezers, will pass me by, while the squeezers themselves will chuckle over my adventurous career, as thieves read the police reports, partly on account of the affectionate interest they take in the profession, and partly in the hope of picking up a wrinkle or two for future use and guidance.

Having taken the liberty, with a frankness which I regret formed no part of my original character, but which my approaching dissolution has suggested to me as expedient, to address these and all other classes of my readers, I will now endeavour to convey to them some idea of the process of my inception. I wish it, however, to be distinctly understood, that while I carefully veil the mystery of my identity, I am not altogether a mythical character; that the facts of my existence are real, and not imaginary; and that there is nothing I am about to relate which has not actually occurred: at the same time, any attempt of the most experienced promoter or knowing broker to discover exactly who I am, or rather was, will be utterly futile, so artful is the disguise behind which this record of my varied fortunes has been concealed.

Disdaining to take refuge in a fictitious name, and scorning the subterfuge of a sham prospectus, I will merely say that I first received the rude outlines of my subsequent shape in the ingenious brain of a needy and adventurous speculator. This gentleman, who had passed through the various phases of an officer in the army, a member of the House of Commons, and a broker on the Stock Exchange, from all of which he had, in one form or other, been practically, if not by any formal process, expelled, had been driven to earning a precarious livelihood by taking up what he called one "little business" after another. He was popularly known as the "Captain;" and in consideration of his natural predatory habits, I will venture to introduce him to my readers as Captain Hawk. His style of "little business" consisted in arranging for concessions, acting apparently as principal where it was too dangerous for the real principal to appear; playing the part of spy or detective between business friends at the request of either, or both; dealing in horses and carriages; trying to obtain contracts for large contractors; and introducing people who had "good things" to sell, or valuable ideas to impart, to capitalists likely to invest in them, and *vice versa*: on all which transactions he received commissions varying in amount – sometimes, indeed, very trifling – or was remunerated in other underhand methods well known to the craft. I don't think he was originally a dishonest man, and he still possessed many amiable and generous traits – such, for instance, as that of freely lending his friends the money which did not belong to him, and being always ready to put them into "good things," a service which they rarely returned. The fertility of resource and ingenuity of invention with which this worthy was gifted was something amazing; and I shall never forget the first time I saw myself in manuscript. He was in very low water at the time, and lived in a small lodging in a street off the Strand; but he shared the peculiarity of other members of the same fraternity, of rising and sinking with extraordinary rapidity and facility. There never was anything to equal his elasticity in this respect. The contrast between his gay and jaunty appearance when he was dashing down Piccadilly behind a pair of high-stepping bays, when his luck was good – and the seedy sort of swagger with which, a few months after, in an almost starving condition, he would secretly visit financiers who were ashamed to see him openly, – was a perpetual marvel to me. His external appearance was that of a somewhat dissipated "plunger." Heavy sandy moustache, from which volumes of smoke perpetually issued, concealed a not unpleasant mouth; and as he wrote me out impregnating me with his filthy tobacco, I remember looking up with astonishment into his calm blue eyes, and wondering how such an apparently vacuous countenance could ever have imagined such a complicated and incomprehensible prospectus as I felt myself, even in that first down of consciousness, to be.

Poor man! He deserved to get something for his trouble; for the effort of producing me cost him hours of concentrated thought, six tumblers of brandy-and-water, and as many cigars; and though, of course, I cannot say I have any recollection of it, I have a dim sort of consciousness that I have, so to speak, been incubating in his brain for many weeks before I saw the light.

At last, after innumerable corrections, modifications, and final polishings, I was folded up, put into his pocket, and entered upon the next stage of my still infantile existence.

This gentleman is known in the phraseology of finance as my *Promoter*; and in spite of his many bad habits and general laxity of morals, after an extensive experience of city men engaged in providing investments for the public and managing them after they have been provided, I am proud to say that I can think of him with a certain feeling of filial tenderness and even respect, for he did not conceal unknown villainies under the guise of respectability: having no profession he certainly made none; he was contented to live on the outskirts of the society to which he really belonged, instead of forcing his way into the society to which he did not belong – and rather picked up the remnants after the leaders of the profession had robbed the public, than stole from them himself.

Although I naturally did not know where I was going to, or what the next feature of my existence was to be at the time, it will make it clearer if I explain, which the light of my subsequent experience enables me to do, the plan of my Promoter. In order to give me any real value, it became necessary for him to obtain certain concessions and permissions from foreign Governments and municipalities – for I was a vast conception with ramifications all over Europe, and my success depended upon the construction of divers works involving contracts; in fact, there was a great deal of money to be made out of me by my Promoter, if he was only careful in his manipulation of me in my earlier stages. The first difficulty, and indeed the one, poor man, with which he had most frequently to contend through life, was impecuniosity.

He now stood in need of cash with which to pay his travelling expenses, and which should enable him to deposit the necessary caution money. Now there were two courses open to him: he could either go to a capitalist, explain the merits of the scheme, and go as his agent, having to give an account of his expenses, and receiving a stipulated sum; or he might take a partner from among the unwary youth of the West End.

The objections to the first course were obvious. The City capitalist would use him and throw him aside with a beggarly remuneration when he had no further need of him. The poor Captain knew this from bitter experience; but the obstacle in the way of the other course was, that the Captain had exhausted the tribe of fast and rich young men whom he had known in his fashionable days. He could only think of one man with whom he had a chance in this direction; if this failed, he would have to do the best he could in the City. A few weeks before, he had observed in the papers the death of a rich baronet, who had made his fortune in trade, and whose son had been a cornet in my Promoter's regiment, where he was noted for his weakness of intellect and extreme vanity. This youth had now become Sir Twig Robinson; and to him with a sanguine and even triumphant air my Promoter addressed himself, though I could feel the sinking presentiment of failure agitating his breast as I pressed against it.

Inexperienced as I then was, I was literally thunderstruck at the skill with which my Promoter flattered, tempted, and cajoled Sir Twig. That young gentleman, inflated with the newly-acquired consciousness of great wealth, was dazzled by the prospect of his name being connected with the brilliant and gigantic enterprise which my Promoter expatiated upon with extraordinary eloquence. Not only was there great profit, but there was great credit to be got out of it; and if the truth is to be told, with management, there really was both. Sir Twig was, after all, not by any means such a fool for taking me up, as he has been since on many occasions; and he exhibited a certain degree of cunning in the tenacity with which he insisted that if he advanced the whole of the capital necessary for these preliminary expenses, the concessions should be taken out in his name alone. The

Captain was afraid of exciting his suspicions if he objected too strongly: so it was finally settled, that in consideration of my Promoter undertaking the by no means simple task of securing the concessions and permissions, Sir Twig was to find the money requisite, and the profits were to be equally divided; or, as he elegantly expressed it, "We'll go halves in the pull."

I am obliged, in order not to prolong this veracious history to undue limits, to deprive the reader of the exciting narrative of my adventures in various foreign capitals. Indeed I have some excuse for this; for although I was generally in his pocket, they were not so much my adventures as my Promoter's. He it was who lingered and gambled at Monaco, and justified it afterwards to Sir Twig on the plea that he was obliged to go there in order to meet a lady who was supposed to exercise a paramount influence over a certain well-known minister who dispensed concessions. An admirable linguist, my Promoter was eminently qualified for the duty on which he was now engaged. His easy assurance secured him a favourable reception in society; and although he was somewhat shyly regarded by our own embassies and legations, he succeeded in winning access to the authorities with whom he had to deal, generally by means of his popularity with the fair sex. My readers would indeed be surprised to learn the names of certain distinguished foreign dames to whose powerful advocacy the Captain owed more than one concession, and whom he, in consideration thereof, allowed to "stand in" for a certain number of fully paid up shares in the Company when formed. For more than six months did my Promoter dine, bribe, flirt, and intrigue, to his own great content; for he spent Sir Twig's money as freely as if it had been his own, while he graduated his bribes with a most delicate discrimination. It takes a great deal of patience and diplomatic skill to secure a concession; for any small *employé* can put a spoke in the wheel if he is not "squared" in some shape or other, and they know their power but too well. But my Promoter was more than a match for them, and returned triumphantly just as Sir Twig was beginning to take a gloomy view of things, and to think that the whole affair was a *ruse* of the Captain to live luxuriously abroad at this expense. It was with a surly grunt, then, that he received my Promoter, as the latter, in faultless attire purchase with Sir Twig's money, and with a radiant smile, burst into his room one morning to announce his success.

"I thought you were never coming back," growled Sir Twig. "I suppose you thought there was no occasion to hurry, considering that I was paying the piper. I kept writing to tell you to come back, but you took no notice of my letters; and now you have got these precious concessions, I don't believe they are worth anything. Who is going to buy them? People who know about these things tell me the public are shy of going in for a thing of this sort, and that there is not a chance of its going down."

"Of course it won't go down, my dear Twig," said the Captain, with a delightful impudence.

"Then why did you get the concessions, and what do you propose to do?"

"Form a syndicate to be sure, – what else should I do?"

"A syndicate! what's that?" asked Sir Twig.

"I'll explain in a moment," replied the Captain; "but before we go any further, we have a little business to settle between us. You will observe that all these concessions are, as you stipulated they should be, taken in your name. Now I want you to sign a little agreement to the effect that whatever money is given for the concessions, if we sell them, is to be equally divided between us. This is only fair, you know – an ordinary matter of business routine. After you have done that, I'll explain to you the nature and functions of a syndicate."

Sir Twig had a vague feeling that it was never safe to sign his name, but he could see no valid objection to this proposal of the Captain's; and moreover, he felt himself in his ignorance so completely in that plausible gentleman's power, that he did as he was told, with a sigh.

"Now," said the Captain, with a glance of amiable compassion, "I will proceed to teach this young idea how to shoot. We have an invaluable packet here of concessions and permissions. The great object is to induce the confiding country investor to think that his or her future happiness and prosperity depend upon their obtaining possession of them. Now if you or I were to offer them for sale, their reputation for value would be ruined, because the public never look into the intrinsic value of the article to be purchased, but are influenced entirely by the manner in which it is presented to them, and the financial standing of the persons who offer it for sale: a poor, honest man will utterly fail to sell them a good thing in a straightforward way, while they will jump greedily at a bad thing, dangled skillfully before them by a rich rogue. The first thing for us, therefore, to find, is the rich rogue. He will become the syndicate manager. And his business is to induce a number of gentlemen of the highest standing he can find to become the directors of the new Company, and an eminent contractor to engage to carry out the works, upon the certain assurance that money will be found; and at the same time to induce the public to subscribe the money upon the no less certain assurance that the directors and contractor have been found. This looks like a vicious circle, because you can only obtain one essential condition on the distinct understanding that the other has been already secured."

"And how do you manage to get out of it?" asked Sir Twig.

"Why, we offer the scheme in the first instance, not to the public, but to an influential combination of capitalists called a syndicate."

"But why should the capitalists take the shares which the public will not take?"

"Because," replied the Captain, "they will get them much below their nominal price; and by being only a few holders, and all known to each other, they can put up prices on the Stock Exchange, and easily rig the market, and then clear out at a profit."

"Excuse my stupidity," said Sir Twig, "but how do they rig the market?"

"That is very simple. A says to B, don't sell your shares under ten per cent premium. I will buy them publicly at that price through a broker, if you will privately give me back my money afterwards, and take back your shares. The next day B buys from A, and so on. This keeps up the price on the official quotations on the

Exchange, and the outside investor comes in and buys; then the syndicate can quietly unload."

"I see," said Sir Twig, with more humour than I gave him credit for; "it seems to me that this syndicate, as you call it, is itself the 'vicious circle' of which you were talking just now; but where shall we find a syndicate who will be sufficiently respectable to inspire confidence, and yet be guilty of such practices?"

"My innocent Twig, have you lived so long in this world," said the Captain, with calm superiority, "and not found out yet that confidence in matters of finance is not inspired because a man deserves it, but because he has accumulated vast wealth by a long and successful career of fraud? Leave this to me – I will find the syndicate: they will pay for the concessions; and whether they are afterwards 'stuck' with the shares, or succeed in palming them off on the public, surely does not concern us."

"And how much shall we ourselves make out of it?" asked Sir Twig, with an eye to the main chance.

"Can't say. We shall ask £250,000, and probably take £50,000, which makes £25,000 each. However, put yourself unreservedly into my hands, my dear Twig, and you won't have any reason to complain." Saying which, the Captain nodded in a reassuring manner, took up his hat, and swaggered off, soliloquising thus as he went along. From my advantageous position in his breast-pocket I could hear him plainly.

"This little matter looks tolerably healthy. I shall get £25,000 for my half of the concession. Considering I deposited no caution money, and I bled Twig pretty freely in the matter of expenses, I shan't lose on that. If I introduce my syndicate man to a good contractor, the latter will have to pay me at least one per cent commission on the contract price, which certainly does not concern my Twig. After all, he has only paid £15,000 in caution money and expenses, and he will make, without any exertion of brain, £10,000 on that, which, considering that he has no brains to exert, ought to satisfy him."

I wondered, as we went along, where my Promoter was going to, but was soon enlightened, as he turned in to some handsome offices, and I observed the names of Chisel Bros., the well-known contractors, on the door. Mr. Chisel was engaged; but my Promoter waited patiently to see the great man, who was evidently in no hurry to see him, and made him a cold suspicious bow, as he offered him a chair. "What I am about to say," remarked the Captain, with the bold assurance of one about to confer a favour, "must be considered absolutely private and confidential. A certain friend of mine, who is of the highest respectability, and moves in the first social circles – in fact I may tell you, under the pledge of secrecy, that he is a baronet, is the possessor of certain most valuable concessions" – here the Captain explained in general terms their nature, and went on, – "Now I have come to tell you that some City friends of mine, a most powerful combination of capitalists – men, I need scarcely say, of first-class financial standing, as you would yourself acknowledge if I was permitted to divulge their names – are inclined to take up the scheme. I thought that the project was one which would just suit you, and that if you felt inclined to undertake the contract, it would be useful to you to be introduced to the capitalists interested. I should be glad to present you to them; but in order to be able to talk to my friends, I should be happy to know what your prices are for carrying out the proposed works."

Mr. Chisel here fixed my Promoter with his eyes, and asked him bluntly for the names of his financial friends. With an air of profound secrecy, but with an appearance of absolute *bonâ fides*, the Captain as steadily retuned the glance, as he replied, "I have already said I am not at liberty to give you their names; but if you keep it entirely secret, I may say this, that one of the partners of Cash, Bullion, & Co. is interested in the matter." I literally trembled in his pocket as my Promoter uttered this unblushing falsehood; but he evidently knew his man. The name of the firm, combined with the imperturbable calm of the Captain's manner, seemed to affect the contractor; and with a furtive side glance at him, he said, as he carelessly turned over the leaves of a book on the table, "Do you want our prices net, or will they include any commissions?"

"They will include one per cent commission for me," replied the Captain, coolly, but firmly.

Mr. Chisel seemed prepared for this, and quietly dismissed his visitor with the assurance that he would soon hear from him, and that he would make an estimate of the prices.

My promoter instantly hurried eastward, murmuring, as he went, "Chisel bites – and so he ought, for there has not been a sounder or a better thing put on the market this long time; now the only thing is to find the powerful combination of capitalists I told Chisel I had found already. I suppose there is not a chance of Cash, Bullion, & Co. going into it. But, confound it! When he pressed me so hard, I had to give some name, and under those circumstances there is no reason why one should not give the best; but I must see them first, just to save appearances if Chisel ever calls on me to explain my statements." And to Cash, Bullion, & Co. he accordingly went. A frigid reception and still more frigid refusal was all he got there; but he seemed rather to enjoy the joke than otherwise, and, with a chuckle to himself, proceeded in quest of that less scrupulous class amongst whom he knew that his powerful combination could alone be found.

I will not weary my reader with a narrative of all the conversations to which I listened during the various visits which my Promoter now paid; and, indeed, if I have been obliged to go into so much detail hitherto, it has been because it is impossible to convey any just idea of how these negotiations are carried on without it. First he tried Squeezer, a powerful man well known in the world of finance; but though he acknowledged the excellence of the scheme, his terms were too high, and it was evident that he would be satisfied with nothing less than the lion's share. This worthy had been successful in bringing out about a hundred companies, at least ninety of which had since become bankrupt, though he himself had realised an immense fortune in giving birth to them. Next he dangled me in vain before the eyes of Shaver, who generally victimised his dupes with a joke, but who, at this particular juncture, had too many irons in the fire to take me up.

He was unable to come to terms with Rigger, because that gentleman demanded that £60,000 should be set aside out of the preliminary expenses for "making a market," which, as the Captain has already explained, consisted in dealing in the shares of the future Company, the moment the prospectus had appeared, and before the shares had been allotted, at figures much above what would have been taken for them except from purchasers eager to maintain a fictitious high price; which operation, the Captain knew, was ordinarily carried out at about one-sixth of the money asked by Rigger, who intended to pocket the balance. This process seemed to me not only novel, but immoral; but when I saw the evidence which was taken the other day before the Foreign Loans Committee, I found it was as common in the floating of foreign loans, as in the bringing out of joint-stock companies. Sharper seemed more hopeful, and at one time I thought we should come to terms; but he had his own contractor; and my Promoter, fearing the loss of his commission, hurriedly terminated the interview, and pushed on in search of some more pliant gentleman.

I was surprised at the number of his acquaintances: without describing them *seriatim*, I may give a general outline of our mode of procedure. We always seemed desirous to shun observation, and to approach the great man we were in quest of as quietly as possible. The very clerks seemed to entertain a certain feeling of contempt for us, and knowing looks passed between them as my Promoter's card was taken to the sanctum of the millionaire. At first I used to feel this humiliation; but as I saw my inventor was perfectly stolid, I soon ceased to feel sensitive on the subject. On no one occasion that I remember were we at once admitted, but generally kept waiting in some dingy little back room for an hour or two, during which time my Promoter was preparing his part. I now, to my great delight, became aware, by the contrast which his manner presented to the personages to whom I was submitted for inspection, that my Promoter was a gentleman. There was a delicate combination of dignity, mystery, and reserve which struck me as very effective; and I used to wonder how any one could resist the low persuasive tones and explicit definitions with which my great advantages were described. I even myself really believed that I should be the means of making the fortunes of all who had anything to do with me; and felt quite irritated at the cold suspicious manner in which my merits were treated, the objections which were raised to me, and the evident doubt with which I was often regarded. The peculiarity of all these magnates seemed to be that they were very purse-proud, very grasping, very overbearing, and generally more or less vulgar; the richer they were, and the more convinced they became that I really was of some intrinsic value, the more unreasonable they seemed to get, and I quite sympathised with my poor Promoter's repeated disappointments. By degrees he dropped from the eminent financier to the eminent stockbroker, from the eminent stockbroker to the doubtful financier, from the doubtful financier to the German Jews; and it was among this latter fraternity that at last he found a man willing to take me up. His name was Mire. He was a person of great activity, great perseverance, parsimonious habits, grasping in his transactions, and one who, although possessed of great affection for all the members of his family scattered about in various countries, was not averse to cheating them when he could realise a respectable margin thereby. He took me up coolly at first, but grew warmer and warmer over me as he spent some time in considering my merits. Finally, he told the Captain that he would give him an answer on the following day; as he wanted to consult his solicitors, the eminent firm of Twister, Wriggle, Sly, & Wriggle.

The Captain occupied the interval by seeing Chisel's manager, explaining to him that Mire had taken up the affair, and that circumstances had arisen in consequence which made it advisable that Cash, Bullion, & Co. should not be mixed up in it; and he received from the manager the prices which had been promised, and a great deal of technical information, primed with which he kept his appointment with Mire. That gentleman began by making difficulties, said that the public were not ripe for enterprises of the sort, that the capital wanted was very large, the state of the market very bad (the Captain happened to know that the market had never been more buoyant), and that it would be difficult to find a good contractor willing to take it up. At this point the Captain interrupted with great effect, and poured out his recently-acquired knowledge with a volubility which somewhat disconcerted Mire, to whom he explained that for certain technical reasons connected with the nature of the works, there was in fact only one contractor in England who was really competent to carry out so magnificent and gigantic an enterprise, but that he fortunately was prepared to undertake it practically without making his legitimate profit, as it was indispensable to him to crush a rival firm, who were seriously threatening his pre-eminence in that particular line. Mire gave a deliberate wink, as if he distrusted this latter piece of intelligence; but his intense desire to get a good bargain overruled his better judgment, and he relented. After a prolonged negotiation, in which some very pretty fencing took place, showing great wariness, coolness, steadiness of purpose, and self-control on both sides, Mire agreed to take up the matter and to form a syndicate, on condition that he should be syndicate manager. The following terms were agreed upon: The contact was given to Messrs Chisel Bros. Mire here asked, "What is the price net?" The Captain replied, £1,500,000. "I understand you," said Mr. Mire, "to say this is absolutely net?"

"Absolutely," said the Captain, with a calmness which caused me a painful feeling of distress, well knowing as I did that it included one per cent commission to himself. After a long and searching look into the Captain's inscrutable physiognomy, Mr. Mire seemed evidently satisfied, and said, with a knowing look, "My dear sir, have you mentioned this price to anybody but me?"

"I have not," rejoined the Captain.

"Then," said Mire, "let us tell the contractors they must ask for £1,515,000. I must have something for my troubles."

"I presume," blandly remarked the Captain, "one-third of this will go to me."

Mire seemed to undergo a convulsion; he sprang from his chair and violently paced the room. "I thought, sir," at last he remarked, planting himself firmly before the Captain, "that you acted on behalf of the concessionaire, and you will have to look to that gentleman for your remuneration."

"Very well," drily replied the Captain. "As nobody knows what the contractor's net price really is, if you make any difficulty about my standing in, I shall take care that the contractor will refuse to ask for a higher price than the one he actually receives. Indeed, although I am aware that this practice is not uncommon with other contractors, it will be difficult in this case, anyhow, to induce so respectable a firm to consent to it."

Finally, it was arranged as a first condition that the Captain would agree to overcome the contractor's scruples on this point for a percentage of one-sixth of the commission to be given by the contractor to Mr. Mire. Second, that Mr. Mire should be syndicate manager, which post, as it afterwards turned out, involved a variety of commissions. Third, that the concessions of Sir Twig Robinson should be bought for £50,000. On this point there was also considerable haggling, the Captain having begun by asking £150,000 for the concessions. "The little business" being so far settled, Mr. Mire produced a box of cigars and a bottle of capital sherry; and, fifteen minutes later, the Captain left the office in high spirits, with the promise of an interview with Mr. Mire on the following day at his solicitor's. From all of which you will perceive, O my investing readers, how much trouble it takes to prepare the gaudy fly by which you are ultimately to be hooked. Nobody knows what running about, and worry, and meetings, and appointments, and disappointments, and wrangling, are involved in the promotion of a company – what patience it requires, what constant watchfulness, lest by one false move the labours of months are neutralised, and the profits swept away by a stoke of sharp practice on the part of a friend and a brother. My Promoter's anxiety of mind during this trying period involved a perpetual recourse to stimulants, and he almost lived in Hansom cabs.

His next interview with Mire was in the office of the eminent solicitors already alluded to. There he met a small closely-shaved gentleman, with sharp pinched features and an oily manner – Mr. Wriggle, to wit; and there also were present several of Mr. Mire's powerful financial friends, whose names are of no importance. For many successive days did this little group meet in close conclave, their principal duty being to write to, and produce their correspondence with, their financial friends abroad, whom they had urged to join them in the enterprise, and become members of the syndicate, and who wished to be informed in regard to sundry details. At one of these meetings the contractor and his solicitor appeared on the scene. The contractor insisted that the whole of the capital of the intended Company should be "taken firm" by the syndicate before the prospectus was issued; which, I find out, means, that the various financial gentlemen who form the syndicate are required to sign a letter, which is called a syndicate letter. The skeleton of this letter ran as follows:

The X. Y. Z. Co. (Limited).
(Of course my real name was given here.)
To be incorporated under the Companies Acts 1862 and 1867.
Capital £____, in one hundred thousand shares of £____ each.

To the Manager of the Syndicate.

Sir, – We authorise you to place our name on the syndicate for raising the cash capital of this Company for a subscription of £____. We understand that Sir Twig Robinson, Bart., is prepared to sell several valuable concessions from foreign Governments and municipalities for the sum of £____, and Messrs Chisel Bros. are prepared to enter into a contract for the construction of . . . at a total contract price of £____ in cash, and £____ in fully paid up shares of the Company. We guarantee to the extent of our subscription the raising of the whole of the above-mentioned capital of £____; and further, that if the whole of such capital shall not within one month from the date hereof be otherwise applied for, the members of the syndicate will themselves subscribe for a sufficient number of shares to make good the deficiency; on the understanding that, by way of remuneration for our trouble and influence in establishing and bringing out the Company, and in raising the capital, and as a consideration for our entering into the above-mentioned undertaking, Messrs Chisel Bros. will pay to bankers to be agreed upon on behalf of the syndicate, a sum of £____, which is equivalent to seventeen per cent of the capital of the Company, that sum to be appropriated as follows: Two per cent on the capital or the sum of £____, to be paid to the syndicate manager for syndicate management and expenses, and the remaining fifteen per cent or £____ to be divisible *pro rata* among the members of the syndicate. – We are, Sir, your obedient servants.

This somewhat complicated document was printed and shown to the eminent financiers assembled, in a guarded manner, as productions of this sort are of too delicate a character to leave the hands of the initiated few who are promoting the Company. Its real purport only became clear to me after I had overheard the following explanation of it by the Captain to Sir Twig, to whom he showed a copy of the letter, the intelligence of the hon. Baronet being quite unequal to grasping its meaning on a bare perusal.

"My dear fellow," said Sir Twig, after having laboriously endeavoured to master its contents, "you might as well have expected me to understand an Egyptian papyrus as this long-winded yarn. What does it all mean?"

"Well, Twig, it becomes plain enough when you have had as much to do with promotion work as I have. We want to be paid for the concession; it is an essential preliminary to this that the capital of the Company be found: if you advertise the prospectus, the public may or may not subscribe to it. To make it a certainty, we find a small lot of financiers first, which, as I before explained, is called a Syndicate, to subscribe for the whole of the shares. The shares are then offered to the public for subscription. Whatever amount is applied for by the public is allotted to them at par; whatever amount remains is taken up by the members of the syndicate, in the proportion of their original subscription, so that a man who figures in the syndicate as a subscriber for one-tenth of the capital has to take one-tenth of the shares which have not been subscribed for by the public. In consideration of this risk he receives a syndicate commission of, say, fifteen per cent on the whole of his original subscription in the syndicate; so that if he has subscribed £50,000, and the public take all the shares, he receives £7,500 for having affixed his name to a syndicate letter, and without having disbursed a farthing. If the public subscribes half, he receives the same commission, but has to take up £25,000 worth of shares, and so on."

"That is clear so far," said Twig; "but I don't see who is to pay them the fifteen per cent. Who do they get it out of – the public?"

"Of course out of the public in the long run, but in the first instance out of the contractor. It is clear that the Company cannot openly allot shares to the public at par, and to the syndicate at 85. That would be illegal. The situation therefore has to be turned. This is easily managed by sticking the syndicate commission secretly into the contract price which appears in the public prospectus; and the contractor equally secretly hands back this commission to the syndicate when he receives his first instalment from the Company."

After many days spent in negotiation and preliminary haggling over further details too minute and complicated for me to go into here, and sundry financial firms had risen freely at the tempting bait offered to them, some boldly dashing at it, others shyly coquetting with it, a certain number were sufficiently firmly hooked to be brought to the point of signing; and a meeting was held of all those intending to become members of the syndicate with the contractor, the Promotor, Mire's solicitor, who was to become the solicitor of the Company, and the contractor's solicitor.

The syndicate was to consist of upwards of seventy members, of whom, however, only thirteen attended, acting for themselves and their friends. Mr. Mire had in the meantime prepared and finally settled the memorandum and articles of association of the future Company – a contract for the conveyance of the various concessions of Sir Twig Robinson to the new Company, and the contract to be entered into between Messrs Chisel Bros., on the one part, and Mr. Mire, acting on behalf of and for the future Company, on the other part, and a deed of transfer of such contract from Mr. Mire to the future Company.

Printed copies of all these documents were profusely scattered over the table. Their backs were neatly lined with red tape, as though to impart an air of respectability to their contents.

While they were assembling, these gentlemen collected in groups and talked finance until they were called to order by a sort of admonitory cough from Mr. Mire, who took a chair which happened to be at the top of the table, and addressed the meeting as follows: –

> "Well, gentlemen, you are all aware of the nature of the business which has brought us together today: the valuable concessions of Sir Twig Robinson, who is represented by our friend Captain Hawk, are to be taken over by the Company which we propose to form. Mr. Wriggle, the deeds of transfer are, I presume, in order?"

Mr. Wriggle nodded assent. "The contract with Messrs Chisel Bros.," pursued Mr. Mire, "has been in your hands for the past week, and I should be glad of any observations referring thereto which any of you, gentlemen, might desire to make."

At this moment a funereal-looking individual in a suit of black, gaunt and scraggy, with high cheekbones and a sanctimonious expression of countenance, interposed and said in unctuous tones, which seemed rather more appropriate to a meeting in a dissenting chapel than of a syndicate Committee: –

> "It appears to me that the 45th clause of the contract does not sufficiently provide for the penalty to be incurred by the contractor in case of the completion of the works being delayed for more than two days beyond the time specified in clause three. I observe that the contractor is not bound to pay any forfeits, not only in the case of an interference by *force majeure*, to which, of course, nobody amongst us could object," and he threw a glance reverently upwards, "but also in the case of a strike amongst his workmen; it appears to me that in a Christian country like ours, it is utterly unnecessary if not injurious to public morality to secure the contractor against a contingency which cannot arise if he chooses his workmen only among converted and God-fearing men."

The contractor maintained that this observation was founded on fallacy, and that his experience had proved to him that workmen were pretty much alike when it came to the question of a rise in their wages, no matter what their professions might be.

The contractor's solicitor here interfered, and produced a number of similar contracts entered into with other companies which all contained the same clause, and to which no such objection had ever before been taken. It was finally overruled. The gaunt gentleman observed that there were a great many other points in the contract to which he could not assent, and he proposed therefore to take the contract clause by clause. As his name was down on the syndicate list for by far the largest amount, no serious objection could be raised to this. It would weary the reader, as it certainly did the syndicate, were I to attempt to enumerate the objections raised by this perverse and pious millionaire to almost every point contained in the contract. He was only finally interrupted by a portly and jovial-looking personage declaring he felt faint, and that it was time to adjourn for lunch. At this meal the contractor managed cleverly to sit next the lugubrious objector, whose name was Sarmist, and a whispered conversation took place between them, which I managed to overhear, and which resulted in a secret offer from the contractor of a commission of two per cent on the contract price if the scruples of that high-minded man could be overcome on all the points raised by him, and the contract could be admitted as it stood now. Mr. Sarmist rejoined that two per cent was not enough, and that he could not possibly waive his scruples for less than three. I now understood the motive which had prompted his obstructive conduct throughout. The contractor refused absolutely to accede to this, feeling sure that the other was only "trying it on," and would ultimately take two.

The sherry at luncheon seemed to have a salutary effect upon the transaction of the business, for Mr. Samrist retained an attitude of dogged silence during the subsequent proceedings, while the jovial gentleman was smoothing away difficulties and winning over waverers whose natural dispositions were not so sanguine as his own, until, as the day closed in, the meeting was adjourned, and everybody seem to feel a certain amount of relief in the reflection that matters had been nearly brought to a head, and that one more sitting would at last give me definite existence, crown the hopes of my Promoter, and line the pockets in various proportions of the gentlemen who so kindly and disinterestedly invented for the public its latest want, and now modestly undertook the means of supplying it.

It was proposed to meet again on the following day. Mr. Sarmist, however, with an expression of profound regret, announced that a meeting at Exeter Hall demanded his presence, and begged those present, in solemn tones, to adjourn reassembling for two days. This was agreed to. With a light and buoyant step my Promoter wended his way homewards. He calculated as he did so what this, his last venture, was likely to prove worth to him. The schedule which he worked out in his mind, if put on paper, would read thus: –

Price of concession, . . .	£50,000
Old Twig out of pocket, . . .	15,000
Leaves to be divided . . .	£35,000
Half of that for me, . . .	£17,500
One per cent on contract price, . . .	15,000
One-sixth of old Jew's commission, . . .	2,500
Total, . . .	£35,000

As this figure presented itself to his imagination, a radiant smile overspread his countenance, and I felt his heart beat faster with the throb of pleasant anticipation. For a moment, but only for a moment, this feeling was checked by the sad recollection of the numerous former occasions on which a cup equally overflowing had been rudely dashed from his lips; but he regained confidence as he recalled the instant when his sharp eye detected the contractor in secret conversation with Mr. Sarmist, and the change which it affected in that pious gentleman's subsequent demeanour.

I must here remind my reader that having been printed in so many forms, I now filled the pockets of all the syndicate members, and that it was owing to this circumstance that I overheard the following conversation in Mr. Mire's office.

That gentleman was engaged in affixing his valuable signature to sundry invoices for a large cargo of tallow, when Mr. Sarmist's name was announced by a seedy-looking junior clerk with a hooked nose. Mr. Mire quietly turned on their faces all the letters which happened to be lying open before him on his desk, and signified his willingness to receive his visitor.

"I have come to speak to you, Mr. Mire," said the gentleman, with whom it had been my misfortune to be present at the meeting which we had just quitted at Exeter Hall, "about the contracts to be entered into for the X. Y. Z. Co. I have received distressing information this morning that several of my Continental friends have changed their minds about joining the syndicate, as they first intended. This would entail (if the Company for which we are working is to succeed) the contractor's taking a certain amount of his price in fully paid-up shares. From confidential inquiries which I have had made, it appears that Chisel Bros., though excellent contractors, have already rather more paper than they like, and that they would hardly be in a position to take anything but a cash contract. I have called, therefore, on Messrs Gouge & Co., limited, who are willing to execute the works for £1,350,000 in cash, and £250,000 in shares."

"This is about £100,000 more," Mr. Mire replied, "than Messrs Chisel Bros. have asked; and as to their taking part of the contract price in shares, I have no doubt whatever that they could make as favourable terms as Gouge & Co.' besides, Mr. Sarmist," he added, with a grave countenance, "it would be hardly fair and business-like – and certainly injurious to my reputation for straightforward dealing – to throw over at the last moment a contractor with whom we have gone so far."

After a good deal of skirmishing, Mr. Sarmist, who seemed to have good reason for preferring Messrs Gouge & Co., limited, drew his chair close up to Mr. Mire's, and having assured himself that the door was locked, said to him –

> "I may tell you, my dear sir, that in point of fact their price is rather lower than Chisel's, being only £1,250,000 in cash, and a quarter of a million in shares – £100,000 being available for distribution amongst their friends."

"In cash, or in shares?" asked Mr. Mire.

"In cash," replied Mr. Sarmist, watching the effect that this announcement would produce upon his antagonist.

"Well," said Mr. Mire, "this looks like business: how much of that would go to me?"

"Half," responded the other.

"Done," said Mire, unhesitatingly.

My heart sank when I thought of my poor Promoter's schedule, and heard this nefarious bargain struck. The two worthies then engaged in minute calculations as to the distribution of the funds. It was found absolutely necessary to reduce the price of the concession to £25,000. This gave me another pang on the unlucky Captain's behalf; and for the first time I became aware that the *concessionaires* were practically powerless, and that those who had most capital at their backs really divided the spoil, and dictated their terms to everybody else. After a long and close confabulation, a schedule was drawn up and agreed to between Messrs Mire and Sarmist.

This version of the schedule was, as a matter of course, kept perfectly secret between the two gentlemen, who, with a smile of mutual respect, congratulated each other upon "standing in on the ground-floor," as they significantly expressed it. A second schedule was then prepared for the benefit of the syndicate and *concessionaires*, to be submitted to them at the meeting on the following day. This body was only to be allowed to stand in on the next floor, and of course knew nothing of what took place on the ground-floor. And lastly, a third schedule was prepared to form the basis of the prospectus which was to be offered to the *bonâ fide* investors among a confiding public, who naturally were not to be allowed to stand in on any floor.

I give the three schedules side by side for the better edification of this last class of my readers, who will appreciate their position on the tiles

THE X. Y. Z. COMPANY, LIMITED.

***Capital* £2,000,000.**

Schedule for Miro and Sarmist (*ground floor*).		Schedule for Syndicate (*first floor*).			Schedule to be used for public prospectus (*on the tiles*).	
Contract price shares,	£250,000	Contract price shares,		£250,000	Concession,	£25,000
,, cash, .	1,250,000	,, cash,		1,350,000	Working capital,	45,000
		17% on £1,750,000, .		297,500	Contract,	1,930,000
	£1,500,000	Prel. Ex.—				
Wanted in cash—		Making market, .	£20,000			£2,000,000
17% on £2,000,000		Law, .	2,000			
Less 250,000 shares.		Brokerage,	3,000			
£1,750,000 .	£297,500	Press, .	2,000			
Contract, . .	1,250,000	Advertising,	5,000			
X X X, . .	100,000	Contingencies,	500			
Working Capital, .	45,000					
Concession, . .	25,000		£32,500	32,500		
Making market, .	20,000					
Law, . . .	2,000	Concession, . .		25,000		
Brokerage, . .	3,000	Working Capital, .		45,000		
Press, . . .	2,000					
Advertising, . .	5,000			£2,000,000		
Contingencies, . .	500					
	1,750,000					
Shares, . .	250,000					
Capital, . .	£2,000,000					

Fair female investor, youthful scion of nobility, confiding officer on half-pay, gentle curate, dull squire, do not turn from an examination of this dreadful-looking sheet of figures because it is dry and complicated, but try to understand the explanation I am now going to give of it. You will see from the first column how a company is started with a capital of £2,000,000 to get works done which only cost £1,500,000, to acquire concessions which cost £25,000, and to retain a working capital of £45,000. The difference of £430,000 is spent as follows: £100,000 are absorbed by what Mr. Sarmist delicately styles X X X, in order not to do violence to his own religious sentiments, but by what is called, according to the individual tastes of financing men, "loot," "plunder," "faux frais" (an expression used by the more travelled and cosmopolitan financiers), "pull," swim," and "margin." In the particular instance you are investigating, the Jew and the Christian each stole half of this amount, which rightfully belonged to my shareholders.

From this example you will perceive that the highest aim of every financier engaged in work of this description is "to stand in on the ground-floor." £297,500 were spent in a syndicate commission, the nature of which my Promoter has already carefully explained to Sir Twig; £20,000 were spent in "making a market" – a swindling process also I hope made clear to you. Lawyers, brokers, advertising agents, and a small contingency fund, absorbed legitimately enough £2,000, £3,000, £ 5,000, £500 respectively; and £2,000 were distributed among the gentlemen of the independent press, in order to impress them favourably with my undoubted merits. The greater part of this sum, however, was refused by all the more respectable members of journalism, and Mire and Sarmist of course pocketed what remained. The second schedule only differs in so far from the first that the contract appears to be £100,000 higher, as this amount, which has already been secretly appropriated by the two gentlemen living on the ground-floor, could not be disclosed to the lodgers on the floor above. The third schedule differs very widely from the two former, as it only contains what can in common decency be mentioned to the public. The contractor here appears as taking for his contract, and for preliminary expenses, a sum which exceeds his real price by exactly £430,000; and many a time, when his friends congratulated him upon his gigantic enterprises and advantageous contracts, he mournfully thought to himself how little of the first instalment of his nominal price ever found its way into his banker's account. However, he had no reason to complain, because when my works came to be made I found to my surprise that they really did not quite cost a million. So that, for doing work which, in fact, scarcely cost a million, and for holding his tongue about what happened to the other half million, he was paid a million and a half.

Hence my total capital came to be two millions.

On the following day, the powerful influence of Mire and Sarmist carried their scheme. The syndicate did not raise much objection to the change of contractor, as they got their seventeen per cent. The poor Captain, who neither got his one per cent from Chisel Bros. nor his part of Mire's commission from the same firm – they having been dropped at the eleventh hour – and who only got at last £25,000 instead of £50,000 for the concessions, saw his bright dream of £35,000 vanish, and found himself a winner of only £5,000 on the whole transaction. Sir Twig, of course, received the same, but immediately lost it at the next Derby. Chisel never forgave himself for having gauged his man so badly, and not having been more wary in his dealings with one so profuse in Christian profession as Mr. Sarmist; and his former antagonism to Gouge & Co., Limited, has derived a bitterness all the more intense because he so nearly carried off the prize himself.

This practically terminated my existence as an embryo. I shortly after saw the light of day, and received my formal name at the hands of the Register of Joint-Stock Companies.

One more step, however, had to be taken on my behalf before I could be introduced in a complete shape to the investing British public. My Board had not yet been constituted, and my success now mainly depended upon the air of respectability which might be imparted to me by the names of the gentlemen who could be induced to sit on it. Messrs Mire and Sarmist were, of course, among the number; but unfortunately their names inspired no confidence in the City, and were utterly unknown anywhere else. It became necessary to find persons who possessed the two rare and valued attributes of a director – a high social standing and an entire ignorance of business: this latter somewhat negative quality being thought indispensable by Mire and Sarmist, to enable them to exchange their functions as members and managers of the syndicate, for the equally dignified and not less lucrative position of wire-pullers – in other words, they wished to retain in their own hands the control of the Company's fortunes for the purpose of manipulating its operations with a view to their own private aggrandisement.

The process of forming a Board has been so recently revealed in the columns of the daily press, that it is not necessary for me to go into any detail in regard to it. I was no exception to the general rule. A noble lord, an ex-Minister of a foreign State, a Right Honourable, a General K.C.B., and four Members of Parliament, were secured mainly by the exertions of a well-connected young man of fashion, who received the usual commission; and duly qualified themselves by accepting a present of the necessary number of fully paid-up shares, in return for the dazzling effect which it was confidently and not unreasonably anticipated their names would produce upon the country public. It is due to these gentlemen to say that they were so firmly convinced of their own value, that it did not occur to them that there was anything wrong in selling themselves in this way; and I have always felt that any reflection upon their honesty was most unfair. It is natural that a duped public should be indignant with every one connected with the cause of their disasters, but let me assure you that nearly all these gentlemen sinned purely through ignorance and indiscretion. I found them invariably struggling to be honest all the time they were on my Board, and vainly attempting to comprehend and thwart the nefarious schemes of Mire and Sarmist. That they did not succeed, and ultimately drew upon themselves the anathemas of an exasperated public, was the result of being tempted by a plausible touter, with the prospect of increasing their limited incomes, into engaging in matters of which they had no experience, and of a certain fascination which the idea of directorial responsibility and dignity exercises upon certain weak minds.

A prospectus setting forth my merits in the most glowing terms, and promising a return of unheard-of dividends, was now printed in all the papers, and freely circulated through the means of an advertising agency, which had a list of all the names of unhappy shareholders in other companies. So well was my prospectus drawn, so overwhelming was the brilliancy of my Board, that my shares were greedily subscribed for; and I found myself established in handsome offices, with a board-room which became a favourite lounge with sundry of my directors, and a manager, secretary, and an array of clerks and officials which made me the envy of my neighbours. I need scarcely say that my manager was the nominee of Mire and Sarmist. This gentleman possessed an invaluable physique; his flowing grey locks, and general air of matured sagacity and intense respectability, which he heightened by wearing a white tie, produced an invariably reassuring effect upon shareholders. But he lived in a perpetual thraldom, for he was bound with chains which had been dexterously thrown round him by the two cunning intriguers to whom he owed his position, and who, while they never allowed him to forget the debt of gratitude he was under, had taken care to place him still more absolutely in their power by the loan of one thousand pounds, which his extravagant habits made it impossible for him to think of repaying.

We were now in a position to usher in our prosperous career by a magnificent banquet. This was by no means an original idea. Messrs Mire and Sarmist had already upon previous occasions proved by experience the splendid effect which a display of this kind has upon the public, and no pains were spared to secure the presence of a distinguished company; the services of the young gentleman who had helped to provide the directors were again in request, and the result was a plentiful sprinkling of noble lords, scientific men, distinguished *litterateurs* and gentlemen of the press, city capitalists, and Members of Parliament. There was the usual amount of speech-making, consisting mainly of mutual compliments which were paid by the scientific gentlemen to the capitalists on their wonderful enterprise, and by the capitalists to the scientific men on their no less remarkable attainments; the General K.C.B. returned thanks in a facetious speech for the army, which thus found itself unexpectedly allied to commerce and science; the peers whose presence "graced the auspicious occasion" felt themselves "honoured by being allowed to take part in an undertaking which reflected so much credit upon the spirit and enterprise of Englishmen;" and the Members of the House of Commons who responded for that body, committed it recklessly in all future time to watch over and protect my interests; the literary men pretended that they regarded with envy the more distinguished career on which their fellow countrymen had entered; and the gentleman who replied to the toast in behalf of the fifth estate, was profuse in his eulogium of Messrs Mire and Sarmist, and in his predictions of the future success of the company, – all which proceedings were duly chronicled in the papers of the following morning, as my readers may verify by an examination of the press of the period.

The sober, and as it would appear to the world the legitimate work of the undertaking of which I was the embodiment, now commenced. The works were executed one by one, as the shareholders were informed at the first public meeting, in the most brilliant and satisfactory manner; but frequent discussions between the contractor and my Board convinced me that the former was endeavouring to do as little as possible for the price, and was attempting to put on "extras" whenever opportunity offered. A period of about a year and a half was thus spent, at the expiration of which time my works were completed, and I entered upon my functions as a public benefactor. My operations were a decided success, in spite of the high remuneration set aside for the directors' services, and of the appointment of a numerous staff of ignorant connections and nominees of the directors, irreverently termed by the really efficient employés "Directors' puppies." My intrinsic merits were so great that large receipts were taken, and there was every prospect of a high dividend being paid at an early date.

I was surprised to find that my anxious shareholders were by no means well informed by my Board as to my excellent prospects, but that profound secrecy was maintained in regard to my actual position. From the frequent conversations which I overheard between my manager and sundry gentlemen who rushed in and out of his office gaily dressed, and with a noisy and impudent air – whom I, by degrees, discovered to be brokers – I became aware, to my intense regret, that my shares were being freely knocked up and down in the market; and after having listened to frequent extraordinary conversations carried on in the slang peculiar to all engaged in Stock Exchange transactions, I finally realised that Mire and Sarmist were ultimately becoming what they styled "bulls" or "bears" of my shares. They carried out their operations by spreading rumours sometimes detrimental, sometimes favourable to my interests. They never failed to take advantage of the turn of the market which had thus been influenced by them. Their best *coup* was made immediately prior to the declaration of my first dividend. My earning had been so large that a high dividend should have been paid. Mire and Sarmist, however, obstinately insisted upon the absolute necessity of laying by a large reserve fund; and so strongly objected to what they termed "stuffing shareholders with dividends," that for some time it really appeared that only a low dividend would be declared. This prospect, of course, soon finding its way into the Stock Exchange, depressed my shares considerably. Mire and Sarmist thereupon bought largely, and relented at the next Board meeting in their objections to a high dividend, which was eventually declared. My shares flew up with a bound, and the clever pair cleared out with a large profit.

Up to this time my career had, although not free from the influence of all the refined forms of swindling which our advanced civilisation makes possible, and almost encourages, been one of unbroken prosperity. Indeed my success was so palpable that rumours soon reached me of a competing company being promoted. My old friend the Captain easily overcame the scruples of Messrs Gouge & Co., who at first thought it unfair to assist in starting an opposition company to the one out of which they had made so much profit; and after the usual sharp practice, and the many vicissitudes of promotion had been successfully encountered, my competitor was at last fairly started.

The state of terror which was now created amongst my Board was pitiable to behold; while Mire and Sarmist experienced the most intense indignation at anybody's daring to invade what they considered their private field of enterprise. These two worthies, however, eventually consoled themselves when they found a congenial friend on the Borad of the rival company in the person of Sir Verrikute Trimmer, who made common cause with them, furnished them with all possible information regarding my young enemy in return for being well supplied with the latest news about my own health and circumstances; and they all three operated cleverly in harmony, so as effectually to plunder the shareholders in both companies. When my competitor's works were completed a brisk competition ensued. My rival's Board addressed themselves to the public in the capacity of general benefactors – the same work which had been performed by me at a remunerative rate to my shareholders was to be done by my new-born rival much more cheaply. The effect of this was a great loss to both of us, and a consequent fall in our shares. This went on for some time; everybody connected with either of us, whether shareholder or director, felt profoundly miserable. Even the very managers, who, as enjoying fixed salaries, cared little for the amount of the dividends earned, began to yield to the general feeling of gloom; only the recently-constituted triumvirate of Mire and Sarmist on my Board, and Sir Virrikute on the other, chuckled and rubbed their hands in an unostentatious and modest sort of way as they agreed upon one move after the other, which had the effect of still further depressing our revenues, and proportionately drove down our shares. All this time the three conspirators were heavy "bears," and made large amounts.

It was during this period that I for the first time understood what it meant to be a bear. The process of operation is as follows: Sir Verrikute, for instance, operating for joint account as a bear, calls into his sanctum in his City abode, one fine morning, one of his junior clerks. "Mr. Jones," says the chief, "will you send for one of the partners of Contango, Backwardation, and Margin, and tell them to sell £100,000 of X. Y. Z. for you." Mr. Jones, who is a rosy-cheeked, guileless youth, with a flower in his button-hole, drops his not over-intelligent countenance very considerably indeed. "Beg your pardon, sir; sell what?" "Send for the broker," says Sir Verrikute, gruffly; "I want *you* to sell a bear.: The broker arrives, and Mr. Jones tells him – having been ordered to do so by his chief – to sell for him, Jones, £100,000 worth of X. Y. Z. shares, wondering all the time how on earth he could sell such a fortune in securities of which he never owned a single pound's worth in his life. Nor had his principal the shares either in his possession. The intelligent transaction simply consisted in this: Sir Verrikute sold through an impecunious clerk, who acted as nominee, £100,000 of X. Y. Z. shares which he did not possess. The purchaser paid £100,000 for them. The shares would, in the ordinary routine of business, have to be delivered about a fortnight hence or later; and Sir Verrikute knew well that by that time he might buy them for £90,000, as he was running them down in conjunction with Mire and Sarmist by proceedings injurious to both companies, but justified by them on the ground of exigencies of competition, public convenience, and so on. So, at the last moment, he bought himself for delivery at £90,000 what he had sold fourteen days previously for £100,000, thus getting the advantage of the unwary purchaser, who was, of course, not "in the swim," to the tune of £10,000.

At last the ruinous effects of competition began to tell so severely upon both companies that the directors revolved to open negotiations for an amalgamation. This, again, was done in the most secret way; and while terms were being negotiated which could not but raise the price of my shares enormously whenever they should become known, Mire, Sarmist, and Sir Verrikute were buying shares, to the full extent of their available cash balances, at a low figure; and, as it afterwards turned out, again realised largely when the amalgamation was consummated and the shares rose in consequence.

It must not, however, be imagined that all the proceeds of their enterprising speculations went into their own pockets. It was necessary to "square" other directors, to put them in for a call" of shares; in short, the weak and respectable fractions of both Boards had to be persuaded that they ought to agree to certain measures – hold their tongues, and participate in the illicit plunder, as it was "a sort of thing which every business man did."

My chairman, who was elected to that office chiefly through Sarmist's efforts, because he was a noble lord, and because he had the qualification, still more important to Sarmist's eyes, of the most charming and absolute ignorance of business, was, shortly before the completion of the amalgamation, confidently taken into a corner by Sarmist.

"It will be necessary, my lord," Mr. Sarmist said, "that our company should increase its capital and create new shares. The new shares will be given in exchange for the shares of the opposition company. This it will be easy enough to carry at a general meeting of shareholders. Our capital being two millions, and that of the other company one, we should require to make ours three millions; but I should strongly recommend that it should be made six."

"What!" exclaimed the noble lord; "six? – for what?"

"Well," said Sarmist, complacently smiling, "it will halve the dividend – that is, our shareholders will receive £200 of share certificates for every £100 invested, and their dividends will apparently look only half as big as they are, and this will deter further competition."

The noble lord was not quite able to follow the argument; he rather thought there was something wrong about it, but the idea of doing away with further competition, and the business authority of Sarmist, at last made him yield.

Thus my competitor was bought; my capital was first increased to a sufficient amount to represent the shares of both companies, and the joint capital doubled, or, as they call it on the Stock Exchange, "watered," and we jogged on unitedly as one concern, and yielded half our former dividend.

My share now became very much the instrument of gambling on the Exchange, and I am afraid that my directors gradually began to assume a less and less dignified position, as my shares passed into the hands of speculators far more knowing than the majority of them were. In vain Mire and Sarmist, who were no doubt "up all to the dodges," attempted to keep my Board as well in hand as they had them formerly; the disastrous results of their general malfeasance and of the "watering" of my stock were only too perceptible. The high figure at which my capital now stood made "market operations" in my shares safe, and therefore attractive, and the bold speculator began to divide the controlling power with the wire-pulling.

A violent struggle now took place between a powerful combination of speculators, who bought large quantities of my shares, and Mire and Sarmist, as to who should control my destinies. The latter soon found that they would have to appropriate a very much larger amount of their own capital than they cared to lock up towards purchasing my shares, if they wished to retain their hold upon me. In order to meet this danger, and to find large sums of money belonging to other people which could be used for their own purposes, they conceived the brilliant idea of starting a trust company. The capital of this company was fixed at three millions. It was set forth in the prospectus that the trust company would exchange its own certificates against the certificates of various other companies at a given figure calculated upon the average market price of each security. The holder of one trust certificate would by this means become a part-proprietor in a large shareholding concern which owned a variety of securities, receiving their dividends and paying to its own shareholders the average on all the dividends it had taken. It was very plausibly urged that even the smallest investor would by these means always obtain a fair return for his outlay, no matter whether some of the companies, the shares of which were owned by the trust, were paying well or not. Mire, Sarmist, and Sir Verrikute naturally made themselves directors of the trust, completing their Board from the ranks of the necessary fashion and ignorance. The new trust was readily taken up by the public; large quantities of all the shares which had been selected as eligible for the trust were exchanged for the new certificates. Mire and Sarmist, by pointing out how very low my shares stood at that moment in the market, considering my intrinsic merits, easily induced their colleagues to sell the best of the securities which had been tendered for exchange by the public, and buy with the proceeds of the sale large quantities of my own shares. Before long, half a million sterling was invested by the trust in me. This practically gave to the trust – or, in other words, to the three directors who controlled it, once more an overwhelming influence over my fortunes. This was the culmination of the power of the triumvirate. They again were in a position to bull and bear my shares with an almost absolute certainty of success; and whenever adverse circumstances or unforeseen difficulties upset their calculations and involved loss, they immediately represented themselves to have undertaken the speculation on behalf of the trust, and "stuck" that unhappy company with the transaction. Their purse-proud arrogance and insufferable insolence at this period procured them great consideration in commercial circles, which unfortunately even extended to fashionable society in the West End. While my directors were thus triumphantly magnifying my stability and grandeur, I myself was becoming painfully conscious of the seeds of incipient disease; the water seemed to be pressing upon all my vital functions. My works were allowed to fall into disrepair, and every consideration of prudence in management was sacrificed to giving the shareholders the highest possible dividend. My reserve fund was little more than nominal, and it was very evident to me that additional capital would soon be required to renew my already decaying system and make good my numerous deficiencies. At the moment when I was regarded with envy by my enemies, with pride by my friends, and was encircled with a general halo of respect, I began to feel myself tottering on my swollen limbs, and to have a dark presentiment of the final crash.

Meantime Messrs Chisel Bros. had not been nursing their vengeance in vain. Following with a watchful eye my rising fortunes, their quick experience soon detected the internally rotten condition I have just described; and they suddenly appeared as contractors of a rival company, which had been financed with unusual secrecy and honesty. Chisel himself was averse to the fraudulent dealings in which he had nearly become involved in my case, and determined, in order the more effectually to crush me and my contractors Gouge & Co., to content himself with moderate profits. The consequence was, that the A. B. C. Co. started with a capital of only one million, and with works almost as extensive as mine. It was utterly unable, however, to contend against the overwhelming forces which Mire and Sarmist brought to bear against it; they invoked the aid of their influential shareholders, of the Peers and Commoners who had assisted at my banquet, and, above all, of the Press. Many baser members of the journalistic world wrote up those gentlemen and their enterprises on every possible occasion, and opened upon my rival with a chorus of slander like a pack of hounds on a hot scent. Every disgraceful transaction of which they had themselves been guilty, Messrs Mire and Sarmist darkly insinuated was practiced by the Directors of the A. B. C. Co. These latter gentlemen did not happen to have been obtained by the same method as mine; but were quiet business men – not much known either to the world of fashion or of finance – their praises had not been sounded at banquets, nor had the public been made familiar with their names in articles written in their laudation. The consequence was that the poor A. B. C. Co. had a very rough time of it, and was generally regarded as one of the most dishonest, gambling, stock-jobbing concerns in the city – an impression which certain of the less reputable members of my Board found it easy to produce, by getting up "rings" to bull and bear its shares, heaping discredit upon it thereby, while they at the same time filled their own pockets. Another favourite device was that of spreading false reports about it; and when they were found to be false, they accused the A. B. C. Directors of having invented them in order to "rig" the shares. I knew the A. B. C. Co. intimately; and I used to tell it that I felt like a skunk who squirted its own vile odour all over it, and then cried aloud to the passers-by to shun it on account of its noxious effluvium. So successful were these tactics, that for a year or two the poor A. B. C. Co. scarcely got business enough to pay its working expenses. In the meantime, Mire and Sarmist could not shut their eyes to the danger which was slowly but surely threatening – not my existence alone – for which after all they cared very little – but their position as wire-pullers of a large joint-stock company, which had enabled them to accumulate so much ill-gotten wealth. They ceased, therefore, to be content with slandering the A. B. C. Co., but intrigues were secretly set on foot for the purpose of acquiring it. In this case, however, my competitor was not so easily absorbed as on the former occasion. No congenial friend was found on the Board who was willing to go halves in the plunder. The negotiations between the Boards failed. The unprincipled attempts of broken-down speculators, who at the command of Mire and Sarmist, and with their money, brought shares in the A. B. C. Co., and appeared at that body's public meeting in the characters of distressed shareholders, and insisted upon the necessity of coming to terms with me – the powerful rival – were frustrated by the firm attitude of the A. B. C. Board; and even the threat of the still powerful Trust Company to acquire a controlling influence in the A. B. C. shares and extirpate that Company's Board, unless they came to terms, was of no avail with my rival, and practically never carried out by the Trust Company for want of funds.

A feeling of intense irritation now took possession of Mire and Sarmist; but the despondency to which, for a moment, they almost succumbed, was succeeded by a reaction to their old arrogance and self-confidence; and with a boldness which was characteristic of their palmy days, they determined to infuse new life into me by supplying me with new works. This had, indeed, become absolutely necessary; for the contrast between my efficiency and that of the A. B. C. Co. was dawning even upon the outside public.

With feverish anxiety they rushed a resolution through my Board for the raising of additional capital. With agitated anticipation my prospectus was placed before the public, inviting that never failing source of money to subscribe to my seven per cent first mortgage debenture bonds. This time, alas, the appeal was made in vain. Just as my prospectus appeared, a serious financial crisis had shaken the confidence, not only of the money circles in the city, but of the investing public at large. As a last resource, my shareholders were called together, and a piteous appeal was made to them by the noble lord who occupied the chair. My shareholders, however, – who had been in a fool's paradise up to this time, and only looked forward to receiving dividends, instead of being called upon to furnish additional capital, – indignantly demanded further explanations from the chairman, which the utter want of knowledge, on the part of that nobleman, of my affairs prevented him from affording in a satisfactory manner; and eventually a stormy meeting was brought to a close by the adoption of a resolution, moved by a powerful speaker, that a committee be elected from amongst the shareholders to inquire into the Company's position.

Now, for the first time, I became perfectly aware of my utter want of vitality. The weak and credulous part of my Board was even more astonished than I was myself at the revelations which were the result of this inquiry. On the second day of these investigations large defalcations were discovered, and upon summoning the elderly and highly respectable manager to account for them, it was found that he had not yet arrived in his office. The day passed without this functionary making his appearance – indeed, it has since been ascertained that he spent the afternoon in a passage to Boulogne, and is to this day a subject of interesting but fruitless inquiry to the police. Sick at heart were the unhappy shareholders when they understood the real position of their fine property, and even Mire and Sarmist were crushed in spirit when they saw the proud Temple of Gambling, which they had reared to themselves, about to crumble to dust. It was some consolation to them doubtless to reflect upon the thousands they had made out of me, but even of this they were soon to be deprived. The Committee's report was submitted to a second meeting, recommending my immediate liquidation; and the necessary legal steps were at once taken, which landed me in that bourne from which no company returns – the Court of Chancery.

Inexorable fate, which had already overtaken me through the agency of Chisel Bros. and their friends, who had started my triumphant rival, dealt the final blow at the hand of my old friend and promoter the Captain. With the *coeur léger* which characterised that gentleman, he had applied at the outset for a few of my shares, which he retained through my varied fortunes; and now he appeared in a court of law in the since famous suit of "Hawk v. Mire and others," claiming to be reimbursed the purchase money for his shares, on the ground that a certain sum was paid to Mire and Sarmist, being directors, by Gouge & Co., being contractors, under a contract which was not disclosed in the prospectus, and which contract related to the X X X or plunder money with which my readers are already familiar. This revealed the whole of the fraudulent transaction I have narrated. The high-minded judge who presided on the occasion ruled that Mire and Sarmist should repay to the shareholders the sum of £100,000; and he expressed himself in unequivocal language as to the corruption which had crept into a certain class of the commercial community of London.

My melancholy history is now closed. If I have wearied you, my patient readers, and still more patient investors, my apology must be that it would have been quite impossible for you ever to have obtained the valuable information which has been disclosed in this veracious history, excepting through the medium of an abstract being like myself. I now bid you farewell with that feeling of remorse akin to tenderness which those in their last moments are generally supposed to entertain towards persons whom they have irretrievably ruined in purse and character. I look mournfully for the last time upon the Captain as he dashes past the office in which I am now lying, behind his high-stepping bays, bent on the promotion of a new Company. Only yesterday I overheard Sarmist say to the official liquidator in greasy tones that he had been sorely chastened by Providence, but that he intended to kiss the rod and profit by the lesson he had received, by which I understood him to mean that for the future he would take proper precautions to see that X X X was so contrived that the law could not lay hold of it. Mire, I am informed by the remains of the Trust Company now lying under liquidation in the next room, took to his bed when the decision of the high-minded judge was communicated to him, at the fearful prospect of having to disgorge several millions of pounds, under the precedent just created by the said decision. He sunk gradually and never rallied. He now lies in the cemetery of a synagogue not far distant, and on his tombstone, engraved in choice

Hebrew, is a correct translation of the thirty-eight clause of the Companies Act (1867), 30 & 31 Vict., cap. 131.

N.B. – The 38th clause runs as follows: "Every prospectus of a Company, and every notice inviting persons to subscribe for shares in any Joint-Stock Company, shall specify the dates and the names of the parties to any contract entered into by the Company, or the promoters, directors, or trustees thereof, before the issue of such prospectus or notice, whether subject to adoption by the Directors, or the Company, or otherwise: and any prospectus or notice not specifying the same shall be deemed fraudulent on the part of the promoters, directors, and officers of the Company knowingly issuing the same, as regard any person taking shares in the Company on the faith of such prospectus, unless he shall have had notice of such contract."

28

LAW REPORTS

Twycross vs. Grant

Source: Twycross v. Grant and Others, June 2, 1877, *Law Reports, Common Pleas Division,* Vol. 2, 1876–1877 (London: William Clowes and Sons), pp. 469–77.

EDITORIAL HEADNOTE

Among the most notorious company promoters was Albert Grant (1831–1899), who during the 1860s and 1870s floated a number of foreign railways, mines, and public utilities. Grant bribed newspapers to secure favorable reviews of his promotions, and he rigged the market by secretly buying up shares in his own companies to stimulate demand and inflate prices. Many of Grant's companies were over-capitalized in order to provide hefty promotional fees for himself and his allies.[1]

By 1877 Grant was bankrupt and many of his companies were in disarray. Disgruntled shareholders instituted scores of lawsuits against Grant. One of these suits, Twycross v. Grant, became a landmark case in company litigation. The plaintiff, James Twycross, alleged that Grant had violated the 1867 Companies Act by failing to disclose in the prospectus of the Lisbon Tramways Company certain contracts, in particular, a secret agreement between Grant and the builders of the tramway to pay Grant £45,000, in effect a "kickback." Arguing that he would not have purchased shares in the company had he known of the undisclosed contract, Twycross demanded repayment of his £700 investment. The court found for Twycross, and in so doing, established the principle that promoters were fully responsible for information in the prospectus and that they must disclose all contracts which affected the new company in a significant, material way.[2]

Notes

1 P.L. Cottrell, "Grant, Albert," *Dictionary of Business Biography*, vol.2, pp. 623–29.

2 George Robb, *White-Collar Crime in Modern England* (Cambridge University Press, 1992), pp. 101–2.

DOI: 10.4324/9781003713890-32

TWYCROSS V. GRANT AND OTHERS

Joint Stock Company – Fraudulent Prospectus – Concealment of Contracts affecting the Company – Companies Act, 1867 (30 & 31 Vict. c.131), s.38 – Words "Knowingly Issuing" – Measure of Damages.

Action brought by the plaintiff under the Companies Act, 1867, s. 38, to recover the amount paid by him on certain shares taken by him in the L. Company on the ground of the fraud of the defendants (promoters of the company), in omitting from the prospectus two contracts entered into by them as promoters – the one a contract between the defendants C. & P. and one S., for the purchase of certain foreign concessions for the construction of tramways which the company was afterwards incorporated to make and work; the other a contract between the defendants, C. & P. and the defendant G., as to certain payments to be made by C. & P. to G. in consideration of his obtaining for them a contract from the company for the construction of the tramways, by means of which fraud the plaintiff had been induced to take shares, which proved worthless. The jury found that these contracts were material to be made known to the intended shareholders of the company:

Held, by the Common Pleas Division and in the Court of Appeal by Cockburn, C.J., and Brett, L.J., that the contracts ought to have been specified in the prospectus, and that the defendants were liable; Kelly, C.B., and Bramwell, L.J., dissenting:

Held, by the Common Pleas Division and in the Court of Appeal, by Cockburn, C.J., Bramwell and Brett, L.J.J., that the words "knowingly issuing" in s. 38 mean intentionally issuing a prospectus without inserting the contracts which are required by that section to be specified, although they are omitted under the bona fide belief that it was unnecessary to specify them.

At the trial the judge directed the jury that if the real damages occasioned to the plaintiff by the defendants' fraud was the price he paid for the shares he was entitled to recover that amount. The jury assessed the damages at the price paid by the plaintiff:

Held, by Cockburn, C.J., Bramwell and Brett, L.J.J, affirming the judgment of the Common Pleas Division that the direction was right, and that the shares taken by the plaintiff being worthless he was entitled to recover the amount paid by him for them: Kelly, C.B., dissenting.

This was an action founded upon s. 38 of the Companies Act, 1867 (30 & 31 Vict. c.131), which enacts that "every prospectus of a company, and every notice inviting persons to subscribe for shares in any joint-stock company, shall specify the dates and the names of the parties to any contract entered into by the company, or the promoters, directors, or trustees thereof, before the issue of such prospectus or notice, whether subject to adoption by the directors of the company or otherwise; and any prospectus or notice not specifying the same shall be deemed fraudulent on the part of the promoters, directors, and officers of the company knowingly issuing the same, as regards any person taking shares in the company on the faith of such prospectus, unless he shall have had notice of such contract."

The first count of the declaration (delivered 5th July, 1875) stated that the defendants Grant, Clark, & Punchard, were the promoters of a company called the Lisbon Steam Tramways Company, Limited, being a joint-stock company having a capital divided into shares, and duly registered under a memorandum and articles of association under the Companies Acts, 1862 and 1867 (25 & 26 Vict. c. 89, and 30 & 31 Vict. c. 131); and the defendants, being promoters of the company, before the issue of the prospectus and notice hereinafter mentioned, had entered into a contract with each other in the words and figures following, that is to say,

Memorandum of an agreement made the 6th of July, 1871, between Messrs. Edwin Clark, Punchard, & Co., of &c., contractors, of the one part, and Messrs. Grant & Co., of &c., bankers, of the other part, whereby it is agreed as follows:

1. In consideration of the expenses incurred and to be incurred and the services rendered and to be rendered by Messrs. Grant & Co. in and about the obtaining for the said E. Clark, Punchard, & Co. of a contract upon such terms as shall be satisfactory to the said E. Clark, Punchard, & Co., from the Lisbon Steam Tramways Company for constructing and equipping certain lines of tramways, and also in and about the formation of the said company, and in and about the preparation of and advertising and making public the prospectus of the company, and in using their best endeavors to raise and place the capital thereof, E. Clark, Punchard, & Co. shall pay to Messrs. Grant & Co. the sum hereinafter mentioned at the times and in the manner following, that is to say, the sum of 30,000*l.* in cash out of the first payment which E. Clark, Punchard, & Co. shall receive under or by virtue of the said contract, and the further sum of 10,000*l.* in cash as follows, viz. 5,000*l.* out of the second payment and 5,000*l.* out of the fourth payment which E. Clark, Punchard, & Co. shall receive under the said contract, as and when received; and the said Clark, Punchard, & Co. shall also pay or hand over to Grant & Co. 5,800*l.* in fully paid up shares of that nominal amount, or, at the option of Clark, Punchard, & Co., a similar amount, 5,800*l.* in cash on the second installment being paid to Clark, Punchard, & Co., such option to be declared by them within thirty days after the first allotment of shares shall be made by the company.
2. In the event of Clark, Punchard, & Co. being required by the company to take any part of the payments to be made by them by the company in respect of the works to be executed by them under their said contract in 8 per cent. debentures of the company, Grant & Co. shall take from Clark, Punchard, & Co. one fourth of any debentures they may be called upon to take instead of cash, at the price of 80*l.* for every 100*l.* debenture.

3. Clark, Punchard, & Co. further agree that, in the event of Grant & Co. declaring within thirty days after the first allotment of shares shall be made by the company that they require Clark, Punchard, & Co. to take up shares in the company to an extent not exceeding 4,200 shares in the whole, Clark, Punchard, & Co. will accept a transfer or transfers of such shares as they may be so required to take, and shall pay to Grant & Co. the par value of such shares, that is to say, the sum per share which for the time being shall be called upon the said shares, upon such transfer or transfers being tendered to them duly executed by the transferor or transferors.
4. It is understood that all the shares hereinbefore referred to and which may be taken by the parties hereto shall be held by them respectively, and shall not be dealt with or disposed of until the completion of the contract hereinbefore mentioned. As witness, & c.

And the said Lisbon Steam Tramways Company mentioned in the said contract is the same company as is hereinbefore mentioned; and the defendants, after the making and entering into of such contract, and after the passing of the Companies Act, 1867, and after the 1st of September, 1867, knowingly and fraudulently, and with intent to induce persons to take shares in the said company, and well knowing the premises, issued and caused to be published a prospectus of the said company, and also issued and caused to be published a notice inviting persons to subscribe for shares in the said company, which said prospectus and notice did not nor did either of them specify the dates, and the names of the parties to the contract; and the plaintiff, on the faith of such prospectus and notice, respectively, took shares in the company and paid to the company a large sum of money in respect thereof; and the plaintiff had no notice of such contract, there being a contract within the meaning of s. 38 of the Companies Act, 1867; and the said shares were and are of no value to the plaintiff, and he has lost the money he so paid the company as aforesaid.

Second count, that the defendants were the promoters of a company called the Lisbon Steam Tramways Company, Limited, being a joint-stock company having a capital divided into shares and duly registered under a memorandum and articles of association under the Companies Acts, 1862 and 1867; and the defendants Clark & Punchard, being promoters of the company, before the issue of the prospectus and notice hereinafter mentioned had entered into a contract with His Excellency Field Marshal the Duke of Saldanha, who was the director of the company, and which contract was in the words and figures following:

Memorandum of an agreement made the 5th of July, 1871, between His Excellency Field Marshal the Duke de Saldanha, of the one part, and Messrs. Edwin Clark, Punchard, & Co., of the other part, whereby it is agreed:

1. The Duke de Saldanha shall transfer and make over to Clark, Punchard, & Co. such part and interest of and in the concessions granted to the Duke de Saldanha by royal decrees of the kingdom of Portugal as enables the Duke de

Saldanha to establish, maintain, and work for the term of ninety years from the 15th of May, 1871, railways on the system Larmanjat on the roads from Cascaes to Cintra and Pero Pinheiro, and from Lisbon through Lumiar to Torres Vedras, with all the rights, privileges, and advantages to the said part and interest in the said concession belonging or appertaining, or in any way incident thereto. The Duke de Saldanha shall also transfer and make over to Clark, Punchard, & Co. the existing railway on the road from Lisbon to Lumiar, with all the rolling-stock, materials, implements, and appurtenances thereto belonging.

2. The Duke de Saldanha having made application to the proper authorities in Portugal for the grant of a concession for the like period of ninety years of the right to establish, maintain, and work steam tramways on the road from Lisbon to Cascaes, and having received a formal promise from the minister of public works that the concession so applied for as aforesaid shall be granted to him, hereby agrees to obtain such concession and to transfer and make over the same to Clark, Punchard, & Co., within the space of thirty days from the date hereof.
3. The Duke of Saldanha shall also transfer and make over to Clark, Punchard, & Co., the right and interest of him the Duke of Saldanha of and in the invention of Jean Larmanjat of a new system of mixed railway with a single rail, to such extent as will enable the invention to be used and applied upon the roads mentioned in clause 1 of this agreement, but not further or otherwise.
4. The consideration of price to be paid to the Duke de Saldanha for such transfer as aforesaid shall be the sum of 22,000*l.*, of which the sum of 6,000*l.* shall be paid in cash, and the remainder, viz., 16,000*l.*, in fully paid up shares in a company now in course of formation intended to be called the Lisbon Steam Tramways Company, Limited, for the purpose of constructing, maintaining, and working steam tramways or railways upon the roads of Portugal hereinbefore mentioned upon the system of Larmanjat.
5. The sum of 6,000*l.* so intended to be paid in cash shall become due and be payable to the Duke of Saldanha within three calendar months after the first allotment of shares in the company shall have been duly made to the public and the payment made on such allotment; and the 1,600 fully paid up shares representing the remaining 16,000*l.* to be received by the duke shall at the same time be delivered to him or as he may direct.
6. Messrs. Clark, Punchard, & Co. shall hold harmless and indemnify the Duke of Saldanha against all claims and demands of Larmanjat for royalties, dues, or charges in respect of the use of his invention upon the railways mentioned in clause 1 of this agreement, or in respect of the construction, maintaining, and working thereof.
7. In the event of the capital of the intended company not being subscribed to such an extent as in the opinion of the board of directors thereof, and with the concurrence of Clark, Punchard, & Co. is sufficient to warrant them in proceeding to allot the shares to the public, or in the event of Clark, Punchard, &

Co. not obtaining from the company the contract for constructing and equipping the said railways, then and in such case this agreement shall be of no effect, and every clause, matter and thing herein contained shall cease and be void.

8. It is hereby further agreed that the 1,600 fully paid up shares in the Lisbon Steam Tramways Company hereinbefore agreed to be delivered to the Duke de Saldanha shall not be dealt with or disposed of by him, but shall be held until the steam tramways about to be constructed by the company have been completed and opened for traffic. As written, &c.

And the Lisbon Tramways Company, Limited, mentioned, in the said contract is the same company as is hereinbefore mentioned, and the defendant Grant as well as the defendants Clark & Punchard were before the issuing of the prospectus and notice hereinafter mentioned well aware of the said contract; and the defendants after the making and entering into of the said contract, and after the passing of the Companies Act, 1867, and after the 1st of September, 1867, knowingly and fraudulently, and with intent to induce persons to take shares in the company, issued and caused to be published a prospectus of the company and a notice inviting persons to subscribe for shares in the company, which prospectus and notice did not nor did either of them specify the dates and names of the parties to the contract; and the plaintiff, on the faith of such prospectus and notice respectively, took shares in the company, and paid to the company a large sum of money in respect thereof; and the plaintiff had no notice of such contract, then being a contract within the meaning of the 38th section of the Companies Act, 1867; and the shares were and are of no value to the plaintiff, and he has lost monies he so paid to the company. Claim 1,000*l.*

The defendant Grant and the defendants Clark & Punchard severally pleaded not guilty and a traverse of every material allegation in the declaration. Issue thereon.

There were eighty-seven other actions brought against the same defendants by other persons who like the plaintiff had been induced to become purchasers of shares in the Lisbon Steam Tramways Company upon the faith of the prospectus issued by the company. The aggregate amount of the claims in these several actions was about 36,000*l.* In one only of these eighty-seven actions, viz., *Miller v. Grant and Others*, had a statement of claim been delivered, which charged fraud at common law as well as under the statute. The others had proceeded no further than writ, when (on the 23rd of February, 1876) the following consent was given by the respective solicitors for the defendants in the eighty-seven actions: "We do hereby consent that the time limited for the respective plaintiffs in all the above actions to deliver statements of claim be extended until one month after final judgment shall be entered in the action of *Twycross v. Grant and Others.* This consent, however, to be without prejudice to any application the defendants may hereafter make, upon reasonable terms, in any one or more of the said actions, to compel the plaintiff or plaintiffs to deliver his or their statement or statements of claim at an earlier date. No order or orders to be drawn up upon this consent, unless required by one of the parties to one of the above actions."

The action came on for trial before Lord Coleridge, C.J., on the 26th and 29th of May, and the 7th, 11th, 12th, and 13th of July, 1876. Before the jury were sworn, the counsel for the defendants applied for a postponement of the trial, on payment of costs, and upon the terms of bringing the amount of damages claimed (1,000*l.*) into court, in order to give the defendants an opportunity of entering into negotiations with the Portuguese authorities to obtain further concessions to re-establish the company; or, in the alternative, to allow the defendants to withdraw their pleas. The application was opposed by the plaintiff's counsel; and Lord Coleridge, C.J., declined to accede to it, on the ground that, this action, having been put forward as a sort of test action in order to try the question or one of the questions common to all the eighty-eight actions, the trial of this action, in the preparation for which great expense had necessarily been incurred, must materially affect the trial of the others, and therefore it would be inexpedient in this manner and at this stage of the proceedings to interrupt the ordinary course.

The jury having been sworn, the defendants' counsel formally offered to consent to a verdict for the plaintiff for the amount of the claim in the declaration. This offer being rejected, the case proceeded, the counsel for the defendants intimating to the Court that it was not their intention to appear for their respective clients or take any part in the trial.

The view of the facts taken by the judges respectively is given in detail in their judgments, and this renders a separate statement unnecessary.

At the close of the evidence for the plaintiff his counsel summed up the case. The defendant Grant then, in the absence of his counsel, addressed the jury and contended that there was no evidence to shew that he or his co-defendants had been guilty of any fraud; that the contracts referred to in the declaration were not such "contracts entered into by the company, or the promoters, directors, or trustees thereof," as were required by s. 38 of the Companies Act, 1867, to be disclosed in the prospectus; and that, at all events, the defendants were guilty of no want of bona fides in assuming that they were not such contracts as the Act required to be disclosed.

The defendants Clark & Punchard were not represented. No evidence was offered on the part of the defendants.

Lord Coleridge, C.J., in the course of his summing up observed that it was necessary to determine whether the contracts mentioned in the declaration were contracts entered into by the defendants or promoters, and whether they were intentionally concealed by them when they caused the prospectus to be issued; and he left the following questions to the jury:

1. Were the contracts so mentioned made by the defendants?
2. Were the defendants promoters of the company at the time of making such contracts and of the issue of the prospectus?
3. Did they issue the prospectus?

4. Did they knowingly omit mention of these contracts from the prospectus?
5. Did the plaintiff take his shares on the faith of the statements in the prospectus?
6. If these contracts had been disclosed in the prospectus, or reference made thereto, would the plaintiff have taken the shares?
7. Had the plaintiff any notion of the existence of such contracts?
8. Were the contracts connected with the affairs of the company, and were they such that they were material to be known to a person about to apply for shares?
9. Did such contracts materially affect the interests of the company?
10. Was it known to the defendants, and was it the fact, that the company, when formed, would bear the burden of the payments to be made under such contracts, and that the sums to be paid under them would come out of the funds of the company?
11. Were such contracts made, and the fact of their existence intentionally suppressed in fraud of the company and of persons invited to take shares in the company?

The jury declined to answer the last question; and they answered the sixth and seventh questions in the negative, and all the others in the affirmative.

At the suggestion of the defendant Grant, Lord Coleridge, C.J., put this further question to the jury: "Were the statements of the contracts withheld under the bona fide belief that by law those contracts need not have been set forth?" To this question the jury answered "Yes."

As to the measure of damages, Lord Coleridge, C.J., told the jury: "The plaintiff is entitled, if you think there has been fraud, to recover what that fraud has cost him. He is entitled to recover the real damage occasioned by the fraud. If you think the real damage occasioned by the fraud is the full amount of the shares, give him the full amount of the shares, namely, 700*l.* If you think there is evidence which goes to shew that the result of the fraud is not damage to the full extent of 700*l.*, then give him so much less as in your judgment the fraud has really occasioned him loss."

The jury awarded the damages at 700*l.*

A verdict was thereupon entered for the plaintiff for 700*l.*, with leave to enter judgment for the defendants on the additional findings of the jury.

29

MADAME MIDAS

Fergus Hume

Source: Fergus Hume, *Madame Midas: Realistic and Sensational Story of Australian Mining Life* (London: The Hansom Cab Publishing Company,1888), pp. 17–21, 154–55, 165–66.

EDITORIAL HEADNOTE

Fergus Hume (1859–1932) was a novelist born in England but raised in New Zealand, where his family emigrated during the 1860s. He attended the University of Otago and qualified as a lawyer in 1885. He then moved to Australia where he began writing mystery stories. His first novel, *The Mystery of a Hansom Cab* (1886), became a tremendous bestseller and helped establish the genre of detective fiction. In 1888 Hume relocated to London, where he published dozens of novels over the next few decades.[1]

Madame Midas (1888), like most of Hume's novels, is a murder mystery. It is set in an Australian mining camp, and its title character was inspired by the career of Alice Cornwell (1852–1932), the only woman company promoter of the nineteenth century and a friend of Hume's. Like him, she was born in England and her family emigrated to New Zealand and then later to Australia. Her father was a mining promoter who, with Alice's assistance, made a fortune sinking gold mines. In 1886 Alice returned to England, where she floated the Midas Mine on the London Stock Exchange. She then established the British and Australasian Mining and Investment Company to enable the British public to invest in Australian gold mines.[2]

Notes

1 John Sutherland, "Hume, Fergus," *Stanford Companion to Victorian Fiction* (Stanford: Stanford University Press, 1989), p. 313.
2 D.M. Griffiths, "Cornwell, Alice Ann," *Oxford Dictionary of National Biography*, eds. H.C.G. Matthew and Brian Harrison (Oxford: Oxford University Press, 2004), Vol. 13, pp. 492–93.

DOI: 10.4324/9781003713890-33

In the early days of Australia, when the gold fever was at its height, and the marvelous Melbourne of to-day was more like an enlarged camp than anything else, there was a man called Robert Curtis, who arrived in the new land of Ophir with many others to seek his fortune. Mr. Curtis was of good family, but having been expelled from Oxford for holding certain unorthodox opinions quite at variance with the accepted theological tenets of the University, he had added to his crime by marrying a pretty girl, whose face was her fortune, and who was born, as the story books say, of poor but honest parents. Poverty and honesty, however, were not sufficient recommendations in the eyes of Mr. Curtis, senior, to excuse such a match; so he promptly followed the precedent set by Oxford, and expelled his son from the family circle. That young gentleman and his wife came out to Australia filled with ambitious dreams of acquiring a fortune, and then returning to heap coals of fire on the heads of those who had turned them out.

These dreams, however, were destined never to be realised, for within a year after their arrival in Melbourne Mrs. Curtis died giving birth to a little girl, and Robert Curtis found himself once more alone in the world with the encumbrance of a small child. He, however, was not a man who wore his heart on his sleeve, and did not show much outward grief, though, no doubt, he sorrowed deeply enough for the loss of the pretty girl for whom he sacrificed so much. At all events, he made up his mind at once what to do: so, placing his child under the care of an old lady, he went to Ballarat, and set to work to make his fortune.

While there his luck became proverbial, and he soon found himself a rich man; but this did not satisfy him, for, being of a far-seeing nature, he saw the important part Australia would play in the world's history. So with the gold won by his pick he bought land everywhere, and especially in Melbourne, which was then becoming metropolitan. After fifteen years of a varied life he returned to Melbourne to settle down, and found that his daughter had grown up to be a charming young girl, the very image of his late wife. Curtis built a house, went in for politics, and soon became a famous man in his adopted country. He settled a large sum of money on his daughter absolutely, which no one, not even her future husband, could touch, and introduced her to society.

Miss Curtis became the belle of Melbourne, and her charming face, together with the more substantial beauties of wealth, soon brought crowds of suitors around her. Her father, however, determined to find a husband for her whom he could trust, and was looking for one when he suddenly dies of heart disease, leaving his daughter an orphan and a wealthy woman.

After Mr. Curtis had been buried by the side of his dead wife, the heiress went home to her richly-furnished house, and after passing a certain period in mourning, engaged a companion, and once more took her position in society.

Her suitors – numerous and persistent as those of Penelope – soon returned to her feet, and she found she could choose a husband from men of all kinds – rich and poor, handsome and ugly, old and young. One of these, a penniless young Englishman, called Randolph Villiers, paid her such marked attention, that in the end Miss Curtis, contrary to the wishes of her friends, married him.

Mr. Villiers had a handsome face and figure, a varied and extensive wardrobe, and a bad character. He, however, suppressed his real tastes until he became the husband of Miss Curtis, and holder of the purse – for such was the love his wife bore him that she unhesitatingly gave him full control of all her property, excepting that which was settled on herself by her father, which was, of course, beyond marital control. In vain her friends urged some settlement should be made before marriage. Miss Curtis argued that to take any steps to protect her fortune would show a want of faith in the honesty of the man she loved, so went to the altar and reversed the marriage service by endowing Mr. Randolph Villiers with all her worldly goods.

The result of this blind confidence justified the warnings of her friends – for as soon as Villiers found himself in full possession of his wife's fortune, he immediately proceeded to spend all the money he could lay his hands on. He gambled away large sums at his club, betted extensively on the turf, kept open house, and finally became entangled with a lady whose looks were much better than her morals, and whose capacity for spending money so far exceeded his own that in two years she completely ruined him. Mrs. Villiers put up with this conduct for some time, as she was too proud to acknowledge she had made a mistake in her choice of a husband; but when Villiers, after spending all her wealth in riotous living, actually proceeded to ill-treat her in order to force her to give up the money her father had settled on her, she rebelled. She tore off her wedding-ring, threw it at his feet, renounced his name, and went off to Ballarat with her old nurse and the remnants of her fortune.

Mr. Villiers, however, was not displeased at this step; in fact, he was rather glad to get rid of a wife who could no longer supply him with money, and whose presence was a constant rebuke. He sold up the house and furniture, and converted all available property into cash, which cash he then converted into drink for himself and jewelry for his lady friend. The end soon came to the fresh supply of money, and his lady friend went off with his dearest companion, to whose purse she had taken a sudden liking. Villiers, deserted by all his acquaintances, sank lower and lower in the social scale, and the once brilliant butterfly of fashion became a billiard marker, then a tout at races, and finally a bar loafer with no visible means of support.

Meantime Mrs. Villiers was prospecting in Ballarat, and gaining the respect and good opinion of everyone, while her husband was earning the contempt of not only his former friends but even of the creatures with whom he now associated. When Mrs. Villiers went up to Ballarat after her short but brilliant life in Melbourne she felt crushed. She had given all the wealth of her girlish affection to her husband, and had endowed him with all kinds of chivalrous attributes, only to find out, as many a woman has before and since, that her idol had feet of clay. The sudden shock of the discovery of his baseness altered the whole of her life, and from being a bright, trustful girl, she became a cold suspicious woman who disbelieved in everyone and everything.

But she was of too restless and ambitious a nature to be content with an idle life, and although the money she still possessed was sufficient to support her in comfort, yet she felt that she must do something, if only to keep her thoughts from dwelling on those bitter years of married life. The most obvious thing to do in Ballarat was to go in for gold-mining, and chance having thrown in her way a mate of her father's, she determined to devote herself to that, being influenced in her decision by the old digger. This man, by name Archibald McIntosh, was a shrewd, hard-headed Scotchman, who had been in Ballarat when the diggings were in the height of their fame, and who knew all about the lie of the country and where the richest leads had been in the old days. He told Mrs. Villiers that her father and himself had worked together on a lead then known as the Devil's Lead, which was one of the richest ever discovered in the district. It had been found by five men, who had agreed with one another to keep silent as to the richness of the lead, and were rapidly making their fortunes when the troubles of the Eureka stockade intervened, and, in the encounter between the miners and the military, three of the company working the lead were killed, and only two men were left who knew the whereabouts of the claim and the value of it. These were McIntosh and Curtis, who were the original holders. Mr. Curtis went down to Melbourne, and, as previously related, died of heart disease, so the only man left of the five who had worked the lead was Archibald McIntosh. He had been too poor to work it himself, and, having failed to induce any speculator to go in with him to acquire the land, he had kept silent about it, only staying up at Ballarat and guarding the claim lest someone else should chance on it. Fortunately the place where it was situated had not been renowned for gold in the early days, and it had passed into the hands of a man who used it as pasture land, quite ignorant of the wealth which lay beneath. When Mrs. Villiers came up to Ballarat, this man wanted to sell the land, as he was going to Europe; so, acting under the urgent advice of McIntosh, she sold out of all the investments which she had and purchased the whole tract of country where the old miner assured her solemnly the Devil's lead was to be found.

Then she built a house near the mine, and taking her old nurse, Selina Sprotts, and Archibald McIntosh to live with her, sank a shaft in the place indicated by the latter. She also engaged miners, and gave McIntosh full control over the mine, while she herself kept the books, paid the accounts, and proved herself to be a first-class woman of business. She had now been working the mine for two years, but as yet had not been fortunate enough to strike the lead. The gutter, however, proved remunerative enough to keep the mine going, pay all the men, and support Mrs. Villiers herself, so she was quite content to wait till fortune should smile on her, and the long-looked-for Devil's Lead turned up. People who had heard of her taking the land were astonished at first, and disposed to scoff, but they soon began to admire the plucky way in which she fought down her ill-luck for the first year of her venture. All at once matters changed; she made a lucky speculation in the share market, and the Pactolus claim began to pay. Mrs. Villiers became mixed up in mining matters, and bought and sold on 'Change with such foresight and promptitude of action that she soon began to make a lot of money. Stockbrokers are not, as a rule, romantic, but one of the fraternity was so struck with her persistent good fortune that he christened her Madame Midas, after the Greek King whose touch turned everything to gold. This name tickled the fancy of others, and in a short time she was called nothing but Madame Midas all over the country, which title she accepted complacently enough as a forecast of her success in finding the Devil's Lead, which idea had grown into a mania with her as it already was with her faithful henchman, McIntosh.

When Mr. Villiers therefore arrived in Ballarat, he found his wife universally respected and widely known as Madame Midas, so he went to see her, expecting to be kept in luxurious ease for the rest of his life. He soon, however, found himself mistaken, for his wife told him plainly she would have nothing to do with him, and that if he dared to show his face at the Pactolus claim she would have him turned off by her men. He threatened to bring the law into force to make her live with him, but she laughed in his face, and said she would bring a divorce suit against him if he did so; and as Mr. Villiers' character could hardly bear the light of day, he retreated, leaving Madame in full possession of the field.

He stayed, however, in Ballarat, and took up stockbroking – living a kind of hand-to-mouth existence, bragging of his former splendour, and swearing at his wife for what he was pleased to call – her cruelty. Every now and then he would pay a visit to the Pactolus, and try to see her, but McIntosh was a vigilant guard, and the miserable creature was always compelled to go back to his Bohemian life without accomplishing his object of getting money from the wife he had deserted.

People talked, of course, but Madame did not mind. She had tried married life, and had been disappointed; her old ideas of belief in human nature had passed away; in short, the girl who had been the belle of Melbourne as Miss Curtis and Mrs. Villiers had disappeared, and the stern, clever, cynical woman who managed the Pactolus claim was a new being called "Madame Midas." . . .

At last a time drew near . . . which filled Ballarat with wonder. It began in a whisper, and grew into such a roar of astonishment that not only Ballarat, but all Victoria, knew that the far-famed Devil's Lead had been discovered in the Pactolus claim. Yes, after years of weary waiting, after money had been swallowed up in apparently useless work, after sceptics had sneered and friends laughed, Madame Midas obtained her reward. The Devil's Lead was discovered, and she was now a millionaire.

For some time past McIntosh had not been satisfied with the character of the ground in which he had been working, so abandoning the shaft he was then in, he had opened up another gallery to the west, at right angles from the place where the famous nugget had been found. The wash was poor at first, but McIntosh persevered, having an instinct that he was on the right track. A few weeks' work proved that he was right, for the wash soon became richer; and as they went farther on towards the west, following the gutter, there was no doubt that the long-lost Devil's Lead had been struck. The regular return had formerly been five ounces to the machine, but now the washing up invariably gave twenty ounces, and small nuggets of water-worn gold were continually found in the three machines. The main drive following the lead still continued dipping westward, and McIntosh now commenced blocking and putting in side galleries, expecting when this was done he would thoroughly prove the Devil's Lead, for he was quite satisfied he was on it. Even now the yield was three hundred and sixty ounces a week, and after deducting working expenses, this gave Madame Midas a weekly income of one thousand one hundred pounds, so she now began to see what a wealthy woman she was likely to be. Everyone unfeigningly rejoiced at her good fortune, and said that she deserved it. . . .

The Pactolus was now a perfect fortune, and Madame Midas being sole owner, her wealth was thought to be enormous, as every month a fresh deluge of gold rolled into her coffers from the inexhaustible Devil's Lead. McIntosh, of course, still managed the mine, and took great pride in his success, especially after so many people had scoffed at it.

Various other mines had started in the vicinity, and had been floated on the Melbourne market, where they kept rising and falling in unison with the monthly yield of the Pactolus. The Devil's Lead was rather unequal, as sometimes the ground would be rich, while another time it would turn out comparatively poor. People said it was patchy, and some day would run out altogether, but it did not show any signs of exhaustion, and even if it had, Madame Midas was now so wealthy that it mattered comparatively little. When the monthly lead was small, the mines round about would fall in the share market to a few shillings, but if it was large, they would rush up again to as many pounds, so that the brokers managed to do pretty well out of the fluctuations of the stock. . . .

30

THE PROMOTER

Montagu Williams

Source: Montagu Williams, 'The Promoter,' *Round London: Down East and Up West* (London: Macmillan and Co., 1892), Part 2, pp. 163–71.

EDITORIAL HEADNOTE

Montagu Williams (1835–1892) was a lawyer and writer. He was educated at Eton and called to the bar in 1862. He worked as a Treasury counsel and as a magistrate in London. A colorful character, Williams also wrote theatrical farces and occasionally appeared on the stage. His most famous work was *Round London*, a fictionalized tour of the city featuring sketches of typical urban characters, high and low, such as money lenders, stockbrokers, street singers, and flower sellers.[1]

"The Promoter" profiles a flashy financier, Leopold Stiff, who fleeces gullible investors, but is eventually tried at the Old Bailey and sentenced to prison. As the story implies, by the late nineteenth century, company promoters had become well-known figures in the urban landscape.

Note

1 J.A. Hamilton, "Williams, Montagu Stephen," *Oxford Dictionary of National Biography*, eds. H.C.G. Matthew and Brian Harrison (Oxford: Oxford University Press, 2004), Vol. 59, pp. 261–62.

The company promoter – The gullible British public – Leopold Stiff – His office – I visit him there – He is "so Busy" – A remarkable sight – An invitation to dinner – Mixed company – Excellent entertainment – The Gull Gold Mine, Limited – Wound up – Stiff arrested – Committed for trial – The Old Bailey – A great crowd – The trial – Sentence – From the West End to Millbank.

There is no more remarkable being in the city of London, with its many curious trades and vocations, than the company promoter. He has existed there and

DOI: 10.4324/9781003713890-34

flourished like a green bay-tree for many years past. Though everybody knows him, either personally or by reputation, there is in all quarters much uncertainty as to his origin and antecedents.

The successful company promoters are enormously wealthy, they have palaces at Kensington or mansions in Grosvenor Square, besides charming places in the country, and they are usually aspirants – and, it may be, not unsuccessful aspirants – for Parliamentary honours. They are, as a rule, Conservatives in politics, and have a large circle of titled acquaintances – impecunious lords, baronets, generals, admirals, and the like. The latter, who are termed "guinea pigs," figure as directors of the companies launched by their City friends.

The promoters drive to their businesses in well-appointed broughams, drawn by high-stepping horses. They are remarkably particular in their dress, and wear a good deal of jewelry, their massive rings being particularly conspicuous. Altogether their appearance, both in the City and in the West End, is calculated to impress the casual observer.

Quick at figures, cool-headed, and gifted with a retentive memory, the company promoter is an excellent business man. There is a good deal of variety in his work. He transforms all manner of going concerns from private enterprises into share investments for the public. One day it is soap; the next, candles; then an hotel or a theatre, and so on. He also finds capital for, and works – by syndicate, or as a company – mines, valuable and valueless. His ability in placing an undertaking before the public in an alluring form is marvelous. What prophetic visions of wealth for those wise enough to subscribe! What dividends await the investor – if he will only walk into the parlour! How eagerly the public rushes to secure shares in the Brobdingnagian Diamond Mine, the South African Auriferous Dust Company, and the Borneo Sea Salt Company!

There is no one so gullible as an ordinary member of the British public. He will invest his last penny in an undertaking of which he knows absolutely nothing, although if he reads his newspaper, he must be perfectly well aware that kindred enterprises have, times without number, been exposed as out-and-out swindles. This starting of bogus companies is very like the confidence trick, the ring dropping, and the painted sparrow.

Of course, the "fat," as it is termed, goes in a great measure to the promoter, and between him and the poor investor there are usually several individuals with their minds very wide open.

Many a company promoter, when he has amassed considerable riches, retires from business, and, as one of the moneyocracy, gives sumptuous dinners and splendid receptions, and, by these and other means, gradually elbows his way into fashionable society. With some of these individuals, however, things take a very different turn, as the history I am about to relate will show.

At the time when I was reading for the Bar, and eating my dinners at the hospitable board of the Inner Temple, no man was better known as a financier and company promoter than Leopold Stiff. Scarcely a new venture was launched but he manipulated the ropes. He had a finger in every pie.

Mr. Stiff's office, which was not a hundred miles from the Old Jewry, was more like an enormous bank than a private establishment. The bustle and commotion that went on there were astonishing. All day long people passed in and out, upstairs and downstairs, dozens of clerks hurried hither and thither, doors slammed, bells rang, and everywhere were noise and movement.

The premises themselves were built in the most costly style, and were an ornament to the thoroughfare. Several broughams and hansom cabs were usually to be seen waiting in the roadway outside.

On entering the building the visitor passed up a broad marble staircase, and his progress was likely to be impeded by the number of persons ascending and descending. In the throng were noblemen, officers in the Army, clergymen, fashionably attired ladies, mothers and wives of the middle class, and, in fact, all sorts and conditions of men and women.

At the head of the stairs stood a page in livery, who was available for taking the visitor's card into Mr. Stiff's private office.

On the ground-floor were any number of little rooms, each of which contained a chair, a writing-table, and a sofa or small settee. Anybody who wished to have an interview with Mr. Stiff was shown into one of these apartments, where he had to wait until the great man was able to come to him.

One day I paid him a visit, to enquire as to the value of certain securities. He saw me in one of the rooms I have described, and I must confess that his manner was the perfection of politeness and affability.

He explained that he was so busy he scarcely had time to breathe, but that he would make a note of my enquiry, and get his head clerk to write me on the subject.

"Good-bye," said he, shaking me by the hand. "You must excuse my running away. I have a board meeting going on in room A., and in my large room there are specimens of the gold ore taken from the great Gull Mine, the prospectus of which you may have seen. People from all parts of the country have come up to see it. I wish you had been older, for I would have put you on the directorate. I've put your friend Colonel S. on. He dined with us at home last night."

As we passed out into the corridor a clerk came up and whispered something to him. The next minute he was shaking hands with an elderly gentleman, who was about to be ushered into the little apartment we were leaving.

"I'll be with you in ten minutes," said Mr. Stiff to the new comer; "can't spare a moment now."

He disappeared down the corridor, and the page shut the old gentleman in.

Before leaving the premises I thought I would pay a visit to the large room, being rather curious to inspect the specimens of the Gull Mine ore. Happening to see one of the liveried servants of the establishment I asked him the way thither, and he very graciously volunteered to be my guide.

A remarkable sight met my eyes as I entered the room. It was crowded with men and women of all classes, including country gentlemen, widows, City merchants, and clergymen. Every one was closely inspecting the ore, which lay on tables placed about the apartment, or scrutinising the charts and maps that hung upon the walls.

Standing in the middle of the throng, chatting very affably with those about him, was Mr. Stiff, whom I was surprised to see, as I had fancied he had left me to return to the boardroom. He was admirably dressed for office purposes, wearing a well-cut black velvet jacket and a double-breasted white waistcoat, across which hung a gold and turquoise watch-chain. He had a ruddy complexion and iron-grey hair, and I do not think I ever saw a man more calculated to inspire persons with confidence. He looked a philanthropist every inch of him. For my part, however, I confess that I had no consuming desire to take shares in the Gull Mine.

That evening, as I was about to leave the chambers where I was reading, I received a letter answering the enquiry I had made in the morning, and enclosing an invitation to dinner from Mr. and Mrs. Leopold Stiff. I had never been to their house, and as I had a curiosity to go there, I accepted the invitation.

The house, which was situated in a fashionable quarter of London, was magnificently appointed – in fact, a little too magnificently appointed. As you entered, you were literally mobbed by footmen, who were ablaze with yellow and crimson. The drawing-room was hung with exquisite water-colours, which must have cost any amount of money. It called up a smile to my lips to see the host pointing them out to Lady H., one of the reigning beauties, and discoursing to her on Art.

The company was a little mixed. There were one or two City magnates and their wives pompously marching about the room, the Marquis and Marchioness of A., Lord H.L., whose name, at that time, figured on many boards of directors, and several others *ejusdem generis.*[1]

The dinner was excellent, the wine beyond reproach, and the flowers among the choicest I have ever seen. After dinner there was a concert. It was arranged by Signor P., who was the conductor of the Italian Opera at the time, and among the performers were several of the leading lights of the musical world. In fact, I am bound to say that, could one have only forgotten how the money which procured the entertainment was acquired, it would have been possible to pass a most enjoyable evening.

Years rolled by, and it came about that dark clouds gathered over the London money market. A disastrous drought crippled the finances of a foreign land, two large English houses were reported to be hopelessly involved, a panic spread through the City, and half-a-dozen bubble companies burst in a single day. Several directors were prosecuted, and our friend Leopold Stiff was in an extremely bad way.

It was rumoured that, though apparently ruined, the well-known promoter, having executed some timely settlements, and having in days gone by, sent large sums of money out of the country, was still a wealthy man. Whether this was so or not I am unable to say. One thing is certain – if he had escaped ruin, a large percentage of those who had placed money in his concerns were less fortunate.

Of all the companies that had gone to grief, the Gull Gold Mine, Limited, proved to be the greatest swindle. Remarkable as it seems, though some pieces of very rich ore were found on the estate before the company was floated, not another solitary speck was discovered there after the capital had been subscribed.

Unfortunate individuals in all parts of the country had placed their savings – in some cases to the extent of the last shilling they could scrape together – in the Gull Mine, and the consequence was that when calls were made, prior to the winding up, thousands of persons of all grades were involved in absolute ruin.

It was rumoured one day in the City that Leopold Stiff had sought an asylum in a foreign land; but this, strangely enough, proved not to be the case. Within forty-eight hours a vigilant press informed the country that a warrant had been issued for his apprehension, and that, it having been duly executed, he had made his appearance before the Alderman at the Mansion House.

It would have been an odd coincidence had the presiding justice been one of those City magnates who were guests at the sumptuous entertainment I have described as having been given some years before at the company promoter's magnificent West End house. This was, I am happy to say, not so; but – which comes to very much the same thing – one of these very individuals, actuated, it may be, by a not unnatural curiosity, was seated throughout the proceedings on the bench beside the Alderman.

The proceedings, as is usual in this Court, were of a quiet and businesslike nature. Sufficient evidence was tendered to enable the accused to be sent for trial, and the very able counsel who represented him asked but a few questions. Leopold Stiff was committed to take his trial at the next sessions of the Central Criminal Court.

Bail was applied for and tendered to a very considerable amount, but refused, and the prisoner was conveyed to Newgate in the prison van. An application was afterwards made to the Court of Queen's Bench for the removal to that – the highest court in the kingdom – of any indictment that might be found against the prisoner at the Old Bailey. This application, as might have been expected, was at once refused. I may remark in passing, that so far as these applications are concerned, things have very much changed since that time. The late Lord Chief Justice Cockburn had the greatest objection to sanction such removals, and only did on rare occasions and under very exceptional circumstances; but now, provided the defendant be a man of means, the application is seldom refused.

The day for delivering the gaol of Newgate soon arrived, and the date was fixed for the trial of Mr. Leopold Stiff.

This was, of course, a *cause cèlèbre,* and the rush of persons seeking to obtain admission to the Court was almost unprecedented. The number of witnesses, too, was unusually large.

Has the reader ever visited the Old Bailey while the sessions are on? Possibly not, and he may therefore like me to give some description of the *locus in quo.*

Turning from the left from Ludgate Hill you find yourself in a narrow, unimportant thoroughfare, with less than its fair share of pavement. The roadway is pretty sure to be choked with vans, either lumbering along with Smithfield or some City warehouse as their destination, or hovering about the railway and steamboat goods depot.

On the right-hand side is the Court-house. What an interesting medley of human beings you find inside the lobby and on the pavement! – weeping women in black shawls, a couple of well-drilled, compassionate policemen, shabby Jews with anxious faces, Bill Sikes and his young woman, a few detectives, and any number of nondescript males consorting in groups and talking in a whisper.

Of course there are a few public-houses hard by. You always find them in the immediate vicinity of criminal courts. During the sessions these places do a roaring trade. Witnesses, prisoners' friends, prosecutors, and solicitors' clerks mingle together in a heterogeneous mass, all eager for drink, a few for food. The public-house immediately opposite the Court-house is always so full as to be scarcely approachable. I wonder how many alibis have been concocted on those premises, how many prosecutions have been, as they term it, "squared," and how much false swearing planned!

Of course, when executions were public the proprietors of these houses, in addition to their ordinary profits, received large sums of money from persons who came from the West End and elsewhere to witness those terrible spectacles. The culprits were hanged early in the morning, and it was no uncommon thing for parties of men and women to proceed to these public-houses overnight, provided with hampers of food and champagne, with which, by way of killing time until the "show" took place, they kept up the most disgraceful orgies throughout the small hours. I was told by the late Mr. Jonas, who for a great many years was governor of the gaol, that the scenes which used to be enacted on those premises were a disgrace to civilisation. Happily executions are no longer public.

There are two entrances to the Old Bailey, one approached from the public thoroughfare, and the other approached from the court-yard of the prison. You reach the latter by passing up some stone steps which are on the right-hand side as you enter through the broad gateway. This entrance is used by the Judges, Aldermen, Sheriffs, and other officers of the Court, by counsel, and, on occasions such as the one to which I am referring, by the few privileged members of the public who have been furnished with tickets of admission. In order to prevent a crush, wooden barriers are erected at the bottom and top of the stone steps, and they were certainly needed on the day of Mr. Leopold Stiff's trial.

On the occasion in question the roadway outside the Old Bailey was blocked with carriages and hansoms, and from half-past nine to ten o'clock in the morning the pavement and lobby were crowded with people, many of them ladies. The moment the doors of the court were opened every inch of available space was seized upon, and the Sheriff ordered the outer gates of Newgate to be closed.

It was a pouring wet morning, and on a rainy or foggy day I don't think there is a more depressing place in the world than the Old Court of the Old Bailey. There are two doors leading into the Court from the corridor. One is used by the Judges, the Aldermen and Sheriffs, and the few selected visitors, who either take their seats upon the bench or in a contiguous enclosure that looks like a huge private box. The second entrance from the corridor is used by barristers and their clerks, solicitors, and other persons having business in the Court. The centre of the chamber is occupied with seats for members of the Bar, and below them is the solicitors' bench. Between the Judges and the jury – both of whom command a fine view of the dock – is the witness-box.

Underneath the jury-box sits the usher, an individual who must enjoy very little sleep in a natural way at night, for while the trials are on he is rarely to be seen with his eyes open. Once or twice during the day, however, he rouses himself by a great effort and, in stentorian tones, shouts "Silence!" and this, generally, at a time when everything is so still that you could almost hear a pin drop.

Over the jury-box are three large windows furnished with reflectors, in front of which hang huge lamps for use in foggy weather.

Just over the dock is one of the most interesting places in the Court. I refer to a little gallery that is principally used by the friends of the prisoners. Most of the celebrated murderers of the century, including Lamson, the Stauntons, Pook, the Mannings, and Catherine Wilson – to take a few names at haphazard – were tried in this Court. What scenes those walls have witnessed! What terrible agony have I seen suffered there myself! The cries of despair that have issued from that little gallery from time to time when a verdict has been pronounced, or a sentence passed, will never be forgotten by those who heard them.

At length there are the two knocks, and the Judge, the Lord Mayor, and the Sheriffs, preceded by the mace bearer, enter the crowded Court. The prisoner ascends from below the dock, steps up to the rail, and is called upon by the Clerk of Arraigns to plead the indictment. "Not guilty," he replies in a firm voice.

Leopold Stiff has very little changed in appearance. His hair has grown a shade or two greyer, that is all. The same scrupulous care is observable in his dress, and the same smile plays upon his face.

The *dramatis personae* in the most interesting act in a remarkable drama have a peculiar interest for me. At the back of the Court I catch sight of two ladies who are among the guests at the dinner-party I attended at Mr. and Mrs. Stiff's house several years before, and there, ready to ascend the witness-box, is one of the very clergymen whom I had seen handling the gold ore of the Gull Mine.

Very distinguished counsel appeared for the prisoner, but the result of the trial, which occupied the whole day, was a foregone conclusion. Mr. Leopold Stiff was found guilty, and sentenced to five years' penal servitude.

From a West End mansion to Millbank is truly a curious transition!

Editorial Endnote

1 Latin: "of the same kind."

31

PROMOTING A COMPANY

Bracebridge Hemyng

Source: Bracebridge Hemyng, "Promoting a Company, or, Shrimps for the Million," *The Stockbroker's Wife, and Other Sensational Tales of the Stock Exchange* (London: John and Robert Maxwell, 1885), pp. 181–96.

EDITORIAL HEADNOTE

Bracebridge Hemyng (1841–1901) was a popular and prolific novelist and journalist. Born in India, the son of a colonial administrator, he was educated at Eton and called to the Bar in 1862. Disliking the life of a barrister, he turned to writing. He compiled the section on prostitution for Henry Mayhew's *London Labour and the London Poor* (1861) and wrote more than fifty novels. His greatest success was a series of adventure stories for boys featuring the character Jack Harkaway.[1]

The Stockbroker's Wife, written in collaboration with the broker John Shaw, included comic and melodramatic stories about the addictive nature of financial speculation. In "Promoting a Company, or, Shrimps for the Million," Hemyng mocks the late Victorian craze for joint-stock schemes via the preposterous London and Provincial Shrimp Breeding, Catching, and Canning Company, Limited. The company's prospectus argued that "the social elevation of the masses was only to be effected by the means of cheap and abundant shrimps."

Note

1 John Sutherland, "Hemyng, Bracebridge," *The Stanford Companion to Victorian Fiction* (Stanford: Stanford University Press, 1989), p. 290.

. . . Though Jeffries was a schemer, we may mention that he was passionately attached to his wife and children, who were all very good-looking; the boys being handsome and manly, the girls beautiful. If he schemed it was for the sake of his

DOI: 10.4324/9781003713890-35

family. Call him a mercenary villain, if you will; it was not for himself he laboured. He stood at nothing where money was concerned. His wife and he had known one another in their youth. He loved her; but they were parted. They met again, and were married. He worked hard, and never took a holiday. If he went abroad it was to make money. If he was harsh to men he was a child to a woman. His wife sings an old song, he turns away his head and cries; yet he would crush a man under his heel in business. On a Sunday he had taken his family to Windsor to see the beeches and the deer, and romped around like a boy in the old park. On Monday he was issuing prospectuses of an undertaking which would ruin hundreds.

He had once been bold enough to stand for Parliament. It was a metropolitan constituency for which he stood, but he retired in disgust before going to the poll. Innumerable deputations of women waited upon him, representing every real and fancied grievance: one lot objected to pictures representing nude stories being exhibited in the galleries; another wanted to regulate the social evil, representing that shop girls should be watched by the police, as comparatively respectable women had taken the place of the professional abandoned creatures of twenty years ago; in fact, he had no idea of the number of busybodies there are ready to ventilate grievances, evils, and abuses, until he endeavoured to become a public man.

His great friend who assisted him in his enterprises was a man of about his own age, named Charles Bayldon, who had been a bookmaker, but was obliged to relinquish that lucrative profession because he one Monday neglected to settle with his creditors, and was posted at Tattersall's Subscription Room as a defaulter. He now described himself as an agent, and did a little business for customers, whom he met principally in taverns, though he was privileged to transact business in one of the two rooms which Jeffries rented in Bucklersbury. One morning in early spring Jeffries arrived at the Cannon Street Station at ten o'clock, and proceeded to his office, where he found Bayldon waiting for him, he having been summoned by letter to attend to new and important business. They shook hands, lighted their cigars, told the half-a-crown-a-week boy, who acted in the capacity of a clerk, that they were visible to nobody, and retired into the inner room, which was marked "private."

"What's in the wind now?" asked Bayldon, expectantly.

"Money, my dear fellow," replied Jeffries, who was always optimistic in his views. "Money, and lots of it, I hope."

"Another company?"

"Just so," said Jeffries, oracularly.

"I should have thought you had had enough of that line of business," remarked Bayldon, "after the Marriage Mart, the Sedan, the Aerated Brick, and the Electric Liver and Lights."

"This time I shall make a hit," interrupted Jeffries, "a palpable hit. The idea occurred to me all in a moment. I had been spending a few days in Southend, and walked over to Leigh. Now, what is Leigh famous for?"

"Mud," replied Bayldon, stroking his moustache with a ruminant air.

"No, my good man, it is where the shrimps come from. I made the acquaintance of a fisherman named Trawler. He has got half a dozen smacks and nets to sell, with an old barn thrown in. We can buy the lot for a song, and have a going concern, lock, stock, and barrel."

"What for?"

"The London and Provincial Shrimp Breeding, Catching and Canning Company, Limited; works at Leigh, Essex," said Jeffries earnestly. "You see, land for breeding purposes could easily be acquired. We shall soon have money in the bank."

"The mud bank, you mean."

"You know what I mean. We will buy a part of the foreshore of the river. Now, pay attention. Shrimps are scarce, shrimps are dear, and they are undoubtedly a favourite article of food with the masses. I ask you what a Bank Holiday would be without shrimps? Would not Hampstead Heath become a howling waste, and Greenwich a desert without its teas and shrimps at ninepence a head? You can get your Souchong mildly tempered with Pekoe at two shillings per pound, but you cannot obtain the indispensable, the appetising, the all-absorbing shrimp for less than sixpence a quart, and the supply is deficient at that. The L. and P. S. B. C. and C. Company will cheapen and tend to still more popularise the shrimp. It will be a food for the people. The eye of the dyspeptic will glisten, for your fine fat fresh shrimp is as easy of digestion as an oyster; the innocent face of childhood will be wreathed with smiles, for what child ever despised the shrimp? The facial muscles of the horny handed son of toil will relax; the Blue Ribbon man will feel his heart expand, and the drinker will become gay, for all know what the shrimp is to a thirsty man; the comely matron will become more comely; in fact, we shall supply a long felt want. It will be a sweet boon to one and all, to rich and poor – the coroneted earl and the ill-fed underpaid artisan. What the people want is cheap shrimps and plenty of them."

John Jeffries paused to get his breath.

"What do you think of it?" he asked, presently.

"Very good," replied Bayldon. "The possibilities of the company are infinite. We could add dabs, and might rise to oysters."

"Of course. I never thought of dabs or natives."

"And yet you are a dab at astonishing the natives," said Bayldon, perpetrating a mild joke.

"Don't be frivolous. Sit down and draw up the usual document. 'Articles of Agreement entered into between Charles Bayldon of the one part, acting on behalf of the London and Provincial Shrimp Breeding, Catching, and Canning Company, and Mr. Timothy Trawler, for the purchase of________' You know how to go on."

"Yes, yes. I've got it by heart."

"Then write out the prospectus. I want to get the advertisements out as quick as possible. Offices of the company, here; bankers, City and Country. Put old File down as solicitor. My father-in-law and your brother will do as directors, with the baronet as chairman."

Taking pen, ink, and paper, Bayldon began to write facilely, for this kind of work was familiar to him, and while he is at work, we will say a word about the directors. Mr. Morley Morley, the father-in-law of Jeffries, was a tenant farmer, of no means, of the Uplands Farm, near Chelmsford, which sounded well in the prospectus. Mr. Christopher Tatton Bayldon kept a grocer's shop at Highgate Rise, and had confined himself to his Christian names for some time past, owing to an irregularity in his accounts discovered by his creditors under his third bankruptcy, which had necessitated his withdrawal from public life for the space of six months on a judge's order. The baronet alluded to was Sir Augustus de Sarcenet Drake, who, for a couple of pounds a week, payable in advance, was always ready and willing to allow Jeffries to use his name in connection with his undertakings. He lodged in a small road, built on an estate called Bolingbroke Park, in a southern suburb, but he was invariably described as Sir Augustus de S. Drake, Bolingbroke Park, S.W., which looked very well in print.

"I've done the prospectus," said Bayldon, laying down his pen after a time.

"Very well; let us see how you've baited the hook," replied Jeffries, who had been busily figuring in a note book as to the estimated profits of the first twelve months, the amount of income over expenditure showing several thousand pounds net, and an approximate dividend of 50 per cent.

He looked as pleased as the young broker who went into the "House," and by a fluke made a sovereign in a minute, and spent the rest of the day calculating, if he made a pound a minute every day, how much he would be worth at the end of the year.

Bayldon handed him a sheet of foolscap paper, on which was written –

"The London and Provincial Shrimp Breeding, Catching, and Canning Company, Limited." Capital, £30,000 in 30,000 shares of £1 each. Payable 5s. per share on application, and 15s. on allotment.

Incorporated under the Companies Acts 1862 to 1880, whereby the liability of shareholders is strictly limited to the amount of their shares.

Directors.
Sir Augustus de S. Drake, Bart., Bolingbroke Park, S.W.
Morley Morley, Esquire, The Uplands, Chelmsford, Essex.
Christopher Tatton, Esquire, The Rise, Highgate, London.
With power to add to their number.
Bankers: The City and Country, Bartholomew Lane, E.C.
Solicitor: W. Sharpe File, Clement's Inn.
Secretary pro tem.: Charles Bayldon, Esquire.
Office: 175, Bucklersbury, London.

"That won't do," said Jeffries.

"What do you object to?" asked Bayldon.

"You ought to know better than to put yourself down as secretary."

"I forgot."

"Of course you did. Hang it all! We must start the company at the expense of the secretary."

"I only put myself temporarily; we will advertise for a victim at once."

"Yes. We want one with about £2,000," said Jeffries.

Bayldon was a practical man, and saw the point at once. He was always sharp, short, and business-like. They said in the City that he was the hero of the longest and shortest correspondence on record.

His tailor had written to him every three months for seven years for his account. At last he replied: – "Sir, – Your letters to hand. If you annoy me any more I shall put the matter in the hands of my solicitor."

He met a lady at a party. She had some money, and he thought he would like to make her Mrs. Bayldon. To take a cab to her home would have cost time and cash, so he wrote:

"Dear Madam,
Do you want to marry?
Yours truly, C. Bayldon."

To which the lady replied:

"Dear Sir,
Certainly.
Yours truly, R. Smith."

He wrote again:

"Dear Madam,
Will you marry me?
Yours truly, C. Bayldon."

The reply came:

"Dear Sir,
Certainly not.
Yours truly, R. Smith."

So Bayldon remained a bachelor.

"The baronet is a good card," remarked Bayldon.

"I count on Sir Augustus to float the company, and the public to support it," answered Jeffries.

"He wants his fees in advance."

"Oh! I always humour Sir Augustus, though I once lost a good director by giving him his money before it was due: he withdrew; it frightened him; he thought the concern looked fishy."

"That's what they'll say of the Shrimp Breeding, Catching, and Canning Company."

"I spoiled a respectable man," sighed Jeffries, thinking of his lost director.

"Good L____! It wouldn't spoil me," laughed Bayldon.

"We can sell for cash and go on credit," continued Jeffries, recurring to his shrimps.

"You can acquire a retail business for a small sum. There is old Loader, who keeps a fish stall near the station, his stock usually consists of two lobsters and a pint of shrimps."

Jeffries laughed.

"It is a very old established business," added Bayldon, "and will go cheap to an immediate purchaser for prompt cash."

There was another laugh.

"By G___! old man, you're in it," Bayldon concluded, "and it will be good news for the baronet."

"Yes, he'll see a chance of paying his washerwoman," remarked Jeffries, "and his eyes will glisten."

"I've heard him say she's a tight 'un."

"I reckon she is about the only creditor he does pay."

"Laundresses and bakers are troublesome, and so are milkmen," exclaimed Bayldon, reflectively.

"Do you speak from experience?"

"Yes, I often drink champagne at home, though I greatly prefer milk."

"Why?"

"Because I can't get milk without money, and I've always plenty of champagne in the house; the wine merchant only sends in his bill once in six or twelve months."

"Well, how do you like my scheme?" asked Jeffries.

"It will be the greatest success you ever invented," returned Bayldon.

"I thought of bringing out a lead mine, but –"

"Bah! Mines are no good; mines stink. Now listen to the prospectus."

"I am ready."

Bayldon began to read the particulars he had jotted down.

This was rather a lengthy affair, so we will only take the heads of it. The directors invited subscriptions for the shares of the above mentioned company, to enable them to purchase the fishing smacks, nets, premises, and plant generally of Timothy Trawler, Esq., fish merchant, of Leigh, Essex, and to extend and develop the already existing large business done in catching and forwarding shrimps to the London and other markets; and to breed, pot, and can shrimps, a very lucrative trade in which could be done by a judicious outlay of capital. All companies engaged in the fishing trade were making enormous profits, and the company would have almost an exclusive field, which justifies the directors in anticipating a most satisfactory return to the shareholders.

"The only contract entered into is one dated the 10th day of May between Mr. Timothy Trawler of the one part, and Charles Bayldon of the other part, as trustee of the company, for the purchase of certain property, which, together with the articles of association, can be seen at the office of the solicitor.

"Prospectuses and forms of application may be obtained from the bankers, solicitor, or from the secretary at the company's offices. In the event of no allotment being made to an applicant, the deposit will be returned in full. If a smaller number of shares are allotted than applied for, the surplus deposit will be credited towards the amount payable upon allotment."

Then followed a dissertation on shrimps, their market value, their fecundity, and their popularity. It was argued that a plentiful supply at sixpence the quart, retail measure, would enormously increase the consumption, and one came to the end of the prospectus with the firm conviction impressed on the mind that the social elevation of the masses was only effected by the means of cheap and abundant shrimps, for which the people of England had long been craving. They were to regenerate mankind, and build up the condition of succeeding generations of this great empire. One marveled why the apostle of shrimp culture had never risen in our midst before, but the gap was to be stopped at last, and the country saved from speedy perdition. The adipose tissue and manly bearing of our shrimp-fed population in Essex was pointed to with pride, and it was clear that halcyon days were in store for us.

Jeffries made a few corrections, excisions, and additions, after which he expressed himself satisfied with the prospectus. The same day he went to Leigh with Bayldon, and bought the property that old Trawler wished to sell. In fact the boats were worn out, the nets full of holes, the boilers leaky, and the barn in a tumble-down condition. Trawler had had enough of shrimping, and wanted to go into the beer-house line, which offered a more congenial sphere to him. He was glad enough to get rid of his plant at any price, but Jeffries was equally pleased to obtain it, because it gave him something to work upon. Returning to London, he gave the manifold copy of the prospectus to the papers and awaited results. The baronet seeing his name in the paper, over his matutinal coffee, was one of the first to call. Having an income, as he would often observe jocosely, of nothing a year, paid quarterly, he recognised the fact that he was entitled to something, and did not deem it prudent to let capital, however small, lie idle. Money was at all times needed by him, for he had an unquenchable thirst, which was as expensive to him as a taste for orchids is to a duchess. Fully expecting him, Jeffries had a cheque ready on his desk, which, after shaking hands, he presented. It was for a month's pay as director at two guineas a week, and Sir Augustus pocketed it with a nod intended to convey his thanks.

"What's this new swindle?" he asked, irreverently.

"My dear sir, how can you talk like that?" replied Jeffries, greatly shocked, "it's the grandest idea of the present century."

"Humbug!" said Sir Augustus, "any one would think you were a Mahdi, going to bring about a millennium; but you can give me some shares if you think they will go to a premium."

"Sure to. We shall have them at three above par before the week's out. I'm having fifty got ready in your name."

"Can I borrow anything on them?" inquired the baronet, his eyes twinkling in a merry manner.

"Why not?"

"Say as collateral security for a bill of £170."

"Try it; they ought to be as good as a bank note to you," said Jeffries.

"Or a new pawn ticket," laughed Sir Augustus; "their value will only decrease with age. Oh, you can do it. I believe you'd take a pence out of a blind man's hat, or runaway with a railway arch if you could carry it."

"How well he knows me," remarked Jeffries.

"Got any specimens? Pegwell Bays are my favourites," asked Sir Augustus.

"You must come down to the fishery," answered Jeffries. "This time we are on the right track, and have a sure fortune in hand."

Sir Augustus de Sarcenet Drake whistled. "Upon my word, Jeffries," he remarked, "I sometimes fancy you tell 'em till you believe what you are saying. However, it does not make a pin's worth of difference to me. All I want is a cheque in advance. When do you hold your first board meeting?"

"You shall have due notice," was the rather dry answer.

"Where's Charley?"

"Bayldon? Oh, he's round the corner, I suppose. You generally know where to find him."

The baronet waved an adieu with his ungloved and not scrupulously clean hands – they said all his landed property was under his nails – leaving Jeffries to speculate as to the success of his new venture. Jeffries looked at his window on which was painted, "Mr. John Jeffries, Financial Agent," and at a slip of paper placed underneath, on which was written the name of the new company. He could not help feeling that he was a clever fellow, but at the same time he wondered how it was he never made a fortune. It was true he lived. But how? From hand to mouth, as it were. Figuratively, the wolf was always barking at his door. He longed for rest; he wanted to get out of the busy, whirling maelstrom of City life. In reality, this man liked pastoral pursuits; he could have been contented in a cottage with a large garden, growing fruit and flowers and vegetables, rearing poultry, and varying the monotony of such a life with a little fishing and shooting, always provided that he had his wife and children with him. But these things were not to be his. Similarly to Ixion he was bound to his wheel, and if he wanted to wear purple and fine linen he must spin to get it.

While he was plotting and planning his clerk brought him a lady's card, which had engraved on it "Mrs. Haydon, Brook Street, Grosvenor Square." He ordered his visitor to be admitted. She was a handsome, middle-aged woman, dressed in deep mourning. She had blue eyes and brown hair, and was of the Irish type. Mary Haydon had married an elderly man for his money. She had not loved him. In fact, she had never yet seen the man she could love. She was a pretty woman and a flirt. Now that her husband was dead she wanted association, feeling that she could not live alone. But she could not find what she wanted, but directly she saw Jeffries she felt she could love him. It is so with many of us. We look round for years. At last we say, "This is the one I want." We know not why; we care not why. Yet it is so. Let each one ask his own heart. Jeffries was not a handsome man for a woman to fall in love with, but he was fascinating, and pleased women. He saw from her facial expression that she liked him, and he determined to take advantage of the weakness and get her money. All the time, however, he was strictly true and loyal to his wife and children. In her hand she held a newspaper, in which she had marked an advertisement of his. It set forth, among other things, that he was prepared to give advice to intending investors, and she explained her business at once by informing him that she was the widow of a physician who had left her fifteen thousand pounds, invested at three per cent., half of which she wanted to speculate with. She wished to see what she could do with seven thousand. At present this sum only brought her in an income of two hundred and ten pounds. What could she do for the best? She had heard that in the City, by taking shares in companies, she could treble or quadruple it. Was this true? Did not Electric Lights show a large profit?

"They did not," replied Mr. Jeffries, "but he had in his hands the very thing that would just suit her," and he presented her with a proof of the prospectus of the L. and P. S. B. C. and C. Company, upon the prospects of which he took advantage of the opportunity to dilate.

"I am willing," said Mrs. Haydon, "to follow your advice, but I do hope you are not mistaken in your estimate of the probable profits of this concern, as I have young children, whose future I have to study."

"My dear madam, the prospectus speaks for itself. Everyone eats shrimps. We shall do an enormous business. You have come just in time," replied Jeffries, "for I expect that by to-morrow the shares will have been applied for twice over."

"I heard of a lady who invested in some oil shares, and after a time the wells dried up."

"Shrimps can never be exhausted, and people will eat them as long as England is a country."

So eloquent and enthusiastic did Jeffries become, that Mrs. Haydon was persuaded to invest her surplus cash in the company. He called several times on her at her house. In the end she gave the promoter a cheque for seven thousand pounds he presenting her in return with a receipt for the amount, promising to have the shares ready for her in a day or two. His first care was to go to her bank and get the money in notes and gold. These he put in his side pocket. He felt as if he was treading on air. The idea of devoting the cash to the interests of the company did not occur to him for a moment. Feeling that it was a time when inspiration might be derived from the consumption of champagne, he strolled into a restaurant, where he met several friends, who congregated around him at once.

"Hullo, Jeff!" cried one.

"Here's old Jeff, in his best stride," said another. "Hurrah for Jeff!"

"He's looking more jolly than he did over Electric Liver and Lights!" remarked a third.

"What will you have?" said a fourth. "Perrier Jouet or Pommery Greno? Anything you like. What's it to be? Pommery or Moet?"

"Have you been to the 'House' – how are prices?" asked Jeffries, while the wine was being opened.

"The markets are firm. Your favourites, Chatham Prefs., are up 2. But I say, what is this new scheme of yours?"

He handed them a prospectus.

"By Jove! That's a glorious idea! Supply a want, you know," exclaimed one of his friends.

"Shrimps are the thing; I always said so," remarked a second.

"They've been neglected too long," observed a third.

"Don't forget us when you make the allotment," said the fourth.

"No, no; Jeff never forgets his friends," replied the first speaker. "By G___! Jeff's a good fellow."

The object of this panegyric was about to raise his glass to his lips when a man in a threadbare coat and a shabby hat looked in at one of the doors.

Two years ago this man had been rich, but he was dazzled by the Aerated Patent Brick or the West-End Sedan – it does not matter which – and he lost his all. Since then he had haunted Jeffries, who always fled at the sight of him.

It was a question of the fly out of the mustard pot; he was off.

"Goodbye," he said hurriedly, setting down his glass. "Pressing engagement – excuse me."

He rushed to a side door, and was soon out of sight.

"Villain!" yelled the ruined speculator, gnashing his teeth.

"Ha! ha!" laughed the friends; "one of Jeff's ghosts," and there was a chorus of "Ha! ha! ha!"

Jeffries walked away eastward until he got into unfrequented streets, and communed with himself. He was inclined to let the company take care of itself now that he had got Mrs. Haydon's money. That the company never could and never would pay he knew perfectly well. It's explosion was only a question of time. If he could get abroad and change his name he would be able to start in some business, and send for his wife and children. To a man like himself, this was an alluring prospect. He could not resist the temptation. What did it matter to him if he betrayed his friend Bayldon, and involved the name-lending baronet in disgrace? Such men as he only live for themselves. The very nature of their business makes them selfish. He would do it. Yes, he would throw care to the winds; and instead of going to the office he went to a railway station, and booked himself to Paris. It was nothing new to leave his wife for days at a time without giving her any notice. She was used to such eccentricities on his part. Bayldon, however, was alarmed when his partner did not make his appearance on the following day. He guessed that something had happened. What it was he did not know until Mrs. Haydon called again at the office in Bucklersbury, finding him there. She had done what she ought to have done before making the investment – that is, she had consulted her friends, who had advised her that she had done the wrong thing; so she wanted to sell her shares, and get her money back. But this was not so easy in practice as it looked in theory. Subscriptions did not come in very fast. The public fought shy of the company, and there was no market for the security. Then she told Bayldon how much money she had given to Jeffries, which opened his eyes.

"You will never see him again," he said, angrily, for he felt that he had been made a fool of, and left in the lurch.

"Why not? I – I do not understand you," replied Mrs. Haydon.

"He is absconded."

"Then he is a swindler."

"Call him what you like. By this time he is in Paris, if he does not go to Monte Carlo direct. That's his loadstone."

Mrs. Haydon wrung her hands tearfully.

"Oh! how cruelly I have been deceived, and my poor children robbed, but I, weak woman as I am, will follow him to the end of the world if necessary and get my money back."

Her pride was wounded and her jealousy aroused.

"If you can. It is sunk in a morass."

"You are in league with him, you are one of the gang of villains."

"I assure you, I have not had a shilling of the money," replied Bayldon, who put his hat on his head and rushed wildly from the office, not knowing what fresh trouble he would have to face if he remained there.

Mrs. Haydon did not attempt to follow him. Jeffries was the man she wanted; she determined to hunt him down, and being a woman of considerable energy she set about it at once. Requiring assistance she engaged the services of a private detective, who ascertained that a gentleman answering the description of Jeffries had gone by the night mail to Paris on the preceding evening. Following up this slight clue, they started together for the French capital, where they found distinct traces of the absconder, but the bird had flown, they knew not whither. On a forlorn hope they went on to Monte Carlo, arriving there about ten o'clock on a beautiful moonlight night.

"You will want rest, madam," suggested her companion.

"No," she replied bravely, "my brain is on fire; to the tables."

They proceeded without making any alteration in their travelling attire to the gambling saloon. Here they saw Jeffries, who rose dejectedly from his seat and muttered, "All is lost! All gone! Oh my poor wife!"

"His wife! He talks of his wife," hissed Mrs. Haydon.

Listlessly he strolled into the gardens, the sound of the music swelling on the night air; he had gambled, and lost, that was evident enough. Mary Haydon pursued him, the detective was close behind. Jeffries paused under a tree, against the trunk of which he leant; his eyes were downcast, and he trembled violently, as if stricken with the ague; the rustle of a dress aroused him; he looked up, Mrs. Haydon stood before him, their eyes met.

"My money!" shrieked she, "the money you robbed me of; I demand it back."

"Go to the croupier," replied Jeffries, recklessly.

"Have you lost it?"

"Every sovereign."

"Wretch!" cried the maddened woman, "you shall pay for this with your life."

She drew a pistol from her pocket, the polished barrel flashed before his eyes, and he saw that she intended to shoot him.

"Hold!" he exclaimed, "do not stain your hands with my blood."

"You think to escape me?"

"On the contrary, I will save you the trouble of killing me."

With a sudden movement, Jeffries snatched the pistol from her hand, put it to his head, pulled the trigger, and ere the report had died away fell down dead at her feet.

The servants of the Casino, accustomed to such scenes, and ever on the alert, came with an ambulance, and took the body away quickly, before the crowd could fix their morbid gaze upon the lifeless clay.

Mary Haydon was avenged!

But at what a price!

She had not meant to go so far, for at the last she had cherished a forlorn hope that she could make the unhappy man love her.

Certainly she felt the loss of her money – women always do feel this kind of thing more than men – but she would have set this off against his love.

Sinking on her knees with an agonised cry, she clasped her hands, and exclaimed, in a voice that quivered with emotion, "Good God! What have I done?"

Then she fell forward on her face in a dead faint.

And still the music floated on the breeze, and the croupier said, mechanically, "Make your game."

32

UTOPIA LIMITED

W.S. Gilbert

Source: W.S. Gilbert, *Utopia Limited; or, The Flowers of Progress* (1893), in W.S. Gilbert, *The Savoy Operas* (London: Macmillan and Company, 1952), pp. 598, 600–602.

EDITORIAL HEADNOTE

William Schwenk Gilbert (1836–1911) was a playwright and librettist, who in collaboration with the composer Arthur Sullivan, wrote a series of wildly popular operettas for the Savoy Theater in London from the 1870s to the 1890s. Gilbert was the son of a naval surgeon who later turned to writing. He was educated at University College, London and qualified as a barrister. He soon abandoned the law for a career as a comic writer. Gilbert penned humorous verse and stage burlesques before embarking on his fruitful partnership with Sullivan.[1]

Utopia Limited is set on a remote island paradise ruled by King Paramount. His daughter, Princess Zara, has just returned from being educated in England, and she brings with her representatives of British civilization – a lawyer, an army captain, a naval commander, and a company promoter – who pledge to transform Utopia from a sleepy backwater into a modern state. The promoter, Mr. Goldbury, intends to float Utopia as a limited liability company, in the process providing ample material for satirizing late Victorian finance culture.

Note

1 "Gilbert, Sir W(illiam) S(chwenck)," in Ian Ousby, ed., *The Cambridge Guide to Literature in English* (Cambridge: Cambridge University Press, 1993), pp. 71–72.

DOI: 10.4324/9781003713890-36

Princess Zara (presenting Mr. Goldbury):

A Company Promoter this, with special education,
Which teaches what Contango means and also Backwardation –
To speculators he supplies a grand financial leaven,
Time was when *two* were company – but now it must be seven.

Mr. Goldbury:

Yes – yes – yes –
Stupendous loans to foreign thrones
I've largely advocated;
In ginger-pops and peppermint-drops
I've freely speculated;
Then mines of gold, of wealth untold,
Successfully I've floated,
And sudden falls in apple-stalls
Occasionally quoted:
And soon or late I always call
For Stock Exchange quotation –
No schemes too great and none too small
For Companification!

Chorus: Yes! Yes! Yes!
No schemes too great and none too small
For Companification!
Ulahlica! Ulahlica! Ulahlica!

. . .

Mr. Goldbury:	Utopia's much too big for one small head – I'll float it as a Company Limited!
King:	A Company Limited? What may that be? The term, I rather think, is new to me.
Chorus:	A Company Limited? What may that be? The term, I rather think, is new to me.

Scaphio, Phantis, and Tarara [Utopian officials] (aside):
What does he mean? What does he mean?
Give us a kind of clue!
What does he mean? What does he mean?
What is he going to do?

SONG – Mr. Goldbury:

Some seven men form an Association
(If possible, all Peers and Baronets),

They start off with a public declaration
To what extent they mean to pay their debts.
That's called their Capital: if they are wary
They will not quote it at a sum immense.
The figure's immaterial – it may vary
From eighteen million down to eighteenpence.
I should put it rather low;
The good sense of doing so
Will be evident at once to any debtor.
When it's left for you to say
What amount you mean to pay,
Why, the lower you can put it at, the better.

Chorus: When it's left for you to say
What amount you mean to pay,
Why, the lower you can put it at, the better.

Goldbury: They then proceed to trade with all who'll trust 'em,
Quite irrespective of their capital
(It's shady, but it's sanctified by custom);
Bank, Railway, Loan, or Panama Canal.
You can't embark on trading too tremendous –
It's strictly fair, and based on common sense –
If you succeed, your profits are stupendous –
And if you fail, pop goes your eighteenpence.
Make the money-spinner spin!
For you only stand to win,
And you'll never with dishonesty be twitted,
For nobody can know,
To a million or so,
To what extent your capital's committed!

Chorus: No, nobody can know,
To a million or so,
To what extent your capital's committed!

Goldbury: If you come to grief, and creditors are craving
(For nothing that is planned by mortal head
Is certain in this Vale of Sorrow – saving
That one's Liability is Limited), –
Do you suppose that signifies perdition?
If so you're but a monetary dunce –
You merely file a Winding-Up Petition,
And start another Company at once!
Though a Rothschild you may be
In your own capacity,

As a Company you've come to utter sorrow –
But the Liquidators say,
"Never mind – you needn't pay,"
So you start another Company to-morrow!

Chorus: But the Liquidators say,
"Never mind – you needn't pay,"
So you start another company to-morrow!

RECITATIF:

King: Well, at first sight it strikes us as dishonest,
But if it's good enough for virtuous England –
The first commercial country in the world –
It's good enough for us.

Sca., Phan., and Tar. (aside to King):
You best take care –
Please recollect *we* have not been consulted.

King (not heeding them):
And do I understand you that Great Britain
Upon this Joint Stock principle is governed?

Goldbury:
We haven't come to that, exactly – but
We're tending rapidly in that direction.
The date's not distant.

King (enthusiastically):
We will be before you!
We'll go down to Posterity renowned
As the First Sovereign in Christendom
Who registered his Crown and Country under
The Joint Stock Company's Act of Sixty-Two.

All: Ulahlica!

INDEX

For Product Safety Concerns and Information please contact our EU representative GPSR@taylorandfrancis.com Taylor & Francis Verlag GmbH, Kaufingerstraße 24, 80331 München, Germany